The Ambivalent Revolution

Frontispiece: Demonstration to reopen churches in Ciudad Las Casas, 7 July 1937. Courtesy of the Archivo Histórico de San Cristóbal de Las Casas, Fondo Fotográfico, Colección C. Arturo Crocker y Arturo Crocker Pascacio.

The Ambivalent Revolution

Forging State and Nation in Chiapas, 1910–1945

Stephen E. Lewis

UNIVERSITY OF NEW MEXICO PRESS

ALBUQUERQUE

Printed and bound in the United States of America
11 10 09 08 07 06 05 1 2 3 4 5 6 7

Library of Congress Cataloging-in-Publication Data

Lewis, Stephen E., 1967–
The ambivalent revolution : forging state and nation in Chiapas, 1910–1945 / Stephen E. Lewis.
p. cm.
Includes bibliographical references and index.
ISBN 0-8263-3601-9 (pbk. : alk. paper)
1. Education—Mexico—Chiapas—History—20th century.
2. Education and state—Mexico—Chiapas—History—20th century.
I. Title.
LA429.C42L49 2005
379.72'75'09041—DC22
2005001617

MAPS: *Jacob Rus*
DESIGN AND COMPOSITION: *Mina Yamashita*

Contents

List of Illustrations

Maps

Figures

Acknowledgments

ALTHOUGH THE PRACTICE OF HISTORY can be a solitary endeavor, this book, happily, was a collective effort. After David Johnston turned me on to history at The Thacher School, Ann Wightman and David Sheinin introduced me to Latin America at Wesleyan University. At the University of Connecticut, Hugh M. Hamill Jr.'s grace, wisdom, and teaching skills set a high standard which I try to emulate. Christine Hünefeldt believed in me and kept me anchored during my first two years in the doctoral program at the University of California, San Diego.

In researching, writing, and rewriting this book, I had three outstanding mentors and friends. Eric Van Young, my dissertation adviser, nudged me toward a better understanding of social history and peasant studies. He meticulously combed over every sentence of the dissertation and dared me to leave a single thought unsubstantiated. More recently, I have thoroughly enjoyed our discussions at noisy academic meetings and over cholesterol-laden breakfasts.

Warm thanks also go to Mary Kay Vaughan, to whom I owe my interest in the social history of rural education in Mexico. Mary Kay also served on my dissertation committee and introduced me to the community of Mexican scholars interested in this topic. Since then, our friendship has grown as we have collaborated on other projects and sustained an engaging, ongoing dialogue about cultural history.

My third mentor is Jan Rus, whose knowledge of nineteenth- and twentieth-century highland Chiapas is unmatched. Without Jan's enthusiastic support, I and other *chiapanólogos* would not be able to decipher the highlands' recent and turbulent history. His pathbreaking ethnohistorical work has set the new standard in the field.

Eric, Mary Kay, and Jan showed me the way, but other friends had to put up with me when the going got tough. I would like to especially acknowledge Susan Blanchard, Ákos Foty, Michelle King, Dave Leheny, Brian Lewis, Odin Soli, Antje Sroka, Peter Tontonoz, Aída Hernández, Shannan Mattiace, and the Center for U.S.–Mexican Studies class of 1995–1996 for the camaraderie and the much-needed reality checks.

I have also incurred professional and personal debts south of the border. In Mexico City, I owe special thanks to the staff at the SEP archive and especially Carlos Carrizales Barreto and Roberto Pérez Aguilar for granting my innumerable requests for information. Raymundo Álvarez and Albertano Guerrero made research at the AGN a profitable and pleasant experience. Luz Elena Galván and participants in her education *seminario* provided intellectual support. At the INI's Centro de Documentación "Juan Rulfo," Ángel Baltazar encouraged me to explore the twists and turns of applied anthropology in Mexico. In Chiapas, Isabel Pedrero Esponda and family were gracious companions and hosts, and Federico Morales and Vicky Jiménez provided intellectual and personal support. Finally, I thank Verónica Arellano, Gabriela Barrios Vargas, Ángel Cabellos Quiroz, John Garrison, Mariam Yitani Baroudi, and especially my *caseros* Juan Manuel Maldonado and Alejandra Pons for their friendship and encouragement over the years.

Several institutions provided generous financial support for this project. Research grants from UCSD's Center for Iberian and Latin American Studies and the University of California Institute for Mexico and the United States (UC-MEXUS) funded preliminary research forays. A Fulbright grant and a dissertation fellowship from UC-MEXUS funded my research from 1994 to 1996. Grants from the Spencer Foundation for Research Related to Education and from the Center for U.S.–Mexican Studies at UCSD supported me as I wrote the dissertation. An NEH Summer Stipend in 2000 funded additional research, and a Spencer Foundation Small Research Grant facilitated substantial revisions. Two grants from California State University Chico's Office of Sponsored Programs also helped support research and writing.

As I began preparing this book manuscript in earnest, my colleagues at CSU Chico's Department of History and the Latin American Studies program encouraged me to press ahead and kindly supported my efforts to obtain release time. Students in my Mexico and Social Revolutions classes engaged this topic thoughtfully and gave me useful feedback. I also thank Patricia O'Connor and the staff of the University Studies Abroad Consortium office in San Sebastián, Spain, for their assistance during fall 2002. Several chapters in the book benefited from Friedericke Baumann's encyclopedic knowledge of Soconusco and Mariscal. Alexander Dawson's innovative work on Indians also shaped key parts of the manuscript. Chuck Churchill, Catherine Nolan-Ferrel, Jessica VandeHoven, and three anonymous reviewers also read my final draft, made useful suggestions, and pointed out mistakes. Naturally I must assume responsibility for any that remain.

David Holtby and his team at the University of New Mexico Press patiently guided me down the homestretch. Special thanks also to Karen

Taschek for her copyediting and to Jacob Rus for preparing the maps.

I have incurred the greatest debts—personal and financial—to my parents, Dennis and Betty Lewis, who gave me a solid personal foundation and never placed limits on my educational ambitions. Somehow, financial aid, loans, work-study and summer jobs, and a public-school teacher's salary combined to provide me with the very best high school and undergraduate education. I'd like to dedicate this book to them. ◆

Introduction

The history of Chiapas is a work in progress.

—*Thomas Benjamin, author of* A Rich Land, a Poor People: Politics and Society in Modern Chiapas

On January 1, 1994, as Mexico officially entered the North American Free Trade Agreement (NAFTA) and its ruling party abandoned decades of economic nationalism, the impoverished southern state of Chiapas exploded in violence. The indigenous rebels wore ski masks and called themselves Zapatistas, and their list of denunciations was long—political corruption, local bossism and officially sanctioned violence, the president's recent decision to end land reform, inadequate medical care, and a useless and culturally insensitive education system, among others. Led by a pipe-smoking mestizo who called himself Subcomandante Marcos, the Zapatistas deftly invoked the name of revolutionary agrarian hero Emiliano Zapata and other symbols of the imagined Mexican nation. They turned a relatively local and isolated rebellion into a challenge of national dimensions. Significantly, this challenge came from a border state that did not experience significant popular mobilization during or after Mexico's armed revolution of 1910–1920. Perhaps it is fitting that on the dawn of Mexico's entry into the North American trading bloc, when its revolutionary institutions and policies were being sacrificed on the altar of free trade, its marginalized population in its most marginalized state rose in arms to demand social justice and the rights of citizenship enshrined in the revolution's most important document, the Constitution of 1917.

Mexico's entry into NAFTA was supposed to be the crowning achievement of Carlos Salinas's presidency. The darling of Wall Street, Salinas had continued the work of his predecessor Miguel de la Madrid by further privatizing and dismantling the corporate state that had grown out of the revolution. But 1994 would not be a year of celebration for Salinas and his supporters. The Zapatista rebellion weakened the peso and complicated the presidential succession. In negotiations with the government, the Zapatistas underscored the illegitimacy of the Institutional Revolutionary Party, or

PRI. Symbolically, they severed the "nation" from the one-party state and challenged Mexican society to envision a society that nurtured indigenous cultures. By the end of the year, two high-level political assassinations further shook the PRI establishment and a peso devaluation triggered a major recession. The Mexican state would never be the same again.

Why did Mexico's most significant rebellion in decades take root and grow in indigenous Chiapas? Scholars, journalists, and casual observers scrambled to make sense of the uprising. It soon became clear that Chiapas's twentieth-century history was relatively unknown, despite a formidable corpus of community studies on the state's highland Maya populations.[1] In recent years, social scientists have published a number of important works exploring the rebellion's direct causes.[2] More historically grounded explanations are still lacking, however, partly because the state's immediate postrevolutionary history (1920–1940) is still largely *tierra incógnita*. With the notable exceptions of Thomas Benjamin's meticulously researched political history *A Rich Land, a Poor People*, Antonio García de León's more schematic and polemic *Revolución y utopía*, and Jan Rus's ethnohistorical work on the highlands, historians have made little headway in the state's recent history.[3] Most archives in Chiapas pertaining to this period have suffered benign neglect, and historians have periodically found their access to certain public records restricted or altogether denied.

This book explores an important gap in our historical knowledge by examining Chiapas's revolutionary and postrevolutionary experience through the lens of the rural schoolhouse. During this time the modern Mexican state was forged, and in most of the country the promises of the Constitution of 1917 were at least partially realized. The federal government's most important state- and nation-building institution was the Ministry of Public Education (SEP), created in 1921. The SEP and its teachers tried to modernize and "nationalize" Chiapas and introduce important federal reforms against a backdrop of grinding rural poverty, inadequate infrastructure, a fiercely independent rancher and planter class, and an ethnically diverse population that vacillated between indifference and open hostility. Thanks to Mexico's longstanding tradition of administrative centralization, most of the documents pertaining to this history are housed in the historical archive of the SEP in Mexico City. Documents at the Archivo General de la Nación, also in Mexico City, helped me flesh out the state's political history. Among several important secondary archives, those in Chiapas's state capital, Tuxtla Gutiérrez, and San Cristóbal de Las Casas allowed me to analyze local politics and local responses to federal education and Indian programs.

Together, these documents illuminate the social, political, and institutional history of Chiapas during a critical thirty-five-year period spanning the revolution, two decades of postrevolutionary state and nation building, and the conservative counterattack of the early 1940s. During the 1920s and 1930s, federal teachers devoted relatively little time to traditional classroom instruction. They were under SEP orders to promote community development, introduce and defend federal labor legislation, and forge the "new Mexican." This would be done by combating alcoholism and religious "fanaticism" and instilling a sense of national identity. In the 1920s, SEP programs rarely resonated with local populations. After Lázaro Cárdenas became president in 1934, the SEP moved to the left and embraced "socialist education" as its pedagogy. Radicalized federal teachers doubled as agrarian reformers, unionizers, political agitators, and social reformers. Governor Victórico Grajales tried to block key components of this program; so did the state's ranchers and planters. In the always contentious highlands, teachers' attempts to combat debt labor contractors, alcohol merchants, and a variety of other local exploiters merely antagonized the local *ladino* (non-Indian) population and did little to win over the Tzotzil and Tzeltal Maya. *Cardenismo*—and socialist education—both ran out of steam even before Cárdenas left office in 1940.

Despite considerable opposition to its programs, the SEP can point to some successes. Federal teachers played important roles in helping Cárdenas outflank Grajales and his supporters in the state's 1936 gubernatorial elections. Many communities that supported SEP teachers were rewarded for their loyalty by the agrarian reform of 1939–1940. Even if the SEP's overt attempts to forge more secular, sober Mexicans produced disappointing or inconclusive results, SEP teachers convinced most rural Chiapanecos of the value of the school and the messages and skills that it taught.

The SEP's shortcomings are more obvious, especially in indigenous communities. Two decades of federal education and indigenista projects did not "incorporate" the Tzotzil and Tzeltal highlands as SEP social engineers had planned. By the late 1930s, the federal government was ceding ground to the Chiapas state government's office of Indian affairs. SEP schools helped train a generation of indigenous scribes who in later years would become the political and economic *caciques* (bosses) of the highlands. These men, nurtured and protected by the state and federal government after 1940, would drive their opposition out of the highlands in the 1970s and 1980s. Many of the refugees ended up in the *Selva Lacandona*, the rain forest of eastern Chiapas, the eventual stronghold of the EZLN (Ejército Zapatista de Liberación Nacional, or Zapatista Army of National Liberation).

Forging State and Nation in Rural Chiapas

The State

In recent years, historians have issued important correctives to previous works that overstated both the social accomplishments and the strength of Mexico's postrevolutionary central government. An important subset of this historiography has focused on the presidency of Lázaro Cárdenas. From 1934 to 1940, his administration expropriated nearly 50 million acres of land, nationalized foreign-held oil reserves, favored workers in their disputes with their employers, and invested heavily in indigenous programs and rural education. In 1938, Cárdenas reformed the structure of the official party and created the Party of the Mexican Revolution (PRM), the direct precursor to today's PRI. The social achievements of his presidency and the resiliency of the PRI convinced earlier generations of historians that Cardenismo was a progressive Leviathan capable of imposing itself on the state and local level.

Historians working in state and local archives are now providing a much more nuanced view of Cardenismo. The "state-as-Leviathan" thesis has been thoroughly discredited. Cardenista weakness in states like Puebla, Sonora, and Yucatán forced the federal government to compromise its goals. At times it pacted with known enemies of agrarian reform and worker mobilization, nurtured regional *caciques* and *camarillas* (networks of informally linked elites), and fostered new kinds of patron-client relationships.[4] In a pivotal article, Alan Knight argued that the Cardenista state was actually more reactive than proactive, more "jalopy" than "juggernaut."[5] Mary Kay Vaughan has shown that the weakness of the federal government and the SEP in the 1930s forced teachers to negotiate the federal blueprint with local communities. Paradoxically, this process of negotiation reinforced state hegemony; in other words, the federal government's weakness became its strength.[6]

This book highlights the inability of the federal government to fully impose itself in Chiapas. Like the aforementioned studies, it finds the central government after 1920 opportunistic, improvised, and easily corrupted. The foundation for a weak federal presence in Chiapas was laid in the nineteenth century. The state's political leaders developed a thesis of state sovereignty based on the state's allegedly "voluntary" incorporation into Mexico in 1824, its geographic distance from Mexico City, and the federation's apparent neglect of the state. When a Constitutionalist army entered Chiapas in

September 1914 and imposed provocative land, labor, and anticlerical reforms, ranchers, planters, and their retainers fought them to a draw in the name of state autonomy. Following Álvaro Obregón's successful coup against Venustiano Carranza in April 1920, the leader of the most important rebel faction in Chiapas became state governor. He continued to defend the state's sovereignty and blocked the major reforms of the revolution emanating from Mexico City, including federal education. However bloody their internal feuds, Chiapanecan ranchers and planters succeeded in frustrating federal reforms and institutions until the middle 1930s.

In recognition of its own relative debility, the Cárdenas administration did not turn its attention to Chiapas until 1936, more than a year after Cárdenas took office. When it finally did, it relied heavily on the loyalty and organizational capacity of federal teachers. Cardenismo had a positive, even transformative impact in Chiapas, but only where teachers had been able to submit agrarian reform requests, unionize and mobilize workers and peasants, and introduce the ideology of the revolution. The popularity and success of federal teachers were critical to the twin successes of the Cardenistas in the state—the ouster of Governor Victórico Grajales and his camarilla in late 1936, and the federal land reform that finally reached the state in 1939–1940. In later years, even after the SEP turned its back on its legacy of social activism, most mestizo communities demanded federal schooling as a right of Mexican citizenship. They tended to identify with the Mexican nation and realized that the school and the literacy skills that it taught were essential to their interactions with the state.

Cardenismo lasted only four years in Chiapas, and much of the last two years was spent in willful retreat. Consequently, the institutions of the Mexican revolution that preserved the social and political peace elsewhere in the country either did not have the opportunity to develop in Chiapas or were so thoroughly corrupted that they exacerbated problems instead of solving them. After 1940, the state that had been part of Guatemala until 1822 would follow a distinctly Central American pattern of political, economic, and social development, culminating in guerrilla insurgency.

The Nation

Most of the Zapatistas' demands in early 1994—clean elections, better schools, an improved health care system—reflected the weakness and corruption of the federal state in Chiapas. Over the ensuing months and years, their demands increasingly pointed to the monocultural, exclusive nature of the

Mexican nation. The nation—not to be confused with the "government" or the "country"—is an identity. It has been variously defined as an "imagined community" or a "large-scale solidarity" based on factors such as ethnicity, religion, language, customs, and geography. Collective memory also binds the nation: according to Thomas Benjamin, "the key is memory, myth, and history, organized remembering and deliberate forgetting."[7]

The year 1821 signified the troubled birth of the Mexican state—an administrative and territorial unit—not the Mexican nation. Early republican state-builders embraced the nation-state model, which assumes a relationship between a sovereign government, a territory, and a unified, relatively homogenous people. Such unity simply did not exist in Mexico. Although the colonial caste system had been legislated out of existence, Mexican society was still hopelessly divided along ethnic, class, ideological, and regional lines. The creole nationalism so eloquently examined by David Brading remained the domain of elite dreamers who failed to convert their devotion to the Virgin of Guadalupe into a national program of political or ideological unity.[8] Caudillos like Antonio López de Santa Anna frequently invoked Mexican patriotism each time the territory was invaded (this happened forty-three times between 1821 and 1915).[9] However, this patriotism was usually ephemeral and self-serving.

In recent years, Florencia Mallon and others have made a convincing case for mid-nineteenth-century peasant nationalism and patriotic liberalism in central Mexico stemming from the country's wars of national liberation. In Guy Thompson's words, the weak Mexican state "hid behind a progressive, secularising, liberal-patriotic discourse of nationhood which achieved a precocious ascendancy after 1867."[10] John Hart takes the argument farther, claiming that Mexican nationalism, linked to anti-foreigner sentiments, helped spark the revolution of 1910.[11] However, despite these rather particular cases of peasant and working-class nationalism, the Mexican "nation" before 1910 was largely unrealized. As Knight tells it, Mexico on the eve of the revolution was "less a nation than a geographical expression, a mosaic of regions and communities, introverted and jealous, ethnically and physically fragmented, and lacking common national sentiments."[12] There were "many Mexicos," and Mexicans in 1910—especially in outlying states like Chiapas—were more likely to identify with ethnic, regional, ideological, class, community, family, and clientelist allegiances (or some combination thereof) than with a Mexican "nation."

Many competing visions of the Mexican nation clashed on the battlefields of the revolution. As the fighting gave way to state building, the task of forging a nation, of "inventing" secular national traditions, fell to the postrevolutionary Mexican government.[13] As Eric Hobsbawm has written, "'National consciousness' develops unevenly among the social groupings and *regions* of a country . . . [and] whatever the nature of the social groups first captured by 'national consciousness,' the popular masses—workers, servants, peasants—are the last to be affected by it."[14] The SEP promised to give the Mexican population the cultural uniformity that the nation–state model demands. It would bring its schools and its message of revolutionary nationalism to the most remote corners of the Mexican state. The tremendous scope and urgency of the SEP's task did not escape North American educator John Dewey in 1926:

> The difficulties in creating a moral and political entity out of Mexico are so enormous that they often seem insuperable. . . . Add to this fact that the Indians are anything but homogenous among themselves . . . intensely self-centered, jealous of their autonomy, prizing an isolation which is accentuated by geographical conditions, and we begin to have a faint idea of the problem which the revolutionary government is facing as systematically as all previous regimes dodged it.[15]

The SEP's most vigorous state- and nation-building campaign was its socialist education program, launched in December 1934. This populist, nationalist crusade attacked the perceived enemies of the emerging nation-state—among them the landed class and the Church—and attempted to "modernize" and "Mexicanize" the country's heterogeneous population. Part of the struggle entailed gaining control over the calendar and replacing the cult of the saints with the cult of the state. SEP documents tell of teachers in Chiapas preparing civic, patriotic, and/or sporting festivals at a frantic rate of roughly one event per week during the mid- to late 1930s. Inside the classroom, teachers used new official textbooks that celebrated popular agency, class struggle, sobriety, patriotism, and secular thought. Local response to socialist education varied widely in the state, partly because its implementation was far from uniform, partly because local circumstances greatly conditioned local responses. In general terms, however, this agenda (which also included agrarian reform) won the support of most mestizo communities and was the key to Cardenista grassroots mobilization in the state.

The most novel dimension of postrevolutionary Mexican state and nation building was *indigenismo*, official Indian policy written and implemented by non-Indians. Indigenismo called for the revindication of indigenous Mexicans and their inclusion in the new nation. Four hundred years after the fall of Tenochtitlán, Mexico was still home to as many as 6 million indigenous people out of total population of roughly 15 million. Divided into at least sixty distinct ethnic and linguistic groups and residing in the country's most remote regions, these populations were marginalized politically, economically, and culturally from the national mainstream.

During the 1920s and 1930s, Mexican indigenismo was almost exclusively the realm of the SEP. Utopian politicians, anthropologists, and pedagogues launched several highly acclaimed projects meant to "incorporate" indigenous Mexicans into the national, mestizo mainstream. In Chiapas, these projects had no impact in the 1920s and seemed only to provoke the Indians' exploiters in the 1930s. In 1936 the SEP admitted defeat. More than a decade would pass before the federal government would again try to introduce comprehensive indigenista policies to the Chiapas highlands.

Indeed, Chiapas is a uniquely challenging laboratory for the study of Mexican state and nation building after 1920. Geographically, it is a marginalized border state with long-standing political, economic, cultural, and historical ties to neighboring Guatemala. Its population is ethnically diverse, overwhelmingly rural, impoverished, and scattered into various distinct regions. The state's autonomous tradition adds a particularly thorny dimension to federal state and nation building. Even the state's physical setting presents formidable obstacles. The foreign surveying companies that charted and sold enormous tracts of Mexican land during the regime of modernizing dictator Porfirio Díaz (1876–1880, 1884–1911) complained of the state's "rugged mountains . . . impassable rain forests . . . epidemics of measles, scarlet fever, whooping cough, typhus, cholera, and smallpox" and the "absolute lack of roads."[16] Nowhere in Mexico would the SEP face greater challenges to its state- and nation-building designs.

Chiapas by Region

As the Porfirian land surveyors noted, the topography of Chiapas is varied and often spectacular. It has given rise to several clearly defined regions, each with its distinct history, demographic base, climate, and means of production. Juan Pedro Viqueira has argued that Chiapas can only be understood as a sum of its regions, even if scholars cannot agree to a common "regionalization" of the state.[17]

Taking its cue from Viqueira and others, this book takes a regional and

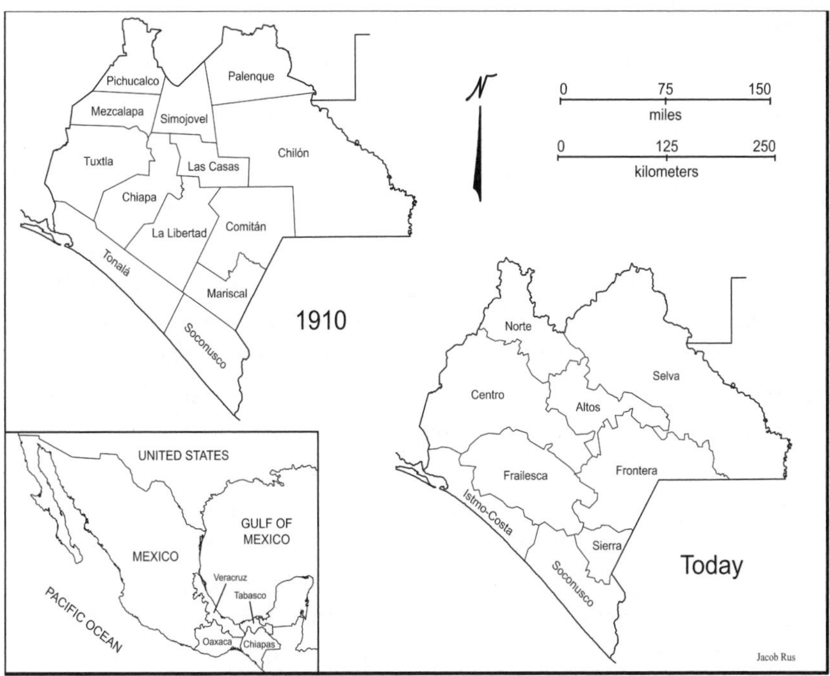

Map 1. Chiapas by region, 1910 and today.

chronological approach, concentrating on the parts of the state that received the most attention from the SEP. Chapter 1 surveys a century of Chiapas's history from its separation from Guatemala in 1822 until the arrival of SEP director José Vasconcelos's first "missionaries" exactly one century later. Chapter 2 focuses on three regions. The first is Mariscal, which defines part of Chiapas's border with Guatemala. Marsical's most important towns—Amatenango, Motozintla, and Mazapa—had actually been part of Guatemala prior to the 1882 border negotiations. A region of barren, rocky soil, Mariscal's ladino and Mam inhabitants typically supplemented their meager incomes with work stints on the coast every fall. These peasants, petty ranchers, and coffee pickers generally supported the armies of Venustiano Carranza during the revolution and were sympathetic to the SEP's program of action pedagogy in the 1920s. Federal teachers tried to use the school to support their Socialist Party of Chiapas (Partido Socialista Chiapaneco, or PSCH). They—and their schools—were eventually targeted for repression.

Our attention then shifts to the steamy lower Grijalva River valley, home to the state capital, Tuxtla Gutiérrez, the nearby city of Chiapa de Corzo, and cornfields and extensive cattle ranches. The population here is ladino. By

1930, SEP schools in this region were benefiting from the land reform program of state governor Raymundo Enríquez (1928–1932) and provided hope for the future of federal education in the state.

Last we consider Soconusco, the southeastern portion of the state's Pacific coast. Here, in the shady, humid, fertile hills of the Sierra Madre de Chiapas, national and foreign entrepreneurs built coffee and tropical fruit plantations beginning in the late nineteenth century. This region's seasonal labor needs forced it into uneasy partnership with indigenous and ladino populations in Mariscal and the central highlands. In the 1930s, Soconusco was the scene of an explosive showdown between planters, who often refused to support the schools that they were required to provide for under the terms of Article 123 of the Constitution of 1917, and the SEP, which attempted to enforce compliance.

Chapters 3 and 4 move our attention to the *Altos* (central highlands), a place of great geographic and human diversity. The western part of this region rises abruptly from the Grijalva valley, boasting pine forests and elevations of 2,400 meters. The northern and eastern limits of the Altos descend gradually toward the Caribbean and the Lacandón rain forest, respectively, supporting livestock and coffee production. San Cristóbal de Las Casas had traditionally been the commercial and political center of the highlands, and after 1920 *coletos* (ladino residents of San Cristóbal) fought to keep it that way. Their lifestyles depended on their ability to control and exploit the hundreds of thousands of Maya-speaking people who resided in the hills, plateaus, and valleys to the north and east. Residents of the western highland municipalities generally speak Tzotzil, while those in the eastern municipalities speak either Tzeltal or Ch'ol.

As chapter 3 illustrates, the first decade of SEP indigenismo failed roundly in the highlands, as it did in other indigenous regions of Mexico that lacked a tradition in schooling. Chapter 4 represents the first close look at anticlericalism in postrevolutionary Chiapas. Then as now, San Cristóbal was the administrative and spiritual stronghold of the Catholic Church in the state. Although Chiapas was relatively calm from 1926 through 1929, when the Cristero war raged in western Mexico, it flared into a hotbed of iconoclasm in the early 1930s. The initiative came not from the SEP but from Governor Victórico Grajales, who managed to close every church in Chiapas and expel or drive underground every priest *before* the SEP officially embraced socialist education. An enemy of SEP activism, Grajales unwittingly did federal teachers a favor by sparing them an inflammatory, ultimately counterproductive campaign. In 1936, when Cardenistas finally made their move in Chiapas, they would turn Grajales's anticlerical demagoguery against him.

Chapters 5 and 6 consider the impact of socialist education on the entire state. In February 1935, radical pedagogue Elpidio López became the state's director of federal education. After purging the teaching corps, he boldly attempted a top-down imposition of socialist education in all its populist dimensions. Ranchers and planters responded with lethal violence. Although López tried to soft-pedal the program that summer, he was soon transferred out of Chiapas. Chapter 6 examines the nation-building aspect of socialist education. This campaign was especially intense in Guatemalan communities that passed to Mexican control following the 1882 border negotiations. Teachers also found themselves involved in a quixotic campaign to reduce or altogether eliminate alcohol consumption in the state, especially in indigenous communities. This campaign initially met with considerable grassroots support, especially from women. However, it was soon undermined by the state government itself, which depended on state alcohol tax revenues and sought to protect alcohol producers and distributors.

Chapter 7 takes us back to the central highlands and evaluates the impact of socialist education and SEP indigenismo on the Tzotzil and Tzeltal Maya. Federal teachers attempted to initiate agrarian reform, close illegal company stores, and attack the well-entrenched system of *enganche* (debt contracting) by which lowland planters obtained highland Indian labor during harvest season. Ladinos reacted vigorously, using every means—legal and illegal, passive and violent—at their disposal. Meanwhile, the SEP's ladino, mainly monolingual teachers still labored without the support of the indigenous people themselves. By the middle of 1936 the SEP was in clear retreat.

Tuxtla Gutiérrez and the former state capital, San Cristóbal de Las Casas, renew their historic rivalry in chapter 8 after Cardenistas seize control of the state's branch of the National Revolutionary Party (Partido Nacional Revolucionario, or PNR), win the primaries, and impose Efraín Gutiérrez as governor. Highland ladinos took immediate action to prevent Cardenista indigenismo from threatening their political and economic grip over "their" Indians. They managed to blunt the Cardenista offensive, but they also learned that they could no longer prevent a federal presence in Tzotzil and Tzeltal communities. The federal government, for its part, would be forced to work through influential ladinos who compromised and corrupted indigenista projects. Anthropologists who believed that they were describing relatively autonomous, "closed" corporate communities in the 1950s and 1960s were actually witnessing communities that had been subjected to indigenista programs and outside political control and manipulation since the 1930s.

Chapter 9 takes us back down to the plantations of humid Soconusco. Reforms to the Federal Labor Law (Ley Federal del Trabajo) in 1934 brought the Article 123 schools under SEP control just months before the SEP endorsed socialist education. Two years later, 5,460 students attended 133 Article 123 schools in Chiapas. Article 123 teachers were state-building shock troops for the central government, bringing the revolution's reforms and institutions to the virtual fiefdoms of resistant rural proprietors. Many planters and ranchers sabotaged these schools. Although the SEP was in steady (and perhaps willful) retreat by late 1938, Cardenistas a few months later would execute major land reform on plantations where SEP teachers had mobilized workers, enforced federal labor laws, and promoted agrarian reform.

Chapter 10 considers the fate of SEP programs after 1940. Clearly it was a mixed harvest. Socialist education (and its practitioners) became unfashionable. In the highlands, SEP indigenismo ceded ground to ambitious state indigenista Erasto Urbina. In Soconusco, the recent beneficiaries of Cardenista land reform complained of manipulation by the government's agrarian credit agency. The SEP allowed the remaining Article 123 schools to wither and die. But there was also a silver lining. As SEP budgets shrank and national commitments shifted, parents' groups and union members spoke up in defense of their teachers and schools. Suddenly and dramatically, grassroots demand for federal schooling outpaced supply. Thanks to the mass orientation of socialist education, the SEP had won over most rural Chiapanecos. This legacy has been one of the SEP's most enduring achievements.

The conclusion carries our story up to the present, when Tzotzil and Tzeltal migrants from the central highlands and the eastern lowlands joined Tojolabal and Ch'ol settlers from the south and north of the state, respectively, in creating a uniquely democratic, multiethnic frontier society in the Selva in eastern Chiapas. Ultimately, the state that most resisted postrevolutionary state and nation building in the 1920s and 1930s hatched the most novel challenge to the PRI and presented a compelling proposal for indigenous autonomy within a new, more plural Mexican nation. ◆

Part One

LEARNING to CRAWL

State, Nation, and Schooling to 1930

Chapter One

Revolution(s), State Autonomy, and Public Schooling to 1922

> In view of the vandalous acts which have victimized the Chiapanecan Family by the odious armed group that has invaded Chiapanecan soil, sent by the Carrancista government without any objective other than to destroy our political institutions, foundation of our Sovereignty, and make themselves masters of our lives and haciendas . . . we the undersigned have resolved to rise up in arms in defense of society, with the men that the indignant Chiapanecan people can provide.
>
> —*"Acta de Canguí,"* 1914

In 1935, the SEP in Mexico City sent a circular instructing teachers how to commemorate Chiapas's 1824 incorporation into the Mexican federation. The plebiscite held to determine Chiapas's fate was absolutely transparent, the circular read; the Mexican army did not intimidate the pro-Guatemalan vote and played no role in shaping the outcome. Teachers were also told to emphasize that the outcome of the plebiscite was met with the "jubilation . . . of a free and virtuous people."[1] Since none of these assertions was actually true, why was the SEP so intent on propagating these fictions?

Given its historical ties with its southern neighbor, Chiapas's commitment to the Mexican state and nation has often been suspect. Following independence from Spain, both Mexico and Guatemala attempted to control Chiapas's fate. Later in the nineteenth century, the annexation fantasies of various Guatemalan presidents and the ill-defined border brought the two countries to the verge of war several times. In the early twentieth century, no state resisted the reforms of the revolution as resolutely as Chiapas. The SEP apparently hoped that a concerted nation-building campaign in the classroom would paper over past divisions and tensions.

This chapter traces the historical roots of the thesis of Chiapanecan sovereignty. It then discusses the development of Soconusco by largely foreign planters with autonomist aspirations of their own. After a brief discussion of Porfirian education, it explores how rebel ranchers and planters known as *Mapaches* ("raccoons," because they moved at night) resisted the Mexican revolution. Relations between the state of Chiapas and the Mexican federation since 1920 must be understood in the context of the Mapaches' victory, the state's geographic and economic marginality, and the continuity and relative autonomy of a landed elite of pre-Porfirian and Porfirian origin.

"Chiapanecan Sovereignty" and the Mexican State

When the wars of independence broke out in New Spain in 1810, Chiapas was a marginalized, impoverished intendancy of the *capitanía* of Guatemala. The region's only "natural resource" was its indigenous population. Leading residents purchased the colonial post of *alcaldía mayor* (provincial governor) and forced indigenous communities to produce sugar, cotton, cacao, and dyes as *repartimientos de mercancía* (a form of tribute used to artificially stimulate market production and consumption). Indians were forced to accept rum and other commodities in return. Indians also paid a head tax and met labor obligations. Exploitation of the indigenous populations by the provincial governors and other colonists was so severe that it brought them into prolonged conflict with the clergy. The friars were motivated in part by their consciences and in part by their own economic interests, since the governors left the communities too poor to sustain parish priests through tribute payments, alms, and fees.[2]

In this atmosphere of economic stagnation and neglect, a spirit of separatism took hold among the province's oligarchy during the late colonial period. "Chiapas has been under the Guatemalan government for three centuries, and in all this time it has not prospered," wrote Ciudad Real's town government in 1821. "Guatemala has never provided this Province with science, industry, or any other utility and has looked upon it with much indifference."[3] Ironically, Chiapas's elite would lodge similar complaints against Mexico throughout the nineteenth and twentieth centuries.

After Spain recognized the independence and sovereignty of the Mexican Empire in August 1821, Chiapas's provincial assembly declared independence from both Spain and Guatemala and solicited annexation with its northern neighbor. Aggregation with Mexico made perfect sense for Chiapas's oligarchs. The considerable distance from Mexico City would afford them the autonomy they desired. At the same time, as part of the Mexican Empire their commercial opportunities would increase and they could escape the restrictions of Guatemala City's Consulado de Comercio (Commerce Council). Agustín de Iturbide's Plan de Iguala, published in February 1821, seemed a sufficiently conservative guarantee against Spanish republicanism and "caste wars," and if it came to a caste war, Chiapanecan oligarchs reasoned, the Mexican army would be more capable of crushing rebellious Indians.[4]

Chiapanecos were forced to reconsider their union with Mexico following the abdication of Emperor Iturbide I in March 1823 and the subsequent collapse of the Mexican Empire. Chiapas's twelve-member provisional assembly split into two factions. Representatives from Tuxtla, Chiapa, Comitán, and Tapachula favored union with newly sovereign Guatemala. They feared exclusion from the Guatemalan market and the continued economic and political domination of Ciudad Real's oligarchy. Furthermore, nineteen months of Mexican statehood had brought with it few advantages and an ominously large army of occupation. The commercial and ecclesiastical elite of the Altos, however, continued to favor union with Mexico. A third faction advocating autonomy formed a sovereign Suprema Junta Provisional in June 1823. With Mexican troops still stationed in Chiapas, the junta declared full, if temporary, independence from Mexico, at least until the imperial government was restored.[5]

Anxious to avoid the permanent loss of Chiapas, the Mexican government resorted to bullying tactics. Under orders from then Secretary of Foreign Relations Lucas Alamán, the army dissolved the Suprema Junta in September 1823 and revived a pro-Mexico junta. As Chiapas teetered on the verge of civil war, the plebiscite was held. The results showed over 96,000 votes in favor of union with Mexico to only 60,400 for union with Guatemala. Only the temporary secession of Soconusco—in reaction to pro-Mexico vote rigging—tarnished the Mexico camp's victory. Chiapas, minus Soconusco, was formally annexed by Mexico on September 14, 1824.[6] In no uncertain terms, Benjamin writes that the annexation "was engineered by the oligarchy of Ciudad Real for the purpose of extending its political domination within the province, maintaining its economic domination of the Indian population of the Central Highlands, and promoting [its] commercial and business interests."[7] The highland oligarchy would maintain its political grip over the state until 1892; its control over the central highlands would not be challenged by the federal government until 1936.

Throughout the remainder of the nineteenth century, successive Guatemalan governments attempted to recover Soconusco and the rest of Chiapas. Scores of writings repeated the accusations—most of them true—that the plebiscite had been rigged by Ciudad Real's elite, that the indigenous vote had been manipulated by the pro-Mexican clergy, and that the Mexican army's presence in nearby Tehuantepec had intimidated voters, among many other charges. Bad blood between Mexico and Guatemala postponed the first serious attempt to fix the international border until 1874. Given Guatemala's historical claims to Chiapas, the extremely vague colonial boundary markers, the lack of topographical data on the region, and the highly mobile populations that inhabited both sides of the border, de Vos calls it "almost a miracle" that the two countries were able to sign a boundary treaty in 1882. Both countries agreed to use straight cartographic lines where boundaries were especially obscure. Consequently, Mexico ceded parts of Tabasco, Campeche, and the southernmost tip of Soconusco; Guatemala, for its part, relinquished the northernmost tip of the Petén rain forest to Campeche and ceded Motozintla, Mazapa, and other Mam communities to Chiapas. Guatemala also "renounced forever the rights that it believed to have over the territory of the State of Chiapas and its District of Soconusco, and, consequently, considered said territory to be an integral part of the Estados Unidos Mexicanos."[8]

This declaration did not put an end to Guatemala's claims on Mexican territory, however. After the euphoria of the 1882 signings died down, the Guatemalan government arrived at the exaggerated conclusion that it had suffered a net loss of four thousand square miles, or 6 percent of its national territory, and 12,500 inhabitants. Bitter that it had again suffered humiliation at the hands of the Mexicans, in 1884 the Guatemalan government began obstructing the work of the two companies that had been commissioned to complete the cartographic work. After logging companies entered the fray over disputed claims in 1892, both countries put themselves on a wartime footing. After the Guatemalans backed down, Mexican president Porfirio Díaz resolved to build a coastal railroad to Tapachula as a matter of national security. In 1895, Guatemala and Mexico signed the final border treaty, but even that did not stop Guatemalan military figures, politicians, and intellectuals from dreaming of reincorporating Chiapas during the revolution and beyond.[9]

Guatemala's persistent attempts to recover lost territory motivated postrevolutionary Mexican governments, through the SEP, to embark on intense nationalization campaigns in areas ceded by Guatemala in 1882 and populated by people considered to be Guatemalans. Beginning in 1930 the

SEP established frontier schools along Chiapas's southern border. A few years later the SEP purged border schools of Guatemalan teachers and launched social campaigns meant to instill in students and their parents a love for Mexico. Meanwhile, the national government invested heavily in infrastructure development projects along the southern frontier. It also offered Mexican citizenship to Guatemalan workers residing in Chiapas and granted them land during the major expropriations in 1939 and 1940. It was this co-optive federal strategy—both cultural and economic—that finally secured Mexico's southern border and put to rest any serious concern that Chiapas could or would be lost to Guatemala.

The Development of Soconusco's Export Sector

If Chiapas was slow to incorporate itself into the Mexican federation, Soconusco waited even longer before casting its lot. For nearly two decades following Chiapas's 1824 incorporation with Mexico, the district of Soconusco experienced almost unfettered autonomy. Following a minor Guatemalan incursion in 1842, Soconusco's caciques formally solicited annexation with Mexico. Later that year Mexican president Antonio López de Santa Anna incorporated the region and declared it a department within the state of Chiapas.[10]

After Guatemala renounced all claims to Chiapas and Soconusco in 1882, Porfirians took steps to encourage colonization of the region by immigrant entrepreneurs. Two survey and colonization companies (one British, the other North American) were granted the right to sell land and colonize Chiapas. While the state reported only 501 ranchos in 1877, by 1895 Soconusco alone counted 530 ranchos; Tuxtla 240, Tonalá 368, and Pichucalco 529.[11] European, North American, and Mexican entrepreneurs bought land at giveaway prices. They established cacao, corn, and tropical fruit plantations in Pichucalco; cattle and corn haciendas in the lower Grijalva Basin; hardwood mills in Lacandonia; coffee and rubber plantations on the coast; and coffee, sugar, and tropical fruit plantations elsewhere in the state. In Soconusco, German entrepreneurs played a preponderant role, and by 1900 German immigrants owned or managed three-quarters of the region's coffee groves. Many were experienced growers who had thrived in Guatemala and were attracted to Chiapas by the liberal land policies of the Porfirian government. Their expertise and financial connections placed them in an ideal position to transform the social and economic landscape of Soconusco and nearby areas.[12]

The development of the export sector in Soconusco (and the rest of

Chiapas) was further facilitated when Porfirio Díaz appointed a succession of modernizing governors, beginning with Emilio Rabasa in 1892. In an act suggestive of the growing importance of lowland ranchers and planters, Rabasa moved the state capital from San Cristóbal de Las Casas to the steamy lowland commercial town of Tuxtla Gutiérrez. Not only did Rabasa seek to escape the interference of conservative coletos and the well-entrenched highland clergy, Tuxtla was also better positioned to take advantage of growing trade opportunities with the rest of Mexico. Rabasa also invested heavily in productive infrastructure in order to nurture the state's budding export economy. He improved river traffic and seaport facilities and built a highway connecting San Cristóbal and Tuxtla to Oaxaca in order "to open [Chiapas] to becoming Mexican."[13]

To further assist the emerging rancher and planter class, Rabasa also approved the division and privatization of all remaining *ejidos* (communally held lands) in the state. The *reparto* was intentionally double-edged. While it provided economic advantages to ranchers and planters, indigenous residents of at least sixty-seven village ejidos were suddenly forced to find less secure work as migrant laborers or debt peons on lowland plantations. Those who chose to remain on the land were reduced to a serf-like status known as *baldiaje*. As *baldíos* they worked several days a month for the new landowner in exchange for the right to keep their houses and farm their plots. Some baldíos north of San Cristóbal endured grueling conditions on the cacao plantations of Pichucalco; those who inhabited the Central Highlands were contracted by highland ladinos (*transportistas*) to work as load-bearers (*cargadores*). Cheaper, more expendable, and more reliable than mules, they moved goods like wheat flour, bread, refined sugars, preserved meat, and *aguardiente* (literally "burning water," a rough cane alcohol) from San Cristóbal north to the lowland valleys of Simojovel and Chilón; they also carried coffee, tobacco, henequen, cacao, and rubber grown in these departments to the Gulf of Mexico port of Villahermosa, Tabasco. So lucrative were the profits made off the load-bearers that the highland transportistas that controlled them offered Governor Francisco León a thirty-thousand-peso bribe *not* to build a cart road from San Cristóbal north to Chilón.[14]

After 1890, as export agriculture became increasingly important to Chiapas, the ability of rural capitalists to affect policy and extract concessions grew accordingly. By the turn of the century coffee planters successfully lobbied for tax reductions when the price of coffee fell. The state government also took steps to facilitate the flow of labor. This was absolutely essential, since coffee planters typically saw the size of their workforce increase by four times during the harvest. Initially the state government attempted to force indigenous workers into the wage economy by increasing their tax burden and forcing them into debt. Beginning in 1892–1893, the state government revived the head tax and added new police and school taxes and municipal fees. As Rus notes, those who could not produce a tax receipt on demand were subjected to a new vagrancy law that mandated immediate arrest and a fine, following which the hapless Indian could be turned over to an *enganchador* (debt labor contractor). Figures for the highland community of Cancuc show that the total burden of these new taxes in 1907 came to 10.87 pesos for each male over the age of twelve. Given the prevailing wage on the lowland plantations, this translated to more than forty days per year of state-obligated labor—a modern-day *repartimiento*.[15]

But taxation alone could not rationalize the flow of labor in Chiapas so long as highland ladinos monopolized indigenous workers. This set the stage for another clash between Chiapas's traditional highland elite and lowland planters both foreign and Mexican. When Governor León called a Congreso Agrícola (Agrarian Congress) in 1896, the struggle over Indian labor ended in a stalemate. Díaz then gave León permission to redraw departmental boundaries in the highlands. Consequently, highland ladinos lost administrative control of (and the right to tax) the Tzotzil municipalities immediately north of San Cristóbal in 1896. León placed the municipalities in a new *departamento* or province called the "Partido de Chamula," to be administered by a ladino *jefe político* (political boss) of his choosing. As Rus concludes, "90 percent of the Tzotzil population of the department of Las Casas [fell] under the direct control of the federal and state governments—and the lowland planters."[16]

In the struggle over indigenous labor, the planters, most of whom were of foreign origin, had long argued for a system of free labor whereby fair wages and decent working and living conditions would attract workers. This fact is often lost in the historiography, which—drawing closely from nationalist and xenophobic sources written in the 1930s—portrays foreign planters (and especially Germans) as ruthless exploiters of "our" Indians. In fact, following the deadlocked Congreso Agrícola of 1896, planters had to settle for enganche, a system of debt labor contracting managed by the highland ladinos.[17] Indians who had previously carried loads north to Simojovel, Chilón, and Villahermosa were now directed south every fall to the plantations of Soconusco, an eight-day (unpaid) walk. Under enganche, Indians were offered wage advances that they repaid by working on the plantations. Although some Indians willingly availed themselves of this form of credit in order to buy candles, farm tools, and other products in the city, many others were victimized by *enganchadores* who used alcohol, guile, and even force to "hook" a workforce.[18] Over time, lowland planters with seasonal labor needs grew to appreciate the enganche system because it spared them the responsibility of maintaining a workforce during the off–season.

The linchpin to enganche was the highland municipal secretary—typically ladino—who worked in cahoots with the enganchadores. Appointed by jefes políticos, municipal secretaries collected taxes, controlled labor flows, enforced debt labor contracts, returned runaway debt peons to the plantations, and managed the manufacture and distribution of alcohol in Indian villages. Indigenous *ayuntamientos* (town councils) and scribes were enlisted to help collect the taxes that often forced individuals into debt, a reality that provoked nasty internal divisions in many communities. In the short run, at least, this system worked. By 1910, ten thousand men (or 80 percent of the male Tzotzil and Tzeltal population in the old Department of Las Casas) were making the seasonal trek down to the coffee plantations of Soconusco.[19]

But Chiapas was a powder keg about to explode. Highland ladinos prepared for the day when they could exact revenge upon their lowland rivals. Rumors told of conservative rebels stockpiling weapons and training in the hills above San Cristóbal for an uprising. As the partnership between lowland politicians and planters solidified, Díaz's modernizing state governors were targeted for assassination.[20] Finally, the exploitation of the highland Tzotzil reached extreme levels. According to oral histories conducted by Rus, many men found themselves indebted for two or three years at a time without the possibility of returning to see their families in the highlands. During the years preceding the revolution, the drain on the adult male population in some communities was so great that the wives of absent plantation workers had to serve important religious posts known as *cargos*. Most irksome to the Tzotzils was the knowledge that their own native town governments often collaborated with the ladinos and profited from the "sale of their brothers."[21] They too would soon take their revenge.

Porfirian Schooling in Chiapas

The history of rural education in Chiapas begins, for all practical purposes, with the Porfiriato (1876–1911). During this time, states with healthy export sectors like Sonora, Coahuila, and Yucatán established and funded school systems that in many ways outperformed the SEP's schools into the 1930s. Chiapas, however, came late to the table of Porfirian economic development, and its public education sector languished until roughly the turn of the century. Schools were rarely found outside of towns and municipal centers, and the few rural schools established were usually unpopular, underfunded, and ephemeral. The state received a collective black eye in 1892, when the abuses of a particularly entrepreneurial rural schoolteacher in Tumbalá (in the northeastern district of Palenque) caught the attention of the national press. After several German colonists bought land in the area and established coffee plantations, they quickly learned that Tumbalá's "teacher," the cousin of the municipal president, doubled as a labor contractor and tax collector. The Germans paid their indigenous workers 1.06 pesos, but the teacher collected 0.25 pesos of that amount daily. When the Germans tried to contract the Indians directly, offering them a relatively generous daily salary of 1 peso, the teacher threatened them. The Germans then learned that the teacher collected marriage, burial, and baptismal fees, charged Indians (and even ladinos) a fee when they slaughtered their animals, taxed Indians for their fiestas, and so on. Like a colonial *encomendero*, he demanded weekly deliveries of corn, beans, eggs, and chickens. Needless to say, the "teacher" did not hold class; his "students" were his personal servants.[22]

Despite the efforts of Rabasa and a succession of Porfirian governors, progress on the educational front was slow. In 1896, Governor León claimed that lack of money in the state treasury forced him to prioritize spending commitments, with education taking the leftovers. "Finding myself in the painful position of spending a paltry sum on education, with a budget that amounts to not one-twentieth of the required sum, or abandoning other branches of vital importance for the development of the state, I opt for the first option," he wrote, with the hope that economic development would educate and "civilize" Chiapas's rural, largely Indian majority.[23] Two years later the governor claimed that 124 schools were operating in Chiapas, serving 5,267 students, less than one-tenth of the more than 64,000 school-age children in the state. León explained that "the indigenous race . . . resists the schools, because in the past they were victims of the wicked exploitation of teachers."[24]

This is not to say that the current crop of teachers was an improvement. In a private letter to Díaz, León complained that the "teachers" in Chilón and Simojovel were "the worst type of ladino," not content to simply exploit the Indians. They were also doing the coletos' bidding, agitating the Indians as part of their campaign to bring the state government back to San Cristóbal.

"I am getting rid of these employees with the hope of improving the teaching corps, but their replacements are even worse," León wrote.[25]

León's successors took small steps toward institutionalizing and professionalizing the state's school system. In 1902, Governor Rafael Pimentel inaugurated the Women's Normal School (Escuela Normal para Profesoras de Instrucción Primaria) to complement the state's normal school for men, founded during León's tenure.[26] By 1908 Governor Ramón Rabasa (older brother of ex-governor Emilio Rabasa) had the state government again taking an active role in establishing schools, increasingly for girls and women. Of 172 state-funded primary schools in Chiapas, forty-three were for females, fifty-two for males, and eighty were coeducational, serving a total of nearly 9,000 students. Municipal schools taught only 230 students, and only 378 students attended the poorly developed private schools.[27]

The expansion of state-funded schooling in Porfirian Chiapas looks impressive on paper, if only because public education had been so neglected by previous state governments. Between 1884 and 1907 per capita expenditure on public primary schooling in Chiapas increased 667 percent, the third-highest increase among Mexican states. School enrollments increased 289 percent during that same period, the fifth-greatest increase nationally. By any other measure, however, the education system in Chiapas was woefully inadequate. In 1907, after years of growth under Porfirian governors like the Rabasas, the state's per capita expenditure on primary education placed it twenty-third among twenty-seven states; with only 13 percent of the school-age population enrolled in public primary schools, it ranked last; and its 9.12-percent literacy rate ranked it ahead of only Guerrero.[28]

One of Porfirian Mexico's most illustrious educators was Justo Sierra, minister of the educational branch of the Ministry of Justice and Public Education (Secretaría de Justicia e Instrucción Pública) from 1901 to 1905, when he became the first director of the Ministry of Public Instruction and Fine Arts (Secretaría de Instrucción Pública y Bellas Artes). Sierra believed that education was the key to modernizing and unifying Mexico, a country that had endured multiple foreign invasions and civil wars and suffered mightily for its economic backwardness. Sierra also hoped that schools would assume the restraining and disciplining role occupied by the Church, an institution officially out of favor during the last third of the nineteenth century. In many regions Porfirian economic development triggered land expropriations, mass migrations into the cities, and a decline in working conditions; it also provoked the dissolution of family and community life and traditional, pre-capitalist forms of social control. Sierra and his peers turned to the schools to control this increasingly mobile, potentially unruly underclass. Teachers taught obedience to authority, honesty, and abnegation while providing literacy skills and encouraging the development of traits suitable for Mexico's economic development, like a capitalist work and savings ethic, a sense of individual responsibility, punctuality, and self-discipline.[29]

The controlling nature of Porfirian schooling was most evident in the realm of classroom discipline. Corporal punishment was liberally employed. Courses in civics, history, and physical education were steeped in a militaristic rhetoric of order and discipline. In some classrooms, students were subjected to potentially humiliating hygiene reviews. Teachers themselves were carefully monitored by school directors and local education committees both in their professional and personal lives, and those who "failed to uphold the dignity of their profession [were] dismissed."[30]

Civic education lessons also clashed with the realities of the Porfiriato. A teachers' instructional pamphlet in the neighboring state of Tabasco stated that "in a democratic country such as our own, where sovereignty resides in the people, all citizens should know their obligations and their rights . . . [such as] equality before the law [and] respect for individual liberty," even though the Díaz dictatorship granted effective citizens' rights to very few and placed palpable restrictions on individual expression.[31] Students living under the dictatorship were also taught to take "aversion to bad citizens, to traitors, to despots and to all that violate the rights of free men and oppress the weak and dispossessed."[32]

As schoolrooms in Porfirian Mexico provided some students with literacy skills and a notion of citizens' rights and obligations, they may also have given disenchanted future "citizens" the ideological and practical tools for rebellion. The capacity to read and write was potentially subversive, granting students access to the late Porfirian opposition press and political movements. Many of those who taught the mixed Porfirian message participated in the movement that swept Mexico after 1910, prompting one prominent observer to write that "it is possible to measure the value of public primary school in Mexico simply by recalling the decisive role played by teachers during the Revolution."[33]

The Mexican Revolution and Education in Chiapas

Understanding the idiosyncratic course of the Mexican revolution in Chiapas is the key to understanding the strength of reaction there after 1920.

When revolution finally came to Chiapas, it lacked a popular grassroots component—even the state's Zapatista division was in the hands of a wealthy rancher, Rafael Cal y Mayor, who espoused a peculiarly feudal and paternalistic version of Zapatismo.[34]

As Benjamin has written, Chiapas experienced three "revolutions" between 1910 and 1920, though none was truly "revolutionary." The first was simply the latest battle in the protracted political and economic war between the conservative elite of San Cristóbal and their liberal rivals in the lower Grijalva valley. Following months of disputes and an election in August 1911 that failed to produce results favorable to the coletos, San Cristóbal withdrew recognition of the state government in Tuxtla and prepared for war. With the help of Bishop Francisco Orozco y Jiménez, coletos recruited a few thousand poorly armed Maya highlanders and eight hundred ladinos. Most of the indigenous recruits were commanded by the Chamulan cacique Jacinto Pérez, also known as El Pajarito. After the coleto forces quickly seized several highland towns, Maya peasants began to settle scores with their brothers who had administered the tax and labor recruitment policies of the preceding fifteen years; according to Rus, "by far the bloodiest actions of the entire episode . . . were those directed against other Indians."[35] The federal government saw it differently, however. Acting to prevent another so-called caste war, it intervened on behalf of the one thousand or so state troops in Tuxtla and bloodily suppressed the insurrection in October 1911. Although divided politically, economically, and ideologically, lowland liberals and highland conservatives were united in their fear of indigenous *jacquerie*.[36]

Chiapas's second "revolution" began in September 1914 and was imposed from without by Carrancista general Jesús Agustín Castro and his troops. A native of Durango, Castro was one of First Chief Venustiano Carranza's young, radical proconsuls in the vein of Francisco Múgica and Salvador Alvarado. Hostile to privilege, hierarchy, and the clergy, Castro believed in top-down "revolution" and social justice. He immediately abolished the state's congress and Supreme Court. On December 14, 1914, he passed an anticlerical law that prohibited confession, legalized divorce, closed convents, restricted the celebration of mass to once a week, and confiscated all Church property, including that of Bishop Orozco y Jiménez. Crosses were also to be removed from the rooftops of private residences. In early 1915 Castro abolished the Porfirian post of jefe político and passed laws initiating limited land reform. A firm believer in central government, Castro's efforts in Chiapas were intended to break the power of the *familia chiapaneca* and liberate the masses of mestizo and indigenous peasants and workers from the priests, *finqueros* (plantation owners), and ranchers who had previously controlled their lives.[37]

Castro's most significant reform was his October 1914 Ley de Obreros (Workers' Law, also known as the Ley de Liberación de Mozos, or Peon Liberation Law). It represented the first federal attempt to regulate labor in Chiapas by ending debt peonage and enganche and abolishing outstanding worker debts and the *tienda de raya* (company store). The law also set minimum wages according to occupation and geographic location and created a corps of labor inspectors. It established rudimentary accident and disability insurance for workers, set a ten-hour day, and stipulated, vaguely, that rural proprietors establish schools for the children of their workers.[38]

Castro also undertook major educational reforms meant to wrest public schooling from the hands of pro-clerical coletos. He closed professional schools in San Cristóbal and moved them to Tuxtla Gutiérrez. Castro also called the first Pedagogy Congress in Carrancista Mexico. The conference was held in Tuxtla, of course, and featured the participation of directors, school inspectors, and teachers. Fifty-nine men and forty-two women answered the call. Men were well represented in all three occupational categories, while all forty-two women were teachers, indicating a "glass ceiling" for women in the education hierarchy. In attendance were future directors of the SEP in Chiapas, Mauro Calderón and Raúl Isidro Burgos, as well as future SEP zone inspectors Daniel Tamayo and Epigmenio de León.

For over six weeks congress participants engaged in lively, democratic debate as they charted the course for "revolutionary" schooling. Participants questioned the rigid disciplinary regime of Porfirian classrooms and the utility of Porfirian-era textbooks, considered how best to educate children on haciendas and ranches, and discussed the need to teach indigenous languages at normal schools. Like their colleagues nationwide, Chiapanecan pedagogues vowed to discontinue "authoritarian" practices that awarded prizes to a few while others suffered corporal punishment.[39]

On the highly polemical theme of coeducation, heated debate occupied several days and participants had to be called to order multiple times. Numerous teachers testified that parents withheld their daughters from male teachers' classrooms, fearing molestation, and withheld their sons from female teachers' classrooms, fearing they would develop homosexual tendencies. It was agreed that resistance to coeducation was fiercest in rural and indigenous communities, where the vast majority of the state's population were to be found. Participants resolved that coed classrooms were tolerable on haciendas and ranches only, because rural proprietors (under the terms of General Castro's 1914 Ley de Obreros) could not be expected to support a school for each sex. Another resolution stipulated that only women should teach at these coed schools in order to increase the enrollment of girls.[40]

Following the Pedagogy Congress, Constitutionalist budgets reflected the new regime's commitment to education. In 1915, half of the state budget was dedicated to road construction and schools. One year later the Constitutionalist governor, General Blas Corral, claimed 474 schools, a number no doubt inflated for public consumption. Less than one fourth of these alleged schools were to be found in rural Chiapas.[41] As Constitutionalist pedagogues would learn, ambitious legislation and larger budgets only went so far; implementation was quite another matter.

The Mapache Response

Castro's reforms—political, anticlerical, agrarian, labor, and educational—might well have provoked revolt in any state, but conditions in Chiapas made rebellion practically inevitable and widely popular. To begin with, Castro lacked a popular rural constituency in Chiapas except in Soconusco, where his top-down revolution struck a chord among permanent workers on the heavily capitalized coffee plantations, and adjacent Mariscal, where the plantations recruited many seasonal laborers.[42] For the most part, his provocative legislation simply made it easier for his enemies to rally around the banners of family, church, property, and state sovereignty.

If Castro's radical reforms initially provoked a conservative backlash, Carrancista abuses throughout the war that ensued granted the rebels a degree of popularity they would not have otherwise enjoyed. Their propensity to pillage was reflected in the coining of the verb *carrancear*, meaning "to steal," and in the present-day Tzotzil word for the common Norway rat, *caransa*.[43] Carrancista troops executed scores of so-called enemies of the people, such as jefes políticos and others identified with the Porfiriato. They also killed El Pajarito, who had peacefully retired following the cessation of hostilities in October 1911, fearing that he was still capable of igniting a race war. In a prelude to the rabid official anticlericalism of Governor Victórico Grajales (1932–1936), troops stole from sacristies, destroyed religious art, and converted churches into stables. Bishop Belisario Trejo described the scene in Comitán, where Carrancistas sacked various parishes in 1914. "All the pews were removed to make beds, stained-glass windows were broken, twelve elegant chandeliers and almost all of the altars were destroyed, and so was the Archbishop's throne, made of silver," he wrote. "Decorations, candelabras, and vases were lost" and "confessionaries were ripped apart." Soldiers then sold religious artifacts "at laughable prices" in the streets and plazas of Comitán. According to Trejo, most of the buyers were "pious people" who hoped to eventually return the objects to their parishes.[44]

On December 2, 1914, Chiapas's third "revolution" began. Tiburcio Fernández Ruiz and about forty other landowners met on the banks of the Canguí River, near Chiapa de Corzo, and declared themselves in rebellion against Carrancista occupation. Only twenty-six years of age, Fernández Ruiz had been studying law in Mexico City under former governor Emilio Rabasa when the revolution broke out. He then fought in the División del Norte under Pancho Villa's command. Although he had Villa's blessing to head a Villista movement in Chiapas, Fernández Ruiz was single-mindedly concerned with the defense of state sovereignty. Most of the Mapache leaders were frontier finqueros and ranchers of modest means.[45] Their dependent workers, or *mozos*, typically joined them in battle. The Mapache manifesto, the Acta de Canguí, promised to "expel the Carrancista filibusterers from the State, and place our destinies in the hands of a legitimately Chiapanecan government, product of a people who—more than any other that forms the Mexican Federation—has the right to demand due respect for its sovereignty."[46]

For the next six years, the Mapaches fought the Carrancistas to a draw, even though their numbers never exceeded more than a couple of thousand and in 1918 dropped to as low as six hundred. In 1915, their cause received a boost when several finqueros from Comitán joined their cause, including Abelardo Cristiani and Ernesto Castellanos, father of writer Rosario Castellanos. One year later coleto Alberto Pineda and his "Las Casas Brigade" joined the rebellion. Another source of logistical and financial support came from Guatemala, new home to exiled clerics and former Porfirian officials. They were joined in their efforts by Guatemalan president Manuel Estrada Cabrera, who supplied arms to various rebel factions.[47]

In this hard-fought civil war of attrition, the warring parties took pains not to mobilize Chiapas's rural masses, especially Indians. The highland ladinos' political mutiny of 1911 had already been recast as a menacing Indian uprising, a "cautionary tale about the dangers of mobilizing and arming the 'semi-savage' Maya peasants."[48] In the highlands, where the troops of Pineda did battle with the Carrancistas, the Maya were often pressed into service as guides, load-bearers, cooks, and servants, but never as soldiers.

As told by Miguel Ordóñez, a Tzeltal from Cancuc, the Carrancistas took men not to fight ("*tirar bala*") but rather "to care for the generals' women, to care for the horses and kill the bulls that the generals ate."[49] As Jan Rus has written, the revolution in Chiapas was "little more than a civil war among ladino elites—a civil war in which Indians were considered not allies, but part of the spoils."[50] Actively discouraged from taking a more direct role in the conflict, Indians still suffered its consequences as the warring parties passed through their towns and fields, wreaking havoc and destruction, stealing money, corn, chickens, and sheep, and raping and murdering at will.

The Mapaches were able to grab victory from the jaws of defeat in February 1920. Just days before Fernández Ruiz entered into peace negotiations with the Carrancistas, Constitutionalist general Carlos Vidal met Fernández Ruiz and his depleted forces at a ranch on the Nandayacuí River. Vidal, a finquero from Pichucalco, offered peace to the Mapache caudillo if he would back General Álvaro Obregón's anticipated coup against President Carranza.[51] In such an event, Vidal promised to recognize Fernández Ruiz as the state's revolutionary boss (much to the subsequent dismay of Pineda).

In April 1920 the much-anticipated rebellion against Carranza materialized at Agua Prieta. Fernández Ruiz seconded the movement and became first chief of Obregonismo in Chiapas, as planned. After several federal military garrisons declared their support for Obregón, Carrancista general Alejo González abandoned Tuxtla on May 18. Four days later, Fernández Ruiz and his troops occupied the state capital. The Mapache victory was confirmed in June when interim president Adolfo de la Huerta named Mapache commander Francisco Ruiz interim governor of Chiapas. In September, Alberto Pineda made peace after extracting several concessions from de la Huerta, including payment of debts that he owed residents of San Cristóbal and a promise to construct a highway from Pineda's stronghold of San Cristóbal north to Salto de Agua, near Palenque. The restless Pineda was then incorporated into the Mexican army. The victory of the Mapaches and especially Tiburcio Fernández Ruiz was sealed in November when he won an uncontested election for state governor. He took office on December 1, 1920.[52]

As Benjamin has written, "Mapache reconstruction in the area of labor and agrarian reform was exactly that—the reconstruction or restoration of the Porfirian social order as much as possible."[53] During his four-year tenure, Fernández Ruiz successfully eluded enforcement of Carrancista labor law by budgeting no funds for inspection and enforcement. Although debt peonage, company stores, and enganche never actually disappeared during the

Carrancista occupation, under Fernández Ruiz they were once again sanctioned. Mapache politicians and the state judiciary also crippled the federal agrarian reform program. In 1921, the state government passed a law declaring that properties of less than eight thousand hectares were considered "small property" exempted from expropriation. This left only about seventy *fincas* (farms or plantations) unprotected. State and federal legislation also declared *peones acasillados* (resident laborers) ineligible to receive land. Fernández Ruiz and his supporters were able to control the pace of land reform in the state because petitions had first to be approved by the state's Local Agrarian Commission (Comisión Local Agraria), entirely in the hands of unsympathetic landlords and the governor.[54] They also received help from the federal government in 1922. Anxious to protect productive estates from zealous reformers, the Obregón administration (1920–1924) stated that coffee, cacao, vanilla, rubber, and other plantations would be exempted from agrarian reform. As late as 1936, none of the coffee plantations in Soconusco had been expropriated. Finally, as we shall see, Fernández Ruiz consciously undermined the crippled state education system and opposed the federalization of existing schools.

The Failure of Constitutionalist Schooling, 1915–1922

During the period of revolutionary violence in Chiapas, the Carrancistas had little opportunity to implement their education agenda. General Castro's most notable innovation was the creation of a body of delegates of public instruction. Each municipality in the state was assigned one delegate, who technically served as an intermediary between the schools and the town council (*ayuntamiento*) on the one hand and the education zone inspector on the other.[55] Through this body of delegates Carrancista pedagogues hoped to address a number of ills that had plagued Porfirian schools, such as poorly provisioned classrooms, abusive teachers, obstructionist local governments, and the abysmal attendance rates of both students and teachers.

Yet old habits die hard, and surviving documents speak to the ineptitude and corruption of many delegates and the persistence of obstacles to educational reform. In 1915 San Cristóbal's delegate wrote that "there are delegates and teachers who live in the arcades of the town hall, drinking themselves into a stupor; schools without a single student; teachers of both sexes who cannot even sign their names." Other delegates and teachers showed a true entrepreneurial spirit "as telephone operators, town council officials and tax collectors; in other words, all of the public positions in a town can be in the hands of one enterprising person." The delegate at the municipality of Jitotol, for example, also held the posts of municipal treasurer, cemetery guard, and postman.[56] In May 1915, just a few months after the creation of the body of delegates, the state government published a decree prohibiting them from working other jobs.[57] This proved unenforceable, since the delegates answered to no one except one of the state's six overextended zone inspectors.

In the end, Castro's delegates and inspectors were powerless to prevent teachers from extorting economic resources and otherwise abusing their authority in their communities. At the Tzotzil community of San Andrés Larráinzar, for example, teacher Manuel Molina Morales practiced the age-old custom of "selling" excused absences to the parents of school-age children. When told to stop by the municipal delegate, Molina replied that "no one tells him how to run his school." Molina also used the school's furniture as his own and housed his livestock in the schoolroom at night. On top of these abuses, Molina taught religious history.[58] In another case, at the town of Santiago (near San Cristóbal) the inebriated, well-connected male teacher at the boys' school broke into the home of Maurilia Villafuerte, the teacher at the girls' school, and sexually assaulted her in late 1915. The male teacher told his victim to keep the matter quiet, so as not to stain the honor of either of them. Local law enforcement and the nascent education bureaucracy proved unable and unwilling to prosecute the matter seriously. The only person to testify on behalf of Villafuerte was her servant, who heard the screams. The male teacher fabricated an alibi and had students, their parents, and the municipal president testify to his good conduct. In frustration Villafuerte wrote a letter to the Director of Public Education in Tuxtla. "Mr. Ramos considers it his right to insult the honor and decorum of a lady because he is Municipal Secretary, telephone operator, tax collector, judicial scribe and director of the school," she wrote. "Since he holds these positions, it comes as no surprise that to this date he has enjoyed absolute impunity." Villafuerte requested a transfer to another school, then offered her resignation.[59]

The Carrancistas' most notable foray into indigenous education was the ill-fated School of Indigenous Regeneration (Escuela de Regeneración Indígena), a boarding school established in San Cristóbal in 1919. Students were to learn Spanish and an appropriate skill. According to the government's official bulletin, they would also learn to behave like *gente decente*.

> [Students will acquire] domestic and social habits superior to those of today's indigenous pueblos. . . . Students will become accustomed to the use of pants and a jacket . . . to eating at fixed hours, at a table

> with a tablecloth and silverware, with correct manners . . . to all of the practices of washing, posture and hygiene used by civilized people, without forgetting that which refers to salivation, spitting, and urinating. . . . [Students will learn] to love work, the truth and temperance, and to repudiate the vices most common among *indígenas*, which are laziness, lying, and drunkenness.[60]

Students were not allowed to visit their home villages until they had been enrolled in the school for two years. Recruitment methods for this school were often violent. As SEP "missionary" Federico Corzo later wrote, Chamulan children "were practically pulled out of their homes by force" and fled the school whenever they could. The students' home villages were taxed so that students could be fed.[61] Subsequent state and federal boarding school projects in the 1920s and 1930s would try to live down the notoriety of this school, but would frequently resort to the same coercive recruitment techniques.

The education system that Carrancistas in Chiapas worked so hard to build in 1914 and 1915 was abruptly dismantled by Constitutionalists at the federal level in February 1916. Responsibility for funding schools fell to municipal governments, many of which were coping with the disastrous consequences of war. This shift had its roots in Carranza's decree of December 25, 1914, which proclaimed the principle of the self-governing municipality.[62] Based on the success of the free municipality in his home state of Coahuila, where local governments were seemingly able to continue funding and managing their schools, Carranza believed the independent municipality to be the (low-cost) foundation of future democracy in Mexico. Delegates at the Constitutional Convention in Querétaro ratified educational decentralization by voting to suppress the federal Secretaría de Instrucción Pública in 1917.

In Chiapas, Constitutionalist decentralization had the effect of turning back the clock to pre-Porfirian times. Mauro Calderón, appointed Chiapas's first director of federal education in December 1921, wrote of the collapse of public schooling throughout the state. Of the 474 schools claimed by Governor Corral in 1916, only 136 primary and rural schools remained in 1922, and these were in terrible condition. "Only two or three municipalities have been able to sustain their schools, but every day it becomes more difficult to do so," he wrote.[63] "Locally funded education is a disaster." Echoing his words were teachers in Tuxtla Gutiérrez, who wrote "we are convinced that teaching conditions in this corner of Mexican soil will improve only with the help of the federation."[64]

Although Chiapanecan pedagogues favored federalization, more powerful interests in the state were loath to relinquish power to the political and military faction that claimed the spoils of victory in 1920. Some even asserted that José Vasconcelos's proposal to establish a national Ministry of Public Education in 1921 was a violation of states' rights.[65] Historian Luis Espinosa, one of Chiapas's representatives to the national congress, argued that states should have veto rights over federal education policies. Espinosa's objections were brushed aside, and the SEP was established in 1921 with the power to direct matters in its schools throughout the country—even in Chiapas.

Conclusion

The Mapaches' military and political victory in 1920 boded ill for the immediate future of public schooling in Chiapas. An adamant defender of state autonomy, Tiburcio Fernández Ruiz made no secret of his desire to limit federal influence in the state during his tenure. In his second annual address to the state legislature in 1921, Fernández Ruiz dismissed Constitutionalist rule as "abnormal and irregular" and "foreign." He praised the ultimate outcome of the fighting, which produced "an authentically Chiapanecan government, with origins in the sovereign will of its people."[66] Although states like Chiapas were unable to prevent the establishment of the federal SEP in 1921, the collapse of central authority during the revolution gave governors like Fernández Ruiz in the early 1920s considerable freedom to obstruct federal education programs in their states.

The Mapache governor also attacked what remained of Chiapas's crippled state education system. Believing it to be a vestige of Carrancismo, Fernández Ruiz purged the state's teaching corps shortly after assuming power. Claiming that many teachers had become embroiled in politics and had forgotten their true mission, he closed down the state's Department of Education (Dirección General del Ramo). He also dismantled the network of zone inspectors established during Constitutionalist rule.[67] Chiapas therefore entered the postrevolutionary era with a woefully inadequate education infrastructure and a state leadership bent on resisting federal intervention in state affairs. The SEP would have to tread lightly in the state. Its first step was to send "missionaries" in 1922.

Chapter Two

Action Pedagogy and Political Realities

> There is . . . a world of economic problems to resolve and literally mountains of material obstacles to remove before the work of the school can bear fruit. . . . Teachers will keep teaching. Governments will continue paying for schools. Effort and money will be wasted . . . until we have a more comprehensive educational program and a social philosophy that requires the school to project itself definitively into the community.
>
> —*Moisés Sáenz, "El paisaje social en la sierra de Puebla,"* 1927

Throughout the twentieth century, revolutionary states emerging from civil wars sought to consolidate and institutionalize their rule through ambitious federal education systems. In the Soviet Union and postrevolutionary China, schools strove mightily to carve nations of productive, nationalist citizens out of ethnically heterogeneous, traditional, and predominately illiterate populations. In Latin America, Cuba and Nicaragua consolidated their leftist nationalist revolutions through schools and highly publicized literacy campaigns. In all four settings schools anchored state control, disseminated official ideology, and attempted to create a sense of national identity and unity. Meanwhile, the revolutionary regimes took credit for extending the gifts of literacy and schooling to the masses, and education became part of the official revolutionary nationalist ideology.

Mexico's SEP intended to use education to similar ends. Although the *outcome* of the violence of 1910–1920 was not "revolutionary" in a Marxist sense, the *process* was highly popular, and many participants believed they were indeed fighting for revolutionary ends.[1] The victorious Sonoran dynasty looked to the SEP to exercise the same controlling and didactic functions that schools were to have performed during the Porfiriato. But times had also changed. The SEP was to "forge the fatherland" in unsettled, war-torn regions where armed locals demanded resolution of their long-standing grievances and where powerful governors and caciques resisted federal intervention. Rather than attempt to suppress the revolutionary impulse, the SEP tried to harness and appropriate it through the rural school, also known as the Casa del Pueblo.

Despite the fanfare surrounding the SEP's early efforts, its record throughout rural Mexico in the 1920s was rather spotty. In Chiapas, the odds were certainly stacked against success. Mapache governor Tiburcio Fernández Ruiz not only opposed federal education in principle, but his brutal electoral impositions throughout the state generated instability and threatened SEP teachers. Lukewarm or nonexistent community support and racial and ethnic tensions also vexed the SEP's teachers. Even under the best of circumstances, many teachers lacked the basic skills and training to succeed. Just as the SEP's project was getting off the ground, the de la Huerta rebellion of 1923–1924 swept away teachers and schools. The SEP returned to the state in late 1924 still smarting from its initial failures. In this, its second attempt to win over rural Chiapanecos, it would deploy a new weapon—action pedagogy.

"Missionaries" of Education

The founding of the SEP in 1921 is intimately linked to its creator, the enigmatic José Vasconcelos.[2] As director of the SEP, Vasconcelos implemented innovative, populist programs for rural education in spite of his elitism. His first step in 1922 was to send normal school graduates to rural, often indigenous areas to study the socioeconomic and cultural condition of the people, to interest community members in education, and to recruit prospective teachers. In Chiapas, these educators, known confusingly as "ambulatory" teachers, "*conferencistas*," and later "missionaries," traveled to remote corners of the state on horseback and on foot, sending reports to federal education delegate Mauro Calderón. In late 1922 Calderón's synthetic report spoke of the "complete decadence of the municipal schools." Although municipalities levied taxes in support of public education, rarely was this money spent on schools. Conditions were most deplorable in indigenous pueblos, he wrote, because the few existing schools "serve no function at all, other than to torture the Indians."[3] Despite the efforts of the missionaries, only fifteen federally funded Casas del Pueblo were established in the state in 1922, most of them in relatively developed Soconusco and Mariscal.

In 1923 and 1924, missionaries in Chiapas founded many more Casas del Pueblo by incorporating and federalizing dozens of existing municipal and state schools. Most of these had been abandoned or closed due to economic hardship. Elsewhere in Mexico, communities often resisted federalization of their schools because they feared losing control over a vital local institution.[4] In Chiapas, however, most schools were of recent vintage and had not operated regularly enough to have cultivated local traditions in education. Communities entrusted their schools to the missionaries willingly, even gladly. The jealous state government, though, did not cede these schools to the SEP without a fight. In a letter to Vasconcelos in 1923, it made it clear that the missionaries' actions constituted an unwanted federal intrusion. Missionaries had "usurped schools formed by the Municipalities or established by the State, taking with them the students, the classroom supplies, and even some teachers, changing only the name of the school."[5]

The state government even raised the banner of indigenismo in a cynical attempt to discredit federal teachers. "The so-called missionaries of the twentieth century bear no relation to the sixteenth-century apostles," wrote the interim governor in May 1923.[6] In indigenous towns they allegedly engaged in "the barbaric custom of demanding emoluments and cash subsidies, animals and personal services under the pretext that they were needed to constitute schools."[7] There was probably a certain degree of truth to these charges, since communities were expected to contribute land, building materials, and other resources to the school; it may also have been true that many missionaries and teachers abused their positions. But it was most certainly true that the "barbaric customs" of extraction had been perfected by municipal presidents and other agents of the state government. Municipalities large and small continued to petition the SEP for federalization throughout the 1920s and early 1930s.[8]

The hostility of the state government in Chiapas exacerbated working and living conditions for missionaries. Indeed, when Vasconcelos labeled his pioneering teachers "missionaries" he had the example of the sixteenth-century Franciscans in mind. His missionaries would endure trials and tribulations too as they imparted a secular message of redemption to their flock. This religious imagery clearly appealed to Ernesto Parres, the missionary based in Tapachula, who in his reports made frequent reference to the "Franciscan patience" and "abnegation" of his best teachers. For Parres, who became locally known as a novelist, poet, and historian, some missionaries were true martyrs, suffering countless deprivations in a hostile and unforgiving wilderness. Consider his description of Pedro Juárez Carranza, missionary at the Casa del Pueblo at Niquivil, Mariscal. "Although Citizen Carranza already combs gray hairs, has stoically suffered the constant frosts in the region, for which he now has acute rheumatism, and has suffered a thousand inconveniences from the building he occupies, [he possesses] a constant desire to obliterate illiteracy and pull the inhabitants of the village out from darkness and ignorance."[9] Missionary life in Chiapas approached the Franciscan example in other ways as well. Until the fledgling SEP normalized payment of its teachers, missionaries were essentially forced into a vow of poverty. In late 1922, Parres noted that he was "obliged to resort to a thousand subterfuges to ensure my subsistence, which violates my pedagogical principles."[10] In May 1924, after his teachers had not been paid for four months, Parres complained, "our stoicism has reached the limits of martyrdom!" Chiapas's missionaries still had not been paid by October of that year, prompting SEP Undersecretary Moisés Sáenz to intervene on their behalf.[11]

Carrying the Franciscan analogy a bit further, Vasconcelos's missionaries often found communities indifferent (if not hostile) to their redemptive, "civilizing" mission. Often, the SEP's blueprint was unsuitable to local realities. In the town of Tuxtla Chico, located in the heart of Soconusco's coffee-, sugar-, and cacao-producing region, SEP teacher Octavio Ángel Soto complained that villagers regarded the school with "glacial indifference" and refused to construct facilities for instruction in apiculture and livestock husbandry. Parents wanted reading and writing taught, not farming and ranching, especially since their children gained firsthand experience in agriculture when they worked alongside their parents on the coffee plantations every fall.[12]

Still, the missionaries' greatest obstacles in Chiapas were ethnic and cultural, especially in indigenous communities. As the next chapter will explore in greater detail, few Maya welcomed their ladino redeemers with open arms, the legacy of centuries of oppression and exploitation. In many highland villages, language and cultural barriers were insurmountable and interethnic relations so tense that scores fled at the mere sight of Vasconcelos's missionaries. As Federico Corzo wrote in 1922, "The Chamulans seem to be refractory to civilization, or at least they fear or hate civilized people, maybe because they have been subjected to exploitation or because they have been trampled . . . and abused and disregarded. Those that spotted me from afar changed their course and avoided me and those that I managed to surprise up close were terrified at the sight of me."[13] Another missionary in Chiapas wrote:

> The mestizo teacher will not be accepted because the Indian is suspicious, distrustful and does not tolerate the "ladino," who he considers to be his enemy, capable only of doing harm and never good: in

> order to convince him that we are his brothers, sons of the same motherland, an arduous and prolonged campaign will be necessary. . . . Only with love, good faith, and honor we will incorporate and civilize our Indians.[14]

Although a handful of missionaries were bilingual, all were ladinos. Native teachers—the logical answer to indigenous distrust of ladino teachers—were not used in Chiapas until the 1950s, in spite of the recommendations of several missionaries.

By late 1923 most missionaries in Chiapas who were not recovering from malaria, kidney stones, and other ailments concentrated their efforts in the lowlands or in indigenous communities where at least a few ladinos resided, under the assumption that ladinos would take the lead in endorsing the Casa del Pueblo in their towns.[15] Only in the ex-department of Mariscal could it be said that the SEP's initial project was embraced by teachers, peasants, and workers.

Activism, Education, and Repression in Mariscal

Mariscal's politically active, experienced teachers viewed federal education as a means of outflanking the Mapaches, mobilizing workers and peasants, and advancing their progressive political agenda through the Partido Socialista Chiapaneco (Socialist Party of Chiapas, or PSCH). Ultimately, the combination of political activism, independent unionization, and federal education proved too explosive, and the socialists (including teachers) paid a high price for their courage.

Mariscal's peasants and small-scale ranchers were relatively cosmopolitan. Many came from Guatemala and spoke K'anjobal, Chuj-Jacalteco, and Mam. They settled in Mariscal after Soconusco's landowners convinced Porfirio Díaz to pass a colonization law in 1883. They typically supplemented their incomes with annual stints on Soconusco's coffee plantations, just a day or two away by foot. These migrants, both Maya and ladino, became radicalized by their experiences in the capitalist export economy. When General Castro introduced the Ley de Obreros in 1914, Mariscal was as politicized as any district in Chiapas, and many of its workers and peasants enlisted in the Carrancista army.[16]

In January 1920, teachers and others from Motozintla turned their liberal democratic political club into the Partido Socialista Chiapaneco. When Carrancismo collapsed a few months later, the PSCH—with help from Obregonistas like Carlos Vidal—overturned several local municipal

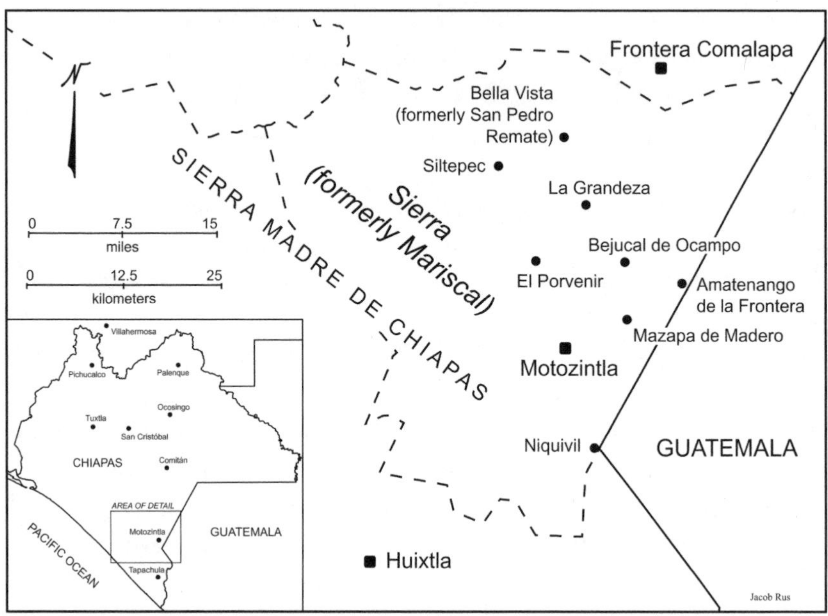

Map 2. Sierra, formerly Mariscal.

governments and installed socialist party members. The Mapache state government quickly retaliated by stripping "socialist" municipalities (like San Pedro Remate) of their municipal status and turning them into administrative appendages (*agencias municipales*) of more docile municipalities.[17]

For the next few years, members of the Partido Socialista Chiapaneco demanded compliance with the terms of the Constitution of 1917 as a means of improving working conditions for the thousands who migrated annually to Soconusco's coffee plantations. They also fought in the electoral arena to remove local authorities who controlled labor contracting. As they tried to explain to President Obregón, they did not consider themselves a threat.

> Here, sir, Bolshevism does not exist; it's true that we are socialists, but our socialism is evolutionary, which calls for social transformation through school books, through the free diffusion of the sciences and the regeneration of the Indians, for whom we ask for the suppression of alcoholism and the masked slavery that is practiced here by "habilitators" [debt labor recruiters].[18]

Federal schooling became an integral part of the political struggle in

Mariscal. Not only did teachers help create the party, but the father and brother of the party secretary, Ricardo Alfonso Paniagua, were both federal teachers who participated actively in the party's electoral struggles and unionization drives. In January 1922, shortly after the creation of the SEP, residents of San Pedro Remate requested a school for themselves and for each of the sixteen municipalities that roughly constituted Mariscal. No doubt Juan Eduardo Paniagua (Ricardo's father) was behind the petition. The elder Paniagua and his wife had directed San Pedro Remate's boys' and girls' schools, respectively, during the years of revolutionary violence. In February, Juan Eduardo Paniagua was appointed teacher of this ethnically mixed former municipality. Although 75 percent of the population was Mam, more than half of its residents spoke Spanish, and of the roughly fifty-five students that attended class regularly, forty were indigenous.[19]

Paniagua's eloquent reports provide us with a glimpse of life in a SEP rural school in early 1922. His classroom lacked desks. Nowhere could students buy the chalk, pens, and ink that they needed. Paniagua had not received guidelines or regulations from the SEP, not to mention a pedagogical orientation. He was forced to improvise his lesson plans because the SEP had not sent any books. He had no teaching tools for the monolingual Mam children in his classroom. He remained optimistic nonetheless, inspired by a missionary spirit. "Not everything can be fixed with theoretical methods and systems," he wrote. "Perseverance and the faith of a Pedro de Gante or a Motolinía [two Franciscan evangelists known for their work with indigenous peoples] are also needed." He concluded that in Mariscal, "teaching is a true apostolate and the only ones who can dedicate themselves to it are those that feel a true calling to bring the light of learning to these remote mountains, not for individual gain or bastardized ambitions, but for love of the career and of humanity."[20]

Juan Eduardo Paniagua's faith and perseverance (and that of his two sons) were tested in 1922. Believing themselves supported by President Álvaro Obregón, the Socialists formed the Workers' and Peasants' Union of Soconusco (Sindicato de Obreros y Campesinos de Soconusco) early that year and allied themselves with the Obregón administration's official labor union, the Regional Confederation of Mexican Workers (Confederación Regional Obrera Mexicana, or CROM). The SEP did not approve; in May of that year, responding to complaints lodged by the Chiapas state government, it threatened Paniagua with dismissal if he did not desist in his political activities.[21] In response, Paniagua bitterly labeled La Grandeza's municipal authorities "enganchadores . . . modern slavers who distrust the Rural School, because now they cannot send the unhappy peons to the coffee plantations whenever they feel like it, since the peons will not pull their children out of school until they have taken their year-end final exams." Paniagua invoked more imagery in closing his report. "I feel like a sentinel advancing against illiteracy and if my superiors abandon me, believing the attacks of my adversaries, I will necessarily succumb in the battle."[22]

The "battle," of course, involved much more than a literacy campaign. Juan Eduardo Paniagua's school had become an integral part of life and the struggle in San Pedro Remate. In May 1922 he managed to obtain a vaccine against chicken pox and vaccinated many of his students, only to contract hemorrhagic malaria himself two months later. Once restored to health, he participated in the Sindicato's September 1922 strike to force the authorities to abide by the terms of the Constitution of 1917. Although seven thousand workers supported the strike and forced the coffee planters to negotiate, its end result was ambiguous. While the planters agreed to an eight-hour workday and agreed to establish schools on their plantations, they found ways around the workers' demand for a wage increase.[23] Shortly after the Sindicato's strike, Paniagua's direct superior, Ernesto Parres, spoke with the authorities in Motozintla (once again in Mapache hands following that year's extraordinarily violent elections). As Motozintla's municipal president reported to the SEP in Mexico City, the purpose of Parres's visit was to "investigate the latest socialist activity that has affected the region."[24] According to one of Paniagua's contacts, Motozintla's municipal authorities told Parres that Paniagua had misused SEP funds[25] and was "preparing the *indígenas* for the practice of citizenship." Parres obligingly found someone to replace Paniagua. Once again, Paniagua defended his conduct in a dramatic letter to Mexico City, writing, "If I succumb in the struggle, it won't matter—I will be one more martyr and I will fall like the gladiators fell, with their faces to the sun, lamenting only the fact that I was not supported by my superiors."[26]

Three months after the strike, municipal elections were held in Chiapas that unleashed a new round of violence. Mariscal's socialists strengthened their alliance with General Carlos Vidal, who could now offer them protection in his new capacity as chief of the General Staff Division of Obregón's War Ministry. Over the short term, at least, this relationship paid dividends. When Vidal became governor in 1925, he staffed his state bureaucracy with socialist party members. Ricardo Paniagua became president of the state's Agrarian Commission (Comisión Local Agraria) and the Socialist

Confederation of Workers of Chiapas (Confederación Socialista de Trabajadores de Chiapas), created by Vidal to unify and control his allies. But this alliance exposed the socialists to new dangers, as we shall see.

Mapaches vs. the Center, Part II

The Mapaches' struggle with Mexico City did not end in 1920; it merely assumed different dimensions. As Benjamin notes, postrevolutionary state politics became much more complex as 12 powerful jefes políticos made way for dozens of weak municipal presidents.[27] Local elections became wild free-for-alls as factions fought for control of these municipalities. For many other reasons, Chiapas was in a state of nearly perpetual unrest during the tenure of Fernández Ruiz (1920–1924). Expatriated Mexican generals and politicians continued to plot and agitate against the Obregón regime from Guatemala, the Mapache state government and ladino municipalities in the central highlands struggled to reassert their political and economic control over indigenous villages, and theft and generalized violence were endemic along the state's northern and southern borders where the presence of state and federal institutions was minimal.[28] One of Vasconcelos's missionaries along the southern border was Elpidio López, soon to become Director of Federal Education in Chiapas. By March 1922, he had been robbed and assaulted so many times in his zone of La Libertad and Mariscal that he began making his rounds in the company of two or three armed escorts and, occasionally, federal troops. Local politics added another layer of difficulty for the missionaries. As López explained, "Some of my colleagues have been fired due in large part to the political intrigue of small villages." During elections "one is considered an enemy if one declares his neutrality."[29]

Matters came to a head in the tumultuous municipal elections of fall 1922. A heterogeneous coalition including the PSCH, former Carrancistas, highland finqueros, and a small but vigorous contingent of lowland *agraristas* and coffee pickers joined General Carlos Vidal in opposing Fernández Ruiz in what were quite possibly the most contentious elections of the decade. The governor resorted to the old Porfirian trick of arresting opposition candidates before votes were cast. Several pro-Mapache municipalities simply named "winners" rather than hold elections. In the indigenous highlands, voting was orchestrated by ladino officials who owed their jobs to the governor. Nevertheless, the opposition succeeded in winning over two-thirds of the fifty-eight municipal governments where elections were held.[30]

Shortly after the elections, two of Chiapas's representatives to the national Chamber of Deputies, Luis Espinosa and Jaime A. Solís, penned a letter to then Interior Minister Plutarco Elías Calles, decrying what they described as the state's "asphyxiating environment of official imposition." The "Chiapanecan Caesar" was using his control of the state legislature to nullify pro-Vidalista election victories. His thugs resorted to shoot-outs, hangings, and assassinations to reimpose Mapache control in Vidalista and socialist municipalities like Motozintla. In one celebrated case, an estimated seven hundred residents of Tuxtla Chico, Soconusco, grabbed rifles, muskets, pistols, machetes, and sticks and repelled gunmen sent by the state government to remove their elected officials.[31]

Fernández Ruiz may have sealed his fate (and that of his *camarilla*) in February 1923, when Calles paid him a visit in Tapachula. Much of the state was still in post-electoral upheaval, and the strike called by the PSCH had still not been fully resolved. Carlos Vidal's brother Luis had formed an armed group called the Re-organizing Army of the Free and Sovereign State of Chiapas (Ejército Reorganizador del Estado Libre y Soberano de Chiapas). Several hundred rebels—most of them coffee workers affiliated with the PSCH and most of them Carrancista veterans—had taken up arms in Soconusco, Mariscal, and nearby areas. The insurgents demanded the immediate resignation of the governor, asked that the results of recent elections be respected, and pledged their loyalty to Obregón's government.[32] The encounter between the stubborn Mapache and the future president was tense. Fernández Ruiz wanted Calles to authorize the use of the federal army to restore order to the state and safeguard his electoral impositions. Calles refused, recommending that the governor either hold new elections or grant concessions to his opposition. After Fernández Ruiz dismissed both suggestions, a frustrated Calles wrote Obregón that "given the standpoint of the Governor, I don't think a practical solution can be reached and the current abnormal situation will prevail."[33] Obregón called Fernández Ruiz to Mexico City. The Mapache general, a declared Obregonista, eventually agreed to name a provisional governor and respect the results of the elections. By the time Fernández Ruiz returned to Chiapas, he was willing to grant an amnesty to Vidalistas accused of criminal acts. Obregón, the master of compromise and reconciliation, had forced the standard-bearer of Chiapanecan sovereignty to cede some ground.

Fernández Ruiz initially miscalculated again in fall 1923, with the national presidential succession looming. On the heels of his clash with Calles and Obregón, it appears that he initially cast his lot with finance minister and presidential aspirant Adolfo de la Huerta.[34] When President Obregón instead endorsed Calles, de la Huerta declared himself in rebellion. One-fifth of the Mexican army's generals seconded the de la Huerta movement, as did twenty-four thousand of the army's fifty-three thousand troops and numerous state governors and opportunists.

The fighting ravaged much of southeastern Mexico, including Chiapas, where violence and looting were particularly pronounced in the central highlands and northwestern municipalities. Fernández Ruiz was placed in an impossible position, as former enemies and allies alike took the opportunity to renew long-standing local feuds or start new ones. After flirting with the notion of joining de la Huerta, the municipal president of Chiapa de Corzo, Colonel Victórico Grajales, revolted against Fernández Ruiz while affirming his loyalty to President Obregón.[35] The most serious fighting took place after General Alberto Pineda and his 2,500 mounted troops invaded the state from Tabasco and took San Cristóbal, his former highland stronghold, in the name of de la Huerta. Fernández Ruiz moved the state capital to the coastal city of Tapachula, far from the strongholds of Grajales and his erstwhile ally Pineda. Though the delahuertista threat was finally defused on the national level by late spring 1924, some rebels in Chiapas (like Pineda) did not surrender until year's end.[36]

The political conflicts in the early 1920s in Chiapas had far-reaching consequences. Not only did Obregón and Calles succeed in undermining Mapache "sovereignty," but three key participants in these struggles—Carlos Vidal, Raymundo Enríquez, and Victórico Grajales—would cash in their anti-Mapache chips and use their contacts in Mexico City to become governors of Chiapas. Vidal had long cast his lot with Obregón and Calles, and his supporters had proven their loyalty and utility during the de la Huerta rebellion. He prevailed over Fernández Ruiz's candidate and became governor in 1925. Two years later Governor Vidal took a leave of absence to direct the presidential bid of General Francisco Serrano, who had recently defended Obregón and Calles during the de la Huerta revolt. When it became clear that President Calles simply intended to pass the presidency back to former president Obregón, Serrano's team tried to hatch a plot against both men in Mexico City. The plot was revealed, however, and Vidal, Serrano, and ten members of their staff were murdered near Huitzilac (on the highway between Cuernavaca and Mexico). During the ensuing purge of Vidalistas in Chiapas (a time when, in the words of a Callista, the Vidalistas "fell like little lambs"),[37] interim governor Luis Vidal was executed, as was Ricardo

Paniagua. Although municipal presidents known to be Vidalistas or Socialists were purged, others survived, suggesting the extent to which Calles needed allies in Chiapas strong enough to counter the Mapaches.

Following the purge, Senator Tiburcio Fernández Ruiz seemed poised to retake control of the state. Progressive workers, peasants, and educators held their collective breath, fearing the worst. As it turned out, President Calles was as eager to disenfranchise the Mapache faction as they were. His choice for governor, the young agronomist Raymundo Enríquez, had impeccable agrarian and labor credentials. He had helped create the Partido Socialista Chiapaneco and had been a close friend and political ally of Ricardo Alfonso Paniagua. As governor, Enríquez's political enemies accused him of the practices that had long been standard for governors, like rampant nepotism (favoring his extended family, the Enríquez-Cruz-Domínguez clan), using terror and thuggery to dominate municipal governments, and profiting personally from infrastructure development projects. He also turned against the Partido Socialista Chiapaneco, which he had helped create. On the positive side of the ledger, Enríquez promoted agrarian reform in the state's most politicized and mobilized regions, especially Mariscal and the lower Grijalva valley. Even as Calles withdrew support for agrarian reform at the national level, Enríquez redistributed some two hundred thousand hectares of land to fourteen thousand families during his four-year term. It is worth noting, however, that this reform bypassed not only the coffee plantations of Soconusco (where land reform was still prohibited by federal law) but also key Mapache strongholds and the indigenous highlands.[38]

Victórico Grajales also used his loyalty to Calles during and after the delahuertista revolt to become governor in 1932. Unlike both Vidal and Enríquez, who generally supported the labor, agrarian, and education programs emanating from Mexico City, Grajales would oppose these programs once in office and would suffer the consequences in 1936. As Grajales would learn, the "sovereignty" of Chiapas, though considerable, was no longer absolute.

The Demise of Vasconcelos's Missionaries

The delahuertista rebellion effectively dealt the knockout blow to Vasconcelos's missionary program in Chiapas. Dozens of schools were closed as entire communities took cover from the fighting. Arnulfo E. Niño, a missionary stationed near Arriaga, wrote in March 1924 that rebels from Oaxaca entered his zone "without the slightest fear of encountering federal troops." As the rebels committed their "misdeeds," haciendas in the region were abandoned and schools closed. Shortly after filing his report, Niño disappeared. Parres later wrote that Niño had been a Mapache captain during the revolution and that he (and many other teachers) had abandoned his post to fight for Fernández Ruiz. SEP officials in the state later learned that Niño had established phantom Casas del Pueblo in connivance with local elites with whom he split the phantom teachers' salaries.[39]

Other missionaries and rural teachers joined the fray, leaving their schools at the mercy of rebel and federal troops. Parres lamented that the Casa del Pueblo at Huehuetán (just outside Tapachula) "featured a magnificent cornfield ready for harvest, but now not a single plant remains, because the soldiers destroyed it." The school's teacher joined the National Army as captain. Nor was the Casa del Pueblo in Motozintla spared. "It would seem a lie!" Parres wrote, "but the garrison commander ordered the municipal government to convert the Casa del Pueblo—horror!—into a barracks."[40]

Occasionally schools suffered as locals settled old scores. At Acapetagua, in the rubber zone in northern Soconusco, residents targeted the local Casa del Pueblo because they identified the teacher with the unpopular municipal president whom they had killed at the height of delahuertista unrest. When the teacher returned from an extended absence, he found the Casa in shambles. Locals had allegedly used the Casa "for political meetings and for drunken orgies with public women, leaving the school in ruins . . . uprooting and destroying all of the fruit trees and setting the flowers on fire . . . and the authorities offered neither guarantees nor support."[41] Shortly thereafter the teacher was attacked violently and abandoned his post.

In April 1924, as the fighting peaked in Chiapas, the SEP's director in the state Mauro Calderón had little to report. Most of the missionaries' federal schools had been forced to close, the state's schools did not even bother opening that year, and most of the municipalities were "in the hands of the rebels." Postal service was not available even in those areas still controlled by the government. To complicate matters, Calderón was "required to perform nightly military service when an attack by rebel forces [on the state capital, Tuxtla Gutiérrez] seemed imminent."[42] In August 1924, Calderón finally produced a report for his superiors at the SEP, showing just 1,733 students attending only twenty-two state and federal primary schools. The state capital supported just two schools, as did the former state capital, San Cristóbal. Other major population centers like Tonalá and Comitán supported only one school each.[43] Delahuertista violence, in a single stroke, pushed public education in Chiapas back to its pre-Porfirian days.

The SEP Steers a New Course

Once the de la Huerta rebellion was suppressed, the SEP in Chiapas took steps to regroup. Conditions in the ravaged countryside called for urgent action. In 1925 there were only seventy-eight rural and semi-urban federal schools in the state, and not a single federal rural school could be found in the remote, heavily indigenous northern ex-departments of Pichucalco, Simojovel, Palenque, and Chilón. In the central highlands of Chiapas, home to tens of thousands of Tzeltal and Tzotzil Maya, there were only twelve federal rural schools and a handful of state-funded schools in 1926.[44] Many teachers hired in the mid-1920s had not even finished grade school, and most lacked formal training as teachers or were otherwise incapable of realizing a transformative education agenda.

The introduction of action pedagogy provided the SEP with a fresh, more popular approach to rural education and community development. Action pedagogy was best articulated by North American educational philosopher John Dewey.[45] It was formally introduced in Mexico by one of his former students, Moisés Sáenz, who received a master's from Teachers College, Columbia University, and became SEP Undersecretary in 1924. Action pedagogy evolved in the United States in response to the needs of an increasingly urban and socioeconomically stratified society. Progressive educators sought to soften class conflict and create a sense of community and purpose, both of which were perceived to be lacking in modern industrial life. Although Mexico was not nearly as industrialized or urbanized as its northern neighbor, Sáenz and other SEP officials were attracted to various aspects of action pedagogy, including its emphasis on pragmatism, community development, the internalization of discipline and work habits, and the diminution of class conflict.

Action pedagogy in Mexico required teachers to foster small-scale industry, provide technical training in agriculture and animal husbandry, facilitate the sale and consumption of locally produced products, and coordinate civic festivals. In a country still struggling to feed itself, teachers "inculcated the love of the soil" and encouraged campesinos to stay rooted to the land, planting and harvesting grains. Teaching (and learning) the three Rs was secondary to community development, as Tapachula missionary Ernesto Parres learned after an anonymous source alleged that his Casas del Pueblo had not embraced action pedagogy. The SEP's Director of Education and Indigenous Culture, Enrique Corona, lectured him that "schools that are exclusively dedicated to teaching reading, writing, and counting mean little for this Department."

Instead, "the new social state demands that the teacher's work spill into the pueblo, especially the humble homes where the need for knowledge is greatest."[46] Teachers were also expected to exert a vague moralizing influence, stressing a work ethic, solidarity, and respect for others, as if such qualities did not otherwise exist in rural Mexico. Despite the progressive elements of action pedagogy, SEP officials in the mid-1920s still tended to attribute peasant unrest and miserable living conditions to alleged deficiencies in moral character rather than to overarching socioeconomic and political factors.[47]

Action pedagogy in Mexico received national and international attention and praise. As Sáenz confidently wrote in 1926, in the new Casa del Pueblo "one never knows where the school ends and where the village begins, nor where village life ends and scholastic life begins, because once it assumes its role as an agent of real social change, this school is one with the community."[48] Dewey himself concurred that same year, adding "no educational movement in the world . . . exhibits more of the spirit of intimate union of school activities with those of the community." John Collier, future commissioner of Indian affairs in the United States, wrote that the SEP's schools represented "a flowering, an incandescence of the community, and a communal tool for improving life."[49] Other foreign observers showered praise on the SEP's rural schools, even as the SEP itself became increasingly demoralized by the myriad problems associated with extending federal education (and federal control) to isolated, impoverished, indifferent, or downright resistant communities.

In 1927, inspectors were asked to evaluate teacher performance and community support at each of the schools in their zone. Did the school feature experimental gardens and orchards? A workshop? A poultry coop? A library? Was there a parents' association? An education committee? Had the teacher led pro-hygiene or sobriety campaigns? Was there cooperation between the community and the school? In most cases, the answers were "no." Inspectors were also asked to evaluate the schools' nation-building programs. How many students spoke Spanish? How many civic and religious holidays did the community celebrate? Did the school have a Mexican flag? How many students knew of Mexican heroes Hidalgo, Juárez, and Madero? How many knew the name of their state and country? In a great many cases, teachers reported that students had no concept of either Chiapas or Mexico—and rural schools in the 1920s had not yet entered the most remote regions of the state. Just outside of Tuxtla Gutiérrez, in the Zoque village of Ocuilapa, for example, villagers celebrated many religious holidays but no civic holidays, students at the federal rural school all spoke Spanish but had no concept of the Mexican republic, and no dimension of action pedagogy had been developed, owing to the "despairing indifference with which community members regard the school."[50] The SEP recognized a lost cause and closed the school in 1927. The teacher was transferred to another community.

Indeed, the rate at which SEP schools were closed and teachers moved suggests the precariousness of the SEP's presence in many towns. Teachers often challenged the prestige of local authorities, especially if the latter were illiterate. Often, too, class differences were at work. Many teachers were from the urban lower middle class and lacked both knowledge and respect for country living. As outsiders advocating change, they were often blocked by local authorities.[51] Reports in the 1920s were crammed with complaints against authorities that either saw the school as a potential source of personal enrichment or regarded it as a threat to their authority. Ernesto Parres, working among Mam and Tojolabal communities along the Guatemalan border, remarked that "not only do the authorities not help but they obstruct the education effort. . . . And this is what the civilized classes do! What can one expect from those of lower rank?"[52] For their part, campesinos destined to spend their lives in the fields saw little reason to go to school. Action pedagogy had not taken root in rural Chiapas.

A Promise of Better Times Ahead?

One important exception could be found in Chiapa de Corzo and much of the lower Grijalva valley. This zone was administered by Epigmenio de León, a founding member of the PSCH who had also spent many years with the SEP as a "missionary" and teacher in Chiapas and Michoacán. Communities in his zone were generally mestizo, secular, and politicized, given their proximity to the state's political and economic hub, Tuxtla Gutiérrez. De León reported that schools in his zone were building outdoor theaters (for civic activities) and pursuing hygiene and anti-alcohol campaigns (largely through sports and parades) as the SEP recommended. Most dramatically, these schools were active participants in (and beneficiaries of) the Enríquez administration's agrarian reform program. De León noted with satisfaction that "when the majority of peons or *baldíos* decide to leave a ranch where there is a school, the teacher is the first who leads the pilgrimage, carrying books and other school supplies. This action suggests a better future for the Mexican people."[53] Nine *colonias agrarias* had acquired ejidos in his zone, and another thirteen had applied for land reform, promising (as part of the process) to send their children to school and to refrain from drinking aguardiente.

Although community members generally supported SEP schools and social campaigns in the lower Grijalva valley, de León commented extensively on his efforts to improve attendance. He advocated a soft touch. He and his teachers would visit homes one by one, talking to parents and their children and "winning friends." Once inside, de León and his teachers advised the peasants on how to improve their homes, their diet, and their hygiene. Once the parents were won over, the children gladly attended school. As de León wrote, "Many times the desire to learn a trendy song or play soccer is much more effective than the rigorous methods of authorities and the police." Selling coeducation was another matter, especially in rural communities. As he detailed in a 1929 report, attendance figures for girls and women in his zone were still low "given the resistance of their parents and society in general, which do not approve of the coeducational classroom. If the number of girls is to ever equal or exceed that of boys, we must wait for society to convince itself that coeducation is harmless to morality and good customs." Again, de León suggested a remedy. "Social activities are a powerful ally that makes society see that the school is a center for work, morality, and decency and not a center of perversion, as is often thought."[54]

Inspector de León also criticized the unrealistic expectations of action pedagogy. Teachers were so busy trying to protect themselves and implement all of the recommended programs simultaneously that no single dimension was executed properly. "The chickenhouse will have only two or three chickens, the pigeon pen a couple of pigeons," he wrote, "and if the earth has been moved at all they say it's a garden." De León recommended that his teachers concentrate their efforts on those programs that could truly benefit their community and hoped that each school could bring five hectares of land under intensive cultivation.[55]

De León took action pedagogy to its fullest expression in his zone because he enjoyed support both from above and from below. Zone inspectors elsewhere in Chiapas were unable to take such bold measures. In nearby Soconusco, where the private sector was expected to pick up the tab for public schooling, teachers would find their hands tied.

The Evolution of a "Revolutionary" School on the Pacific Coast

When delegates at the 1916–1917 constitutional convention in Querétaro considered measures to regulate labor conditions, curb the power of the landed elite, and increase access to public education, they seemingly met all three demands with one legislative initiative—Article 123 of the Constitution. Education authorities used this article to oblige factory owners, ranchers, planters, and other entrepreneurs to provide schools for the sons and daughters of their resident workers. In some parts of Mexico, such schools were not without precedent. During the Porfiriato, *hacendados* in several of the more prosperous northern states had been required to establish schools for their workers. In Coahuila, these schools were managed by municipal governments; among those sustaining schools were Francisco I. Madero and members of his family. By 1910 most states—including Chiapas—had passed laws mandating privately funded schooling. In some states it was an obligation; in others it was merely an appeal to landlord philanthropy.[56]

Privately funded hacienda schools became a fairly common sight in the north, but such schools were rarely seen in Chiapas. The situation hardly improved during the revolution, when only a handful were established under the terms of General Castro's polemical Ley de Obreros. Proprietors typically hid school-age children in the fields whenever delegates or zone inspectors were rumored near. Since many delegates at the constitutional convention rejected a proposal for exclusive federal jurisdiction over labor matters, implementation of Article 123 was left to the discretion of the states. The law was applied unequally and produced drastically different outcomes. Guanajuato, for example, boasted 453 privately funded schools in 1928, and all but 2 were sustained by agriculture. In that same year Coahuila, with its legacy of hacienda schools, had 338 schools sustained by ranchers and hacendados, and another 45 by assorted industrial and mining ventures.[57]

In Chiapas, where postrevolutionary state governors would not or could not inconvenience rural elites, the Article 123 schools had a difficult infancy. Although the PSCH's strike settlement in late 1922 called for plantation schools, none were built during the tenure of Tiburcio Fernández Ruiz. His successor, Carlos Vidal (1925–1927), felt it necessary to reiterate in 1926 that the state's Ley Reglamentaria del Trabajo (Statutory Work Law) originally issued in 1918 "has been and continues to be in effect."[58] Article 94 of that law ordered proprietors to establish a rudimentary school whenever the number of families on their property exceeded twenty and whenever the distance to the nearest public school exceeded two kilometers.[59] This made little difference, as federal education inspector Benjamín Martínez reported in December 1926. "It's a lie to say that there are schools on the coffee plantations," he wrote. Even if a school was eventually built, "the owners harass the conscientious teacher so much that he must either resign or become a simple employee of the plantation who will submit falsified attendance information." State education inspectors rarely made their rounds, "and if they do it's to become accomplices of this arrangement."[60]

The number of schools established in Chiapas under the terms of Article 94 of the state's labor law grew slowly, if we are to believe the Enríquez administration's figures. In 1929, there were fifty-nine schools; in 1930, sixty-four; and in 1931, seventy-five. Even when the schools functioned, they could hardly have made a positive impact on the lives of their students. Of the fifty schools established by 1928, forty-six offered only the first grade. Regardless of the size of the student population or the financial means of the provider, all schools in Chiapas were one-room schoolhouses where no more than one teacher labored.[61]

The future of the Article 123 circuit in states like Chiapas appeared to brighten in 1931 when *Jefe Máximo* Plutarco Elías Calles introduced the Federal Labor Law (Ley Federal del Trabajo) to draw workers to his recently established Partido Nacional Revolucionario (PNR). Among many other things, this law took important steps to correct the anomalies and deficiencies of the private schools operating in the spirit of Article 123. Matters of school administration and curriculum were placed in the hands of state education authorities, while hiring became the prerogative of SEP officials. Anticipating the complete federalization of these schools, the SEP conducted a nationwide survey in 1932 to determine how many should function under the spirit of the law. Nationwide, there were 1,572 schools, while another 1,684 had yet to be established. In Chiapas the ratio was much worse, testimony to the strength of planters and ranchers and the impotence of state educators. In Comitán, federal zone inspector José Inés Estrada reported that the private sector should establish 37 schools. In October 1932 only 3 such schools were in operation; two of the teachers had studied through the fourth grade, and the other had not even finished second grade. In the northern districts of Simojovel, Palenque, Mezcalapa, and Pichucalco, Inspector Benjamín Rojas wrote that the private sector should create 22 schools; none existed to date. Finally, Benjamín Martínez reported 48 schools in operation in Soconusco and surrounding areas, with 79 more to be established. All told, Chiapas's Director of Federal Education reported that 252 private establishments in Chiapas met the student population and distance requirements for an Article 123 school, but only 55 such schools were in existence.[62]

In that same year, a little-known immigration official named Erasto Urbina accompanied a federal labor inspector on a tour of forty-nine plantations in Soconusco. None complied with the Federal Labor Law that had been legislated into existence one year earlier. Every plantation featured an anti-constitutional company store; many lacked infirmaries and hygienic lodgings. Urbina reported that "workers are poorly fed and are treated, without exaggeration, in a manner which recalls the encomenderos of the colonial period, for we saw evidence of whippings on the backs of many of our Indians." Many plantations featured private subterranean jails "where they are locked up after getting drunk on the wine sold to them at the company store." Urbina blamed foreign planters, specifically "the Spaniards, the Germans, the English, the French, the Turks, the Chinese, and the Guatemalans," for the worst anti-constitutional infractions and for corrupting local government. "Local labor inspectors, municipal presidents, police chiefs, and the rest of the official apparatus were at the service of those who exploit the indigenous race," he wrote.[63]

The SEP was powerless to address these glaring social issues until 1934, when another series of reforms to the constitution and the Federal Labor Law brought the states' Article 123 schools into the federal fold. The SEP offered financial incentives to encourage its personnel to establish these schools. By December 1934 the SEP in Chiapas had added 104 Article 123 schools to its roster, and inspectors would go on to establish 96 more schools during the first eight months of 1935.[64] As we shall see, 1934 is also the year that the SEP adopted "socialist education" as its operating pedagogy. The schools and teachers that the planters resented supporting in the first place would radicalize. The stage was set for a major confrontation pitting a largely foreign plantocracy against activist federal teachers in a state where federal laws and institutions historically carried little weight.

Two Steps Forward, One Step Back: Action Pedagogy in Chiapas, 1922–1932

After a 1932 tour of several federal rural schools in Michoacán, Moisés Sáenz wrote despairingly of the fruits of his own invention. Critics had dismissed his poorly managed and provisioned "schools of action" as mere centers of reading, writing, and arithmetic. What Sáenz found in rural Michoacán was, in his words, "not even deserving of that contemptuous epitaph."[65] Few schools functioned regularly. Those that did failed to embrace the larger objectives of action pedagogy. Experimental gardens went untilled, new techniques in animal husbandry were never practiced, peasant households were not being "modernized," and student and teacher absentee rates were stubbornly similar to those registered during the Porfiriato.

Indeed, by the late 1920s the heady optimism of the Vasconcelos-era SEP had given way to grim realism. Federal education budgets had been the first to be cannibalized in times of national crisis (like the de la Huerta and Cristero rebellions and the Great Depression).[66] In Chiapas, untrained personnel, local politics, violence, and the narrow reformist aims of the federal government also conspired against action pedagogy. Where it did take hold, it usually represented an unacceptable threat to the political and economic status quo.

What most damaged the cause in Chiapas was the almost complete withdrawal of the state government from rural education under governors Tiburcio Fernández Ruiz and Carlos Vidal. While states like Baja California and Sonora earmarked 25 percent and 50 percent of their 1930 state budgets to education, respectively, Chiapas only set aside 10 percent. By 1930 there were only thirty state-funded primary schools and sixty-eight municipal schools in the entire state. The total percentage of school-age children enrolled in *all* schools in Chiapas actually dropped from 13 percent in 1907 to 10 percent in 1928. In both years, which span two eventful decades of late Porfirian, revolutionary, and postrevolutionary educational experiences, the state ranked last nationally.[67]

Though the SEP's performance in Chiapas in the 1920s was far from spectacular, the number of *federal* rural schools increased from just 15 in 1922 to 151 six years later, ranking Chiapas eleventh among thirty states.[68] Bankrupt municipal schools ignored the admonitions of the governor and continued to join the federal circuit, and the eventual federalization of education in Chiapas seemed imminent. In spite of the increasingly conservative orientation of Jefe Máximo Calles, progressive anthropologists, pedagogues, and politicians throughout Mexico continued to introduce new ideas about nation building, community development, and grassroots mobilization through education. Although action pedagogy had seemingly run its course, its legacy would blossom in the middle 1930s. ◆

Chapter Three

SEP Indigenismo

The Early Years

> Now more than ever we must vindicate the remains of that race with such glorious traditions, to make them feel like Mexicans, so that they think and feel like us, in a word to make them *cultos* (civilized).
>
> —*Mauro Calderón, Chiapas's first Federal Director of Education, 1922*

While action pedagogy met with some success in the lower Grijalva valley and Mariscal, it failed roundly in highland Chiapas. SEP schools were not necessarily doomed in indigenous Mexico; in fact, some prospered in central Mexican indigenous communities well on their way to becoming acculturated into the political, economic, and social mainstream. They generally floundered in more remote indigenous areas where there had been no local tradition in schooling.[1] In Chiapas, most teachers were monolingual ladinos. The "otherness" of Tzotzil and Tzeltal communities and their historic distrust of ladinos and ladino culture presented additional social and cultural challenges for the SEP. Although the SEP was forced into a tactical retreat during this period in Chiapas, the evolution of pedagogy, nation-building ideology, and Indian policy at the national level prepared the groundwork for a second, more radical and more integral attempt to transform indigenous Chiapas beginning in 1935.

The Path to SEP Indigenismo

Indians were the objects, not the authors, of Mexican indigenismo. In the words of Alan Knight, indigenismo was "an elitist, non-Indian construct" that "cannot be attributed to any direct Indian pressure or lobbying; in this, it resembled anticlericalism or economic nationalism (comparable elite 'projects') rather than agrarianism (which enjoyed genuine popular roots and, indeed, encountered strenuous elite resistance)."[2] It reflected the convergence of several intellectual and cultural trends current among influential Mexicans during the 1910s and 1920s, including the artistic renaissance, the popular legacy of the revolution, and the movement of the social sciences toward more culturalist (Boasian) explanations for difference in aptitude and behavior. Indigenistas sympathized with the Indians and wanted to incorporate them into a new, more egalitarian and just nation. However, most indigenistas were not content simply to celebrate indigenous Mexicans; they also wanted to modernize, "civilize," and otherwise "improve" them.[3]

Postrevolutionary indigenismo was motivated by several factors. Manuel Gamio, the founding father of Mexican anthropology, was famous for writing, "One cannot govern that which one does not know."[4] In 1915 Gamio proposed using anthropology as a nation-building tool. He called for the creation of a centralized institution capable of studying an entire territory and its people in order to facilitate their social transformation and "improvement." For Gamio, the Indian "problem" was cultural, not racial. He believed that social scientists like himself could classify cultural traits as beneficial or harmful for the unity and progress of the nation, then preserve the positive traits and eliminate the negative.

Indigenismo was also a response to more immediate concerns. It was part of the postrevolutionary state's attempt to extend federal authority throughout the national territory after a period of protracted civil war. The federal government would use indigenismo to address the glaring social inequalities that might disturb the peace and disrupt Mexico's capitalist growth.[5] From a more defensive standpoint, indigenismo (and related campaigns) granted legitimacy to a regime that took power in 1920 by force of arms, intrigue, and assassination. It also aimed to instill loyalty in a population that generally did not identify or sympathize with the nation-state.

Last of all, indigenismo was part of an elite aesthetic movement that had its origins in the salons and art galleries of Europe. During the violent stages of the revolution artists like Doctor Atl (Gerardo Murillo), Adolfo Best Maugard, Roberto Montenegro, and Diego Rivera spent time in Europe, where they participated in the modernist art scene, pondered the collective subconscious (especially nationalism and national identity), and witnessed the new intellectual and artistic interest in the French peasantry. When they returned to Mexico, the indigenous population so commonly dismissed and disparaged "now seemed exotic, romantic, and *muy nuestro*."[6] Indians also seemed beautiful: in 1921, Gamio endorsed a national "India Bonita" ("Beautiful Indian") contest that represented an attack against the "aesthetic tyranny" that permeated white beauty contests. Key figures in this aesthetic movement believed that the inspiration derived from Mexico's diverse rural populations could drive a distinctly Mexican art that would earn Mexico a place among modern nations.[7]

Gamio hoped that the inspiration for the future Mexican nation would come from the rural classes themselves. But he would be eclipsed by the SEP's founder, José Vasconcelos. Though never an indigenista, Vasconcelos played a crucial role in shaping early SEP indigenismo. Like Gamio, he worried that Mexico's cultural heterogeneity impeded the "making of our soul." Unlike Gamio and many of his contemporaries, however, Vasconcelos had no interest in contemporary indigenous cultures. An unapologetic Hispanophile, he openly lamented that the Spanish colonizers had not discovered empty land. For Vasconcelos, the bedrock of the modern Mexican nation had to be the mestizo inspired by the classics of antiquity and Spanish culture.[8] Vasconcelos argued that the mestizo or "cosmic" race enjoyed all of the benefits of hybridization. With this stance he did not refute the racial determinism[9] of earlier decades; he merely inverted it to prove the superiority of the mestizo.

Despite his racial determinism, Vasconcelos's education policies suggested that Indians could, in fact, shed their "Indian-ness" and join the cosmic race. He and other Latin American thinkers were beholden to neo-Lamarckian eugenics, after the early nineteenth-century French naturalist, Jean Baptiste de Lamarck, who believed that changes to an adult organism caused by environmental factors could become part of that organism's genetic code. In other words, "improvements" could be passed to future generations. This kinder, gentler, more flexible school of eugenic thought underlies Mexican indigenismo. For Vasconcelos, Indians had no future as Indians, but their decadence was not a fixed hereditary characteristic. Over time, they could be improved through environmental intervention and assimilation, or what he called "spiritual eugenics." *Mestizaje*, therefore, could be both a racial and a cultural process.[10]

For Vasconcelos, the key to indigenous incorporation was the inclusionary national schoolhouse. He explicitly rejected the North American practice of establishing separate schools for the so-called races, which, in his words, "exaggerates racial differences and makes the savage a creature apart, a kind of link between the monkey and man."[11] Vasconcelos's successor, José Manuel Puig Casauranc, concurred. He wrote that the North American solution to the Indian "problem"—reservations—was flawed because "the Indians continued to form a separate social group, absolutely apart from the rest of the components of the American union. Racial difference was also social separation," he wrote.[12] In 1922 Chiapas's first Director of Federal Education, Mauro Calderón, also rejected North American "social separation," writing, "Nobody can deny the extraordinary cruelty of the reservation system in a civilized society."[13] In a predominately mestizo nation like Mexico, the idea of "social separation" was a disturbing one, even if it existed in practice. The celebration of the "cosmic race" reflected the sentiments of a society and a ruling class uncomfortable with the divisive colonial legacy of caste separation, unsure whether autonomous native peoples could be controlled, and hopeful that *indígenas* could be incorporated and the nation "improved."

Naturally, Spanish was to be the only language spoken in Mexico's educational "melting pot." Here early SEP indigenistas took a cue from their Porfirian predecessors. Justo Sierra had maintained that the destruction of indigenous languages was a necessary step toward national integration. This position was endorsed in 1910 by Comtean positivist Agustín Aragón and again in 1916 in Gamio's classic call to Mexican nationhood, *Forjando patria*. Furthermore, SEP pedagogues feared that bilingual teachers would "go native." As the SEP's Director of Rural Education Rafael Ramírez cautioned Mexico's rural schoolteachers,

> if you speak to [your indigenous students] in their language, we will lose the faith that we had in you, because you run the risk of being the one who is incorporated. You will begin to habitually use the language of the children, later without realizing it you will adopt the customs of their ethnic group, later their inferior ways of life, and finally you yourself will become the Indian, that is, one more unit to incorporate. For that reason I consider it very important that you teach Spanish as it should be taught (*como Dios manda*), that is to say, without translating the language into that of the children.[14]

Implicit in Ramírez's warning was his appreciation of the complex ethnic makeup of the Mexican population. In rural areas, often language was the only characteristic distinguishing self-identifying mestizos from Indians. Anthropologists and pedagogues estimated that between one-fifth and two-thirds of the national population was indigenous. These wildly divergent estimates suggest a profound confusion over what constituted an "Indian"; they also underscore the subjective nature of ethnic labeling in Mexico.[15] Since virtually all mainstreamed Mexicans claimed at least some indigenous ancestry, the possibility existed that the remaining Indians could be "incorporated." With this in mind, Vasconcelos embarked on his redemptive mission.

The SEP Meets Indigenous Chiapas

Beginning in 1922 Vasconcelos's missionaries combed indigenous Chiapas, establishing rural schools and conducting basic anthropological studies. Many understood the needs of the region and its people and proposed forward-looking indigenista strategies later adopted by the National Indigenist Institute (Instituto Nacional Indigenista, or INI) in the 1950s, while others—imbued with prevailing ladino attitudes—were contemptuous of a people they considered refractory, uncivilized, and practically beyond redemption. Far from the literary salons and art galleries of Mexico City, few SEP educators found qualities worth saving. In fact, they believed it their job to rescue the Indians from many of the "primitive" qualities celebrated by artists and intellectuals.

Missionaries in Chiapas came to believe they were working with two very distinct types of Indians. Federico Corzo reported that the Zoques and the Chiapanecas who inhabited the western lowland regions along the Grijalva River "have forgotten their prior life and now dress well, speak Spanish and have acquired some culture." The Mam, who lived along the Guatemalan border, were also "more or less civilized"; only the absence of schools had stunted their development. The highland Maya, however, were "indifferent to progress" and "live[d] like savages." "The race possesses the great virtue of its love for work, they have good souls, and they are noble, obedient, [and] very respectful," Corzo wrote. However, "among their defects is their exaggerated ignorance, their apparent denial of ideals, and their love of liquor."

Corzo proposed three major redemptive strategies for the highland Maya. Taking his cue from Vasconcelos, Corzo first proposed miscegenation as a "civilizing" process but realized that this was unlikely to happen in the highlands "because the mestizo repudiates the Indian woman, and the Indian man never aspires to the mestiza."[16] Later, as director of the state's education circuit, Corzo wrote that "we know . . . that the only way to achieve a slow but firm progress of our race and the construction of a nation is *mestizaje*; yet, we have done nothing to [promote it.] This thwarts our civilizing activity."[17]

Given the unlikelihood of miscegenation on a grand scale in highland Chiapas, Corzo elaborated a second strategy that involved a combination of hard work and education. Young Chamulans[18] would be distributed to the homes of ladinos in San Cristóbal, where they would perform domestic tasks, learn Spanish, and attend schools. Corzo also advocated bilingual teachers in highland indigenous communities, an idea appropriated by the INI nearly thirty years later. Corzo proposed building a university in San Juan Chamula, writing, "If one hundred Chamulan teachers [were] trained, I think the problem would be solved."[19] Not only was a Chamulan university never built, but SEP officials did not recruit indigenous people to the federal rural normal school that finally opened at Cerro Hueco in 1931.

If all else failed, there was incorporation through grunt labor. True to his times, Corzo lauded the strength and resistance of the Tzotzils, hardworking primitives who had lost touch with their noble, glorious past. At times, though, he echoed the Porfirian entrepreneurs and politicians who had "sold" a cheap, hardworking labor pool to potential investors. "In spite of their poor diet, the Chamulans are, in the great majority, of regular height, strong, with muscular legs, and their large backs demonstrate the potential of their lungs," he wrote. "Their constitution is enviable and especially their extraordinary energy for work. With heavy loads on their backs they can follow a horseman moving at a trot all day long."[20] Two years later, Corzo's replacement, Ricardo Sánchez, remarked that from a very early age Chamulans could carry huge loads of wood on their backs for up to twenty kilometers for a daily wage of twenty-five centavos. Sánchez reported that some unscrupulous SEP missionaries had taken advantage of the Chamulans' willingness to work for so little. Mauro Calderón also placed faith in the productive capacity of Chiapas's indigenous populations. Despite their chronic drunkenness, he wrote, they had "an unbeatable physical constitution and their endurance for work and fatigue is enormous." For Calderón, education was the key to restoring "nobility" to indigenous Chiapas. "Now more than ever we must vindicate the remains of that race with such glorious traditions," he wrote, "to make them feel like Mexicans, so that they think and feel like us, in a word to make them *cultos* (civilized)."[21]

But did Indians in Chiapas want to be "saved?" The SEP's first missionaries could not have picked a worse time to "proselytize" in the highlands. The entire region was embroiled in political conflict. During the revolution Carrancistas suppressed the Porfirian-era political bosses in 1915, and their Ley de Municipio Libre one year later gave each municipality the right to name its own officials. Many highland communities like Chamula and Chenalhó successfully recovered municipal power from ladinos. Once the fighting ended, however, the labor-starved finqueros of the lower Grijalva valley and Soconusco resurrected enganche and forced the reimposition of a political and administrative structure capable of controlling labor flows and enforcing contracts. The Fernández Ruiz administration demoted indigenous towns to the status of *agencias municipales* and incorporated them into the nearest ladino municipality. Chamula, for example, became one of San Andrés's agencias municipales in 1921, even though its population was five times greater and, according to several Chamulans, "more civilized and industrious."[22] With a small resident ladino population, Chenalhó also became a full-fledged municipality, administering to four nearby indigenous towns through municipal agents. Ladino-controlled towns like San Andrés and Chenalhó sought large agencias municipales because their only significant source of income was the one-peso "contract fee" assessed each indigenous worker that departed annually for the lowland plantations.[23]

Key to the "reconquest" of the Chiapas highlands were the ladino municipal secretaries reimposed by the state government. Many were alcohol distributors and labor contractors; a few were even murder suspects. In the words of education inspector Jesús Ixta, schools could hardly thrive when "mestizo municipal secretaries act like little kings in indigenous pueblos . . . always looking to exploit the Indian and relegate him to semi-slavery. This evil can only be remedied by removing these enemies of progress from their posts."[24] But this was easier said than done. By the middle 1920s, the ladino governing elite had reestablished their ascendancy over the highlands, thereby ensuring a steady flow of workers and their own financial well being.[25]

Given this tumultuous backdrop, federal teachers and inspectors struggled to convince the Tzotzil and Tzeltal that their redemption lay with the schools. Complicating the educational mission were the abuses of past and present teachers. Indian schools were big business in the highlands. Parents were willing to pay teachers and local authorities for the right to keep their children out of school, so that their labor might be used in the fields, at home, or as carriers of wood, coal, lime, and other articles. Some parents simply wanted to "free their children from the punishment of school," wrote missionary Ernesto Parres in 1923. "That is, they see the school as a prison."[26] At the opening of a state–financed indigenous boarding school in San Cristóbal, the state's director of education, Marcos Becerra, elaborated:

> Victor Hugo's saying—that in every village there was a torch, represented by the teacher, and a mouth [that tried to blow out the torch], represented by the priest—is inapplicable and foolish here, because there would be two mouths blowing, with perhaps the teacher blowing hardest. The story is well known: some poor devil . . . paid the local

> authority anywhere from one hundred to five hundred pesos to become teacher in a village where he would earn eight to ten pesos monthly. How would he live on that? . . . The [students] . . . formed a platoon of servants who served the teacher in his milpa, his pastures, his orchards, and who looked after his horses, sheep, goats, and other animals. Naturally the parents of the children saw the school for what it was and realized that it was in their interests to arrive at an understanding with the so-called teacher. [They] liberated their children from scholastic obligation for one or two pesos monthly.[27]

Eduardo Zarza's Highland Tour

In 1928 fewer than two dozen federal rural schools were operating in the expansive Chiapas highlands. Most were in municipal centers where ladinos controlled local commerce. As director of federal education Eduardo Zarza learned as he toured several of these schools in the summer, local histories, demographics, and the popularity of the SEP's teachers produced widely varying results. At San Andrés Chamula he found thirty-three boys and twenty-eight girls in the boys' and girls' day schools, respectively, and eleven adults taking night classes, but all were ladinos. Zarza implored the teacher (a woman) to convince Indians to attend, gave a class in Spanish and arithmetic, and corrected the students' singing of the national anthem.

From San Andrés Chamula he proceeded on to San Juan Chamula. Here, where the only ladinos allowed in the town were the teacher and the municipal secretary, only eight boys attended school, even though several thousand Chamulans were dispersed throughout the surrounding area. These boys were likely being prepared to be the municipality's future scribes (*escribanos*). They spoke and read in Spanish and claimed to like their teacher, a ladino who spoke Tzotzil. Zarza tried to convince the students, their parents, and community leaders that not all mestizos were exploiters and that, to the contrary, a great majority sympathized with their plight and were trying to redeem them through education.

Zarza found a good deal more community support just a few kilometers down the road in the Tzotzil town of Zinacantán. A regular number of students of both sexes attended school, and the teacher enjoyed the support of their parents. When Zarza arrived, students, parents, and local authorities were busy constructing a schoolhouse (*casa-escuela*) on the condition that their teacher not be switched out of Zinacantán. Zarza felt that Zinacantán's more densely populated center facilitated school attendance, as did its proximity to the main

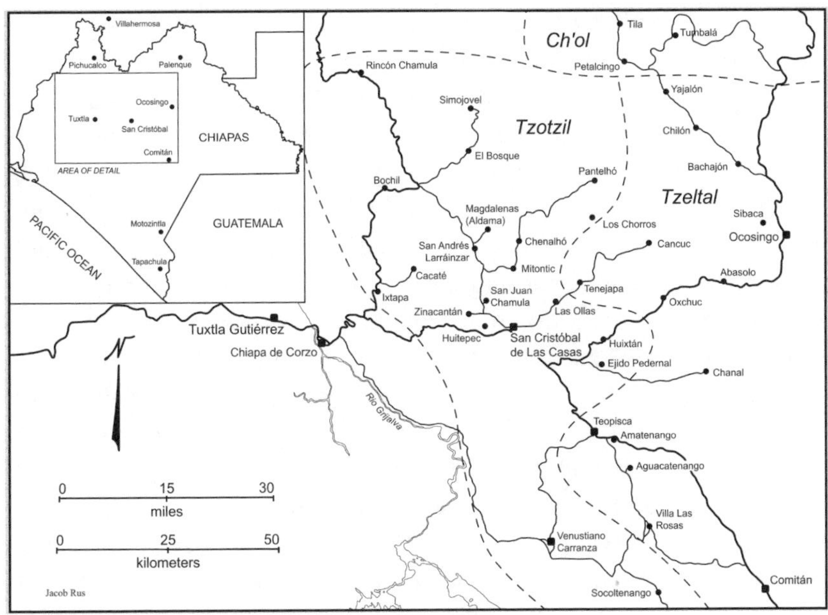

Map 3. The highlands of Chiapas today.

trade route between San Cristóbal and Tuxtla. This gave Zinacantecos more opportunities and a less defensive, less conservative worldview.

Despite the success that he found in Zinacantán, the trip was a real eye-opener for Zarza. He could hardly blame the Tzotzils for living in dispersed settlements. "The Chamulan Indian lives in the mountains to get away from the mestizos from whom they have received the greatest offenses and humiliations," he observed. "Whoever visits the region notes the great crosses that defend, three by three, the entrances into the Chamula region. For the Chamulans these are more than religious symbols, for they are also a warning to those that are not of their race."[28] Zarza watched with indignation "as strong, vigorous [Tzotzil] men prostrated themselves before the municipal secretary and ladinos and did not get up until the ladino placed his hand on their forehead." Zarza concluded that "the Revolution has still not arrived to the interior of this state to break the chains of slavery that the Indians have endured for so many centuries."[29]

Zarza's sensitivity to the economic plight of the highland Maya and his critique of highland ladinos anticipated the more mature version of SEP indigenismo that crystallized under Cárdenas in the mid-1930s. Unfortunately for the SEP, many federal inspectors in Chiapas tended to "blame the victim" rather than situate the plight of Indians within a larger context of political domination and economic exploitation. Take the case of José Macías Padilla, who visited San Juan Chamula in 1926. Using an interpreter, he tried to convince Chamulans "of the comforts of the cities, of the advantages of the Spanish language and enlightenment in general, of the need to instruct themselves, and [the virtues] of cleanliness, a proper diet, and well-paid work." Macías essentially blamed them for living in remote areas, for eating poorly, for unhygienic living conditions, and for working low-paying jobs. After this rather remarkable display of ignorance and paternalism, Macías admitted, "Only by the use of force have we been able to populate the school."[30] He employed similar tactics to improve attendance at Magdalenas, a Tzotzil community not far from San Juan Chamula. The municipal secretary told the hamlet's traditional indigenous leaders that if they did not help the teacher improve attendance, "General Calles would send his troops after them. They had no choice but to obey."[31] Macías then handed out coins and pencils to local children and told them to go to school.

For every Zarza there was at least one Macías; for every school that functioned more or less to SEP specifications there were others that failed for any number of reasons. SEP teachers and inspectors in Chiapas learned that "redemption" would not come easily, especially in the highlands. By the late 1920s, the SEP's rigid insistence on a single schoolhouse for all Mexicans regardless of ethnicity or gender had given way to more practical applications. When Federico Corzo's brother Ángel toured several schools just south of Teopisca in February 1927 as federal education inspector, he made casual reference to the fact that San Bartolomé had one rural school for ladinos and one for Tzotzils. In the ladino town of Socoltenango the girls' school existed in an ex-convent and the municipal government constructed a schoolhouse for boys. At Pinola, the school for boys occupied an ex-convent, and a rural school for girls existed in a private home. Although these towns had violated the SEP's mandate against single-sex schools—which implied added expense, since it usually meant paying extra teachers—the federal government absorbed the costs.[32] Some SEP teachers and inspectors also used native languages in the classroom in defiance of the SEP's Spanish-only policy. In spite of these local adaptations to SEP policy, federal schools in the highlands generally failed to resolve (and sometimes even aggravated) long-standing land disputes, they were powerless to stop enganche and combat alcoholism, and they lacked the resources to "modernize" the countryside and stimulate small industry.

Fig. 1. Cultural missionaries pose with federal employees from Comitán, 1928. The cosmopolitan bias of the Mission was clear. Courtesy Archivo Histórico de la Secretaría de Educación Pública.

Itinerant Missions of "Culture"

In the 1920s, as the logistical shortcomings of the Vasconcelista project became apparent, educators and reformers searched for new ways to bring education to the indigenous countryside and to train teachers, impose high standards, and impart a new pedagogical vision. In the words of José Gálvez, the federal deputy who proposed the creation of itinerant Cultural Missions in 1923, the lack of effective training and supervision allowed many missionaries to "degenerate and succumb to vice, which has discredited the Ministry of Education and sowed mistrust in their zones."[33] Gálvez's Cultural Missions were to be part traveling normal school, part anthropological survey team, part agrarian and home economics workshop, and part country fair, conducting brief but intensive workshops in indigenous communities. Peasants were expected to join local teachers in attendance. For Gálvez, the ideal mission would consist of a doctor, an agronomist, a carpenter, an ironworker, a construction worker, a potter, a master tanner, a soap maker, and a cook who would introduce new dishes and teach rural Mexico's corn tortilla eaters to make bread. Ideally, instructors in aesthetic culture and crafts accompanied the missions. They were charged with finding original examples of the decorative arts in the regions they visited and combating the corrupting influence of contemporary popular art.

Although the Cultural Missions were intended to address the shortcomings

Fig. 2. Departure of the Cultural Mission from Teopisca. Courtesy Archivo Histórico de la Secretaría de Educación Pública.

of Vasconcelos's missionary program, in many respects they suffered from the same philosophical and logistical constraints. All instruction was conducted in Spanish by mestizos. Missions rarely reached their target population; despite the claims of official SEP publications and several sympathetic histories, institutes in the late 1920s were actually held in cities as large as Guadalajara, Toluca, and Villahermosa. In 1926, only one institute was held in Chiapas, and this was in the state capital, Tuxtla Gutiérrez. One year later the state hosted three institutes in medium-sized predominantly mestizo cities. This mission taught the *jarabe tapatío* (Mexican hat dance) and the Yaqui Deer Dance. Of Jaliscan and Sonoran origin, respectively, these dances were to be introduced in schools throughout Mexico as part of the SEP's attempt to transform regional traditions into *Mexican* national traditions. Yet it is impossible to determine whether they instilled in teachers (or their students) any greater sense of national unity.[34] A total of 247 teachers attended the institutes in 1927 (female teachers constituting a slight majority), but less than half taught in the federal rural schools. Others in attendance included federal urban schoolteachers, zone inspectors, and several teachers from state-funded and private schools.[35]

In 1928, four-week institutes were held in the smaller predominately mestizo towns of Berriozábal and Chiapa de Corzo, both near Tuxtla, as well as Teopisca, near San Cristóbal, and La Grandeza, near Motozintla. That year, the Cultural Mission encountered obstacles both physical and human. Institutes usually

Fig. 3. Male teachers at Berriozábal's Cultural Mission construct basketball hoops and posts. Courtesy Archivo Histórico de la Secretaría de Educación Pública.

started several days late because Chiapas's miserable roads became practically impassable during inclement weather. On several occasions, oxen were needed to haul the mission's truck through raging rivers and along muddy, rutted roads. Once they finally arrived in Berriozábal, institute social worker Sara Valero de Marines went about setting fair prices in local stores. This aroused the opposition of the municipal president and municipal secretary, both of whom had profited from a near monopoly on retail goods. Their noisy resistance to the institute provoked a direct response from the fledgling Enríquez administration in Tuxtla, which sent police to restore order and subdue the authorities. At Teopisca, the authorities refused to even greet the mission.[36]

At Chiapa de Corzo, Valero apparently spent most of her time with the town's politicians and their wives. In a meeting with the town's Feminine Action Society (Sociedad Femenil "Acción"), she "tried to interest them in being as useful as possible, as individuals and as a group." She reminded them that "altruism is a quality found in the most cultivated people and nations," emphasizing that generalized misery could affect the upper classes in the way of contaminated milk, unsanitary tortillas, and infected fruits and vegetables. Valero also met with the governor and with local representatives to the state legislature. In other tasks, she struggled to convince disdainful male teachers to help out with domestic chores; they claimed that "domestic work is only performed by the Chamulan race [*sic*]."[37] During the month-long institute Valero also taught hygiene, sewing, and child-rearing classes to

Fig. 4. Two couples dance the *jarabe tapatío* at the closing ceremonies of Berriozábal's Cultural Mission. Courtesy Archivo Histórico de la Secretaría de Educación Pública.

Fig. 5. Teachers perform a calisthenics routine at the closing ceremonies of La Grandeza's Cultural Mission, 1928. Courtesy Archivo Histórico de la Secretaría de Educación Pública.

Fig. 6. Teachers and students at the Cultural Mission's Social Institute at Berriozábal, 1928. Courtesy Archivo Histórico de la Secretaría de Educación Pública.

teachers. Residents of Chiapa could not attend the institute because the school (a former convent) was in such dilapidated shape that it was feared a large gathering might trigger a roof cave-in.

The only institute held in rural, indigenous Chiapas in 1928 was established at La Grandeza, a small village in Mariscal. It was undermined by factors both geographic and political. Its remote location in southern Chiapas implied elevated transportation costs for the rural teachers, most of whom rented horses. Missionaries had trouble purchasing food from locals, who produced principally for their own subsistence. Since La Grandeza's population was so small, the mission's workers recruited residents from neighboring ranches for their courses on agronomy, small industry, and civic education; these people responded "weakly" to the invitation. The fact that the institute was held at all in La Grandeza is puzzling. Perhaps it was a tribute to the close ties that bound Mariscal's socialists and teachers with the Vidal and Enríquez administrations. On the other hand, since Mariscal had been heavily Vidalista, perhaps officials at the federal level felt a Cultural Mission was necessary following Vidal's assassination and the ensuing purge of socialists in fall 1927. This might also explain La Grandeza's lukewarm response to the mission. Either way, the difficulties at La Grandeza highlighted the problems involved in actually taking the Cultural Missions to their target population.[38] Several years after the mission at La Grandeza, Chiapas's exasperated director of federal education conceded that "none of the communities that really need the Missions can be visited."[39]

In 1933, the SEP recognized that "unfortunately and in spite of the enthusiasm of the [individual missionaries], their work has been diffuse, lethargic, and therefore deficient."[40] Despite decisions to lengthen the period of stay to six weeks and then to four months and to create permanent missions in key regions, the missions did not transform the Mexican countryside as their creators had envisioned. Among the institutes' enemies and critics were the attending teachers themselves, many of whom complained of wasting several weeks "singing and dancing" and painting signs for the SEP's sobriety campaigns. Others claimed to have learned "the elegant and modern way to pull students' ears when they do not learn" and were told "never to fail the children of politicians and government workers."[41] In Chiapas, the missions probably had their greatest impact in the late 1920s and early 1930s, before the state's first rural normal school, inaugurated in 1931, began graduating teachers in significant numbers. For many teachers, Cultural Mission institutes were the closest they would get to formal training. They provided hundreds of teachers in Chiapas with at least an introduction to the SEP's evolving pedagogical philosophy and represented the first practical step toward implementing a national education agenda.

Two National "Experiments" in Indigenous Incorporation

While the SEP dispatched its itinerant missions to the countryside in an attempt to bring "culture" to rural, often indigenous people, it also brought select indigenous boys to Mexico City for a fascinating experiment in nation building and social engineering. The stakes were high when the SEP opened the Casa del Estudiante Indígena, a boarding school for native boys, in 1926. As told by Gonzalo Aguirre Beltrán, "The failures of the rural school in monolingual indigenous communities caused many to have serious doubts about [the Indians'] intellectual capacity."[42] The Casa's purpose was two-fold: it served an important public relations function for the SEP's project of indigenous incorporation, and it trained a native elite that, upon graduation, would return to their home communities to impart "civilization" and modernity to their brethren. Success at the Casa would vindicate SEP policy. Failure, warned Casa director Enrique Corona in 1927, "would damage terribly, profoundly, the SEP's policy of indigenous incorporation in the periphery. . . . It would postpone for dozens of years any new attempt at regeneration by similar institutions."[43]

Recruitment for the Casa was difficult. Vasconcelos's successor, José Manuel Puig Casauranc, asked each state governor to send ten boys to the Casa. Not surprisingly, recruiters found few native families willing to send their sons to the far-off cosmopolitan capital, where it was rumored they would be drafted into the army. Most of the initial recruits were actually mestizos, many of them relatives or favorites of politicians. "Of course, since this was a psychological experiment the material had to be pure Indians," explained Puig, "so we had no choice but to reject the mestizo children."[44]

Later in the summer of 1925 the Casa tried again to recruit "pure Indians." This attempt sometimes degenerated into state-sponsored kidnapping. In highland Chiapas, for example, five Tzotzil boys from Mitontic were seized in August and taken to San Cristóbal, where they managed to escape. Three months later the SEP's zone inspector in the highlands, José Macías Padilla, tried again to answer Puig's call by seizing five Tzotzil orphans. When asked whether they were intelligent, yet also "without culture" and "refractory to civilization," Macías replied in the affirmative and requested that the SEP send money quickly for their train tickets because the boys were trying to run away.[45] In the fall these "pure" Indians and dozens of others arrived at the Casa. Puig was pleased, since "many of them were true little savages, who did not speak a word of Spanish."[46]

During its first two years the school aimed merely to "incorporate" its students into the urban mestizo mainstream. To this end it was hugely successful—too successful, in fact. In addition to a core curriculum consisting of Spanish, history, math, and civics, students took courses in auto repair, electrical work, plumbing, metallurgy, and ironworking. These courses not only taught skills that lacked practical application in rural, indigenous Mexico in the late 1920s, but they provided students with the means to remain in the urban environment they came to call home. Sure enough, most students chose to stay in the city after graduation. To counter this tendency, the Casa attempted (in vain) to streamline its course offerings and became a rural normal school—in the middle of Mexico's largest city—in February 1928.

Although few Casa students ended up returning to their communities of origin, politically and symbolically they were extremely useful for the SEP. The Casa came to embody the postrevolutionary regime's declared commitment to indigenous Mexico and its claim that natives could be made useful citizens. Shortly after the Casa was officially inaugurated in January 1926, students took part in a well-attended outdoor patriotic celebration, probably the birthday of Benito Juárez (March 21). President Calles, Puig, and other members of the cabinet came out to the field to meet the students and hand them the Mexican flag. Jacobo Dalevuelta, correspondent for *El Universal*, described the encounter.

> A young, strong Papago Indian, dressed in the gray uniform he had been given and glistening with sweat, approached the President in the company of two of his comrades. And as the young Indian looked at the Chief of the Nation with the serene gaze of those of his race and extended his hands to receive the flag . . . a long tear slid from his tranquil eyes. We saw a slight tremor in his lower jaw. He bent his knee and placed on the flag the most saintly kiss his lips had ever given—perhaps it was this Indian's first kiss—and he was wrapped in the folds of the flag. . . .
>
> The First Magistrate, visibly moved, said to those who accompanied him, "These are my Indians."

Noble-savage imagery also figured prominently in *El Universal*'s report of the festivities on May 5, 1927. After Casa students performed a series of human pyramids, testimony to the physical strength of the Indian "races," correspondent Manuel Ramírez wrote, "The bronzed bodies, the stern and melancholic faces of the sons of our mountains, home to savage tribes, were hymns of glory and hope in front of the hypnotized crowd."[47]

By 1929 certain SEP officials, like Director of Rural Schools Rafael Ramírez, felt that the Casa had run its course. It had proved the feasibility of indigenous incorporation to one and all. The international financial crisis provided Ramírez with the excuse to trim the Casa's budget. Furthermore, as Ramírez wrote, "the type of incorporation achieved by the Casa del Estudiante went far beyond what was desirable." Most students did not return to their places of origin "because they felt repugnance for rural life and repulsion at the thought of living with their brothers."[48] Those who did return often satisfied the "parasitic aspirations" they had learned in the city, according to SEP educator Rafael Molina Betancourt. Some displayed "a sick tendency to become exploiters and caciques by means of their superior cultural preparation."[49]

The Casa was closed in 1932. Part publicity stunt and part proving ground for an indigenous elite, it represented a pivotal moment in the history of Mexican indigenismo and education policy. The Casa proved to a national audience that natives could be and, in fact, chose to be incorporated into urban mestizo life when given the material means and know-how to do so. True "incorporation," in other words, required more than Spanish-only cultural campaigns. Results from a second highly touted SEP "experiment" pointed to the same conclusion. Shortly before the Casa was closed in 1932, former SEP Undersecretary Moisés Sáenz established his own "experimental station of Indian incorporation" at Carapan in rural Michoacán. As discussed in the previous chapter, Sáenz's faith in the Vasconcelista rural school was shaken after his visit to native communities in Puebla in 1927. The traditional language-only incorporative strategy will not be able to complete the task alone, he wrote. "The organized cooperation of other agencies of social improvement is required.... Unless all of them assist the rural school, the work of today's school will be as useless as that of yesterday's, and in a few years, we will explain the failure by once again blaming the Indian."[50] Several months at Carapan in 1932 brought Sáenz's ideological evolution full circle. The empty classrooms, the grinding poverty, and the prevalence of *caciquismo* (bossism) in the area convinced him that the SEP's incorporationist strategy was "simplistic." In place of "incorporating" the Indian, he proposed "integrating" all of

Mexico. An integrated Mexico, in Sáenz's mind, was a nation that respected its indigenous and mestizo campesino roots and institutions while appropriating the progressive elements of Mexico's "white" population.[51] The conclusions drawn from the Casa and Carapan were unequivocal. After 1932 the SEP would take a more holistic approach to education in indigenous areas, as we shall see. But would Mexico's indigenous populations respond any more favorably to the SEP's grand designs?

Conclusion

For a variety of overlapping reasons, artists, intellectuals, social scientists, politicians, and pedagogues placed indigenismo high on the list of national priorities in postrevolutionary Mexico. In part, it was celebratory; in part, it was controlling. Above all, it entailed "improving" and "incorporating" indigenous populations. Nowhere was SEP indigenismo challenged as it was in Chiapas.

During the 1920s and early 1930s SEP inspectors and teachers in Chiapas were unable and often unwilling to confront the structures and institutions that profited from the exploitation of the indigenous people. The following passage from Eduardo Zarza in 1928 underscores the staggering political, economic, and cultural obstacles to SEP indigenismo in the highlands.

> The following factors hinder, stagnate, and retard the progress of the schools and the effective involvement of the communities: enganche, which depopulates entire regions . . . the tenacious resistance of the parents to send their children to schools; the indifference with which the municipal authorities in the pueblos, with few exceptions, view the schools sustained by the Federation . . . the economic state of the pueblos, which obliges many parents to submit their children to the tyranny of servitude; the dispersed settlement patterns of the inhabitants in indigenous regions, who live an autonomous and obscure life; the unrestricted use of alcohol; the lack of roads . . . which keeps pueblos largely incommunicado and makes commercial activity difficult and products costly; the participation of mestizos in governing indigenous pueblos, the former exploiting the latter due to their ignorance, to the point where parents pay them to keep their children out of school; the lack of hygiene and cleanliness which afflicts entire communities, causing epidemics that decimate their inhabitants; and other factors that one could mention.[52]

Two months later, at year-end festivities at a school in San Cristóbal, Zarza was reduced to imploring ladino students, their parents, and local authorities to combat the exploitation of the Tzotzils. Such exhortations were meaningless in a town that lived off enganche, the Indians' consumption of alcohol, and the low wages paid for their goods and services. Mexican indigenismo still lacked the resources and the will to challenge entrenched political and economic interests.

The Casa del Estudiante Indígena produced no tangible benefits for Chiapas. Only a handful of students from Chiapas graduated and returned to the state as teachers. Seven were still studying at the Casa when it was closed in December 1932. All subsequently enrolled in Chiapas's rural normal school; by June 1933, all were forced to drop out after failing the first semester of the degree program.[53] At a more abstract level, however, the lessons learned at the Casa and at Carapan nudged the SEP toward a more holistic indigenismo. By the middle 1930s, indigenistas believed that Mexico's indigenous people could be incorporated into the national mainstream once they had the necessary material and institutional support. Indigenous Mexicans were subsumed within the larger category of campesinos; their plight became more commonly expressed in terms of class exploitation. In highland Chiapas, socialist education and the appointment of Manuel Castellanos as federal zone inspector in January 1935 would shake the highland elite to their core. This more potent version of SEP indigenismo implied a direct confrontation with local authorities, enganchadores, alcohol merchants, and resistant indigenous communities. ◆

Part Two

STATE and NATION BUILDING GO LOCAL, 1930–1935

Chapter Four

The Battle for the Hearts and Minds

> Thanks to the energetic dispositions of the state executive, all temples were closed without altering the state's tranquillity in the slightest, because . . . the proletariat has arrived to the just conclusion that it was victimized by clerical exploitation; later, the federal government decreed that all temples in the state should . . . be made available for use as schools, libraries, and workshops. Therefore, in very little time we will see in the naves of the church not the lamentable spectacle of a pueblo on its knees before the macabre figure of a bloody christ or before a mysterious window of a confessional, but rather desks and benches occupied by today's children.
>
> —*"El Obispo y todos los curas salieron de Chiapas,"* Liberación, *October 1934*

Many histories remember Mexican nation building in the 1920s and 1930s as a relatively benign process of self-discovery. And much of it was. Vasconcelos celebrated the "cosmic race," which vindicated mestizos; Diego Rivera's murals portrayed the glories of past indigenous civilizations and the folkloric beauty of contemporary Indians; and social engineers promoted the popular arts and sought inspiration from them and their creators. In the 1930s, the crusade often involved media, typically in conjunction (or competition) with the private sector. The Cárdenas administration subsidized Mexican film producers, Carlos Chávez and others at the National Conservatory wrote scores that included indigenous themes, and the SEP promoted nationalist programming (including *La Hora Nacional*) on its radio station, XFX.[1]

But Mexican nation building also had its darker, more destructive side. Although the anti-Chinese campaigns of the 1920s and early 1930s fall beyond the scope of this book, it bears remembering that the federal government triggered these ugly episodes by tapping into long-standing racial tensions, xenophobia, and economic nationalism. During the Calles presidency, Chiapas was one of several states to prohibit mixed Chinese-Mexican marriages and confine *chinos* to certain neighborhoods. Tapachula's sizable Chinese merchant community was especially targeted during the Depression years by the PNR-backed Mexican Anti-Chinese League (Liga Mexicana Antichina). The League—with its motto "United we will eliminate the Chinese from Mexico" ("*Unidos deschinatizaremos México*")—flourished into the 1940s, calling boycotts and agitating for mass expulsions.[2]

Anticlericalism constituted another provocative, ultimately counterproductive nation-building campaign. On the face of it, the anticlerical crusade was sheer madness. In a country divided historically by ethnicity, caste, and conquest and where class, linguistic, and ideological distinctions persisted, Catholicism united rich and poor, creole and Indian, *norteño* and *sureño*, banker and peasant. Even the renowned Reforma anticlerical Ignacio Manuel Altamirano recognized that without the Virgin of Guadalupe "the Mexican nationality" would cease to exist.[3] So why would postrevolutionary nation builders attack Mexico's most compelling institution of national cohesion in the wake of a devastating civil war that killed or displaced well over 1 million people?

As Adrian Bantjes has written, anticlericalism in Mexico is "another chapter in the history of Western secularization" not unlike the anticlerical episodes seen in Latin Catholic countries like France, Italy, and Spain. Anticlericalism is "an essential component of most modern revolutions" as "impatient elites, eager to quicken the pace of history . . . impose modernist utopian blueprints."[4] In Chiapas, as in the rest of Mexico, the schoolhouse and the teacher were expected to take over the leading roles in communities, replacing the church and the priest. Revolutionary festivals would supplant Catholic rites, and the civic calendar with its secular heroes would replace the religious calendar so bloated with feast days. Revolutionary ideologues believed that a new culture could not be established without first eliminating preexisting and competing belief systems, symbols, and rites. Iconoclasm, or the burning of saints' images, became the most direct way to physically "desacralize" the old cultural order and facilitate the "transfer of sacrality" to a new civic, secular, and "revolutionary" cultural project, one that would forge the new Mexican.

Anticlericalism and the State: The View from Mexico City

Ever since Mexico achieved its independence in 1821, official anticlericalism had been a key component of liberal state and nation building. On the one hand, it targeted the institution believed capable of challenging the moral authority and organizational capacity of the Mexican state. On the other, it was part of a long-standing cultural project aimed at creating rational, hard-working, and modern Mexicans. Both motives explain the intensity of postrevolutionary anticlericalism in Mexico.

During the 1850s and 1860s, the Catholic Church and its allies suffered a series of political, economic, and military defeats at the hands of liberals. However, during the Porfiriato the Church began to reenter political life. Taking its cue from Pope Leo XIII's 1891 encyclical "Rerum Novarum," which called for fair wages, mutual aid societies, and moderate agrarian reform as a hedge against socialism, the Church held social welfare congresses in Puebla (1903), Morelia (1904), Guadalajara (1906), and Oaxaca (1909). Shortly before Díaz was overthrown, the archbishop and other prominent Catholics founded the National Catholic Party. This party elected four senators, four governors, and twenty-nine federal deputies, and won the majority of seats in seven state legislatures (including Chiapas) during its first two years of existence. The Constitution of 1917, however, especially Articles 3, 5, 27, and 130, invalidated many recent Church advances by declaring its participation in political and social affairs (including education) unconstitutional. Rather than retreat, however, the Church pushed forward, and by 1922 its National Catholic Labor Confederation (Confederación Nacional Católica del Trabajo) boasted eighty thousand members and represented a clear threat to the official CROM, which had about one hundred thousand members at the time. It unionized agrarian workers, hitherto neglected by the CROM, and challenged official *agrarismo* by launching its own agrarian reform program.[5]

"Since the goals of the [Catholic] social action movement and the social goals of the revolution overlapped," Patience Schell writes, "the Church presented a serious political and cultural threat to the revolutionary state-in-formation."[6] In 1926 President Calles, whose anticlerical zeal stemmed from his illegitimate birth and his involvement in late Porfirian liberal politics, began enforcing Article 3 of the Constitution of 1917. He prohibited clergy and members of religious orders from directing and teaching in primary schools, banned religious instruction, and forced all schools to use SEP textbooks and teaching methods. He fanned the flames during the summer of 1926 with his Ley Calles. Section 19 of the decree required priests to register with civil authorities and was designed to force the ultimate subordination of the Church to the state.[7]

The Church retaliated by suspending religious services on August 1. For the first time in four centuries, public mass was not heard in Mexico.

Churches remained closed for the next three years. Calles took heart, believing that 2 percent of Mexico's believers would lose their faith for every month that services remained suspended.[8] Soon the Cristero War erupted, ravaging much of western Mexico. The National League to Defend Religious Freedom (Liga Nacional Defensora de la Libertad Religiosa) led the urban response to official anticlericalism. It launched a nationwide boycott of official primary schools beginning in October 1926. In Mexico City, Guadalajara, and other large cities, where the bulk of official schools could still be found, the boycott enjoyed significant support. Parents and clergy organized clandestine schools in private homes, and thousands of students successfully avoided official, lay schooling.

The Cristero war dragged on for three years and claimed tens of thousands of lives. In Colima, Jalisco, Michoacán, and other states in the Cristero heartland, federal teachers often paid the ultimate price for their association with the SEP. In many other cases, however, teachers who did not agree with Calles's anticlerical crusade either maintained neutrality or joined the Cristero cause. Only in the election year of 1929 did the Mexican government's intransigence soften, and U.S. Ambassador Dwight Morrow was able to broker a temporary truce.[9]

Calles rekindled the flames in late 1931 with the appointment of Narciso Bassols as director of the SEP. Bassols was the first self-proclaimed Marxist to hold a major post in Mexican government. He felt that the "religious opiate" belonged neither in the classroom nor in the lives of twentieth-century Mexicans. Arguably, this renewed anticlerical campaign was timed to distract rural Mexicans from the cessation of agrarian reform and represented part of a larger tendency—perfected by the PNR—of substituting cultural and nationalist campaigns for tangible political and economic reforms. On December 29, 1931, shortly after the Church's audacious celebration of the 400th anniversary of the apparition of the Virgin of Guadalupe, President Pascual Ortiz Rubio issued a decree that invalidated diplomas granted by religious secondary schools and banned the use of religious symbols in the classroom. In 1932 and 1933, Bassols's inspectors toured the country, incorporating some schools, fining others, and closing still others, which earned Bassols the wrath of the vociferous Unión Nacional de Padres de Familia.[10]

Bassols's tempestuous thirty-month tenure as head of the SEP has received mixed reviews from historians. On the one hand, he built rural normal schools (including the school at Cerro Hueco outside of Tuxtla Gutiérrez), revived popular pedagogy, and took steps to improve the physical health of Mexicans.

Teachers took charge of vaccination and public health programs, including sobriety campaigns, and attacked games of chance, prostitution, blood sports, and "wasteful" religious rituals, offering sports, theater, and patriotic festivals in their place.[11] Yet his uncompromising stance on secularization and his endorsement of sexual education created much ill will among many teachers, parents, and clergy, and intensely politicized public education in Mexico.

Anticlericalism and the State: The View from Chiapas

Despite the important political, economic, and social roles played by the Church in Chiapas since colonial times, its institutional strength can be easily exaggerated. As Juan Pedro Viqueira notes, the religious conquest of the highlands during the colonial period was a failed enterprise. Missionaries never succeeded in replacing pre-Hispanic belief systems with orthodox Catholic practice. In the nineteenth century, the Church did battle with anticlerical Liberals and lost. Religious orders were expelled from the state, extensive church lands ended up in Liberal hands, and many indigenous communities stopped paying religious dues and shunned priests altogether. During this period, Chiapas went forty-nine years without a bishop. Indigenous communities took charge of their religious lives and developed an elaborate *cargo* system. Traditional healers began to offer their services publicly without fearing persecution by the Church. The Church's institutional power was further eroded when Rabasa moved the state capital to Tuxtla in 1892.[12]

Nevertheless, successive governors in Chiapas in the late 1920s and 1930s scapegoated and attacked the Church. Whether they actually believed the Church to be a threat to state power and the federal government's modernization project is hard to ascertain. Catholics in Chiapas were spared the first wave of Callista anticlericalism but languished later under Callista governors Raymundo Enríquez (1928–1932) and Victórico Grajales (1932–1936). Governor Carlos Vidal (1925–1927) refused to initiate a concerted anticlerical campaign during his term. Nevertheless, in early 1926 he expropriated San Cristóbal's seminary and turned it over to the SEP. This move was meant to relieve the pressure for classroom space, but in a town like San Cristóbal, it was tantamount to lighting a fuse. Highland inspector José Macías Padilla complained that "the clergy attack our schools in the most impudent way, accusing them of being godless and disruptive and hurling excommunications against whomever sends their children to them. This hurts attendance figures. . . . Only 14% of the school-aged children actually attend school." Months later, as fighting was about to break out in western Mexico, Macías circulated a petition among local civil servants pledging support to Calles. Many refused to sign, prompting him to recommend a purge. First identifying women as the "most tenacious fanatics," Macías suggested that the SEP root out "those who are allied with our eternal enemies" because they "try to make life difficult for the few revolutionaries who live in this Biblical town (*población levítica*)."[13]

After Vidal was assassinated in fall 1927, interim governor Federico Martínez Rojas limited the number of publicly officiating priests in Chiapas to twenty-five.[14] Another interim governor, Amador Coutiño, announced that only one priest would be allowed to officiate for every forty-thousand inhabitants, but this restriction seems to have gone unenforced. During this time of confusion at the state level and demagoguery at the national level, the SEP in Chiapas pursued a rather limited campaign against the few private schools in the state. In 1928, state and federal education inspectors directed their attention to a school in Tapachula named "Constancy and Work." What appeared to trigger the inspection was the fact that the school, formerly known as the "Guadalupan Academy," had been conspicuous by its absence at a public commemoration honoring the birthday of Liberal nineteenth-century president Benito Juárez. A few days later, the inspectors visited the school and found a fully functional convent catering to 147 girls. The interior was adorned with saints' images and portraits of priests. Nuns and most students wore habits and religious training was given twice a day. As if this weren't enough, the state and federal inspectors found the school "anti-hygienic, lacking light and air." Days later, state education director Marcos Becerra closed the school.[15]

It was Governor Raymundo Enríquez (1928–1932) who, owing his position to Calles, took state anticlericalism to new levels. After Calles and SEP director Bassols initiated the second wave of anticlerical activity in 1931, Enríquez followed suit, closing down scores of "under-utilized" churches and limiting the number of official priests to eight.[16] Five of these were Roman Catholics and one was Evangelical. The remaining two were members of the slowly disintegrating Orthodox Mexican Church, a schismatic state church created by Calles and CROM boss Luis Morones in 1925 to challenge the Roman Catholic hierarchy. In an attempt to further weaken the highland church hierarchy, Enríquez's law assigned one man to an impossibly huge zone encompassing San Cristóbal, the Tzotzil communities to the north, and the Tzeltal region lying to the east, including Ocosingo.[17]

Worried by the escalating attacks on the Roman Catholic Church and religion in general, Bishop Gerardo Anaya, who resided in San Cristóbal, issued a circular in March 1932 to the five Roman Catholic priests legally assigned to churches in the state. He asked "the sacred heart of Jesus for grace and blessings so that we may suffer with Christian resignation the pain and bitterness of the present hour."[18] The ensuing months surely tested their "Christian resignation." Municipal presidents throughout the state were told to enforce laws regulating the use of church bells. The cathedral in San Cristóbal was allowed to ring its bells three times daily for no more than one minute to call the faithful to mass, to announce the dawn, and to issue the call for prayers. Any additional ringing was allowed only with written permission from the municipal president. Priests were not allowed to bless town and barrio fiestas, and the faithful had to pay a tax if they wanted to set off fireworks.[19] In early October, Governor Enríquez gave orders to expel Anaya because "the so-called Bishop in this city has been officiating and preaching the Catholic faith without authorization."[20] What happened next is not clear, but correspondence between Enríquez and Anaya in November suggests that the two men came to an understanding allowing the bishop to remain in San Cristóbal for the time being.[21]

In the early 1930s the anticlericals' long-standing campaign against the institutions, power, and influence of the Church broadened as they attacked the very notion of religion. Like the radical liberals of the nineteenth century, they "pushed the debate beyond the problem of clerical power and property and criticized Catholic culture itself as an obstacle in the path toward the creation of a new, secular morality."[22] Individual SEP teachers (and the institution in general) were becoming radicalized as the Church responded to official attacks by becoming more defensive and intransigent. Take the case of Inspector José Vázquez Luna, who was based in Comitán, a town that ranked second to San Cristóbal in importance for the Church hierarchy. In 1933 he attacked not only the institutions and organization of the Church but also the "fanaticism" that threatened to stymie the modernization process in Chiapas. Vázquez Luna decried the "fifi, aristocratic teachers who do great damage" and promised a purge of "fanatic fossils." "Caciquismo, fanaticism, misery, and mass ignorance are ubiquitous," he wrote. He concluded with a familiar refrain: "I can state without reservations that the Revolution has not taken hold in these latitudes."[23]

Governor Grajales and Anticlericalism in Chiapas

Anticlericalism in Chiapas evolved into full-scale antireligiosity under Governor Victórico Grajales (1932–1936). A well-off finquero from Chiapa de Corzo, he was the official PNR candidate for governor in 1932 and won the election without a single dissenting vote. Grajales and his chief of staff (Secretario Oficial), the "reformed" Mapache Fausto Ruiz, placed over fifty family members in the state government as judges, municipal presidents and treasurers, newspaper reporters, and alcohol tax collectors. Distant relatives and friends from his hometown of Chiapa de Corzo filled other posts. Seven of the nine representatives to the state legislature were also from Grajales's hometown. Still other jobs went to people whose only identifiable merit was their enmity toward Grajales's predecessor, Raymundo Enríquez. Among those disgraced during the previous administration was Ángel M. Corzo, former SEP inspector and representative to the local legislature. Grajales rehabilitated him by naming him director of the state's education ministry.[24]

Grajales's virulent anticlericalism gave him powerful Callista credentials. He may have been personally inspired by Tomás Garrido Canabal, a fellow Callista who governed neighboring Tabasco directly or indirectly from 1922 to 1935. For Garrido, anticlericalism was a means of amassing personal power and forging a modern, docile citizenry. Grajales may have had similar aims. In the words of a presidential adviser, he "subordinated his social agenda to Garrido Canabal, burning saints in public plazas and creating a guard of red-shirts; he decreed democracy among the dead; and he raised seeds, pigs and goats to the status of icons."[25] Grajales especially targeted San Cristóbal and used anticlericalism to rekindle the conflict between liberals of the lower Grijalva valley and pious conservatives in the highlands.

In February 1933, shortly after Grajales took office, the state government in Tuxtla limited the number of practicing religious ministers in the state to four. Public outrage forced the government to partially back down and pass a revised law placing the limit at fifty.[26] Even this revised measure—which in the words of the official PNR newspaper "reduces the number of vampires who suck the blood of the people"—was widely resisted by "fanatics" in Villa de las Rosas, Simojovel, and other municipalities in or near the central highlands.[27] Resistance occasionally took the form of armed clashes between enraged churchgoers, PNR provocateurs, and local authorities charged with enforcing the law. Typically, however, the devout simply met in private homes, where priests conducted clandestine services at the risk of five-hundred-peso fines and jail sentences.

Nowhere was mass disobedience greater than in San Cristóbal. Two months after Grajales took office the town's municipal president, Ciro Domínguez, issued a circular stating that municipal employees who attended religious ceremonies would be fired.[28] In November 1933, San Cristóbal's questionable commitment to anticlericalism raised the suspicions of the state government in Tuxtla. Municipal president Domínguez was scolded because "the Law of Religions [restricting the number of practicing priests] is being violated to a scandalous degree."[29] Although the law had been in effect for nearly a year, San Cristóbal's police had not reported a single violation. Meanwhile, an official propaganda organ of the PNR alleged that Domínguez had turned a blind eye to the masses, confessions, and baptisms taking place in private homes. In response to increasing pressure from Tuxtla, San Cristóbal's municipal authorities stepped up raids on clandestine religious services. In one such raid, police caught and immediately released the mother of municipal president Domínguez.[30]

In January 1934, Grajales dealt another blow to the Church. After trotting out the worn-out charge that "the clergy has always been the obstacle to progress in the Republic," he called the number of priests allowed by the decree of February 1933 "excessive and useless" since "the great majority of inhabitants of this state no longer believes in the rancid teachings diffused from the pulpit and through the confessional."[31] He authorized the state congress to limit each religious creed in the state to just one representative. One month later, Grajales's cronies in the legislature decreed that saints' names were to be dropped from all place names, street signs, and public places. For several years, San Cristóbal de Las Casas was known as Ciudad Las Casas, San Pedro Remate became Bella Vista, San Martín Mazapa became Mazapa de Madero, San Andrés Larráinzar became simply Larráinzar, and so on.[32] This measure was not reversed until 1943. In some cases, the reformed name stuck: San Bartolomé de los Llanos became Venustiano Carranza and is still known by that name today, just as San Miguel Mitontic is still known as Mitontic and San Martín as Abasolo.

The Grajales administration disingenuously cloaked its next anticlerical offensive under the veil of a public health campaign. Citing an "alarming" outbreak of smallpox and whooping cough, the administration in April 1934 ordered the closure of all churches in the state allegedly to prevent further contagion; many would remain closed for over three years.[33] In San Cristóbal over two hundred women signed a collective letter to municipal president Domínguez, stating that "even the most ignorant citizens understand the motives behind this measure." Needless to say, the number of reported smallpox cases was negligible, and public schools, theaters, and markets remained open.[34]

Anticlericalism in Chiapas reached a feverish pitch in the summer and fall of 1934. In October, the bishop and all but one priest were expelled from Chiapas by decree. "Nothing could give more satisfaction to Chiapas's revolutionary family . . . [than to witness the] departure of these ominous and despicable parasites of society," crowed an official PNR publication based in Tuxtla.

> Never again will the churches in Chiapas open for congregations to gather before a priest who preaches lies and spreads ignorance. And in the precise place where the Chiapanecan proletariat used to place its offerings to enrich the clergy's coffers, today they will go, free of religious and class prejudice, to receive culture and learning from the school's teachers.[35]

This move received a vote of confidence from the national congress in Mexico City, still solidly Callista. Two months later, literally days after Cárdenas's inauguration, the state's remaining priest, a schismatic named José Ramírez, renounced his profession of twenty-six years in an event well publicized by the state's PNR. After burning some of his religious paraphernalia, Ramírez claimed that idol worship was at the heart of Catholicism. An official PNR publication took pains to stress that Ramírez's conversion had not been forced upon him.[36]

The fall of 1934 was, indeed, chaotic in Chiapas. The state government sponsored public bonfires to incinerate religious artifacts in Tuxtla Gutiérrez and dozens of other towns. PNR activists and state troopers, with the help of some state and federal teachers, sacked and burned parish archives and stole valuable artifacts from sacristies. At Rincón Chamula and other towns, federal teachers presided over bonfires where saints' images were burned. The town's gutted church building would later house the SEP's first indigenous boarding school in the state. At Chamula itself, however, just a few kilometers north of "Ciudad" Las Casas, the Tzotzil residents were prepared to confront Grajales's "*quemasantos*" (saint burners). They hid saints' images in private homes and maintained a small army for several months to repel a rumored attack of provocateurs from Tuxtla Gutiérrez.[37]

The SEP's role in occupying and using gutted churches came at a price. During this time, dozens of church buildings—including the bishop's residence in Ciudad Las Casas—were converted into schools.[38] As told by Héctor Eduardo Paniagua, zone inspector along the Guatemalan border, many church buildings in his zone were "being used by schools and communities as small school workshops because we have attempted to make the school the center around which all community activities revolve."[39] This created good press for the state PNR and occasionally solved the short-term needs of communities that could not otherwise fund school construction, but the education effort in Chiapas no doubt suffered over the long term as villagers correctly perceived the schools to be the beneficiaries of demagogic anticlericalism.

Certainly the apogee of SEP anticlericalism came in early 1935. Shortly after Cárdenas was inaugurated, Chiapas native Elpidio López became the state's new director of federal education. He soon published *La escuela socialista en Chiapas*. This pamphlet spelled out in no uncertain terms the steps to be taken to combat clerical influence. Themes to be discussed by teachers included religion as a means of exploitation, the role of violence in the spread of world religions, the reciprocal relationship between the aristocracy and the Church, and the priest as social parasite. Armed with the laws of science, teachers were to combat local superstitions and critique the curative miracles attributed to certain saints. Teachers were also expected to challenge the spiritual traditions of the agricultural calendar, especially the campesinos' custom of praying to San Isidro Labrador for rain and honoring St. John at harvest time. First- and second-year students were to compare the productive sectors of their towns with local churches to underscore the "uselessness" of the latter. López's history courses placed heavy emphasis on the blotches on the Church's record, including the Crusades, the Inquisition, and its "conspiracies," including its alliance with the Conservatives during the mid-nineteenth-century Reform Wars and its role in provoking Chiapas's "Caste War" of 1867–1870. López also gave his blessing to anticlerical bonfires and went so far as to order teachers to skip the second stanza of the national anthem because it contained references to heaven, the "divine archangel," and God.[40] Lastly, López modified the religiously inspired school names of forty-three additional federal schools in Chiapas. Usually names of local or national heroes were substituted for the names of saints. The runaway winner in the renaming sweepstakes was Francisco I. Madero, who had three schools named after him. No schools were named for either of the "fathers" of Mexican independence, renegade Catholic priests Miguel Hidalgo and José María Morelos y Pavón.[41]

Although the SEP in Chiapas marched in step with federal policy and intensified its anticlerical activity briefly with the arrival of López, its teachers and inspectors rarely matched the enthusiasm and devotion of Grajales's partisans. Given the relative weakness of the SEP at this time, the intensity of its anticlerical campaign naturally varied by region, inspector, and teacher. One of the most dogmatic inspectors was P. Arturo Mota. A product of Chiapas's state normal school in Tuxtla, Mota had been radicalized in the 1920s when he worked as one of Vasconcelos's missionaries. As a federal inspector in late 1934, Mota made sure that all plantation chapels in his zone were converted into schools. He convinced indigenous workers on the fincas to burn the crosses they were accustomed to placing in public places. He also purged all teachers in his zone who professed to be Catholics. Later he reported that these ex-teachers gave "classes to small groups of children, the sons and daughters of reactionaries, in private homes on a rotating basis in order to avoid being caught."[42] Despite the illegal activities of Catholic ex-teachers and the opposition of "recalcitrant fanatics . . . and rich landowners [*latifundistas*]," Mota informed López that Comitán's federal schools in 1935 were nearly full.[43]

The year 1935 witnessed crucial changes in federal anticlerical policy. Although President Cárdenas sponsored a number of anticlerical measures early in his presidency, his fervor never matched that of Jefe Máximo Calles. During the course of 1935, most SEP inspectors sensed that they could back away from this provocative, unpopular campaign. In April 1935, highland zone inspector Manuel Castellanos wrote that school attendance had suffered in his zone due to the "campaign of slander and lies developed by clerical elements and exploiters, as well as the general resentment that exists against the defanaticization campaign, especially the expulsion of priests and the burning of religious objects carried out at the end of last year." Castellanos then urged his teachers to temper their anticlerical activity. By year's end his teachers were going about their defanaticizing activity "with necessary prudence."[44] Manuel Fernando Molina, inspector for the northern zone of Simojovel, reported that his teachers "maintained their ideology with prudence and serenity. Pushing aside all demagogic attitudes they defanaticized children and adult campesinos through persuasion, offering examples from real life and providing rational, accessible scientific explanations of the phenomena of nature."[45] Finally, Héctor Eduardo Paniagua wrote that his teachers had developed an anticlerical campaign that was "carefully considered and orderly."[46]

The Property Nationalization Law (Ley de Nacionalización de Bienes), passed by the national congress in August 1935, declared all churches, church schools, and religious objects to be the property of the nation and is often considered Cárdenas's most anticlerical piece of legislation. Yet the application of this law in Chiapas reined in some of the more extreme anticlerical crusaders, including schoolteachers, by claiming religious artifacts to be property of the nation, not kindling wood for demagogic anticlerical bonfires. Teacher Gaspar Díaz expressed surprise when Motozintla's municipal president informed him that bonfires were no longer permitted. Díaz defended his intentions by invoking the SEP's School Work Plan—which called for anticlerical bonfires—and claimed only to have wanted "to incite the revolutionary spirit of the PNR members present with a palpable display of their antireligious attitudes."[47] As Díaz learned, the official attitude toward religion was gradually but significantly changing.

Another slow learner was Inspector Rubén M. Rincón, who was based in the Tzeltal region surrounding Ocosingo. In a mid-1936 report he wrote that "fanaticism" had been mostly eradicated in his zone and that most peasants no longer had religious fetishes in their homes. According to Rincón, the only remaining religion was that of "honest work and fraternity." His superiors at the SEP took exception to these bold claims. After first reprimanding him for placing too much faith in external manifestations of belief (or lack thereof), the SEP's director general wrote that the SEP "does not believe that drastic changes will shape the beliefs of this country's inhabitants. Rather, through the scientific orientation that it provides, unfounded beliefs will be progressively washed away from the mentality of the masses."[48] Though we can hardly blame Rincón for his assertions, which would have been perfectly acceptable and politically expedient two years earlier, most zone inspectors had already perceived the shift in anticlerical policy. Few even paid lip service to official anticlericalism in their 1936 annual reports.

Without official prodding, Chiapas's inhabitants rarely took it upon themselves to conduct anticlerical acts, even in the *agrarista* lowlands; as Bantjes found in his study of iconoclasm in Sonora, saint burnings rarely resulted from spontaneous and genuinely popular initiative.[49] While socialist education left a lasting legacy of organization and mobilization in Chiapas's public schools, as ensuing chapters will detail, the anticlerical dimension of the project had little lasting impact. Despite an arguably successful cultural program aimed at promoting a national civic culture in the 1930s, the SEP failed to fully "transfer sacrality" from the Church to the emerging Mexican state and nation. Rural Mexicans did not become more "rational" or "modern" through anticlerical bonfires and the harangues of defanaticizing inspectors and teachers. As Knight has written, "It was one thing to get bodies on to the streets, another to change the minds inside the bodies."[50] Fortunately for the SEP and its teachers in Chiapas, demagogic governor Grajales was pinned with most of the blame for anticlerical excesses in the state. This would leave the federal schools poised to successfully participate in other more inclusive and constructive elements of educational populism during the Cardenista years.

Anticlericalism in Chiapas: From Evolution to Near Revolution

After Narciso Bassols pushed federal schools further into the contested arena of PNR state and nation building, the SEP found itself at the center of the renewed clash between Church and state. However, by the time socialist education officially became the SEP's operating philosophy, its antireligious component was redundant and largely irrelevant in Chiapas, where Grajales had already shackled Church institutions. If the governor did not convince most Chiapanecans of the folly of religious fanaticism, he *did* succeed in closing down every church in the state and chasing out or driving underground every practicing priest. The outcome of this campaign is laden with ironies. In most of the state, where the Church's presence had never been prominent, Grajales's agents attacked a weak institution that did not threaten state power. In Comitán and the central highlands, where the Church had traditionally played a more political role, anticlerical demagoguery generated sympathy for the persecuted clergy. Grajales's anticlerical campaign had one further unintended consequence—it spared federal teachers in Chiapas an unpopular and inflammatory campaign, and allowed them to concentrate instead on unionizing workers, enforcing federal labor laws, promoting agrarian reform, implementing health campaigns, and fighting local caciques. This in turn won federal teachers the admiration and support of most mestizo communities by the late 1930s. Although the anticlerical campaign began as a project of the central government under Calles, in Chiapas its excesses would be blamed on Governor Grajales. President Lázaro Cárdenas would use this as leverage against Grajales during the showdown between federal and state forces in summer 1936. ◆

Chapter Five

Socialist Education in Chiapas

> The socialist child will not be suckled on legends of kings and slaves, of masters and servants, of executioners and victims, which could wake his rapacious instincts; he won't be incited by conquests or campaigns against other races, creeds, religions, or teachings . . . he will not be poisoned with hate for others, and he will not consider others, nor the work, sweat, and blood of others, to be his own personal property.
>
> —*"La educación socialista y la escuela rural,"*
> El Maestro Rural, *December 1934*

"The education imparted by the state will be socialist and, besides excluding all religious doctrine, will combat religious fanaticism and prejudice," read the December 1934 reform to Article 3 of the Mexican Constitution. "The school will organize its instruction and activities such that youth will develop a rational and exact notion of the social universe."[1] At once bold and vague, these declarations announced the SEP's educational philosophy for the upcoming *sexenio*, 1934–1940. After President Cárdenas's inauguration an unabashedly radicalized SEP worked with a populist federal government to lay the foundation for the modern Mexican nation-state. Although the meaning of socialist education was never clear, even to its primary advocates and practitioners, it represented the apotheosis of the unrealized populist tendencies of the schools of the 1920s and early 1930s.

Socialist education in Chiapas manifested itself through anti-alcohol campaigns, grassroots politicization and unionization, support for agrarian reform, and a cultural project intended to promote rational, scientific thought. Federal teachers challenged the real and imagined enemies of the emerging nation-state and attempted to "Mexicanize" marginalized populations. While the SEP's radicalized state- and nation-building project sparked fierce resistance from planters, ranchers, alcohol merchants, and Governor Grajales, it won the acceptance, if not full support, of mestizo communities that had previously regarded SEP schools with indifference. Cardenistas would mobilize these communities for the political and organizational struggles that would grip the state beginning in 1936.

"Socialist" Education?

No other moment in the history of Mexican education has generated as much scholarly attention as socialist education.[2] For some contemporaries and scholars, it at least partially fulfilled the promise of the Mexican revolution as legions of young, idealistic teachers labored tirelessly in hopes of leveling class distinctions, eradicating the abuses of national and international capitalism, and raising the consciousness of Mexico's dispossessed. For others, socialist education was a foreign model unsuited to the Mexican context, inspired by godless communists and demagogues. This large corpus of work is a function of the unlikely origins of socialist education, its confused articulation, its inflammatory prescriptions, and the violent, occasionally fatal responses to its implementation.

Ironically, socialist education was endorsed in 1933 following years of increasingly conservative political and economic policy in Mexico. In December 1929, following the Comintern's critique of bourgeois regimes, Mexico's Communist Party was outlawed, its headquarters raided, and its members either deported or jailed. Two months later Mexico severed diplomatic relations with the Soviet Union. Another roundup of Communists occurred following the assassination attempt on President Ortiz Rubio. Meanwhile, Calles ordered an end to agrarian reform in 1930 and became increasingly hostile to labor. Still, socialism went from the margins to the center of the Mexican revolution in the space of less than one year—1933.

How can we explain this resurrection of leftist politics and rhetoric? The crises of 1929—both political and economic—forced Calles to reconstitute his popular base, especially as peasants and labor deserted him. When he formally created the PNR in March of that year, the legitimacy and very survival of his regime were being threatened by the Cristero rebellion to the west, the Escobar rebellion to the north, and the electoral challenge of former SEP director José Vasconcelos. Mexico's domestic political crises coincided with the great crisis in international capitalism. For many intellectuals, members of the fledgling PNR, and communist sympathizers in the SEP, the Depression exposed the failings of the liberal doctrine of individualism. Marxism gained new legitimacy. The Soviet Union's apparent success in riding out the crisis also tended to defang socialism's harshest critics. As social and economic policy, Marxism filled the void temporarily vacated by liberal individualism and free-market capitalism; as a pedagogical philosophy, socialism fed the almost mystical belief held by many that the school could create a new society.[3]

Desperate for a popular base in the midst of such crises, the PNR latched onto well-organized grassroots organizers like teachers and appropriated their radical rhetoric. Teachers had already compiled impressive track records as state builders in Felipe Carrillo Puerto's Yucatán (1918–1922), Adalberto Tejeda's Veracruz (1920–1932), Tomás Garrido Canabal's Tabasco (1922–1935), and Michoacán under Francisco Múgica (1921–1923) and Lázaro Cárdenas (1928–1932). In these states, schools interchangeably called *socialista, racionalista, colectivista,* or *de acción* embraced a rhetoric of liberation and scientific thought. Teachers mobilized peasants, workers, women, and youth into unions and cooperatives. They also facilitated land reform and led anti-alcohol and anticlerical campaigns. When Narciso Bassols and the PNR decided to use the educational practices of populist governors as models for party building, they created the conditions for a leftward shift in policy that not even Calles could contain.[4]

In December 1933, PNR delegates met in Querétaro to formally present the Cárdenas candidacy and his platform, the Plan Sexenal (Six Year Plan). Thanks to the leftward shift in the PNR, the educational program for the upcoming sexenio contemplated a reform to Article 3 of the constitution. As told by Samuel Ramos, the congressional commissioners charged with this task "were ignorant in matters of education, blinded by a phrase [socialist education] which they did not bother to understand before making it law."[5] After months of discussion and several revisions, the commission presented a proposal calling for a pedagogy based on scientific socialism and fervent anticlericalism. However, it remained a dead letter until Calles gave the PNR's antireligious faction the green light in July 1934 with his infamous "Grito de Guadalajara."[6]

After more debate and revisions, the amended Article 3 was approved by the national legislature in October 1934, at the height of Callista anticlericalism in states like Chiapas, and became law with Cárdenas's inauguration in December 1934. In its final version, Article 3 was little more than an anticlerical and positivist proclamation. Its "socialist" orientation was open to interpretation. Some drafters wished to socialize the means of production through the schools along the lines of the Soviet Union, while others simply wanted to humanize capitalism without threatening private property. Still others like Cárdenas sought a middle ground, calling for *socialismo a la mexicana*, or socialism adapted to Mexican realities. A *New York Times* correspondent in 1935 claimed to have found thirty-three different interpretations of socialist education. Even Rafael Ramírez, the SEP's Director of Rural Schools, conceded that the program was vague but insisted that in Mexico a "proletarian school" existed that differed markedly from its bourgeois predecessors. For many SEP inspectors and teachers, socialist education was something "felt," not defined.[7]

Not surprisingly, several major ideological contradictions plagued socialist education. Its rhetoric of class struggle flew in the face of the SEP's stated goal of fostering peace and national unity. And the irony of a dependent capitalist country promoting an allegedly Marxist-Leninist educational program did not escape radical university students, teachers, and individuals like Vicente Lombardo Toledano and Diego Rivera. The Mexican Communist Party, in fact, initially dismissed socialist education as a palliative of a "fascist" and "bourgeois" regime.[8] SEP apologists claimed that the state was preparing students for a socialist future, especially since global capitalism appeared to be on its deathbed. But for all its Marxist rhetoric and its emphasis on collectivized agriculture, socialist education taught some of the basic principles of nineteenth-century liberalism, including notions of individual liberty, and the possibility of individual economic advancement.[9]

If an allegedly Marxist-Leninist educational program was improbable in postrevolutionary Mexico, it was especially so in states like Chiapas, which had barely taken the first steps toward industrialization and where pre-capitalist labor relations were still the norm. A broad proletarian consciousness was unlikely to take root in a state where economic and social relations were still determined by ethnic distinctions. Ironically, socialist education in Chiapas would actually pave the way for *capitalist* development by attacking caciquismo and debt peonage.

The socialist experiment represented the culmination of the populist project begun by Moisés Sáenz and rekindled by SEP director Narciso Bassols. The SEP's curricular transformation came full circle as its newly created Institute of Socialist Orientation (Instituto de Orientación Socialista) published texts that celebrated popular agency, class struggle, sports, the ejido, active citizenship, and patriotism, just as they condemned *latifundismo*, religiosity, drinking, and womanizing. Texts written by Alfonso Teja Zabre, Luis Chávez Orozco, and others celebrated popular insurgents like Hidalgo, Morelos, and Zapata, while erstwhile heroes Cortés, Iturbide, and even Madero were subjected to criticism. Campesinos were urged to fight for their rights through popular, democratic organizations. Urban workers were to feel international solidarity with their working-class brethren. Mexican women were told that they were victims of class oppression, not sexism. Some texts went so far as to encourage proletarians to sharpen their tools for eventual use against their capitalist exploiters. These more radical texts, penned by proponents of scientific socialism, went beyond the relatively tame version endorsed by the amended Article 3. Still, even in the realm of textbooks, socialist education represented more continuity than change, more an apotheosis of the latent populist tendencies of earlier years than a drastic break with precedent.[10]

"Socialism" in Semi-feudal Chiapas

Septimio Pérez Palacios laid the foundation for socialist education in Chiapas. He took charge as the state's Director of Federal Education in February 1933, nearly two years before the reformed Article 3 became law. He inherited 333 federal schools distributed among seven zones, two of which were already in the hands of activist inspectors P. Arturo Mota and Daniel Vassallo. Taking his cue from Bassols, Pérez promoted public health campaigns, road building, experimental gardens, and limited land reform. He also conducted relatively timid anticlerical and anti-alcohol crusades. What distinguished populist education under Pérez from the socialist education that followed was more a matter of intensity than content. His successor merely deepened the above-mentioned campaigns and injected the rhetoric of class conflict.

Elpidio López, whom we met in the previous chapter, replaced Pérez in February 1935. López was a seasoned veteran of radical pedagogy and revolutionary politics, having served as head of the SEP in Tabasco from 1927 to 1928 and later in Rodolfo Elías Calles's Sonora from 1932 to 1934. López's antidote for Chiapas was simple, even simplistic. "During the present year," he wrote in his 1935 Work Plan (Plan de Trabajo), "we must forcefully implement [*violentar*] our educational social work."[11]

López and his teachers took full advantage of the schools' expanded social mandate. Since the federal government lacked the resources to staff an effective state apparatus in Chiapas, the everyday functions of the federal bureaucracy fell to the teachers, who became labor inspectors, union organizers, immigration officials, anticlerical crusaders, health care workers, agrarian reformers, agronomists, and agents of Mexicanization. Their schools were still expected to keep chickens, rabbits, pigeons, sheep, pigs, and bees and feature a garden plot, including a greenhouse, an orchard, and a vegetable garden. In an annual survey, teachers were asked to sketch the plot and provide a detailed description of the crops under cultivation. What was being grown? How was the soil? What were the probable dates of harvest? How much did it cost to plant the crop, and what yield could be expected? When were the seasonal rains, and were there frosts? Was the plot part of an ejido, or was it sold, rented, or donated to the school? Meanwhile, López's teachers organized land invasions and helped peasants initiate agrarian reform procedures. Within months his teachers had established fifty agrarian communities primarily on plantations lands. Each community had an agrarian committee charged with overseeing the paperwork that would legalize their claim to the land that they were occupying.[12]

López's corps of teachers and inspectors also monitored a dizzying array of cultural and social programs. They organized patriotic festivals and sporting events designed to "de-fanaticize" the population and "distance youth from the vice of alcoholism."[13] Teachers gave vaccinations as needed and campaigned against dysentery, malaria, smallpox, measles, and a mosquito-borne disease called onchocerciasis ("purple disease"—its victims gradually go blind). They also conducted hygiene campaigns against lice, mites, and tropical fleas and encouraged villagers to drain swamplands, protect sources of drinking water, and burn their trash.

Of course, even the most dedicated "socialist" teachers in the most cooperative communities could not possibly lead this many campaigns. To encourage community involvement, López urged teachers to create the following organizations: the Children's School Community (Comunidad Infantil Escolar), the Education Committee (Comité de Educación), the Young Revolutionaries' Block (Bloque Juvenil Revolucionario), and the Socialist Mothers' Union (Unión de Madres Socialistas). Where applicable, teachers also established a Peasants' Syndicate (Unión Sindical Campesina), a Workers' Syndicate (Sindicato de Trabajadores), and Consumption, Production, and Agrarian Credit Cooperatives (Cooperativas de Consumo, de Producción, y de Crédito Agrícola). The Education Committee encouraged school attendance and monitored teacher performance and behavior both inside and outside the classroom. The Peasant and Worker syndicates were to monitor application of the 1931 Federal Labor Law. Production cooperatives organized to give communities enhanced buying and selling power. They purchased machinery such as sugar presses and grain mills and sold their products at fair prices. Students were also involved in production cooperatives; at Acapetagua, they raised enough money to buy a profitable soft-drink and slushed-ice stand at a local railway station.[14] The SEP's top-down mobilization campaign in the mid-1930s was one of its most important legacies.

Less than two months into his tenure, López realized that implementing socialist education in Chiapas required much more than simply creating grassroots organizations, printing an ambitious work plan, and eliminating saints' names from schools. He was shocked by what he found in his *patria chica.* In Sonora, Governor Calles had aided López by mobilizing teachers, workers, and peasants into a radicalized state PNR. In Chiapas, on the other hand, the state government was indifferent if not downright hostile to the SEP. "The material state of the schools is disastrous and none of them even approaches the most modest schools in other states of the Republic," López wrote. "I can affirm that in Chiapas, the Federal Government for the last fourteen years has wasted more than five million pesos without achieving any favorable results."[15]

In May 1935, after traveling through ten inspection zones, López penned a sober report to the SEP in Mexico City listing the obstacles impeding the realization of socialist education in Chiapas. Many of these impediments—poorly prepared teachers, a large, marginalized indigenous population, the lack of industry, primitive agricultural techniques, and the presence of obstructionist foreigners in the state's most fertile areas—were long-standing and predated the revolution. Other obstacles, however, were largely political in nature. In a veiled criticism of Governor Grajales, López lambasted the state's "personalist politics" and blamed the state and municipal governments for withholding moral and material support from schools. He also critiqued "the bad faith governing the performance of agents who should labor on behalf of the proletariat," like the state's labor and alcohol inspectors and the Inspectors of Indigenous Action and Protection (Inspectores de Acción y Protección Indígena).[16] In López's assessment, resistance to socialist education was greatest in the highlands and in Comitán. The southern frontier zones of Motozintla and Comalapa also ranked among the most difficult, as did Daniel Vassallo's zone, based in the coastal coffee zone and containing a few dozen problematic Article 123 schools.

López's new prescription for Chiapas called for fifty more teachers and state and federal assistance to help poor communities build schools. He also solicited a portable library and movie projector for each of the state's thirteen zones and asked the SEP to provision classrooms with supplies and sporting equipment. His other material requests suggest his strong commitment toward promoting active citizenship. Each classroom was to have copies of the 1917 Constitution, the 1931 Federal Labor Law, the 1934 Agrarian Code, and laws pertaining to cooperative societies, agrarian credit, and idle (expropriable) lands. López also asked the Ministry of Agriculture and Development to send veterinarians and agronomy engineers to the state to improve breeding stock and agricultural methods and asked the Ministry of Communications to provide tools for road improvement campaigns.[17] But he realized that his most urgent need was a well-trained, ideologically and pedagogically sound teaching corps.

Training the Vanguard

As the SEP's campaigns of social engineering became more ambitious, the deficiencies of its teachers in Chiapas became more glaring. The SEP took a step toward improving teacher performance when it finally opened a rural normal school at Cerro Hueco (outside of Tuxtla Gutiérrez) in 1931. Yet even a normal-school teaching certificate could be sidestepped or falsified, as Director Septimio Pérez learned. Formerly head of federal education in Campeche, Pérez fought mightily to combat the nepotism and intense personalism that characterized government in Chiapas. In a remarkable confidential letter to the SEP's Director of Rural Schools, Rafael Ramírez, Pérez complained that a senator, the head of the state's Conciliation and Arbitration Board (Junta de Conciliación y Arbitraje), and other high-ranking officials of the Grajales administration and federal government had made demands of him on behalf of their friends and clients. They issued veiled threats when Pérez denied their requests for jobs and favors. "You asked if I feel frightened yet," he wrote to Ramírez. "I will say without being a *valiente* that I am becoming aware of how things are done in this state."[18]

Pérez then kicked off an unpopular purge of the SEP rank and file. Teachers who had not completed six years of schooling were given the chance to return to school or take a certifying exam. Many chose the latter option and passed. Those who failed were replaced by graduates from the recently established normal school. But much as Pérez had anticipated, the corruption of enterprising SEP inspectors and functionaries was eventually exposed. An official from the teachers' union in Chiapas and various zone inspectors had sold seven hundred falsified normal-school graduation certificates. The ringleaders soon fled to Mexico City. In time, Mexico's attorney general (Procurador General de la Nación) ordered their detention. But those implicated had friends in high places, just as Pérez had suspected. As they were being flown back to Chiapas in the planes of the Ministry of the Interior (Gobernación), the pilot received orders from President Abelardo Rodríguez to land in Tuxtepec and release them. Pérez was forced to recur to the state's normal school and four private schools to fill teaching vacancies.[19]

Elpidio López renewed his predecessor's campaign to weed out unqualified teachers. As he had seen firsthand, a "good percentage" of teachers were chronic drunks, many male teachers behaved more like satyrs than pedagogues, and several female teachers were guilty of *mala conducta* (bad conduct). Worst of all, they could not teach. "Almost all of them are ignorant in matters of teaching and social action," he reported. "Some teachers have worked for two or three years without realizing that *ejidatarios* reside in their community. As an employee of the Ministry of Education and as a Chiapanecan, I lament all of this." López visited dozens of schools where "attendance was low, the teaching method was outdated, and the teachers were walled-up in their classrooms" and lacked presence in their communities. After a sweep through fifteen northern schools, he found that only one had an experimental garden and greenhouse. The rest simply taught the three Rs "in a completely antiquated way" and/or served as Spanish language schools for the predominately Tzotzil and Ch'ol population. López was also distressed to find that parents were not sending their daughters to school.[20]

López was convinced that communities would warmly embrace the SEP's schools once teachers were well versed in action pedagogy and socialist education. After all, most teacher incompetence was more a product of poor training and supervision than of willful negligence. As one inspector wrote in 1933, most of the teachers in his zone were "youngsters who must be guided more with the counsel of a friend than with the orders of a superior." These "incipient social activists" tended to get discouraged, having accepted difficult work far from home in regions where life was both expensive and arduous.[21]

López first purged ideologically incompatible teachers whom he dismissed as "reactionaries" and/or Catholic "fanatics." Then he and his inspectors attempted to root out teachers who had been "absorbed" by their communities and rendered pedagogically useless. Many of these teachers identified too closely with local political and economic interests and resisted the purges. At La Grandeza state and federal education inspectors attempted to remove two teachers who initially appealed the decision through formal channels. Later, General Inspector Andrés Cancúa Neri reported "some twenty to twenty-five gunmen threatened my life if I did not leave things as they had always been." La Grandeza's caciques ordered parents not to send their children to the new teachers' classes. Locals refused food and lodging to the teachers, who spent several nights sleeping under the awnings of the town hall. The inspector insinuated that previous teachers had protected powerful economic interests in the region and local elites feared that new teachers versed in radical pedagogy would challenge the status quo.[22]

López's next step was to take comprehensive measures to promote ideological unity among those teachers that remained. In order to instill a truly socialist orientation, he published *La escuela socialista en Chiapas* and reprinted teacher training material that he had used in Sonora. Each of the state's thirteen administrative zones was divided into three or four sectors, and inspectors held bimonthly pedagogy meetings (Juntas Pedagógicas) with teachers in each sector to discuss the progress of the socialist school. López also promised to bring the SEP into closer partnership with the state PNR, though Governor Grajales's domination of the party would eventually frustrate this relationship.[23]

Last of all, López used the beleaguered Cultural Missions to keep teachers abreast of the SEP's evolving ideological orientation. In spring 1935, fifty-two teachers participated in a four-week institute at Tenejapa. Teachers who successfully completed the institute were credited with one semester toward the eight-semester rural normal-school degree. Among the highlights of this institute was a course on the history of the workers' movement taught by highland zone inspector Manuel Castellanos. Teachers learned of the "disastrous consequences of capitalism," including eighteen-hour workdays, the destruction of the family, prostitution, and war. Castellanos also lectured on the Luddites, utopian socialism, Marx and Engels, the Paris Commune, the Second International, the Haymarket Square massacre of May 1, 1886, and the Russian Revolution. Closer to home, Castellanos discussed the 1907 massacre at Río Blanco, the Flores Magón brothers, and Article 123 of the Constitution. Teachers at the institute were also expected to fulfill a "social action" obligation. At Tenejapa, participants introduced piped water to the village, built a basketball court, held numerous anticlerical and anti-alcoholic cultural events, and constructed an outdoor theater complete with a mural showing a teacher steering indígenas clear of corrupt mestizo politicians.[24] For the majority of Chiapas's rural teachers, the only formal training that they received was through the missions and the inspectors' monthly pedagogy meetings.

After López's purges, who was left? Surviving documents do not provide a convincing collective profile of the SEP's rural teachers. What we can glean suggests that they were either from the urban lower-middle class, sons and daughters of shopkeepers and local functionaries, or from rural villages with a strong tradition of schooling. They were young, most of them in their late teens or twenties. All teachers in Chiapas were ladinos, and only a handful possessed a working knowledge of an indigenous language. By 1934, only 22 percent of the teachers in service in Chiapas had graduated from a normal school. And despite efforts to root "fanatics" from the ranks, there were still devout Catholics in SEP classrooms.

In terms of the gender composition of the teaching corps, Chiapas once again provides the exception to the rule. In what was considered one of Mexico's few "feminized" professions, most rural schoolteachers in Chiapas were men. Many inspectors believed that men were stricter disciplinarians and more competent at leading the sporting activities that might dissuade students from alcohol. In remote, violent Pichucalco, Inspector Jesús Durán Cárdenas preferred male teachers. Of the more than fifty teachers in his zone only five were women, and two of these were married to the school director where they worked. As a result, expressed Inspector Cárdenas, "we perform our work with enthusiasm and virility."[25]

Yet virility did not commend male teachers to certain tasks. Where women taught, girls' attendance rates generally rose and women were more likely to join cooperatives and participate in anti-alcohol campaigns and political organizations. Female teachers enjoyed more success in entering and "rationalizing" the peasant household than males.[26] However, since most female teachers in Chiapas took jobs in cities and towns, their overall impact on rural communities was greatly reduced.

An ideological and pedagogical sketch of López's rural schoolteachers and inspectors is also difficult to create. While some had been imposed by local caciques or owed their positions to political or familial connections, others were career professionals with a strong commitment to social justice. For every teacher who sold excused absences to parents, others prepared land reform requests, organized civic festivals, and unionized workers. Federal inspectors also ran the gamut. Rubén Rivas, for example, was a disaster. According to Education Committee members at Yajalón, he was a habitual drunk "who roamed the streets late at night playing billiards." During a famine he also threatened to dynamite the town's church when residents refused to contribute money for a new schoolhouse.[27] By and large, however, Chiapas's federal inspectors were committed activists dedicated to improving the lives of people in their zones. Take, for example, Benjamín Rojas, who refused to compel the indigenous people in his zone to "volunteer" their labor to build airstrips. As Rojas wrote:

> In this state I have seen that unfortunately the poor class works hardest and never enjoys any benefit; this was the case with the airstrip at Simojovel. . . . I did not send Indians to that job, because the work was difficult, unpaid, and they would see no benefit until very late; the airstrips have been built for the trips of planters, politicians, and more or less bourgeois employees, who use planes as a high-class luxury, something which I detest; while the white man flies long distances, the Indian continues to use bad roads and paths, carrying loads on his back, exposed to the elements.[28]

Activist federal inspectors like Vassallo, Mota, Castellanos, and Rojas combined Carrancista general Castro's commitment to top-down, controlled Jacobin revolution with Vasconcelos's aesthetic vision of self-sacrifice for the cause of "civilization." As missionaries, rural schoolteachers, and inspectors during the late 1920s and early 1930s, they had been frustrated by the inconsistent application of action pedagogy and by locals who resisted SEP inroads. Teachers and inspectors in Chiapas had to confront an entrenched provincial elite, an obstructionist state government, and an often apathetic and distrustful grassroots population in an impoverished state that lacked a tradition in education. Not surprisingly, the turnover rate was high; only the most ideologically committed teachers and inspectors endured. Little wonder that this battle-hardened federal corps were reluctant to retreat from revolutionary pedagogy in the late 1930s and early 1940s.

The class, ethnic, gender, and ideological composition of Chiapas's federal teachers and inspectors made them ideal candidates as agrarian reformers, community organizers, and promoters of sporting and patriotic festivals in ladino communities. Their degree of success as social organizers can be measured by the degree of resistance registered by *aguadienteros*, finqueros, caciques, and others who felt their interests threatened by socialist education. By the same token, these same teachers enjoyed little or no success in indigenous communities where ethnic, historical, and usually linguistic differences impeded mutual understanding. Nor, from what we can tell, did this predominantly male corps succeed in modernizing peasant households and mobilizing women.

Despite serious shortages of personnel and resources, Pérez, López, and other SEP officials succeeded in shoring up Chiapas's federal teaching corps. In distant Pichucalco, for example, Inspector Jesús Durán Cárdenas reported in 1936 that all of the teachers in his zone had sixth-grade diplomas. Most had studied at least one semester of rural normal school through the Cultural Missions, several more had studied at the federal rural normal school at Cerro Hueco, and a handful had actually finished the four-year course there. Teachers in Pichucalco ranged in age from eighteen to forty-six, although most were in their mid-twenties.[29] No longer was it commonplace to find semi-literate teenagers in front of classrooms. With López's blessing, teachers in Chiapas even organized themselves into professional unions. In the space of less than fifteen years, the federal teaching corps in Chiapas had improved dramatically, from a small, haphazard collection of unschooled improvisers to a larger group of nominally prepared professionals, many of whom had received formal training in pedagogy, and most of whom were familiar with the general philosophical orientation of the SEP.

The "Socialist" Vanguard Meets the Opposition

How did Chiapas governor Victórico Grajales respond to López and his teachers, and to socialist education, with its emphasis on popular mobilization and agrarian reform? As López himself wrote, Chiapas had had ten directors of federal education since 1922, and all but two of them had been forced out by locals.[30] His job security hinged on his ability to tread softly. Throughout spring 1935, the two men tried to work together, and their face-to-face meetings were always cordial. Grajales met most of López's financial requests. The publication of López's *La escuela socialista en Chiapas* was financed out of the state treasury, dozens of communities received state funds to purchase building materials for school construction, and Grajales's administration purchased land and materials for indigenous boarding schools and a new rural normal school. Grajales's April 1935 prohibition on the production and distribution of alcohol in rural areas came at the behest of López, several zone inspectors, and dozens of schools. The two men also saw eye-to-eye on the anticlerical campaign.

During these months López went to extremes not to openly condemn Grajales and his supporters for their violent attacks on teachers and popular organizers. He maintained the facade of a united front with Grajales even as he urged the SEP in Mexico City to prosecute perpetrators of this violence.[31] The year 1935 was the most dangerous for federal teachers in Chiapas. Along the coast, plantation owners, local officials, and hired guns clashed regularly with teachers and workers. At Tapachulita, the municipal president ordered teacher José Gutiérrez to be sprayed with gunfire as he slept in the schoolroom one night in 1935. Later that summer, the federal teacher at El Zapotal was assassinated on orders from the municipal president at Pijijiapan, forcing Inspector Vassallo to close down the school.[32] At Escuintla, another one of Vassallo's teachers was assassinated one year after the inspector—fearing for the teacher's life—had requested the school's closure. Following this fatal attack, no other teacher would accept an appointment there. Vassallo again requested closure "rather than sacrifice another teacher." Add to these cases the psychological violence of death threats, incarcerations, miserable working and living conditions, and months without pay and Vassallo's zone becomes a true battleground, pitting a hostile provincial power structure against the agents and institutions of a mobilizing federal state.[33]

Violence also raged against activist teachers in the ex-district of Comitán, home to a fiercely conservative rancher and planter class. Inspector P. Arturo Mota had his hands full during 1934 and the first four months of 1935, when five of his teachers were subjected to non-fatal armed attacks. Amid this wave of violence Mota asked the SEP to allow several teachers in his zone to carry pistols for self-defense. Celso Flores Zamora, head of the Department of Rural and Primary Schools, denied Mota's request as perhaps only a Mexico City bureaucrat could, declaring "the only weapons that should be used by the rural teachers are those of pedagogy."[34]

On April 3, 1935, gunmen in the municipality of Las Margaritas ambushed and opened fire on Mota as he visited local schools, wounding his horse. Mota and the eighty teachers in his zone were quick to pin the blame on "the bourgeois and clerical factions who currently are the worst enemies of the redemptive mission of the present regime."[35] López alleged that Comitán's municipal authorities had no interest in investigating the case. State police found few witnesses willing to testify against the perpetrators. The attack on Mota was quickly followed by the assassination of Gustavo Montiel Pérez, teacher at Piedra Playa in the northern municipality of Pichucalco.[36] Both Mota and López responded to this escalation of violence by again asking the SEP to allow teachers in Chiapas to carry pistols. Although the SEP denied both requests, later that year President Cárdenas ordered the War Ministry to issue arms and ammunition to socialist teachers to protect themselves and their schools.[37] Mota was soon transferred to another zone.

For every violent attack on a federal teacher in Chiapas there were scores of cases where locals employed more subtle forms of pressure. The most typical "weapons of the weak" were high absentee rates, untended garden plots, and poorly attended civic celebrations. Nor were the resistors in this context exactly "weak." Where residents gave clear and consistent signs of disapproval, the SEP closed their school and transferred the teacher to a more promising community. Sometimes it was enough for a community to withhold small gifts of food from unpopular teachers. This happened at Ixtacomitán, Pichucalco, in 1935. While authorities debated whether Pichucalco would pass to the administrative control of Tabasco, they stopped paying teachers' salaries. Cultural Mission delegates reported that desperate, famished, and unpopular teachers "were reduced to feeding on bananas for several months."[38]

Vicious rumors and allegations against teachers were also used with some regularity. Female teachers, especially single women, personified the SEP's "new" Mexican woman—modern, secular, literate, and relatively independent. They were clear threats to the patriarchal social order and challenged traditional gender roles. Villagers, especially in indigenous communities, used allegations of mala conducta to rein in female teachers who violated traditional codes of conduct. In ladino communities, such accusations were rare. Local authorities and communities also accused male teachers and inspectors of public drunkenness and sexual misconduct, including rape, with some regularity. While López paid serious attention to these accusations, he also noted that they were most common where the SEP's agrarian or temperance campaigns provoked ferocious opposition or where resistance to coeducation was high. The inspectors most commonly accused were Daniel Vassallo, federal inspector in Soconusco, and Manuel Castellanos, who worked in the highlands. While the former squared off repeatedly with resourceful coffee planters, the latter clashed with ranchers, enganchadores, and alcohol merchants and had the task of selling the SEP's agenda to culturally conservative indigenous communities.[39]

Resistant authorities had still other subtle means of pressuring teachers. Some withheld support from school-sponsored cultural and sporting events or allowed cantinas to open next door to schools where the teacher was spearheading the SEP's anti-alcohol campaign. Some authorities went even further. At Metapa, a community in Mariscal, president of the local education committee David Fuentes complained in 1937 that the municipal president had dismantled an outhouse built by the school in 1933, using the wood to repair the galley of the local jail. He also destroyed the school's experimental gardens and allowed a butcher shop to be built less than ten meters from the school door. Fuentes complained that the shop "attracts an infinity of flies and other insects as well as disgusting dogs and harassing buzzards . . . [and] the school patio has turned into a stable for beasts."[40] Without resorting to violence or even threats, Metapa's municipal president sent the teacher an unmistakably clear message.

Sometimes teachers found themselves in communities that were split in their support for the socialist school. While many communities in Chiapas strove to preserve internal unity in the face of outside forces, what Eric Wolf called the "closed corporate community" was the exception rather than the rule.[41] Divisions existed even in those highland Maya communities that had succeeded in chasing out ladinos following the revolution. In the 1930s and 1940s, the influence of Protestant missionaries, political parties, and greater economic opportunities contributed to the increasing stratification of towns in Chiapas.

Often the experimental garden plot was at the crux of intra-village disagreements. Teachers often had trouble convincing campesinos and their children to donate their labor to the plot, especially during sowing and harvest season or in times of agricultural crisis. Where land was scarce, communities and/or individuals were reluctant to offer the school a fertile plot near the town's center. Where food was scarce, villagers resented giving up the plot's bounty to the school's general fund. Some insisted on sharing the food with the village's least fortunate members, while others believed that communally grown produce should be used to buy fireworks, food, and drink for community festivals. Such conflicts tested the negotiating skills of even the most talented and perceptive teachers.[42]

The case of León Santizo illustrates the divisiveness of village politics. A resident of the town of Tuixcum (near Motozintla along the Guatemalan border), Santizo wrote the SEP to complain that the federal schoolteacher wanted to expropriate his land for use as the school's experimental garden. One month after Santizo wrote his letter, federal inspector Benjamín P. Martínez demanded Santizo's expulsion from the country. According to Martínez, Santizo was a Guatemalan citizen with no legitimate claim to land in Tuixcum. The town's Agrarian Committee, therefore, had offered to the school land that technically had no owner. Director of Federal Education Erasto Valle agreed with Martínez and took steps to expropriate Santizo's land and expel him from the country. After conferring with immigration authorities, however, the SEP's national director of rural schools, Rafael Ramírez, had second thoughts. "This Department has the conviction that it has committed a great injustice with Señor León Santizo, accusing him, among other things, of being Guatemalan when he is a Mexican citizen," wrote Ramírez in a letter to Valle. "Therefore I recommend in a special way that you repair the damage that has been caused."[43] Valle then wrote to zone inspector Martínez, ordering him to leave Santizo alone. He also recognized that Santizo could not possibly remain in Tuixcum "because he is hated by the whole town, a most furious hatred because it has its origins in religious matters, since Santizo is the only Catholic in a town of Protestants."[44] In a scenario that repeated itself with some regularity in rural Chiapas, the town's teacher and the Agrarian Committee had singled out the town's most vulnerable member—in this case, a Catholic of Guatemalan origin—and had offered him half of the market value for his land.

Given the explosive complexity of village politics, the obstructions of the state government, and the SEP's provocative state- and nation-building program, one wonders why there was not more registered opposition to the socialist school. Remarkably, as subsequent chapters will illustrate, most mestizo communities rallied behind the SEP's teachers and their school. Under SEP socialism the federal rural school finally became part of rural communities in Chiapas, playing the role originally envisioned by Moisés Sáenz one decade earlier.

The Fallout

By summer 1935 it was becoming increasingly difficult for Elpidio López to maintain appearances with Governor Grajales. In late June, López felt it necessary to issue a circular declaring publicly what nobody truly believed—"that the Inspectors and federal teachers are considered intimately connected to and dependents of one single organism [consisting of] the state and federal government, since both governments are striving for the material and social betterment of the working class."[45] This circular proceeded to condition the mobilizing and organizing dimensions of socialist education on a series of bureaucratic hurdles. Teachers could not unionize peasants and workers unless they notified their zone inspector and four municipal and state employees, who were almost certainly unsympathetic to federal unions. Teachers who solicited land reform were required to contact these officials as well as the Forest Inspector (Inspector Forestal) and the Ejidal Zone Organizer (Organizador de Zona Ejidal). Similar stipulations applied to teachers who formed cooperatives. All popular organizations were to belong to the Confederation of Peasants and Workers in Chiapas

(Confederación Campesina y Obrera de Chiapas, or CCOC), which was utterly beholden to the Grajales administration.[46] López also recommended that peasants and workers belong to the PNR, still controlled by Grajales. Finally, as if the point had not been made, López reminded federal inspectors and teachers to maintain "cordial" relations with all state and local authorities.[47] López, who was struggling himself to maintain his "cordiality," evidently believed that a strategic retreat in summer 1935 was preferable to Grajales's open hostility.

López's efforts were futile. In August 1935 he was transferred to the state of Nuevo León. Three months later the governor there was complaining that López had encouraged teachers to go on strike to demand back pay owed to them by previous administrations.[48] He was then bounced to Sonora, where he did battle with another conservative governor with strong regional interests, General Román Yocupicio. The SEP in Chiapas went without a director until Raúl Isidro Burgos took over in October 1935.

Shortly before López became director of the SEP in Chiapas, both Governor Grajales and his director of state education, Ángel M. Corzo, had indicated that the state's schools would adopt federal methods and orientations, with subtle adaptations.[49] During 1934 and 1935, the SEP signed federalization agreements with several state governments and most observers foresaw the imminent federalization of all education in Mexico.[50] But once socialist education was introduced and the full magnitude of its state- and nation-building potential was recognized, such unity became an impossibility in Chiapas. When teachers became radicalized unionizers, political agents, promoters of agrarian reform, and public health crusaders, they simply stepped on too many toes. In a span of less than two years, then, the federalization of Mexico's education institutions suddenly seemed a pipe dream.

So far, we have seen how the SEP's vaguely conceived plan of socialist education empowered Elpidio López to purge Chiapas's teaching corps and introduce an ambitious plan of state building. We have also observed how socialist education radicalized the countryside, provoked the rural elite to violence, and sent López packing just seven months after his arrival. Now our attention turns to socialist education's cultural dimension in Chiapas, which featured an invigorated temperance campaign and a nation-building campaign most enthusiastically pursued along the southern border with Guatemala. ◆

Chapter Six

Forging the New Sober Citizen

We have made Italy, now we have to make Italians.

—*Massimo d'Azeglio at the first parliamentary meeting of the newly united Italy, 1870*

We have to Mexicanize the Mexicans.

—*Andrés Cancúa Neri, federal education inspector in Motozintla, Chiapas, 1936*

On September 16, 1924, federal mail accountant Francisco Fernández attended festivities in Tuxtla Gutiérrez to commemorate the hundredth anniversary of Chiapas's incorporation into the Mexican federation. He was thoroughly dismayed at what he heard that night. The first speaker, a prominent judge, set the tone. He remarked that Mexico was "indifferent" to Chiapas. "He exhorted his fellow Chiapanecos to achieve the emancipation of 'their Chiapas' themselves without waiting for aid from that which had never provided it," Fernández wrote. The next three speakers allegedly agreed that Chiapas had been abandoned. Originally from the northern border town of Piedras Negras, Coahuila, Fernández had been living in Tuxtla for more than three months "with the moral pain of living not among pure Mexicans but among some renegades of my *patria* and my blood." Fernández was not the only federal employee to remark on the Chiapanecos' "renegade" spirit at this event; members of the National Chamber of Commerce, Industry and Agriculture (Cámara Nacional de Comercio, Industria y Agricultura) also made similar observations to President Obregón.[1]

In 1920s Chiapas such observations were commonplace. Not only were the state's "unincorporated" indigenous populations considered anti- or sub-national, but Mexicans of Guatemalan origin in the south of the state appeared to some as potential fifth columnists. Chiapanecos of all political affiliations were believed to harbor resentment toward the Mexican federation. As was so often the case, the SEP was expected to report on these apparent threats to the nation and address them.[2]

Mexican nation building after 1920 also involved creating a healthier, more productive citizenry. Revolutionary hygienists and health reformers strove to rid Mexicans of the three maladies widely viewed as "social diseases"—tuberculosis, syphilis, and alcoholism. Of the three, alcoholism received the most attention. Not only did long-term ingestion weaken the body, but alcoholism often "enabled" the other two maladies: it made the body more susceptible to graver bacterial and viral maladies like tuberculosis, and it was often consumed in social settings where "undesirable" sexual unions were likely to take place. Underlying these public health campaigns was a particular application of eugenic thought common in Mexico in the 1920s. Mexican eugenicists believed that the "race" could be improved by ensuring that those who reproduced were free from disease and vice.[3]

For several years, the SEP's anti-alcohol campaign was its most important attempt at behavior modification in Chiapas. Inspectors and teachers fought an uphill battle against an intransigent state government, entrenched alcohol interests, countless clandestine distilleries, and indigenous communities for which alcohol had deep cultural importance. We begin by looking at this intense, quixotic, and ultimately futile campaign.

"Dry Laws" in a Wet State

In a state of few industries, alcohol production and distribution had long represented a major interest for powerful individuals and an important source of tax revenues for local government. In 1831, shortly after Chiapas joined the Mexican federation, coletos cornered the market on the production of aguardiente. The municipality of San Cristóbal then taxed the sale of aguardiente to the thirteen Tzotzil and Tzeltal indigenous municipalities that fell within its jurisdiction (the Departamento del Centro). In the late nineteenth century, this represented between 15 and 20 percent of the municipality's total revenues. The coletos' dependence on indigenous alcohol consumption did not stop them from passing laws forbidding public drunkenness, however. When coletos needed laborers for public works projects, the call typically went out to arrest Indians drunk, more often than not, on coleto aguardiente. The Indians worked unpaid to earn their freedom.[4]

The situation had not improved much by the 1920s, when the SEP began to take interest in controlling alcohol consumption. In 1929 President Emilio Portes Gil gave a temperance speech that opened a new front in the war to create the new Mexican. "Among the greatest enemies of the race and the future of Mexico is the vice of alcoholism, rooted deplorably in a great part of our campesino and working classes," he proclaimed. "Alcoholism undermines the physical and moral forces of our men, disturbs conjugal happiness, and destroys, with degenerate children, all possibility of future greatness for the fatherland."[5] Portes Gil also stated, with some justification, that "women suffer the saddest and most deplorable consequences of this home-wrecking vice." Although he asked state and local government to forbid the opening of new "centers of vice," the rest of his proposals were based on persuasion. The SEP was to take a leading role. Schools, unions, and other state-affiliated organizations were to encourage sports, display temperance artwork in public halls and theaters, and create women's anti-alcohol leagues. Teachers were also expected to dedicate one hour each week to anti-alcohol instruction and organize weekly "cultural conferences" for the public featuring plays and lectures condemning alcoholism.[6]

In the ensuing months educators throughout Chiapas reported that dozens of peasant and Indian communities (including Chamula) spontaneously declared themselves "dry." Some communities even posted guards along prominent roads to prevent aguardiente from entering their towns. Just as Portes Gil had envisioned, women reportedly played a leading role in this campaign. Most schools held anti-alcohol festivals on November 20 of that year, Day of the Revolution. In Soconusco, students carried posters and banners in anti-alcohol parades. They drew pictures under the theme "The Value of Muscle" showing the degeneration caused by alcohol. Students wrote letters to their parents either thanking them for not drinking or asking them to stop. Sporting events were held "in even the remotest villages," anti-alcohol theater events were sponsored (some of them translated for indigenous migrants workers), and "many drunks publicly renounced alcohol," including Huixtla's municipal secretary. At night, several schools held "Mexican nights," local versions of the Noche Mexicana organized by artist Adolfo Best Maugard in Mexico City in 1921. Like the original Noche Mexicana, these local versions featured "genuinely Mexican" dancing and folklore.[7]

But these grassroots efforts were sporadic and usually inadequate in a state where its leading citizens and the state government profited from the sale of alcohol and where most municipal authorities supplemented their salaries by either manufacturing or selling alcohol. Federal education director Fernando Ximello was given a reality check when agents of coleto *alcoholeros* (alcohol merchants) attacked students from San Cristóbal's Regional Preparatory School while they listened to him give a speech condemning alcohol. The incident presaged future frustrations in the anti-alcohol campaign in and around San Cristóbal and drew the attention of Portes Gil himself.[8] In May the president received a letter from a PNR party member in San Cristóbal attesting to the town's geographic and, perhaps, political and programmatic distance from Mexico City. "Unfortunately in areas far from Mexico City everything becomes lyricism," he wrote. "The poor Indian is persecuted for his drunkenness because he is inoffensive, while the bourgeoisie enjoys privileges and gets drunk day and night in the center of town, and the police do not bother them a bit despite their public scandals and their shoot-outs."[9]

According to Portes Gil's informant, San Cristóbal's municipal president, Mariano Bermúdez, was the town's principal distiller: "He has three distilleries and eighteen retail stands and cantinas located on the town's principal arteries, and in front of every dispensary is one of Bermúdez's girlfriends, as he is the consummate satyr." Indians who got drunk at these dispensaries were arrested and fined by the local police acting under orders of Bermúdez himself, making a farce of the municipal president's high-minded printed proclamations.[10]

Naturally the authorities in Mexico City did not like hearing that their naive campaign of "persuasion" was not producing results. Juan Vidal, the SEP's inspector in the central highlands in 1930, received a reprimand via telegram from the director of federal rural schools in Mexico City. "I wish Rafael Ramírez would be good enough to elaborate a truly practical plan to combat alcoholism, especially here, where the surest and most lucrative source of income for the state and municipal governments is to tax the production and consumption of alcohol," Vidal wrote in reply. "I'm surprised by the ultimatum-like tone contained in his telegram. If I don't inform of successes achieved it's because there are none."[11] Later, in a surprising article published in the SEP's biweekly newspaper *El Maestro Rural* in 1933, a teacher from Coahuila wrote, "We are completely convinced of the impossibility of achieving a 'dry' country, because this wonderful endeavor has already failed in other more developed countries like the United States." Instead, this teacher suggested a campaign urging temperance. The official position was quickly made clear. In the very next issue of *El Maestro Rural*, the editorial staff explained that it did not necessarily agree with the views expressed by the teacher from Coahuila, then printed "The Drunk's Hymn," an article more in keeping with the stridently prohibitionist tone of the newspaper.[12]

Sobriety and Its Discontents after 1934

It is no coincidence that President Cárdenas's first director of the SEP was

Ignacio García Téllez, the man who had directed the federal government's anti-alcohol campaign during the *Maximato* (1928–1934). The SEP's timid campaign of persuasion quickly gave way to one that lobbied state governors to prohibit the sale of alcohol in Indian villages and ejidos, oil fields, mining camps, and along railroad lines. Governor Grajales reluctantly passed these laws, but few SEP inspectors and officials were fooled by his "*palabrería y simple bluff*."[13]

Still unable to attack the alcohol industry at its well-connected core, the SEP in Chiapas reverted to its campaign of prohibition by persuasion. Teachers sponsored sporting events under the explicit assumption that athletic activity and competition might distract both young and old from alcohol. However, as Katherine Bliss has written, many men capped off a day of sporting activity with a trip to the brothel, where they were likely exposed to two of Mexico's three major social ills, alcohol and syphilis.[14] Other means of conveying the SEP's message included patriotic festivals featuring poetry and plays condemning alcoholism. At times, the campaign was reduced to scapegoating and slogans. Teachers taught that alcohol was part of a larger bourgeois conspiracy to keep workers from coming to class consciousness and improving their lot in life. The two slogans below were printed in 1935 by Huixtla's Local Committee of Culture (Comité Local de Cultura) in Daniel Vassallo's zone.

> ALCOHOL SERVES THE BOURGEOISIE
> To Keep Workers in a Stupor, Preventing them from Knowing
> their True Situation and Reclaiming the Fruit of their Labor.
> Comrade, Don't Drink!
>
> ALCOHOL IS AN INSTRUMENT OF THE BOURGEOISIE
> To Maintain the Workers in Idiocy
> Compañero, Don't Fall into the Trap![15]

One of the more pathetic SEP circulars urged state governors in March 1936 to prohibit teachers and students in rural areas from singing songs like "La Valentina" and "La Borrachita" (The Little Drunk Girl), "the titles of which contain a tribute to alcoholism."[16]

Community response to the SEP's sobriety campaign in Chiapas was a function of local politics, culture, and economic interests. SEP archives contain genuine grassroots manifestations of support for the campaign, especially among women, but the strength of the alcohol industry was such that most inspectors conceded defeat by the end of 1936. Villagers were often discouraged to see how local government coddled and protected the alcohol trade. From the border town of Comalapa, zone inspector Héctor Eduardo Paniagua described how initial optimism and progress gave way to cynicism by the end of 1936. "Unfortunately in the last few months the Administración de Rentas has been authorizing the establishment of liquor producers and distributors in rural communities, contravening the decree of April 3 which frees rural communities from these centers of vice, and the work of the teacher in this campaign has been brought to a halt," he wrote. "Measures have been taken to remove these alcohol establishments but now with less enthusiasm on the part of the campesinos who have seen how their efforts have been frustrated."[17]

The SEP's campaign fared even worse in the Tzotzil and Tzeltal highlands, despite the determined efforts of education inspector Manuel Castellanos. In his words, "In no part of the Republic does the Indian consume as much alcohol, nor does he live under such brutish conditions." Castellanos fought with a limited arsenal against the region's formidable alcohol interests. As he told in an April 1935 report, "The [aguardiente] concessionaires in some cases are influential people who pay large sums to the state treasury and have numerous gunmen at their service. They enjoy the support of some municipal authorities in Chamula, Oxchuc, Tenango, and elsewhere." Alcohol also played a pivotal role in enganche, as agents of lowland planters often used it to put highland Indians in their debt before the coffee harvest. As a planter reportedly said in the early 1930s, "Coffee plantations run on aguardiente as an automobile runs on gasoline."[18]

In 1935, Castellanos founded forty-four Anti-alcohol Committees (Comités Antialcohólicos) in his highland zone and asked Governor Grajales to suppress the sale of aguardiente in indigenous communities, an enterprise that was mainly in the hands of ladinos. The campaign culminated in Grajales's halfhearted April 1935 decree, "which is continually violated by the municipal authorities."[19] Later that year, Castellanos helped suppress the sale of aguardiente in eighteen communities, including Cancuc, where the intervention of federal troops was necessary, and Amatenango, where the town's residents expelled the alcohol wholesalers.

The state's alcohol interests did not take the SEP's campaign lying down. One year after the announcement of Grajales's April 1935 decree, General Francisco Múgica, President Cárdenas's Secretary of Communications and

Public Works, visited the SEP's indigenous boarding school in Huixtán, near Ciudad Las Casas. Teachers at the school had been frequently threatened and attacked by "roving alcohol merchants, who are protected by the local PNR representative and the authorities in Huixtán." They and their students urged Múgica to enforce the state's "dry law" in rural areas. The night after Múgica's visit, unknown individuals shot up the boarding school and were repelled by the armed teachers.[20]

Along the predominately mestizo coast of Chiapas, opposition to the SEP's anti-alcohol policy was less violent though equally tenacious. Writing with his usual candor, zone inspector Daniel Vassallo reported that the campaign had not produced the desired results. "The work is slow and we know that we must work against vested interests," he wrote. "At the fairs of Huixtla and Suchiate, our revolutionary authorities permitted the cantinas to open temporarily, since these public poison wells reap handsome profits for the municipal treasuries and the man who controls the distribution of alcohol along the coast." In a later report, Vassallo wrote that it would be tiring to detail all of the obstacles encountered in the anti-alcohol campaign. "But I would renege on my rights to free expression if I did not report that the state and municipal governments encourage the use of alcohol by granting permits for the opening of new cantinas," he wrote.[21] Coffee plantation owners continued to sell aguardiente in their (illegal) company stores and state police were unwilling to enforce laws passed grudgingly by the state government. Article 123 schoolteachers who attempted to close workplace cantinas often learned that the finca owner had a license to sell alcohol from the municipal authorities or the local alcohol tax collector, even though workplace cantinas violated the Federal Labor Law and Article 123 of the constitution.[22]

On occasion, the SEP's teaching corps itself were the primary obstacles to an effective anti-alcohol campaign. In Daniel Vassallo's reports, Rosario Castellanos's fictional tale of a drunken teacher in *Balún-Canán* rings true.[23] Although Vassallo wrote in November 1935, "The percentage of drunk teachers has diminished considerably," his subsequent reports were filled with firings and transfers of hard-drinking teachers. In March 1936 he fired Raúl Blassi Serrano and relocated Rodulfo I. Rincón out of the urban school at Huixtla as punishment for his drunken revelries. Several months later, teachers Sotero Lara and his wife, Candelaria Castellanos de Lara, were transferred to new schools because he was a chronic drunk "and habitually fought with his wife who, out of disgust, became a drunk herself." Interestingly, both teachers were allowed to keep their jobs at a time (1936) when socialist education was still calling for vigorous anti-alcohol activity. Clearly there was still a shortage of qualified teachers in the state. The fate of two other drunks is less certain: Humberto Escobar was removed from a school in Huixtla, where he was "academically detestable and contributed very little in the way of social programs," and Gabriel Ramos was transferred out of Escuintla "because he completely disgraced himself through laziness and drunkenness and by provoking public scandals."[24] Ramos quite possibly was appointed to another village where his reputation had not yet been tarnished.

Anti-alcohol campaigns in rural Mexico predated socialist education and outlived it as well. Indeed, the SEP's campaign of the mid-1930s was noteworthy only in its intensity. Alcohol and alcoholeros were so much a part of life in rural Chiapas that prohibition could only be conjured up in the collective imagination of naive Cardenistas and PNR officials. Aguardiente greased the all-important engine of enganche. It played a pivotal role in the civil and religious life of indigenous communities; everything from *audiencias* (hearings) to marriage transactions involved its ritual exchange. Religious cargo holders encouraged its consumption and profited from its sale, and it was the drink of choice for a brutally impoverished rural population for whom *trago* represented a necessary escape. Last of all, well-placed individuals and politicians had a keen interest in protecting the lucrative networks of alcohol production and distribution, and they tenaciously defended their interests.

Rural Chiapas Meets the Nation

The SEP's sobriety campaign targeted the nation's body; its civic campaign was meant to win hearts and minds. In Chiapas, however, the performance was perfunctory at best in the 1920s. Students saluted the flag, if one existed in the classroom. Indigenous students were force-fed the Spanish language. Patriotic celebrations tended to be lackluster or ignored. The school calendar called for the celebration of only ten state and national patriotic holidays. For reasons particular to the isolation and history of Chiapas, a tradition of patriotic liberalism had not developed. Beginning in the early 1930s, national traditions were "invented" and consecrated in Chiapas by the SEP's schools. Indeed, for all its pretensions of *internationalism*, socialist education marked the beginning of the SEP's *nationalist* campaign to turn Chiapanecos into Mexicans.[25]

The nationalist campaign in Chiapas was focused largely on civic ritual. Public parades, commemorations, dances, and speeches were complex syncretic interactions involving local custom, state ideology, and community mobilization. They reached large, non-scholastic audiences, including illiterate adults and family members who were never able to attend school. In the 1930s, festivals reaffirmed local power and fostered community cohesion while they legitimated the agents and institutions of the new state, including teachers, agrarian officials, schools, and the PNR. The hierarchy of SEP/PNR festivals placed these new agents and institutions far above the power brokers of yesteryear, especially priests and village elders.[26]

In the middle 1930s, civic campaigns almost inevitably involved attacks on the Church. Schools established in church buildings occupied the physical space of religiosity, and SEP personnel attempted to fill the temporal and symbolic space of church ritual. During 1935 and 1936, sporting events and "Cultural Sundays"—the Mexican equivalent of the French "fête décadaire"—were held on alternating weeks in most large towns. Usually co-sponsored by the state PNR, these civic festivals featured poetry readings and dance pieces by students, anticlerical and anti-alcoholic dramas, lectures on socialism by teachers, and musical pieces by a marimba group or the local military garrison's band. PNR party activists used the familiar structure, discourse, and imagery of Sunday mass to craft their "Cultural Sundays" and lend legitimacy and grandeur to the cultural project of the revolution. Teachers were "missionaries of light" who offered "the bread of the Eucharist" to "hungry souls." Schools were "temples" of knowledge. The Cultural Missions "recalled the apostolic work of the founders of Christianity in the time of the Gentiles."[27] Village notables, teachers, and PNR party members constructed altars to national heroes or the flag. Music and dance pieces were sprinkled around more serious "sermons" about the socialist work ethic, socialist pedagogy, proper hygiene, and even religion, as teachers and PNR officials explained Christ's proletarian credentials. Participants paid homage not to the crucifix but to the red-and-black flag of international socialism. The "services" concluded with "hymns," either socialist or agrarian. Presented in a familiar format, the Cultural Sundays attempted to reaffirm community cohesion at a time of serious cultural upheaval. They also provided an officially sanctioned outlet where the socializing function of the church could take place.

Cultural Sundays also fostered the notion of a supra-regional Mexican identity. Elpidio López promoted the marimba as a distinctly Chiapanecan instrument in danger of succumbing to "the jazz invasion," and many of the music and dance pieces practiced and performed by schoolchildren were taken from the folkloric traditions of Oaxaca, Jalisco, and other states of the republic, like *fados*, *tlapehualas*, and the jarabe tapatío.[28]

Naturally, Cultural Sundays were not always well received, especially in highland towns where the Church had been (and continued to be) popular. López warned that resistance to the Sunday cultural programs of the SEP and PNR was high in Ciudad Las Casas, where "secret agents of the clergy" and "pro-clerical women" encouraged residents to boycott the events. Teachers in spring 1935 gradually convinced residents to attend, "but much time will pass before the whole population accepts revolutionary ideology." López reported that the SEP's cultural festivals were more warmly received in lowland agrarista communities. There, not only had the Church failed to sink its roots, but most communities expected to benefit from land reform and were more willing to cooperate with the government's cultural project.[29]

Patriotic commemorations, festivals, and parades were more popular with villagers because they were not perceived as competing with religious services. In 1935, the SEP at the national level published a school calendar crammed with no less than fifty-four *national* holidays commemorating an enormous range of people and events, including the birthday of James Watt (inventor of the steam engine), France's Bastille Day, and the general strike and massacre at Río Blanco, Veracruz, in 1907.[30] The SEP in Chiapas settled on a slightly more streamlined calendar that year that included forty holidays (twenty-five national, fifteen state), a far cry from the spartan calendar of 1928, which featured only ten. With roughly one *fiesta* per week during the school year, teachers, students, and community members were kept continually busy as organizers and participants. Girls and boys marched, sang, danced, read poetry, and otherwise performed in these civic displays. This frenetic civic calendar kept schools and communities focused on the "imagined community" of Chiapanecos and Mexicans of which they were part. Since most children in Chiapas spent less than two years in school, the broadly participative festivals also served as post-scholastic venues for the practice of state and nation formation. Former students continued to attend festivals as siblings and later parents and grandparents of school-age participants. Ejidatarios, municipal officials, school committee members, and musicians also participated in civic events. Seen in this light, patriotic festivals served as "extension courses" of Mexican nationalism.

During the rollback of socialist education in the late 1930s, the Cultural Sundays were abandoned but the patriotic festival survived unscathed. In fact, it may have been strengthened following Cárdenas's expropriation of the foreign-held oil fields in 1938 and Mexico's May 1942 entry into World

Fig. 7. Peasants from Amatenango rally in defense of a rural schoolteacher who was slandered by the town's postal clerk, 1935. Courtesy Archivo Histórico de la Secretaría de Educación Pública.

War II. The SEP in Chiapas continued to encourage athletic competition between neighboring communities as a way to distract both young and old from alcohol and blood sports (like cockfights) and to encourage campesino solidarity. Even as the SEP streamlined its demanding civic calendar after 1938, the number of sporting/patriotic festivals in Chiapas continued to grow owing to the popularity of basketball and footraces.

Teachers blended sports and patriotism such that the two were practically inseparable. At a 1940 basketball tournament hosted by the school at El Carrizal, participants first executed an elaborate flag salute. Then, before competition began, teams from the four schools mingled in an atmosphere reportedly "full of the warmest rejoicing, overflowing to such an extent that some participants burst out in enthusiastic cheers to the flag, the Mexican Revolution, and Socialist Education." After the games, students and villagers attended a lengthy evening program featuring teachers and students from all four schools. The male teachers expounded on the virtues of sports and the vices of alcohol, while the female teacher discussed the role of women in modern society. Students recited poetry praising campesino solidarity, the rural school, President Cárdenas, and Mexico's indigenous peoples. Two marimbas provided music, and students performed songs and dances taken from Chiapas's local traditions as well as from other regions in Mexico. Early the next morning, the visiting teachers and students returned to their respective villages "observing the strictest discipline."[31] This scenario was repeated throughout Chiapas as teachers linked ever-popular sporting events with the "everyday" practice of state and nation formation.

Whether the people of Chiapas felt any more "Mexican" after being subjected to Cultural Sundays and patriotic and sporting festivals is difficult to say. It is clear, however, that by 1940 many mestizo communities were appropriating the ideology and discourse of secular citizenship and the notion of a popular and heroic Mexican past, ideas first and most emphatically introduced by the SEP.

The Southern Front

The long-standing Guatemalan "problem" continued to vex the Mexican government into the 1930s. Guatemalan exiles and adventurers used Chiapas as a staging ground for their intrigues against the dictatorship of Jorge Ubico. Although these plots did not directly threaten Mexico, they antagonized Guatemala and heightened tensions between the two countries. Mexico City was home to the Alianza Popular Guatemalteca, an exile group led by a former colonel of the Guatemalan army, Jorge García Granados. In March 1937 García told Cárdenas of his intention to launch a coup. He claimed to have the backing of current and emigrant Guatemalan military officers; prominent Mexican revolutionaries like General Francisco Múgica, Ramón Beteta, and Vicente Lombardo Toledano; Lombardo's Mexican Workers Confederation (Confederación de Trabajadores Mexicanos, or CTM); and more than one thousand "revolutionaries" from Cuba, Guatemala, and other Central American countries. He seemed confident that many thousands of Guatemalans (especially Indians from the eastern departments) would join the movement once it was launched. He asked Cárdenas for "tolerance and a bit of discreet support" and permission to construct temporary bases in southern Mexico. In return, García promised to protect Mexican neutrality and to invade Guatemala from Belize, not Mexico. Lastly, he took pains to distinguish his movement from another Guatemalan exile group that had also requested assistance. Were his movement to succeed, García promised to build a truly "revolutionary" government. But if Ubico was not toppled, he warned, "he will remain an insurmountable barrier for the progressive currents in Central American countries; what's more, he will be a constant threat to the Mexican Revolution and an enemy of your regime."[32] Whether or not Cárdenas lent support to this movement is difficult to ascertain, but two years later the Guatemalan government requested Mexico's assistance in crushing a conspiracy led by García and another ex-colonel of the Guatemalan army.[33]

Rumors of conspiracy were rife on both sides of the border during the late 1930s. Both Guatemala and Chiapas were home to large, influential German enclaves, and Guatemalan strongman Ubico sympathized with the Nazi regime. In November 1937 the Cárdenas administration was flooded with letters, telegrams, and tips informing him that the Germans had unloaded a major arms shipment in Guatemala. Meanwhile, the commanding officer of the Mexican army in Chiapas wrote his superiors in Mexico City with worrisome information suggesting possible aggression against Mexico. A mysterious ship (presumably Japanese) had appeared off the coast of Mapastepec, Chiapas; several unidentified planes had flown over Chiapas at high altitude, possibly running spy missions; and rumors circulated suggesting that Guatemala's German colony was preparing for war. The astute brigadier general suggested that the best way to safeguard Mexico's southern border was to resolve the agrarian disputes in southern Chiapas.[34]

The Mexican government was also losing the battle for hearts and minds along the border. In May 1935, the SEP's Director of Rural and Primary Education, Celso Flores Zamora, wrote Elpidio López that high functionaries at the SEP "believe that the problem on the southeastern border of our country is in need of urgent resolution . . . because the frontier schools currently in operation do not form a barrier that could impede the influence of the neighbor country." According to Flores, the failure of the frontier schools "resulted in lukewarm patriotic sentiment" among the children and adults of the region.[35] López responded with a request for federal assistance to improve ten existing frontier schools and build an additional seventeen schools. Later that year, Cárdenas and the SEP ordered federal education zone inspectors to conduct extensive surveys of several communities along Chiapas's border with Guatemala.

Taken as a whole, the survey painted a grim picture of a lawless no-man's-land populated by potential fifth columnists. Suchiate, Mexico's southernmost municipality, had been annexed in 1882. Inspector Daniel Vassallo wrote that the police force there did not draw a regular salary but received tips for permitting the clandestine trafficking of alcohol. "Blood crimes are frequent," Vassallo wrote, "and the delinquents easily elude punishment, passing to Guatemalan territory, or the crime is never investigated, even when there are witnesses, because they refuse to testify, fearing reprisals." At Colonia "La Libertad," on the banks of the Suchiate River, which divides Mexico and Guatemala, the problem went beyond a simple matter of law and order. "'La Libertad' is in urgent need of Mexicanization, because although the residents say they are Mexicans, when they are among themselves one senses a wholly Guatemalan atmosphere," he reported. "It is necessary to develop an INTENSE campaign of attraction and nationalization, not a feeble one, as has been the case until now."[36] Vassallo called on the SEP and the state government to construct a school in Suchiate, complete with a radio station and a movie projector. He also recommended that the future teacher develop an active music and dance curriculum to instill Mexican patriotism in these suspect citizens.

Just up the Suchiate, in Tuxtla Chico, Inspector Rubén Antonio Rivas made similar observations in terms far harsher and less sympathetic than Vassallo's. "The populace still has the stamp of old," he wrote. "Its inhabitants are thoroughly Guatemalan [*de ideas y corazón*], they do not love Mexico, and they vegetate without concerning themselves with the improvement of their town." Rivas recommended the construction of a frontier school. The teacher, he said, should be a normal-school graduate from central or northern Mexico, with authentically Mexican habits and customs and a clear notion of the meaning of the Mexican revolution.[37]

The most thoughtful report came from Inspector Andrés Cancúa Neri. He suggested that the "submissive and quiet" residents of Mariscal had been thoroughly colonized and exploited by Mexicans. "They still feel the weight of the conquest. All of them are vilely exploited by the finqueros, the enganchadores, the politicians, and even by some teachers," he wrote. "It's painful to say, but it's true. The few true Mexicans [in the area] are the caciques, the exploiters, the overseers." Not surprisingly, "the inhabitants of Mariscal still feel love for what was their country. When they see the Guatemalan flag, their eyes glisten and their bodies shake with emotion." Cancúa was also struck by the poverty and disease in the area. "The inhabitants live in houses of sticks and mud . . . animals and people live together in horrific promiscuity," he wrote. "THE LABOR ENTRUSTED TO THE MINISTRY OF EDUCATION IN THIS REGION IS ENORMOUS."[38]

Echoing Rivas, Cancúa warned that the federal teachers in the region were not up to the task because most were sons and daughters of Guatemalans and had been trained south of the border. Their commercial and social contacts were Guatemalan. Few had ever traveled outside the region into greater Chiapas, much less Mexico. Cancúa felt he could not teach them how to implement socialist education in his occasional teacher training sessions (Centros de Cooperación).

In response to these and other reports, the SEP in Mexico City took action in March 1936. They declared that teachers trained in Guatemala were in violation of the constitution. Their presence in front of Mexican schoolchildren now "constituted a danger to [Mexico's] national integrity." Those with at least one year of experience were transferred to other schools away from the border; those with less experience were dismissed.[39] On the recommendations of Vassallo and Rivas, the SEP established one frontier school each in Tuxtla Chico and Suchiate. Each coordinated the scholastic and cultural activity of several surrounding schools. Both schools were to be staffed by a social worker, a music teacher, a sports instructor, and a nurse, each of whom would travel to surrounding schools as needed. All staff were to be *norteños*; that is, from north of Chiapas. Finally, Cárdenas promised federal funds to build a military barracks, a railroad station, a power generator, and a federal building in both municipalities.[40]

Outside the municipalities that passed to Mexican control in 1882, the SEP's nation-building program along the border was less urgent. Héctor Eduardo Paniagua's zone, based in Frontera Comalapa, had not been part of Guatemala since the early nineteenth century, and no frontier schools were established there. Still, Paniagua kept his schools busily engaged in state and nation building. To complement the extremely deficient telegraph and postal service in the region, Paniagua established an inter-school mail service. Each federal rural school served as a branch of one of the zone's four post offices, and mail was delivered once a week. Paniagua's teachers also served as labor recruiters for state and federal infrastructure projects. During 1936, 187 kilometers of local roads were built or improved thanks to their recruiting efforts. Teachers also mobilized labor for bridge construction and repair. According to Paniagua, 435 men were recruited to build a bridge spanning the Comalapa River. This enormous undertaking involved transporting five 16 1/2-meter pieces of wood over a distance of 10 kilometers. Eighty men were used to carry each piece. Twenty-five other bridges were built or repaired during the course of the year in his zone. As Paniagua's activities illustrate, the SEP in Chiapas tailored its state- and nation-building campaigns to the perceived needs of each zone. Along the southernmost stretches of the border, the urgent need was for frontier schools and an intense cultural effort; farther north and east along the same border, SEP officials were more concerned with infrastructure than with cultural identity.[41]

Chiapas's long-standing and difficult relationship with Guatemala was again exploited in the late 1930s, this time by planters and ranchers. At issue was whether President Cárdenas would act on the land reform claims of Soconusco's recently naturalized agraristas.[42] In a desperate attempt to shrink the pool of potential agrarian reform beneficiaries, landowners along the border whipped the media into such an anti-Guatemalan frenzy in 1938 that the Guatemalan Embassy in Mexico felt compelled to deny rumors of an impending invasion of sixty thousand Guatemalan soldiers and an aerial bombardment by Guatemala's tiny air force.[43] Later, local papers cited a *Time* magazine article reporting that Guatemala would join the United States in a preemptive attack on Mexico. The Guatemalan diplomatic corps denied the rumor, saying that if the United States wanted to invade Mexico, it surely did not need Guatemala's assistance.[44] In response to local and national tensions, including Cárdenas's expropriation of the foreign oil fields, the SEP sent a brigade of twenty teachers to Soconusco in March 1938 to give special instructions on national integration to federal employees, especially teachers. The brigade taught that Mexicanization along the problematic frontier could only be achieved by offering the social and political benefits of the Mexican revolution to all, including those of Guatemalan descent.[45]

Later that summer the SEP recalled its Cultural Missions (now called Brigades for National Unity [Brigadas Pro-Integridad Nacional]) from Chiapas, allegedly because Guatemala's dictator, Jorge Ubico, had accused the missionaries of fomenting anti-Guatemalan sentiment. Teachers, banana and coffee workers, and others expressed their dismay to President Cárdenas. In the words of banana workers at the finca Ismalapita in Huixtla, "Their presence here is transcendental because they can lift the veil of ignorance that still covers us."[46] It is likely that the SEP and President Cárdenas used Ubico's complaint as a pretext to remove agitators from a sensitive region just ahead of Chiapas's major land reform.

In March 1939, just days before the agrarian petitioners were to take official possession of the land, several prominent ranchers, planters, and politicians in Tapachula began to organize their own campaign for secession in a desperate attempt to head off (or altogether avoid) Cardenista reforms.[47] When major land reform finally came to Chiapas, Mexicans of Guatemalan descent were among the biggest winners as Cardenistas targeted several large and productive coffee plantations in Soconusco and Mariscal. The reparto was a stroke of state- and nation-building genius. These recently naturalized citizens owed a debt of gratitude to Cárdenas and to Mexico. As ejidatarios, they were incorporated into the institutions of the consolidating Mexican state, like the National Peasant Confederation (Confederación Nacional Campesina, or CNC), the Ejidal Bank (Banco Ejidal), and Cárdenas's PRM, and their loyalty to the Mexican nation would never again be called into serious question.

Conclusion

The SEP's nation-building campaign in the 1930s involved an ambitious, quixotic attempt to forge the hearts, minds, and bodies of the new Mexican. It first attacked the foundations of Mexico's "traditional" culture based on Catholicism and rural paternalism. In its place the SEP sought to create a modern, secular, sober culture that emphasized civic and national duty. Teachers and the school were to replace the priest and the church, and an interventionist federal government was to replace the *patrón* (boss).

Historians of Cardenismo disagree over the extent to which this "cultural revolution" was successful. Bantjes called it a failure in his important study of Sonora, Becker saw initial failure in Michoacán but concluded that Cardenistas learned enough from local culture to eventually dominate it, and Vaughan found that the SEP's program generally succeeded in Puebla and among mestizo settlers in the Yaqui Valley. During the 1930s, it failed among the Yaqui themselves.

In Chiapas the SEP's effort to end the manufacture and sale of alcohol in rural communities was an uneven, short-lived fight. Inspectors and teachers soon realized there was little point in combating interests that enjoyed the protection of the governor, the state PNR, municipal authorities, and the state police. Grajales's selective enforcement of his 1935 rural prohibition decree actually favored the creation of the statewide alcohol monopoly that would consolidate under Moctezuma and Hernán Pedrero in the 1940s.[48]

The SEP's campaign of cultural nationalism enjoyed a more lasting legacy, especially after the divisive rhetoric of class conflict and anticlericalism gave way to a focus on social justice and nationalism in the late 1930s. The Cultural Sundays may not have lasted beyond the heady years of 1935 and 1936, but patriotic festivals only grew in importance as international events in the early 1940s called for national unity. Rural Chiapanecos joined the "imagined community" of Mexicans thanks to skits, speeches, music, dances, patriotic celebrations, and sporting events. Along the southern border, the SEP's frontier schools, its enhanced cultural curriculum, and its infrastructure development programs diffused the perceived threat presented by residents of Guatemalan descent. Guatemalans and many

Chiapanecos still share a common history, and many share cultural and linguistic traits, but these are usually not perceived as threats to Mexico's sovereignty. Indeed, for all its excesses, the socialist school sparked the process by which Chiapas's frontier communities, its peasant and working classes, its state and federal schools, and its teachers were incorporated into the consolidating Mexican state and nation. ◆

Part Three

CARDENISMO and ITS DISCONTENTS

Chapter Seven

The Subversion of SEP Indigenismo in Chiapas

> On repeated occasions I have reported on the special conditions in this zone . . . the state of backwardness and misery in which the indígenas find themselves, and the systems of exploitation organized by the enganchadores, alcoholeros, landowners and municipal authorities. . . . Nowhere do so many factors conspire against the school as in this corner of the Chiapanecan mountains.
>
> —*Inspector Manuel Castellanos,*
> *dated from Ciudad de Las Casas, May 11, 1936*

SEP pedagogues and social reformers had high hopes when Mexico's only self-proclaimed indigenista president, Lázaro Cárdenas, took office in December 1934. For the next six years, the Cárdenas administration made indigenismo a national priority. Cardenistas believed that material assistance and federal paternalism were the keys to indigenous redemption: once Indians had land, water, tools, markets, and access to credit, and once their local exploiters were reined in, they could be incorporated into the nation-state. As Cárdenas himself stated, "The program for emancipating the Indian is in essence that of emancipating the proletariat in any other country."[1] In the interests of nation building, Cardenistas conflated ethnicity and class, and the term *cultura indígena* was used to refer to both Indians and mestizos determined to have low levels of culture.[2] Ironically, just as Cardenistas endorsed a broader, de-ethnicized definition of "Indian-ness," indigenista social scientists and pedagogues increasingly recognized Mexico's tremendous ethnic and linguistic diversity. Against the will of Cárdenas himself, who spoke repeatedly of the need to "Mexicanize the Indian," the crusade for monolingual monocultural "incorporation" gradually gave way to calls for bilingual education and a more plural vision of the Mexican nation.

When Cárdenas took office, Indian policy was almost exclusively the domain of the SEP. Indigenismo was thus inextricably linked to socialist education. In the highlands of Chiapas, disparaging comments about the Mayas' lack of "culture" and refusal to "incorporate" themselves became temporarily unfashionable. SEP zone inspector Manuel Castellanos and his teachers portrayed the Maya sympathetically as victims of conniving ladino alcohol merchants, the clergy, and foreign enganchadores and planters. In Castellanos's words, "The distinct subjects of the curriculum were given a socialist interpretation, that is, each subject was used to judge and critique the prevailing socioeconomic conditions in the region and stir sentiments of justice and equality in the children." Students also learned of "the need to destroy the causes that oblige the proletariat to live a life of ignorance and misery."[3]

But nowhere did the best-laid plans of SEP indigenistas and pedagogues clash with local realities as they did in highland Chiapas. Resistance to the SEP's expanded "socialist" agenda and its generally monolingual teachers came from above and below. Municipal authorities, enganchadores, and alcohol merchants who were able to ignore the innocuous federal schools of the 1920s and early 1930s reacted with such violence that highland teachers in 1935 built schools in bunker-like shelters where they could take refuge, feed themselves, and defend themselves with firearms if necessary.[4] The SEP's indigenous boarding schools, largely successful in other parts of the country, were tragically flawed at every level in Chiapas. They were resisted by Indians and ladinos alike. Most highland Maya still considered the federal school an agent of cultural imposition, not a potential tool of redemption. Forced by ladino opposition to scale back their ambitious social programs, even the most dedicated federal teachers had little to offer. In highland Chiapas, schooling remained what it had always been—an unpopular commodity where success was defined in terms of how well select students subordinated themselves to (and did the bidding of) ladinos.[5]

Chiapas's State Government Discovers Indigenismo

While most pedagogues, political reformers, and anthropologists in Mexico evolved toward a more emancipatory, plural indigenista vision, the political leadership in Chiapas remained mired in old habits and ways of thinking. In 1930 coletos fought to maintain day wages in the highlands at less than one-half the national wage mandated by presidential decree. Members of the state government met in San Cristóbal with representatives of local planters and ranchers and the tamed, official state labor union. They agreed that *peones* and day laborers had few material needs and were satisfied with their salaries, which in any case "only serves them for their vices and not the necessities of life." Furthermore, "the work performed in this region in no way compares with that performed in the coffee plantations of Soconusco, and in this Municipality they are treated with benevolence by their employers." Given this happy state of affairs, these coletos agreed that wages should remain as they were.[6]

In 1933, a spike in the demand for seasonal coffee labor forced the Grajales administration to improve existing labor-contracting institutions. In August, at the start of the coffee harvest, the state government issued a circular ordering municipalities and enganchadores to stop charging debt peons the departure tax and other fees, since such measures "constitute an obstacle for the movement of workers who want to go to the coffee zone, damaging their interests and the interests of those who wish to give them work."[7] The state government also took particular—indeed unprecedented—interest in the abuses suffered by Indians at the hands of enganchadores. In 1934 the Grajales administration announced the creation of a state Department of Indigenous Social Action, Culture, and Protection (Departamento de Acción Social, Cultura y Protección Indígena).[8] Not only did the Grajales administration seek to wrest the control of Indian labor from the enganchadores, alcoholeros, and municipal secretaries, but it feared losing control of "its" Indians to the Cardenistas, especially as the pivotal state election of 1936 drew near.

Naturally, the department never sought to eliminate enganche and debt peonage in Chiapas. Rather, it simply tried to regulate these time-honored practices. Governor Grajales candy-coated enganche in his annual report in 1934, noting that "approximately one million pesos are advanced annually to the Indians, which constitutes agrarian credit in indigenous zones and promotes the annual migration of Indians to Soconusco, facilitating little by little their incorporation into culture." All debt labor contracting was to take place in one of the department's offices rather than at fiestas, liquor establishments, and jails. Department officials were to be physically present to record the amount of money advanced by the enganchador.[9] The department oversaw 2,075 individual work contracts in Comitán and 6,034 in Ciudad Las Casas during its first six months. SEP documents tell of the department's agents working together with enganchadores to convince entire communities to migrate to Soconusco for the coffee harvest, and documents in San Cristóbal's municipal archive show the directors of the department in direct communication with planters, sending workers where they were needed most.[10]

The year 1934 also signaled the beginning of a state government campaign of cultural indigenismo that closely resembled federal programs enacted by the SEP. Ángel M. Corzo, longtime indigenista and the state's Director of Education, announced the formation of the Grand Committee to Dress Indian Children (Gran Comité Pro-Vestido del Niño Indígena) so that "no indigenous child will continue wearing the clothes of his tribe; rather, all will dress decently with the garments that civilization has sanctioned."[11] President of the committee was Governor Grajales. Overalls were distributed to boys ages 7 to 14 and girls ages 7 to 12 who attended the state's schools. This paternalist, simpleminded campaign to promote "assimilation" was seconded by SEP teachers and inspectors in indigenous communities; Inspector Rubén M. Rincón, based in Ocosingo, reported in 1935 that "153 indigenous men now wear pants" and "227 indigenous women now wear [Western-style] skirts."[12] This crusade reached grotesque extremes when state and federal teachers, municipal officials, and state PNR agitators forced indigenous people to burn their old clothing in public bonfires.[13] Aída Hernández writes that this campaign was especially extreme along the border with Guatemala. Elderly Mam still recall the state government's bonfires and the prohibition on speaking the Mam language in state schools.[14]

State indigenismo in Chiapas changed forever in December 1936 when Cardenista Erasto Urbina took control of the Department of Indian Protection and created the Indigenous Workers' Union (Sindicato de Trabajadores Indígenas, or STI). But underlying several important political changes was a surprising degree of continuity. For all the fanfare, the STI probably did more to rationalize labor flows than it did to improve working and living conditions for indigenous workers. Meanwhile, Urbina's bilingual indigenous scribes gradually came to dominate highland communities. In the end, indigenismo in Chiapas was more about political and economic control than social emancipation.

The SEP's Indigenous Boarding Schools in Chiapas

After the SEP closed the Casa del Estudiante Indígena, it redirected its budget and attention to the creation of indigenous boarding schools in rural, indigenous regions where they were most needed. By 1937 there were thirty-three such schools in the states. SEP officials hoped that these schools would build on the successes of the Casa while obviating the problems that had plagued the rural schools, Cultural Missions, and the Casa itself. In recognition of the plurality of indigenous Mexico, "brigades" consisting of a teacher, an agronomist, and a social worker were to conduct ethnographic studies of the region before the school was built. Local needs and local culture were expected to guide the school's curriculum. SEP indigenistas hoped these schools would achieve the collective transformation of the entire community instead of the individual transformations observed at the Casa. Built in the nucleus of truly indigenous communities, schools would educate and modernize students without removing or alienating them from their home environments. Although students were to speak, read, and write in Spanish, they would be allowed, even encouraged to speak in their native tongues.[15]

Practically, too, the schools appeared to represent an improvement, at least on paper. Schools were to be situated in areas where at least twenty-five hectares of land were available for agricultural training. Instruction in small industries (*pequeñas industrias*) was a priority, meant as much to create material needs in the indígenas (like the custom of wearing shoes) as to satisfy existing ones.[16] And although the boarding schools were not normal schools, students would be qualified to teach in the federal rural schools upon completing four- to six-year agricultural and technical training programs. For cosmopolitan indigenistas in Mexico City, the schools represented a shift away from "incorporation" and toward cultural and linguistic pluralism. More importantly, according to Dawson, "these new schools became venues where, on a limited level, communities could promote a kind of pedagogy that celebrated and promoted local cultures, rather than seeking their destruction." This would allow the schools "to foment some of the most radical agendas of cultural pluralism seen in the 1930s."[17]

As was so often the case, urban indigenista idealism could not take root in highland Chiapas. Programs that enjoyed success elsewhere quickly succumbed to inadequate budgets, infrastructure, and personnel, not to mention obstructionist ladinos and indígenas. Although the national SEP recommended bilingual, preferably indigenous directors and teachers, only monolingual ladinos were hired to direct and teach in Chiapas, and most lacked teacher training and misunderstood the indigenous communities where they were based.

In March 1933 the SEP opened one of its new indigenous boarding schools in the ceremonial center of San Juan Chamula. The school was housed in an ex-convent and was staffed by ten teachers. Students learned carpentry (specializing in beds and, grimly, coffins), masonry, pottery, and small-scale manufacturing. Two social workers conducted the customary hygiene and anti-alcohol campaigns in nearby hamlets, organizing potentially humiliating contests rewarding the cleanest student and the cleanest family. The school also gave free haircuts and handed out soap. Three months later, five dozen state and federal scholarships supported fifty-seven male students who studied and lived at the school.[18]

But the school quickly ran into trouble. Chamulans had taken advantage of the chaos of the revolution to chase away all ladinos living in their municipality. They opposed schooling because it implied the return of ladinos, and in July 1933 Chamulan authorities blocked the expansion of the school on precisely those grounds. Complicating matters for the school's employees was the presence of enganchadores who occasionally "stole" students from the school and sent them off to work in the lowlands. Notwithstanding these serious problems, SEP director in Chiapas Septimio Pérez Palacios painted a rosy picture of the school based on reports he had received from zone inspector José María López.

An anonymous (but well-informed) SEP official in Mexico City was not fooled. As he scribbled in the margins of Pérez's July 1933 report, "I know that there are mestizos among the students; I know that there are children (under age 14) present when the instruction is only for adolescents; and I know that the students have not sown anything, despite the fact that agriculture should be at the heart of the school." In a critique echoing those made of the Casa, the school at Chamula was faulted for its "terrible and insufficient food" and its sloppy bookkeeping. Pérez was warned to take interest in the institution, "because it would be sad and shameful if we had to close it due to your lack of attention."[19] Pérez replied that he would go inspect the school for himself. Shortly after he confirmed the miserable state of affairs at Chamula, the school was closed and moved north to Rincón Chamula, where it drew students from Ch'ol, Tzotzil, Tzeltal, and Zoque communities.

The failure of the boarding school at San Juan Chamula was repeated at other sites over the next few years. By spring 1935 two other boarding schools were in operation, one at Nopal Cacaté, in the municipality of Ixtapa, the other at Huixtán. Both drew exclusively from Tzotzil communities. Whether motivated by necessity or symbolism, both were established in ex-convents, just like the ill-fated school at San Juan Chamula. Additional schools were soon opened in the Tzotzil town of Chijtón and the Tzeltal community of Bachajón.

Reflecting the resurgent indigenismo of the Cárdenas period, the SEP began subjecting its indigenous boarding schools to closer scrutiny in 1936. In Chiapas, Ángel M. Corzo was named to head the SEP's newly created Section of Indigenous Education (Sección de Educación Indígena). Later that spring he toured three boarding schools. His report portrayed the institutions in varying stages of decay, suggesting the subversion of SEP indigenismo at all levels.

Fig. 8. Indigenous students brought from Cancuc to attend the boarding school at Huixtán, 1935. Recruitment usually involved coercion. Note the ladino recruiter, seated. Courtesy Archivo Histórico de la Secretaría de Educación Pública.

We first turn to the relocated school at Rincón Chamula. Despite its relative success in recruiting female students, the school was already on shaky ground even before Corzo's visit. In February 1936 zone inspector Manuel Fernando Molina found the school terribly underfunded and unhygienic and its students listless. Many staff spoke openly of the director's incompetence and his misuse of funds.[20] Residents resented the fact that the school had been established inside the community's closed church. Later that year Corzo found the place a disaster. It lacked water even for the most basic hygiene. He reported that "the school's toilet is really just a dunghill and is pestilent to the highest degree." There was no land available for agricultural practices. Spanish was literally forced on students. During Corzo's visit the director returned from a recruiting trip. Of the ninety-seven recruits, eighty-two were male. But nineteen males and seven females were younger than fourteen and twelve years, respectively, and were technically too young to attend. Other students were mestizos. Corzo suspected that heavy coercion had been used in recruiting. The last line of his report was unequivocal: "At Rincón Chamula I think it convenient to remove all personnel, including the Director, who has shown little interest and little efficiency in his work."[21]

Conditions were no better at Nopal Cacaté. The school there had no

Fig. 9. Indigenous children "rescued" from an enganchador. They were sent to the indigenous boarding school at Huixtán. Note their new clothing. Courtesy Archivo Histórico de la Secretaría de Educación Pública.

cultivable lands either, the former convent that housed the school had partially collapsed, and "next to the school, in the same building, and separated only by a wooden fence, [was] nothing less than an aguardiente distillery."[22] Nopal Cacaté's recruiting record was even worse than that of San Juan Chamula and Rincón Chamula. Corzo found thirty-two students, of whom only four were female. Other students had recently fled. Only ten of the students met the SEP's age and ethnicity requirements; the others were too young and/or were deemed mestizos. Corzo also learned that former director Nestor Ojeda had been billing the SEP as if one hundred students attended the school; since there were rarely more than thirty students enrolled, Ojeda had simply pocketed the difference. Ojeda's insensitivity had also soured relations between the school and residents of the town of Cacaté when he violated gravesites in the church's cemetery in an unspecified manner. Villagers were so infuriated that all twenty-eight of the students from the town fled the school in February. None of the students that Corzo found in April were residents of Cacaté. Corzo recommended relocating the school to Chenalhó, a Tzotzil town where residents tended to support federal education and where land was available for agricultural instruction. The move to Chenalhó was made shortly after Corzo filed his report, and the school was still in operation in 1941.

Corzo found conditions slightly better at the boarding school at Huixtán. It too lacked cultivable lands, but most of its difficulties stemmed from its neighbors. The school paid a fair price to its indigenous suppliers of food and other goods, which apparently had the effect of roughly doubling prices for ladino residents of the town. According to zone inspector Manuel Castellanos, this "provok[ed] the resentment of the neighbors, bellicose people who are accustomed to resolving their difficulties with bullets and knifings, so that people are continually being wounded or killed." Local ladinos had made a habit of attacking the school after a night of drinking. Castellanos reported that the school, its personnel, and its students had been subjected to multiple armed assaults and that Huixtán's municipal president and the president of the local PNR, among others, had tried to assassinate teachers. Further complicating matters at the school was a typhoid epidemic in the spring of 1936, which had stricken twenty-six students, killing one. When Corzo visited, he found ninety-five male students enrolled, though nineteen had recently fled due to the epidemic. Corzo recommended moving the school to Amatenango, a wholly indigenous town where cultivable lands were readily available. Amatenango was also a logical site because most of the school's students came from that town.[23] The school was moved there in September 1936, but it suffered an inauspicious beginning. The SEP provided no financial assistance for the move, so the teachers and students had to trek forty-eight mountainous kilometers from Huixtán to Amatenango in driving rain, carrying with them the necessary supplies and tools. Once they arrived at their new home, they were met with "indifference."

The SEP's indigenous boarding schools in Chiapas limped on into the 1940s, when financial restraints and a revived interest in monocultural "national unity" forced their closure. Remarkably, the SEP failed to learn the lessons of previous indigenista experiences at the state and national level. SEP officials in Chiapas founded numerous schools in former churches and convents, provoking the resentment of Catholics. They opened some schools in ladino communities lacking water and arable land. Conditions at the schools were so degrading that recruiters usually resorted to coercion. Male ladinos staffed and ran the schools, complicating attempts to recruit students, especially girls and young women. Spanish was the only language spoken, and no effort was made to train the students to become teachers themselves. These shortcomings simply made it easier for meddlesome ladinos and culturally conservative Tzotzil and Tzeltal communities to undermine the schools.

In his study of national indigenismo, Dawson found considerable grassroots

Fig. 10. Students tend to the experimental garden at their school in Teopisca, 1935. Courtesy Archivo Histórico de la Secretaría de Educación Pública.

support for boarding schools in many indigenous communities throughout Mexico. Even where teachers attacked local religious and cultural belief systems, villagers still tended to support the school and welcomed the allotment of resources that it represented. While some of this support might be dismissed as simply a ploy to receive federal largess in the form of tools, trucks, beds, tortilla machines, and possibly land reform, it is important to note that such support was not manifest in highland Chiapas. Thus, while boarding schools in many states produced thousands of indigenous teachers, agronomists, and other professionals who became interlocutors between the state and their home communities, this was much less likely to occur in Chiapas. In 1941 the state's Director of Federal Education, Jacinto Téllez, recommended closing the schools because they had not produced positive and practical results despite the considerable sums of money dedicated to their upkeep and operation.[24] Nine years earlier, Manuel Mesa had recommended closure of the Casa del Estudiante Indígena for identical reasons.

SEP Indigenismo in Highland Rural Schools

When Manuel Castellanos became education inspector of Chiapas's fifth

Fig. 11. Education zone inspector Manuel Castellanos in the Lacandón rain forest in eastern Chiapas, 1935. Following his visit, Castellanos established two short-lived schools in Lacandón communities. The man at center, Chan Kin Viejo, was patriarch of Nahá until his death in 1996. Courtesy Archivo Histórico de la Secretaría de Educación Pública.

zone in January 1935, he assumed administrative control of a vast area encompassing the central highlands and the hills and lowlands of eastern Chiapas, including Palenque, Ocosingo, and the Lacandón rain forest. In this zone, federal education was still at the mercy of local ladinos. The SEP barely had a foothold in the region; according to Castellanos, its schools and teachers were literally under siege by those who felt threatened by federal education's expanded social mandate:

> As enemies of the redemption of the Indian we have entire communities of landowners and their agents, manufacturers and sellers of aguardiente, and secretaries and municipal agents, who on some occasions are the instruments of the exploiters. Until now the Indian problem remains intact and insoluble . . . which is shameful for our country, and represents a negation of revolutionary principles. Federal education has done nothing to incorporate the Indian into civilization.[25]

Teachers were routinely threatened, beaten, shot at, and hauled to court. Schoolrooms were burned to the ground with some regularity, while indigenous parents and students who supported the schools were subjected to a range of abuses. In several towns, SEP schools catered only to the handful of ladinos who lived in the administrative centers of each municipality. But Castellanos fought back with every means at his disposal, sharing with inspectors Vassallo, Mota, and a few others a passion for popular pedagogy. He believed that federal education—broadly conceived—was the key to improving the lives of the highland Maya. Equipped with a more integral version of indigenismo, progressive directors of federal education in Tuxtla (López and Burgos), and a vigorously mobilized federal government, Castellanos launched the first real challenge to the institutions of indigenous exploitation in the highlands.

Castellanos's achievements during his first year as inspector were impressive, as he labored tirelessly to improve school infrastructure. He inherited twenty-seven schools; seven months later, there were forty-four schools. While only sixteen of the schools were housed in buildings in January 1935, indigenous villagers had built thirty-four one-room schoolhouses—with woven straw roofs and walls of mud and sticks—by July. During that same period the number of pit toilets jumped from three to thirty-four. The number of athletic fields more than doubled; the number of desks and benches almost tripled. From nine experimental gardens in January there were twenty-six in July; from no orchards in January there were twenty by July. Castellanos created so many schools in 1935 that the SEP soon added a new zone based in Ocosingo under the supervision of another inspector. His zone was then reduced to the highland municipalities of Las Casas, Chamula, Zinacantán, Huixtán, Larráinzar, Tenejapa, Chenalhó, Cancuc, Oxchuc, Chanal, Amatenango, Teopisca, and Venustiano Carranza.[26]

Once the basic infrastructure was in place, schools in Castellanos's zone launched the first major social campaigns seen in the region. In July and August 1935, teachers and local education committee members shaved, deloused, and cleaned 687 indigenous children. Children and adults alike were vaccinated against smallpox in thirty-two communities, and campaigns against typhoid fever and malaria were conducted in every community where there was a school. Every school had a first-aid kit. Teachers had their hands full during the typhoid fever outbreak in the spring of 1936, especially struggling to explain that the disease was caused by untreated water, not some supernatural force. All schools in Castellanos's zone had Anti-alcohol Committees, although Castellanos admitted that little could be done after they had been established since "The alcoholeros enjoy more guarantees and official support than the teachers."[27]

Although Castellanos significantly improved classroom infrastructure and launched the region's first major social campaigns, he devoted most of his energy to attacking the institutions and structures that kept indigenous highlanders in a subjugated state. This campaign instantly put Castellanos and his teachers at odds with local officials. As he told it, "The authorities are paid by the enganchadores and alcoholeros to help recruit people to go to the coffee plantations. For this reason they are from day one the determined enemy of the teacher who combats this kind of exploitation."[28] Castellanos also confronted Chiapas's modern-day repartimiento, whereby municipal authorities forced indigenous men to work unpaid on public works projects outside their communities. In early 1936 he prevented the municipal government of Huixtán from using free indigenous labor to construct a walkway connecting the village center with the cemetery. Later that year in Tenejapa he joined the state-appointed Attorney of Indigenous Affairs (Procurador de Asuntos Indígenas) to prevent the municipal government (again, entirely ladino) from using forced, unpaid native labor to build a road. At Magdalenas he joined teacher Anastacio Bautista in defending indigenous villagers against Chenalhó's municipal secretary, who had incarcerated and fined those who refused to build a road for coffee planters at Pantelhó. He and his teachers fought similar battles against ladino ranchers and municipal secretaries in Chanal, Yactaclum, Colonia Luis Espinosa, Teopisca, and a host of other places. Finally, Castellanos organized meetings in Ocosingo, Chenalhó, Las Casas, and Amatenango to explain the schools' redemptive mission and the ways the federal government would protect indígenas from their exploiters. Each meeting was attended by more than five hundred indigenous workers of different ethnicities.[29]

Castellanos and his best teachers also struggled to eradicate the various head taxes that ladino municipal governments levied on indigenous communities. Early in 1936, Castellanos prevented indigenous residents at Ejido Pedernal and Chenalhó from paying a head tax to the municipal government at Ciudad Las Casas for prisoner maintenance. The inspector also took action at Bocolum in the municipality of Tenejapa, where residents explained that they were billed fifty centavos monthly by the municipal president ostensibly "because he lights the moon" every night. At Huixtán he stopped indigenous villages from paying an annual two-peso head tax to maintain the municipality's entirely ladino government.[30]

Castellanos also intervened to jump-start the federal agrarian reform program, which had been stalled on all fronts in Chiapas, especially in the highlands. "This revolutionary promise has greatly disappointed the campesinos," he wrote, "with the exception of a few places where with a thousand sacrifices agrarian colonies and centers have been established." Indians had been swindled by unscrupulous engineers in Cancuc, Tenango, Tenejapa, and elsewhere. Agraristas in Ocosingo had been forcibly removed from lands they were soliciting, including national lands, and had been persecuted, incarcerated, and even assassinated "all so that the campesinos might renounce the just rights that the Revolution has conquered for them and return to being submissive and resigned . . . to the yolk of servitude."[31] Elsewhere Castellanos defended indigenous solicitors of land reform from the reprisals of ladino ranchers whose lands were targeted for expropriation. At Tanaté, for example, he worked with the Delegate of Indigenous Affairs to force a rancher to pay for the damage caused when he leveled eighteen houses of indígena agraristas and allowed his livestock to destroy their crops. As Castellanos noted, villagers at Las Ollas, Huitepec, Yashanal, and other towns had been "influenced by [Catholic] fanatics and land owners, and resisted becoming agraristas, in spite of lacking workable lands."[32] Given this degree of resistance, Castellanos managed to establish only a handful of agrarian committees. When major land reform finally came to Chiapas in 1939 and 1940, its effect was negligible in his zone.

Ladino opposition to SEP schools in the highlands continued unabated into 1936. On January 23, teachers Fidencio Flores and Daniel Rojas at the Chamulan parish (*paraje*) of Romerillo were attacked by inebriated Chamulans who tried to hack them to pieces with machetes. After repelling the aggression the teachers fled to Ciudad Las Casas, later returning to Romerillo only with a federal escort. Also in late January three drunken ladinos attacked teacher Rafael Mayorga and his family at the town of Matamoros; Mayorga repelled the aggression with gunfire. During that same week, a group of intoxicated ladino aguardiente vendors entered the school at Bocolum, chased the indigenous students out of the classroom, and insulted the teacher (a woman) for teaching Indians. The ladino attack on the boarding school at Huixtán occurred on February 2, the night after General Francisco Múgica's visit. At Cuxtitali and other schools, workshop tools, doors, benches, and tables were routinely stolen and the schools' enemies destroyed experimental gardens.[33] After more than a year of intense effort Castellanos was no closer to redeeming the Indians than he had been when he first introduced socialist education to the highlands.

In May 1936, Castellanos sounded a note of desperation in his bimonthly

Fig. 12. Federal troops and local authorities at Yashanal, municipality of Tenejapa. Education zone inspector Manuel Castellanos is second from the right. Castellanos requested the troops after teachers and schools were subjected to attacks. Courtesy Archivo Histórico de la Secretaría de Educación Pública.

report to the SEP. "The education problem of the Chamulan is more complicated than that of any other indígena in the Republic," he wrote.

> I say this because I have worked with the Tarahumaras, the Tepehuanes, the Otomís, and other indigenous people from Veracruz and Tabasco, and in no part of the Republic nor in the state are they more brutalized by alcohol, nor is the exploitation of the Indian—through which the greater part of the mestizo population lives—so well organized. As a result, the principal import in these places is the alcohol which is brought from the distillery of [state congressional representative] Belisario Orantes and from Comitán, and the most valuable business venture is that of sending thousands of Chamulans to Soconusco and the Mumunil region. Nowhere, I repeat, do so many factors conspire against the school as in this corner of the Chiapanecan mountains.[34]

With time and experience, Castellanos came to appreciate the scope of factors that obstructed SEP schooling in the region. Indigenous children, he

Fig. 13. A school festival at Amatenango del Valle, 1935. Note the school theatre (Teatro Escolar). Courtesy Archivo Histórico de la Secretaría de Educación Pública.

wrote, could scarcely be expected to learn when most of them suffered from malnutrition, the result of a poor corn-based diet with little or no protein. Many students worked as load-bearers and had deformed craniums from carrying heavy loads at such a young age. Diseases endemic to the moist, cool highlands ravaged these poorly nourished children. School attendance rates were abysmal, especially for girls in the most culturally conservative Tzotzil towns. In May 1936, for example, 2,396 boys and men attended forty-one schools in his zone, compared with just 659 girls. At Huixtán's boarding school the ratio was even worse: 80 boys attended compared with just 2 girls.[35] Inadequate budgets and unprepared and/or irresponsible ladino teachers only complicated matters for Castellanos. By late 1936 he began calling for a more thorough, comprehensive indigenismo program capable of fulfilling the federal government's modernizing state- and nation-building agenda.[36]

By early 1937, a tone of resignation pervaded Castellanos's reports. His condemnations of ladino enganchadores, alcohol merchants, and priests are reminiscent of the reports he submitted two years earlier. But his 1937 report also suggests a flagging faith in the SEP, which only provided 300 books, pencils, and notebooks for more than 4,500 day and night students. Most notable, however, was his shattered faith in the indigenous population. Gone was the sympathetic rhetoric of class exploitation, replaced by the familiar language of civilization and barbarism used by many indigenistas in the 1920s. "They are excessively dirty, since they never bathe themselves voluntarily," he wrote. "They do not cut their hair, and they neither wash nor change their clothes until they disintegrate. They believe blindly in their 'witches,' and their customs are truly savage." For the coming year Castellanos proposed studies "to determine the physical, mental or social causes that have retarded indigenous learning," as if the Casa del Estudiante Indígena and other experiments had not proven the intellectual and assimilative capacity of indigenous students once removed from exploitative relationships in the countryside.[37] While most indigenista pedagogues and social scientists at this time were beginning to embrace a more plural, locally responsive pedagogy, an exasperated, defeated Castellanos was moving in the opposite direction.

Conclusion

Despite the efforts of the SEP missionaries in the early 1920s, the federal rural schools later that decade, the occasional Cultural Missions, the boarding schools, and the "socialist" rural schools of the 1930s, federal indigenismo had not brought tangible benefits to the Tzotzils and Tzeltals. This became painfully clear every time they conducted business in the ladino commercial center of Las Casas. Throughout our period of study, ladino merchants (*acaparadores*) operating with the blessing of the local authorities installed themselves at the town gates and commandeered indigenous goods at a fraction of their market value. Indian sellers who refused to go along with this were often beaten and thrown in jail. Those found in Las Casas after dark were arrested for "public scandals" (*escándalos en vía pública*) or alleged drunkenness under the Ley de Policía y Buen Gobierno. They were freed the next day, but only after cleaning city streets and plazas.[38] Furthermore, despite Article 123 of the constitution, the city was still home to several holding pens where enganchadores kept indigenous "recruits" locked up until the time had come to march to lowland plantations. The state's Department of Social Action, Culture, and Indigenous Protection had been corrupted to the degree that its labor inspector, Alfredo Jiménez Lara, took bribes from enganchadores and tipped them off when more zealous officials sought to inspect conditions in the holding pens or collect the departure tax.[39]

The SEP's impotence was perhaps most evident in the realm of alcohol policy. Despite concerted campaigns since 1929 to reduce or eliminate alcohol consumption and to close alcohol distilleries and dispensaries in or near indigenous communities, ten distilleries in Las Casas alone reaped handsome profits off indigenous consumption. In fall 1936, the state's Attorney for Indigenous Communities reported that ladino alcohol merchants and agents had established cantinas and checkpoints at the gates to the town. Calling themselves *vigilantes de alcohol,* they inspected and frisked all Indians entering the city "without respecting the women." When they found bottles, the "inspectors" made the Indians promise to buy aguardiente from their bosses. Hours later, before the Indians returned to their villages, they were forced to show a receipt proving that they had made their purchase at the specified location. Those who could not had their bottles smashed or were forced to pour out the contents. In many cases, the "inspectors" made indígenas leave their ponchos (*chamarras*) with them in the morning as a guarantee that they would buy their aguardiente at the "right" place. Regardless of where they bought their *trago*, many Indians went home drunk. The Attorney for Indigenous Communities wrote that it was a "true shame to see groups of indígenas of all ages, men and women, drunk as they returned to their pueblos, brutalized by the effect of alcohol. Sadly, young men and even girls can be seen passed out on the road and even in front of these taverns."[40] The cantinas were in clear violation of the state's 1935 law prohibiting the sale of alcohol to indigenous people and made a mockery of Castellanos's attempts to control the sale of alcohol in his zone. The attorney's calls for a police crackdown on these practices had gone unheeded.

In sum, socialist education and SEP indigenismo were beaten back in the highlands even before Cardenistas took control of the state government in September 1936. While the Indians' successful rejection of the SEP's cultural project could be read as a victory in the struggle for autonomy and cultural self-determination, their rejection of SEP state building meant that local indigenistas could later use a deft combination of limited reforms and direct control to harness highland communities into a new form of domination. Federal indigenismo at least offered highland Indians the opportunity to partially free themselves from the bonds of their local exploiters; state indigenismo would eventually tighten these bonds of exploitation and control. ◆

Chapter Eight

Cardenismo *à la chiapaneca*

In early 1936, just as SEP indigenismo in highland Chiapas was running out of gas, President Cárdenas and his allies made their move against Governor Victórico Grajales. Federal schoolteachers campaigned on behalf of the Cardenista candidate during both the state's gubernatorial plebiscite and the July 1936 general election, but their participation in the brief period of Cardenista reforms that followed was quite modest. The initiative in the highlands passed from the SEP to the ambitious local indigenista Erasto Urbina, who used federal reforms and institutions to forge his own power base and reshape political and economic relations, allegedly on behalf of Tzotzil and Tzeltal workers and peasants. As this foray into political history demonstrates, Cardenistas managed to temporarily outflank powerful coletos who sought to preserve the status quo. Over the long run, however, these local interests possessed the resiliency to wear down the Cardenistas and subvert their agenda even before Cárdenas left office in 1940.

The Case against Governor Grajales

By the time Lázaro Cárdenas became president in December 1934, Victórico Grajales was midway through his four-year term as governor. His priorities had been made abundantly clear. He hijacked Chiapas's labor and agrarian organizations by placing finqueros at the head of the Confederation of Peasants and Workers in Chiapas (CCOC). He withheld official recognition from independent or federally affiliated agrarian confederations and labor unions. In many municipalities he refused to staff local labor boards (Juntas Municipales de Conciliación), which made it difficult for peasants and workers to register their complaints.[1] When President Abelardo Rodríguez urged Grajales and other governors to impose a daily wage of at least one peso in order to stimulate an internal market, Grajales balked, claiming that "in many parts of the state there is overproduction, and workers are perfectly paid with a minimum salary of .75 pesos."[2]

Grajales was much more generous to himself and to his friends. As

Tuxtla's municipal president Gustavo López Gutiérrez noted in a letter to Cárdenas, the man who three years earlier needed a loan to travel to Mexico City to lobby Calles for the governor's seat had purchased three urban properties in Chiapas and a "magnificent residence" in Mexico City's fashionable Colonia Roma. He had also acquired three ranches and countless livestock. He farmed out the right to tax products like alcohol, beef, pork, tobacco, and coffee to his closest friends. These men typically used their positions to create local monopolies. Grajales also reduced rural property taxes and used *apoderados* (agents with the power of attorney) to prevent the breakup of several large ranches and plantations owned by his friends, like state education minister Ángel M. Corzo. According to numerous sources, Grajales protected several close friends accused of committing murder, including José Luis Esponda, brother of senator Juan M. Esponda, and state representative Dr. Enrique Ochoa, an alleged serial rapist who arranged the assassination of the agrarista war hero Alfonso Moguel. Grajales also encouraged his fellow ranchers and planters to form "self-defense groups" (precursors to today's *guardias blancas*) to protect their interests.[3]

Grajales's opposition to the presidential aspirations of Lázaro Cárdenas was no secret. He expelled Cardenistas from the state PNR and backed candidate General Manuel Pérez Treviño until he withdrew his candidacy one month before the election. Once he became president, Cárdenas's ability to control Grajales was by no means assured. The governor dominated the state's PNR party apparatus and controlled the legislature and most of the municipal governments.[4]

Cárdenas initiated his offensive against Grajales within days of assuming the presidency. His private secretary, Luis I. Rodríguez, compiled a list of complaints lodged against the Grajales administration by campesino organizations, workers, and politicians in the state. The institution of enganche was "encouraged and protected by municipal authorities, principally municipal secretaries," even though the practice had been outlawed in 1914 by Carrancista general Jesús Agustín Castro and banned by the Constitution of 1917 and the 1931 Federal Labor Law. The anti-constitutional tienda de raya was also a common sight in rural Chiapas. Workers were often paid in company store scrip and overvalued merchandise, not cash. Violations of the minimum wage had become institutionalized. To complicate matters for Cárdenas, Grajales had achieved almost complete control over the state's workers and peasants. As Rodríguez told it, "Workers' organizations do not exist in the state. Those groups that function under this title are formed by the authorities, with purely political ends, and have no class spirit, nor do they struggle for the social and economic betterment of their members."[5]

Extreme levels of violence were used to keep the state's campesinos, workers, and political opposition under control. Several dozen agraristas were assassinated by the Grajales regime, and those who testified against Grajalistas in court became targets themselves. Other agraristas had been beaten, dragged, fined, and incarcerated for trying to attend regional meetings in Tuxtla and Mexico City. Eight colonias agrarias and two ejidal ranches had been burnt to the ground for having applied for land reform, ejidatarios on three ejidos and colonias had been pushed off their land entirely, and countless presidents of agrarian committees had been forced to resign.[6]

Grajales also used violence and imposition to keep the state's municipalities in line. As told by Tuxtla's municipal president, "During the last two years the local congress has withdrawn official recognition from three fourths of the popularly elected municipal governments in the state, sending to these acephalic municipalities citizens not exactly chosen for their honesty but rather favorites who absolutely ignore the needs of the towns that they will govern." Grajales's chief of police was the former Mapache colonel Wulfrano Aguilar, notorious during the revolution in Chiapas for committing atrocities and burning down the state government's buildings in June 1917. The state police had become "a sort of inquisitorial tribunal . . . because [Aguilar] sentences and punishes at his whim. Excessive fines, forced labor and blows are the order of the day," wrote Gutiérrez.[7] Frequently, the victims were members of the Pro-Cardenista Liberal Party (Partido Liberal Pro-Cardenista) or the Mexican Peasant Confederation (Confederación Campesina Mexicana, or CCM). Many members of these organizations paid with their lives for supporting Cárdenas when he campaigned in the state in February 1934.[8]

Cárdenas could not let such blatant attacks on his supporters go unanswered. He initially proceeded with caution against Grajales, especially while he still labored in the shadow of Calles. In March 1935 Cárdenas's private secretary sent a delicately worded warning to the governor.

> I have news that some groups of Producers and Workers who have been organizing themselves in Chiapas have been subjected to systematic hostility on the part of local authorities who have strayed from the norms that surely you have given them. . . .
>
> As you know, these activities are in accordance neither with the

President's orientation, nor with the dictates contained in the Revolutionary Plan, which perfectly specifies the rules of conduct for both the federal and local government. . . . Inspired by the sincere affection that I have for you, I suggest with all earnestness that you lend your personal consideration to this matter, so that the irregularities that I cite may cease.[9]

The Cárdenas-Calles Split and Its Repercussions

Events at the national level made a definitive clash between Grajales and Cárdenas only a matter of time. The break between former president Calles and Cárdenas came in June 1935, amid a climate of worker strikes and unrest. On June 12 Calles called on the federal government to suppress the strikes, accusing the working class of being traitors to the national interest. Calles's statement also alluded to his dismissal of former president Pascual Ortiz Rubio in 1932 following a similar disagreement over social and economic policy. Business leaders, governors, congressmen, generals, and Callista labor unions pledged their support to the Jefe Máximo. With news that Calles was returning to Mexico City for the first time since his inauguration, Cárdenas knew he had to act quickly and decisively.[10]

On June 13 Cárdenas stated his position in the press, reiterating the workers' right to strike in a capitalist system. On June 15 his cabinet resigned at his request. What emerged two days later was purged of Callistas. Gone was the anticlerical Agriculture Secretary, Tomás Garrido Canabal. Calles's son Rodolfo, former head of Communications and Public Works, made way for the radical former governor of Michoacán, General Francisco Múgica. In the national congress senators and deputies scrambled to pledge their newfound allegiance to Cardenismo. Several days before the crisis, ninety-nine deputies and forty-five senators called themselves Callistas; one month after the crisis, only seventeen deputies and five senators proclaimed loyalty to the Jefe Máximo. Calles himself was expelled from the PNR in December 1935, and in April 1936 he was expelled from the country.[11]

Immediately following his showdown with Calles, Cárdenas forced fourteen Callista governors out of power either by nullifying elections, granting mandatory leaves to governors, or closing state legislatures. In seven other states Cárdenas used regularly scheduled elections to purge Callistas. In Chiapas, he was willing to allow Callista governor Victórico Grajales to serve out his term, due to expire on November 30, 1936.

Grajales lasted so long in part because Cárdenas could find few suitable replacements. His ideal candidate would be a Chiapanecan with no ties to the Mapaches and Callistas who ran the state in the 1920s and early 1930s. This candidate would be strong enough to face down Grajalistas, but pliant enough to accept direction from Mexico City. Cárdenas's advisers made it clear that few men, if any, fit the bill. Most of the likely candidates were Callistas with close ties to governor Grajales. Former interim governor Amador Coutiño was one possibility, but he was tainted by charges of corruption. Worse still, Calles had used him to impose the election of Raymundo Enríquez in 1928, an election in which dozens died. Senator Juan Esponda was also unacceptable. A "refined coleto," he had been a protégé of Calles's right-hand man, Fernando Torreblanca. Dr. Samuel León, another possibility, had been general secretary of the state government under Grajales and was linked to the assassination of peasants and workers who refused to join Grajales's CCOC. Aquiles Cruz also had possibilities but was known as a reactionary and a strike buster after serving as president of the Federal Conciliation and Arbitration Board.[12]

Cárdenas eventually settled on Efraín Gutiérrez. During the revolution, Gutiérrez had interrupted his studies at the National Agricultural College to fight with Zapata in Morelos. He later worked for the state government of Michoacán from 1928 to 1932, when Cárdenas was governor. Though born in Chiapas, Gutiérrez had been absent from the state for twenty-four years when he returned to initiate his campaign. Critics labeled him too "bourgeois," too friendly with lowland coffee planters, too close to the Catholic hierarchy, and too ambitious. During the first two years of the Cárdenas presidency he directed the National Bank of Agrarian Credit and served as general secretary of the Agrarian Department, for which he received mixed reviews. He used these posts to make contacts with high functionaries and employees in the immigration, agriculture, forestry, finance, and education ministries.[13] For Cárdenas, Gutiérrez was the best choice among many undesirable options. He would be loyal, and his links to several federal ministries appealed to the Cardenista project of strengthening the hand of the federal government in renegade states. His time away from Chiapas also meant that he was indebted to none of the major factions that had controlled the state since 1920.

Cárdenas realized that his candidate could not prevail without the firm support of the state PNR, still dominated by Grajales. Former president Emilio Portes Gil, now acting as president of the national PNR, initiated an extremely controversial purge of the state party by naming Pedro Torres Ortiz its new director. Cardenista delegates were named to the PNR's state committee. Torres also purged the local party machinery in Chiapa de Corzo, Ocozocuautla, Jiquipilas, Arriaga, Tonalá, and other areas in western Chiapas where former Zapatista Colonel Rafael Cal y Mayor was expected to do well in the upcoming party plebiscite. Despite these maneuvers, Cárdenas and the new state PNR had a difficult time selling their candidate. Many self-proclaimed Cardenistas in the state would remain dubious of Gutiérrez and instead cast their vote for Cal y Mayor or Aquiles Cruz.[14]

During this electoral struggle, the Gutiérrez camp subtly courted the Catholic vote. Many Chiapanecos perceived that their president and his candidate were "softer" on the Church than the Grajalistas. In early 1936, Cárdenas gave clear signs that his administration would drop its anticlerical agenda. In Tamaulipas, he declared that his government had no intention of attacking religious beliefs; later he stated that the federal schools should end antireligious training and concentrate on social reform.[15] Increasingly he distinguished between "fanatics," who promoted ignorance, impeded national progress, and otherwise opposed his agenda, and Mexico's religious mainstream. Clearly he was courting Catholics at a difficult moment, as he prepared to expel Calles from the country. Yet he also backed his words with action. In March 1936 Cárdenas ordered the governors of Campeche, Colima, Guerrero, Nuevo León, Sinaloa, Sonora, and Oaxaca to cede certain churches to their Catholic occupiers. Catholic Chiapanecos took note. At Pijijiapan and other towns, Catholics reportedly opened churches before and after the April 1936 party plebiscite shouting, "Viva General Lázaro Cárdenas!"[16] On the day of the plebiscite, the municipal president in Teopisca claimed he was overwhelmed by five hundred people asking for the keys to the church. "We had no choice but to hand them over," wrote the postal clerk.[17] It is unclear whether Gutiérrez actually promised to reopen the churches if elected, but certainly many voters in Chiapas believed that he would.[18]

Cardenistas took a further step to produce a favorable outcome by turning to the Tzotzils and Tzeltals, who represented fully one-third of the state's population. Prior to 1936, "Chamulans" (probably Tzotzils) had been excluded from voting in PNR primaries in Chiapas on the grounds that they were "intellectually incapacitated."[19] Cardenistas overturned these laws, then placed immigration officer Erasto Urbina in charge of producing a favorable outcome. Urbina spoke fluent Tzotzil and Tzeltal and named bilingual ladinos to staff an intimidating highland "election committee" for the Cardenista candidate.[20]

Grajales, of course, did not stand by idly as the Cardenistas set their plan in motion. In early 1935 he centralized the education budgets of all the state's municipalities. He used the money to fund a reinvigorated state school system as a counterbalance against SEP radicalism. Grajales and his supporters also revived the rhetoric of Chiapanecan sovereignty, claiming with justification that Gutiérrez was an imposed outsider, the candidate of the meddlesome federation. When these methods were insufficient, Grajales resorted to less subtle means of persuasion.[21]

Federal Teachers and the April 1936 Plebiscite

In the hotly contested PNR gubernatorial plebiscite, federal teachers and other Cardenista allies campaigned actively on behalf of Efraín Gutiérrez. For this they incurred the wrath of Grajales and his allies. As told by federal inspector Francisco Ovilla, reporting from the predominantly indigenous town of Bochil (northwest of Las Casas), "We do not have the liberty of orienting the people in plazas or other public places, because interested politicians or the government—or both—will attack us. This is because we almost always threaten the interests of the bourgeoisie."[22]

The accounts of violence against teachers are numerous. In March, Joaquín Zebadúa, captain of the state police, pistol-whipped teacher Ciro Gómez for having allowed supporters of Gutiérrez to take shelter from the rain in his schoolhouse. SEP officials subsequently transferred Gómez to Ocosingo, where Zebadúa tracked him down and again beat him with the butt of his pistol. In the northern town of Sabanilla, teacher Gilberto Vega was attacked while he taught; one child was killed by stray gunfire. In Comitán, inspector Armando Guerra was nearly lynched by a mob. In the central highlands, most violence was the work of the alcoholeros' hired guns. Teachers Artemio Utrilla and Fidencio Flores were shot in Las Casas, and education inspector and PNR representative Manuel Castellanos was fired on and subjected to a separate attack at the hands of a stone-throwing mob.[23]

The situation after the April 5 plebiscite remained tense. Neither Samuel León nor Aquiles Cruz accepted Gutiérrez's victory, and Cal y Mayor was rumored to be preparing a coup against the state PNR, now controlled by Cardenistas. Several peasant and workers organizations in the state withdrew from the PNR and formed a party called the United Revolutionary Front against the Capitalist and Clerical Reaction. Dozens of federal teachers and their families were attacked for collaborating with the Cardenistas. The state government fired eight state teachers for joining an ideologically radical organization of mainly federal teachers, the Chiapas Teachers' Federation

(Federación Magisterial de Chiapas). Manuel Castellanos and others vowed to respond with violence unless local military commanders guaranteed their safety.[24] Finally, on midnight, April 13, the Chiapas Teachers' Federation called a strike to protest the violence, their miserable salaries, and conditions in the state that hindered the SEP's socialist education project.

The state's various feuding factions quickly chose sides. The conflict escalated when striking teachers forged alliances with nationally affiliated peasants and workers and several Cardenista organizations. State security forces retaliated, beating teachers and peasants of both sexes who guarded school buildings. On April 18, they violently broke up a joint demonstration of teachers and workers in the state capital.[25]

After one week, Cárdenas intervened on behalf of the teachers and the strike was lifted. Grajales's interim governor, José L. Burgete, issued a circular ordering municipal authorities to cooperate with teachers and offer their moral and material support to the socialist school. Authorities were also told to punish those who threatened teachers, to cooperate with the SEP's antialcohol campaign, and to observe federal labor laws. Five of the dismissed state teachers were reinstated. But the battle lines had been drawn. Grajales continued to threaten state and especially federal teachers, many of whom continued supporting Gutiérrez in the July 1936 election.[26]

After Grajales lost his battle against the federation in the April plebiscite, he extended his control over the state teachers by creating an official state teachers' union. Governors in Yucatán, Zacatecas, Durango, Tabasco, and other states used similar tactics as they attempted to head off SEP "socialism." In retrospect, the April 1936 strike in Chiapas can be seen as a prelude to future conflicts pitting the state government and its teachers against the more radical teachers and unions of the federation. Grajales's state teachers' union and schools would pay future dividends, helping the state government and the official National Union of Workers in Education (Sindicato Nacional de Trabajadores de la Educación, or SNTE) suppress the Chiapanecan teachers' democracy movement of 1977–1987.[27]

The same federal coalition that backed Gutiérrez in the plebiscite helped him prevail over Grajales's new candidate in the general election. One night after his victory, Gutiérrez survived an assassination attempt by twenty-five gunmen. Grajales then swore that he would never turn his office over to Gutiérrez. On September 22, 1936, Cárdenas acted on the threat and asked the national senate to depose Grajales. Two days later the federal army closed down and occupied state government offices in Tuxtla.[28] Amador Coutiño was named interim governor. He transferred power to Gutiérrez on December 15, 1936.

Needless to say, the political struggles of 1936 created an environment not at all conducive to "socialist education" or even basic classroom learning. As Francisco Ovilla wrote in February 1937, "Very little was done this past year due to the agitated situation created by the electoral struggle in all social circles, in the cities and the countryside." Attendance was weak and irregular, communities apathetic, and "the authorities did not cooperate at all, with few exceptions."[29]

The Struggle for the Highlands

By late September 1936, the Cardenistas had captured the state government in Tuxtla. In highland Chiapas, however, the battle for political supremacy was only beginning. The region still operated like a Porfirian *jefatura política*. Ciudad Las Casas exercised direct and indirect control over the nearby indigenous municipalities of Chamula, Zinacantán, Larráinzar, Zapotal, Huixtán, and Tenejapa. These municipalities were either governed by ladinos appointed by the municipal president of Las Casas or had lost their municipal rights altogether and were governed directly by Las Casas as agencias municipales. Given the realities of local and state politics in Chiapas, the reforms and social campaigns of the postrevolutionary federal government had had little effect in the highlands.

Nothing threatened Las Casas like Cardenismo. Fittingly, two months before the gubernatorial plebiscite, citizens of the highland town were asked to approve a plan to change the city's name from "Las Casas" (after the Dominican friar Bartolomé de Las Casas) to "Mazariegos," after the Spanish conquistador who founded the city, suppressed an Indian rebellion, and pacified the region.[30] The proposal was narrowly defeated, testimony to the resilience of the Catholic vote despite many years of state-directed anticlerical policy. Undaunted by their defeat, municipal president Evaristo Bonifaz and others vowed to continue their campaign, since "every day we are more convinced that it would be an act of justice, a demonstration of gratitude, an affirmation of tradition and an observance of history to give this city the official name of 'CIUDAD DE MAZARIEGOS.'"[31] The timing of this proposal is telling. During the two years that Bishop Las Casas spent in Chiapas (1545–1547), he fought local encomenderos and settlers who demanded excessive tribute and labor from Indians and routinely enslaved them in spite of a 1542 royal decree abolishing the practice.[32] While on the one hand the proposal to drop the name of the "defender of the Indians" was inspired by the Jacobin anticlericalism of the Grajales era, it was also intended as a clear challenge to the Cardenistas and their indigenista agenda. Furthermore, in a town where the ladino population had lived for generations in fear of a race war, the sense of order and domination evoked by Mazariegos clearly resonated in these uncertain times.

In order to blunt the Cardenista offensive, the coletos turned to Alberto Pineda, the general who twenty years earlier had led the defense of the highlands against a different type of federal intrusion—the top-down Carrancista "revolution" of 1914–1920. In 1923 he joined the de la Huerta revolt against Obregón and Calles. Now, in 1936, he would lead the struggle against a new type of federal imposition. Pineda took advantage of the fragility of the Cardenista transition just days after Grajales was thrown out of office. Aware that the state PNR would try to impose its own candidate in Las Casas's upcoming municipal elections, on September 30 Pineda, the local police, and armed supporters broke into the local offices of the PNR, disarmed general secretary Wistano Molina, and threw him in jail while Pineda registered himself as a candidate.[33] Sitting municipal president Evaristo Bonifaz covered for Pineda, claiming that Molina had been "detained and disarmed by the municipal police for creating a public scandal."[34] Interim governor Amador Coutiño made a hurried visit to Las Casas on October 3 and informed President Cárdenas that calm had been restored in the city, but he was unable to prevent Pineda's election on November 15. Because Las Casas controlled directly or indirectly all of the neighboring municipalities in its district and named the municipal presidents, secretaries, and agents, Pineda was perfectly situated to obstruct Cardenista indigenismo in the highlands.

More was at stake in this struggle than simple politics and economic interests. For highland coletos, their latest battle with their lowland rivals in Tuxtla Gutiérrez had taken the form of a religious crusade. Governors Raymundo Enríquez and Victórico Grajales and the state PNR had taken special pleasure in closing Las Casas's churches and driving its priests underground. Although candidate Gutiérrez had hinted that he would reopen churches and restore religious services, he moved cautiously after being elected, reflecting perhaps the continued ambiguity of federal anticlericalism in late 1936 and early 1937.

Pineda decided to make the religious issue his own shortly after taking office. On January 24, 1937, he allowed Bishop Gerardo Anaya to make a triumphant return to Ciudad Las Casas. The Cardenista coalition was outraged at the audacity of both the bishop and his protector. Five days later, at six o'clock in the morning, police from Tuxtla entered the bishop's house and marched him straight to police headquarters.[35] Shortly thereafter, Anaya went into involuntary exile again. When questioned later by state legislators about his role in Anaya's return, Pineda claimed that the bishop entered the city with such ostentation that he thought that Gutiérrez had allowed it or that it represented "a direct attack on the population given the antagonism that used to exist between [Las Casas] and Tuxtla Gutiérrez."[36] The legislators were not fooled. They also learned that Pineda had allowed several priests to officiate in private homes every day, further violating the state's Ley de Cultos (Religion Law). They reported these infractions to the state congress.

Over the next few months, tensions simmered between Governor Gutiérrez and the renegade municipal president. Pineda continued the age-old practice of using unremunerated native labor for public works projects in Las Casas and blocked agrarian reform in the municipality. He refused to cooperate with the federal anti-alcohol campaign. His agents treated federal teachers (especially women) with great hostility in the surrounding indigenous communities.[37] When state and federal indigenistas planned a May Day parade through Ciudad Las Casas, Pineda and his supporters broke it up with insults and violence. In Gutiérrez's words, Pineda also tried "to foment rivalries that no longer exist between the highlands and the lowlands." Some even rumored that Pineda was stashing arms in preparation for a major armed rebellion in the name of religious freedom.[38]

On July 9, 1937, Pineda undertook his most audacious move yet. With the support of the town's economic and social elite and its underground Catholic hierarchy, Pineda ordered his supporters—including members of the town council and the municipal police—to storm fifteen of the town's churches that had been closed years earlier by government decree. He handed over keys to eight of the churches and urged his mob to bust down the doors of the other seven. Several federal soldiers guarding the churches were wounded in the attacks. Days later he planned to storm the jail that held prisoners taken during the July 9 operation. He called off this attack only after the local commander of the federal army warned of dire consequences.[39]

Citing Pineda's "anti-revolutionary activities," "financial irregularities," and violations of the state's Ley de Cultos and Articles 5 and 130 of the federal constitution, Governor Gutiérrez asked the state Congress to withdraw official recognition of the entire town government of Ciudad Las Casas.[40] On July 20, 1937, the federal garrison forced Pineda out of office. One day later the state government named state legislator Isidro Rabasa to head a new town government that included Erasto Urbina as council member. Professor Manuel Castellanos was proposed as municipal secretary but withdrew his name from consideration, perhaps fearing that the struggle was not over. This new local government was applauded by the same Cardenista coalition that had brought Gutiérrez to power—the state PNR, certain peasant and workers' unions from the coast, state and federal indigenistas, and certain municipal presidents.[41] Highland municipalities were rather mute on the matter. Did they too sense that turbulent times lay ahead?

Cardenistas in Action

At long last, Cardenistas controlled the highlands. The next several months passed in a blur of indigenista activity. Gutiérrez's director of the Department of Indian Protection, Erasto Urbina, took steps to tighten the state's grip on the political and economic life of the highlands. His 1936 "election committee" members became secretaries in the most important indigenous municipalities, and he replaced traditional, monolingual scribes with bilingual, literate young native men willing to do his bidding. He staffed the highland police force with some of his indigenous *muchachos*, most of them still teenagers. Many of the men who controlled the highland municipalities after 1940, like Salvador López, Salvador Gómez Oso, Domingo Jiménez, Nicolás Espinosa, and Pascual Pathistán, got their starts as rural policemen under Urbina.[42]

Urbina then took steps to create an indigenous union under his control. With the help of muchachos Salvador Gómez Oso and Nicolás Espinosa, he dismantled the coffee pickers' union that had been run by the Attorney for Indigenous Communities. In its place he founded the Indigenous Workers' Union (STI). Gómez Oso became general secretary of the new union, which soon claimed nearly twenty-five thousand members. (Espinosa became an important agrarista.) In September 1937 the STI was incorporated into the CCOC, now firmly in the hands of Cardenistas. The STI was Urbina's greatest contribution to state indigenismo, as working conditions for its members improved immediately. But it prevented genuine indigenous participation in its collective bargaining agreements with planters and never once called a strike. The STI took over the department's placement offices in the highlands and soon busied itself sending workers down to Soconusco's plantations as requested.[43]

Las Casas's new municipal president, Isidro Rabasa, worked closely with Urbina. Rabasa canceled some of the outstanding debt owed by indigenous municipalities for the maintenance of their prisoners in Las Casas's jails. He also used his influence to challenge highland authorities who compelled Indians to work unremunerated on public works projects. The two men attempted to enforce sobriety laws in the highland villages and lent support to the state and federal plan to encourage villagers to live in densely populated towns so as to facilitate their education and "progress." When he learned that state teachers in Oxchuc were accepting bribes from ladino residents to keep Indians out of the town center, Rabasa wrote a terse letter to that town's municipal president, asking him to punish the teachers. By early 1938, Rabasa's indigenista sympathies were so well established that Indians residing in communities well beyond the administrative reach of Las Casas wrote him letters and solicited his support.[44]

Rabasa and Urbina never forgot that they were playing to a hostile audience in Las Casas. In late 1937 and early 1938 they tried to capitalize on shifts in federal policy to ingratiate themselves with coletos. Following the lead of Governor Gutiérrez, Rabasa and his allies reopened four local churches to worship during fall 1937. Next came the expropriation of the foreign-held oil fields in March 1938. The crowning moment of postrevolutionary Mexican nationalism, it gave Mexicans the opportunity to set aside old antagonisms and unite in the face of exploitative foreign oil companies. Even the Catholic Church urged parishioners to support the government.[45] Urbina took full advantage of the situation and coordinated the local campaign to raise funds to cancel the debt. Proving that nationalist politics can make strange bedfellows, not only did ejidatarios, workers, and students contribute generously, but so too did Mapache ex-governor Tiburcio Fernández Ruiz, who kicked in 907 pesos. Throughout the state, federal teachers urged their students to contribute whatever they could. Somehow, the terribly impoverished native municipalities of Chamula, Chenalhó, Larráinzar, and Tenejapa and the agrarian colonies "Las Ollas" and "Flores Magón" kicked in an astonishing 352 pesos.[46] Yet even a general relaxation of federal anticlericalism and a burst of patriotism could not save Rabasa's municipal government from its local enemies and, ironically, the federal courts.

The Coletos Strike Back

In a state famous for the defense of its autonomy from Mexico City, the highland region has been the most notorious. Yet coletos have been known to selectively resort to the Mexican federation in defense of their interests, as when they led the campaign to incorporate Chiapas in 1824. In 1938, coletos made another selective and successful appeal to the federation, this time of a legal nature.

Alberto Pineda did not simply fade away after being tossed from office. He crafted a viable legal case out of the matter, alleging that Gutiérrez and the state government had violated Article 115 of the constitution. This article, which guarantees the "free municipality," was a legacy of Carranza's crusade for municipal autonomy during the revolution. During the 1920s and 1930s it was routinely violated by presidents, governors, and municipal presidents like Pineda, among others. Now this former enemy of Carrancismo cynically invoked Carranza's principle. He first presented his case to a judge in one of the state's district courts, but to no avail. He then proceeded to the highest court of the land. On March 15, 1938, three days before Cárdenas made his move against foreign oil companies, the Supreme Court unanimously ruled that Gutiérrez and the state government of Chiapas had violated Article 115 when it withdrew official recognition of Pineda's municipal government. That the court ruling went in Pineda's favor is testimony to his stature and perhaps to Cárdenas's desire to promote domestic peace on the eve of a major international conflict with Great Britain and the United States.[47]

The court ordered the reconstitution of the Pineda government within twenty-four hours. Gutiérrez apparently waited until he knew that Pineda was in Mexico City, then proceeded on April 13 to order federal troops into Ciudad Las Casas and initiate the process. Of course, Pineda was nowhere to be found, and his allies in Ciudad Las Casas either hid or refused to participate in Gutiérrez's charade. As Gutiérrez disingenuously wrote, "The Ayuntamiento had apparently been abandoned, for reasons which I am unaware, [and] the state legislature believed it necessary to promulgate a decree withdrawing recognition from the municipal government."[48]

Pineda arrived by plane on April 22. A large crowd greeted him at the airport, including members of his former city council. When he and his supporters reached the municipal palace, they learned that Rabasa had been expecting them. In Pineda's words, "The door of the building, the windows and the roof were filled with people armed with pistols and rifles . . . and the so-called substitute municipal president Isidro Rabasa stood arms crossed on one of the balconies of the council chambers with a smile of satisfaction on his face."[49] Pineda retreated to his home to take stock of the situation. That night, according to the federal army commander and Gutiérrez's allies in Las Casas, Pineda and his followers tried to seize the municipal buildings by force. Municipal employees and a municipal police force that now took

Fig. 14. Erasto Urbina addresses a crowd of indigenous workers in Las Casas, circa 1938. Courtesy Archivo General de la Nación, México, DF.

orders from Tuxtla repelled the attack. Three of the policemen were wounded. Once again, federal troops were called in to patrol the streets of Las Casas. Pineda's supporters, for their part, claimed that they had been subjected to harassment, beatings, and arbitrary imprisonment and that Pineda's home had been fired upon first.[50]

Rabasa and his supporters held on to the municipality for another two and a half weeks, if barely. Locally, Cardenistas in Tuxtla and the coastal lowlands rallied behind him. Urbina also did his part. On May Day, with Governor Gutiérrez and the embattled Rabasa in attendance, Urbina led a parade of more than fifteen thousand predominantly indigenous peasants through the streets of Las Casas. According to partial eyewitnesses, the paraders carried signs reading "Victory with Cárdenas or death" and praised the president's patriotic stance on the oil issue. Marchers also "deliriously" manifested their support for Rabasa and shouted constant "vivas" in the name of Governor Gutiérrez. This impressive display represented the pinnacle of Urbina's indigenista career in Chiapas.[51]

Meanwhile, Pineda took his case to the state courts and demanded that the Supreme Court's decision be respected.[52] On May 8, Gutiérrez and the state government relented and sent agents to negotiate Pineda's return. Later that day Pineda once again took office and called an extraordinary session of his reconstituted municipal government. He crowed about his victory, invoking the long-standing grievances that coletos held against outsiders. He reminded his supporters that their local representative to the state congress, Salvador Coutiño, was a native of the lowland town of Chiapas de Corzo and had cooperated with Gutiérrez by sanctioning the "disappearance" of Las Casas's government on both occasions. Their representative to the federal congress, Dr. Rafael Pascacio Gamboa, was a Tuxtla native who also did nothing to defend Las Casas. Pineda then reached back into history to remind coletos of the town's dignified historical role as provincial capital and state capital until 1892, when Tuxtla native Emilio Rabasa moved the capital to Tuxtla. Since then, Las Casas had "suffered official contempt and despotism," making the current legal and moral victory all the more sweet. Pineda closed with a proposal that the town government pledge its gratitude and loyalty to the Supreme Court and to President Cárdenas.[53]

Immediately after the celebration came the counterrevolution. The state government withdrew its police force from Las Casas, and within days Cárdenas began receiving telegrams from peasants' organizations claiming Pineda's allies were attacking them.[54] Urbina claimed in his inimitable style that Pineda, with the support of the town's landowners and the capitalist bourgeoisie, was plotting a rebellion and causing "great alarm."[55] Pineda wisely sent Cárdenas a telegram of his own on May 11. In what was intended to be an olive branch, Pineda praised the president's patriotism and promised to collect money to pay for the recent oil expropriation.[56] Later that month, as Cárdenas dealt with his erstwhile ally Saturnino Cedillo in San Luis Potosí, he sent telegrams to both Gutiérrez and Pineda urging them to resolve their differences "with necessary serenity and within the terms of the law . . . so as to avoid all agitation."[57]

Meanwhile, Pineda continued to push his agenda. He spent the rest of May reversing previous indigenista legislation, tying up pending agrarian reform requests, and purging Urbina's muchachos from their positions of local authority. For example, the local police harassed and disarmed Nicolás Espinosa, who had served as municipal agent in nearby Ejido Pedernal and secretary of the Liga de Comunidades Agrarias in the state. Espinosa wrote Pineda two days later, calling him "no friend of the proletariat" and asserting that local ladinos had taken Pineda's return as a sign that they could "attack all my class brothers." He offered his resignation "because I am wholly agrarista and cannot enter into arrangements with the reaction."[58] The official paper of the CTM in Chiapas added that Pineda had unleashed "a wave of persecutions against the organized workers and the members of agrarian communities." The paper recognized that organized labor in Las Casas had not been strong enough to prevent Pineda's return but warned that "someday soon the workers' struggle will grow in Las Casas and the masses will impose their will by electing popular representatives born into the working people . . . and taking into their own hands the justice that was denied them by the Supreme Court of the Nation."[59]

In early June, Pineda decided to take action against Urbina himself, who not only directed the Department of Indigenous Social Action, Culture, and Protection, but had also become head of the municipal PNR and was running for a seat in the state legislature. Pineda first alleged that Urbina—under orders from Gutiérrez and in league with Rabasa—was organizing hostile protests and participating in a campaign of dirty tricks against him.[60] Later he may have ordered Urbina killed. On the night of June 11, as Urbina rode his horse across the central plaza in Las Casas, he was shot and wounded by municipal policemen who once again took orders from Pineda. Hired guns from Tabasco may have also been involved; Urbina attributed the attack to enganchadores, alcohol merchants, and Catholic fanatics.[61] The attack was followed by a roundup of Urbina's supporters, accused of public drunkenness and scandal. Two days later Urbina himself was seized in the federal garrison where he had taken refuge to care for his wound. Naturally, coletos told a different story. According to Ciro Coello, who briefly succeeded Pineda as municipal president, Urbina had led several gunmen in an attack on municipal policemen. Although Urbina was not above resorting to *pistoleros* to get his way, it is much more likely that Pinedistas simply attempted to eliminate the most powerful Cardenista in the region. Meanwhile, Urbina's muchachos used the event to further mythologize their leader. According to Urbina's own testimony, five thousand members of the STI marched through the streets of Las Casas to express their support for him.[62]

The attack on Urbina sealed Pineda's fate. Four days later, the national senate asked Pineda to come to Mexico City and granted the state government the right to name a local government as it saw fit. Las Casas was placed under martial law by federal forces under Urbina's command. Although coletos tried to replace Pineda with Coello, they were rebuffed two weeks later when Gutiérrez flew to Las Casas and forced Coello to resign.[63]

Three men would serve as municipal president of Ciudad Las Casas before the end of the year, none as bold as Rabasa. The third was Manuel Castellanos. But the champion of SEP indigenismo in the highlands appeared to function mainly as a figurehead. By February 1939 another teacher was acting as municipal president. Castellanos dedicated himself to school inspections and political organization in the Tzotzil highlands. Although he resumed the municipal presidency in October 1939, he was powerless to push a progressive agenda. At the national level, Cárdenas had assumed a more moderate stance and the SEP was in retreat. At the state level, indigenismo was firmly in the clutches of Erasto Urbina. In late 1938 his Department of Indian Protection announced that it would deal only with bilingual municipal presidents, thereby empowering its own agents and scribes at the expense of the highland communities' traditional monolingual elite.[64] Meanwhile, the Cardenista coalition was coming apart. Efraín Gutiérrez became a weak, absentee governor who spent an inordinate amount of time in Mexico City caring for his health and attending to personal matters. Over time, many of his staunch allies in the state abandoned him. In October 1938 Gutiérrez wrote to President Cárdenas defending himself from attacks made by his close associates, including local representatives Salvador Coutiño, Amet Cristiani, and—most surprising of all—Isidro Rabasa, whom Gutiérrez had just named to head Chiapas's branch of the reconstituted (and renamed) official party, the Party of the Mexican Revolution (PRM). According to Gutiérrez, these men were angry because he had blocked their nepotism and their quest for favors, monopoly rights, and tax concessions. Perhaps his former partners expected paybacks after two years of loyal struggle. In any case, the letter suggests the closing of the Cardenista "window of opportunity" less than two years after Cardenistas took control of state government.[65] The *familia chiapaneca* (and especially the highland elite) had managed to wear down Cardenismo. Confrontation had given way to accommodation.

Conclusion

Although scholars have disagreed over the exact nature and goals of Cardenismo, all agree that it took hold only where Cárdenas was able to build coalitions and mobilize local forces on the ground.[66] This strategy allowed him to assert his independence from Jefe Máximo Calles in June 1935. One year later, in Chiapas, coalition building permitted Cárdenas to purge the state PNR, impose his candidate in the PNR plebiscite, and win the general election. Federal teachers were among the most valuable members of his statewide coalition. But what worked for Cárdenas at the national and state levels could not work in each of the dozens of municipalities in Chiapas. In

Ciudad Las Casas, Alberto Pineda stepped into the breach before Efraín Gutiérrez even took office. From that point forward, the Cardenistas fought an uphill battle against those who had long profited from the exploitation of highland indigenous communities.

It was a battle that neither side won. Pineda made his comeback, to be sure, but he pressed his luck with a president who ran out of patience with coleto counterrevolution. On the other hand, the Cardenista coalition splintered shortly after pushing Pineda out of politics. It became demoralized and ineffective even before Cárdenas left office.

Although Cardenista indigenismo was designed to bind Indians to paternalistic *federal* institutions, their peculiar application in highland Chiapas tightened the grip of the *state* government and ladinos over indigenous populations. Urbina's highly touted STI became a paper tiger within months of its formation, and his labor placement agencies merely replicated the function once performed by the despised enganchadores (and often employed them). Cardenista agrarian reform in the highlands was also double-edged. Urbina and his mounted agents controlled the pace and nature of the reform by keeping radical federal agraristas out of the highlands. When he and his men hurriedly (and often violently) created dozens of ejidos in the late 1930s, conflicts typically ensued within and between communities over competing claims.[67] As they solicited more land into the 1940s and 1950s, all of the Tzotzil municipalities in the central highlands formed ejidal communities tied to the national government. More often than not, the land ended up in the hands of bilingual caciques who headed these communities, and the promise of more land, federal jobs, and concessions was enough to keep community leaders loyal to the state and federal governments.[68] What triumphed in Chiapas, then, were not the reforms and institutions of the revolution, but rather the individuals who accommodated themselves to the new political landscape and used federal reforms and institutions to their own advantage. And the outcome was bitterly ironic: during the most pro-Indian administration in the history of independent Mexico, Indians in Chiapas were incorporated into an extremely effective system of institutional domination that has only recently slackened its grip. ◆

Chapter Nine

SEP Socialism and Article 123 Schools on the Lowland Plantations

> It's sad to say, but it's true. The federal teachers in Chiapas are the victims of the landowners' tricks. Trusting in the support that we believe we have from the SEP, we demand compliance with the law, and these landowners laugh, because neither the Director of Federal Education [in Tuxtla Gutiérrez] nor the inspectors have the support needed to force compliance with the SEP's demands. With all due respect, Mr. Secretary, I ask that you indicate whether or not you will offer us the support that we need, [because if you cannot] I will stop bothering the Ministry unnecessarily. We are tired of fighting against the landowners . . . without the necessary support.
>
> —*From Rafael Ancheita Aparicio to Secretario de Educación Pública, México, D.F., July 26, 1938*

If the SEP's rural schools in highland Chiapas were in retreat by 1936, its Article 123 schools in the lowlands were doomed from the start. The Article 123 circuit throughout Mexico fell under the SEP's jurisdiction in January 1934, one month after PNR delegates initially endorsed socialist education at Querétaro. Efforts to force compliance with Article 123 therefore coincided with the radicalization of the SEP and its teachers. Rural elites who already resented the minimal costs associated with sustaining schools reacted viscerally to the federalized Article 123 schools, which they rightly considered to be hotbeds of social mobilization.

For the federal government, popular education represented the most direct means of intervening in the lives of workers on Chiapas's plantations. Teachers were expected to build a rural constituency *and* check the power of the state's planter and rancher class. Naturally, landowners resented the intrusion of a federal entity bent on scrutinizing labor practices, promoting federal unionization and agrarian reform, and monitoring the quality of life

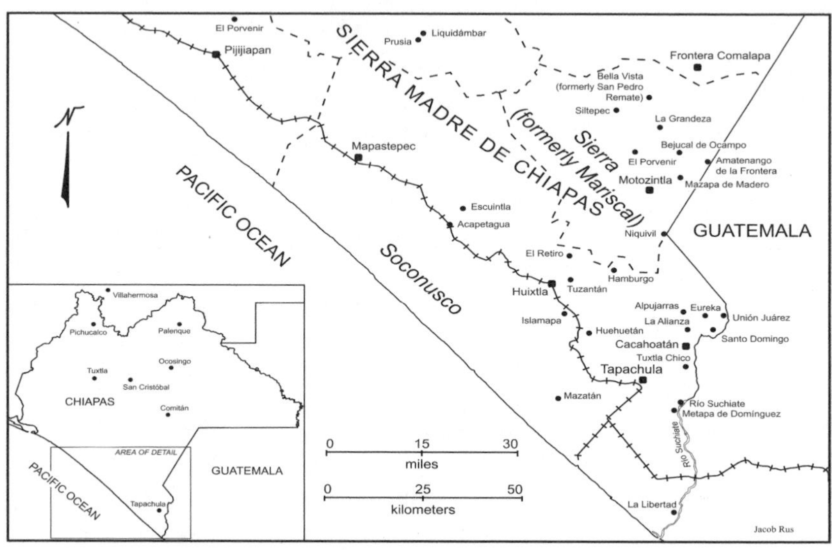

Map 4. Soconusco today.

on their fincas. Article 123 teachers were placed in an unenviable position, charged with implementing an ambitious social program and winning the sympathies of the workers while drawing a salary from hostile planters.

Most of the state's Article 123 schools were established on the coffee plantations of Soconusco, a highly politicized environment where state, federal, and independent organizers fought with planters for effective control of the labor force and the land.[1] The workforce was divided into permanent and seasonal workers and by ethnicity. Permanent workers, for the most part ladinos and ladinoized Indians, were known as *acasillados* because they resided on the fincas. During the harvest season, roughly August to December, seasonal Tzotzil and Tzeltal workers from the central highlands and Mam peasants from Mariscal came to outnumber the acasillados by a margin of three or four to one. Although Urbina and other indigenistas were most interested in improving the working conditions of seasonal indigenous laborers, Article 123 teachers concerned themselves almost exclusively with the smaller, more permanent workforce for three reasons. First of all, the SEP encouraged indigenous students to attend schools in their home villages in the highlands, where they spent most of the year. Second, children brought down to the fincas were put to work and did not attend school. Third, one of the Article 123 teachers' most important tasks was to prepare agrarian reform requests. However, federal law prohibited seasonal nonresident laborers from soliciting land reform, which neutralized the most powerful weapon in the Article 123 teacher's arsenal.

By the late 1930s the Article 123 schools in Chiapas were in full retreat, but not before teachers had unionized plantation workers and helped pave the way for the major Cardenista land expropriations that finally came to Chiapas in 1939 and 1940. When acasillados became ejidatarios, they generally felt a debt of gratitude to federal agrarian officials and the schoolteacher. The complicated legacy of the Article 123 schools in Chiapas's plantation zones is one of struggle, frustration, and futility on the one hand and gratitude and successful state building on the other. A few years later, when the SEP was in the position to rehabilitate the Article 123 program on sequestered German-owned plantations, it passed on the opportunity, in part because the consolidating Mexican state had outgrown the need for radical schools.

Corps and Curriculum

Federalization of the Article 123 schools was a mixed blessing, and not only because it coincided with SEP radicalism. Section VIII of Article 111 of the reformed Federal Labor Law (Ley Federal del Trabajo) stipulated that landowners establish schools whenever the number of students exceeded twenty and the distance to the nearest school was greater than three kilometers.[2] In states where educational cost sharing was a long-standing practice and where more demanding state legislation had created hundreds of schools in the 1920s and early 1930s, the reforms to the Federal Labor Law were disastrous. Coahuila, for example, required proprietors to build schools when the distance from the nearest population was more than one kilometer and the number of school-age children exceeded fourteen. The new federal legislation meant that fewer students officially appeared on school rosters, resulting in mass closures in states like Coahuila. Nationwide, the SEP inherited 1,421 privately funded schools from the states at the time of federalization, only to lose a good portion of these almost immediately because the reformed Federal Labor Law was so sympathetic to the private sector.[3]

In Chiapas, the January 1934 federalization brought far-reaching consequences. The SEP inherited nearly one hundred schools only to lose over two-thirds of them within the year. Furthermore, as told by Alberto Terán, Director of Article 123 Schools, many of the teachers inherited by the SEP in 1934 were hardly dedicated to bringing about a positive social transformation to the working masses. "To the contrary," he wrote, "many of these schools had become, in fact, centers of counterrevolutionary propaganda, constituting stubborn obstacles that impeded the development of the federal rural schools' social and educational programs."[4]

Following federalization, zone inspectors in Chiapas offered their teachers crash courses in socialist education. Teachers were also expected to comply with the SEP's standards for professional preparation. Not only were many Article 123 teachers reactionaries, but many had not attended school through the sixth grade, the minimum level of preparation for a federal teacher. The SEP soon granted an exception for Chiapas, where teachers who had completed at least the fourth grade were allowed to continue in their posts because further schooling was so hard to attain. Insisting on higher standards would have resulted in dozens of vacancies.[5]

Chiapas's Article 123 teachers were drawn mainly from the urban lower middle class. Many had aspired to teach in the federal urban schools but either lacked the preparation or the connections (or both) to work at that level. Instead, they took their often radical agendas to the Article 123 circuit, where they earned only 40 percent of the wage of skilled plantation workers. The most noteworthy demographic characteristic of the Article 123 teachers in Chiapas was their gender. The corps was overwhelmingly male, even more so than the decidedly male federal rural school corps. Of the 125 Article 123 teachers in Chiapas in December 1934, only 13 were women. This is in striking contrast to Coahuila, for example, where in December 1934 215 of 280 Article 123 teachers were women; or Aguascalientes, where all 24 were women; or Jalisco, where 205 of 230 teachers were women.[6] No other state with a significant number of teachers came anywhere near an absolute majority of male teachers. How can the gender imbalance in Chiapas be explained?

As we saw earlier, some zone inspectors expressed a preference for male teachers in light of the adverse, occasionally dangerous living and working conditions at rural schools. In some ways, conditions were even more precarious for teachers in the Article 123 circuit. Many had to subsist for months without pay while plantation owners did battle with the SEP. Some abandoned their posts or renounced the profession altogether. In mid-1935 Chiapas's head of federal education, Elpidio López, closed many schools because new teachers consistently refused appointments at fincas owned by notoriously obstructionist planters. Even when owners paid their teachers, work and living conditions were far from optimal. At the finca Prusia, for example, the new teacher was greeted with the news that he would sleep in the horse stables until the firm completed construction of the school; after construction was finished, he was told that the schoolroom would double as the Casa del Maestro. At Liquidámbar ownership forced the teacher to also work in the coffee groves.[7] At Islamapa, the roof of the tiny, mud-floor schoolhouse/teacher's house "became a colander every time it rained." The frustrated teacher, Rafael Ancheita Aparicio, complained that the SEP was incapable of creating a suitable environment for teaching and learning. "With true sorrow I have seen that neither the Department of Federal Education in this state nor the Ministry of Education [in Mexico City] can force compliance on the landowners," he wrote, "either due to a lack of attention on the part of the education authorities or the Ministry's inability to proceed against the landowners." Ancheita noted that "it is impossible to do one's job in the Article 123 schools in this region, especially at this school, where the landowner's kitchen is a palace compared to the schoolroom, and where even the stables are in better condition."[8]

Like their counterparts in the rural schools, Article 123 teachers asked SEP authorities for permission to arm themselves against local police, guardias blancas (private guards), and the owners themselves. Many, like Javier Rodulfo González, were bullied by armed thugs; at Finca Santa Julia, González received death threats from owner Joaquín García and his foreman, "who threatened the workers with obscenities and approached me with a pistol in one hand and a stick in the other, threatening to end my life if I did not cancel our independence day celebration."[9] Fearing for his life, González spent that night at the plantation's coffee mill. Threats, intimidation, financial difficulties, and miserable working and living conditions were all part of the job description for teachers in Chiapas's Article 123 schools. The SEP's entirely male leadership in the state may have decided that men were better able to endure the hardships associated with these schools.

SEP State Building in the Article 123 Circuit

Socialist education in Chiapas's Article 123 schools differed from that of the federal rural schools. In lowland Chiapas, where most of the Article 123 schools were, the Church had a negligible presence. Itinerant priests occasionally made the rounds on the plantations, but their influence over the transient workforce was never enough to concern Mexican state and nation builders. Consequently, the antireligious campaign was carried out discretely in the Article 123 schools. Not only was the clergy an innocuous threat, but teachers did not want to antagonize workers whom they were trying to organize.

Planters and other members of the rural elite represented a much greater threat to the Mexican state. Accustomed to tax breaks, federal labor-code exemptions, and sympathetic local government, they had never been subjected to federal control. But federal officials were also concerned that certain sectors of labor had shown signs of pursuing an independent, radical course. During the Depression years, from 1928 until 1931, the Communist Party of Soconusco (Partido Comunista del Soconusco) organized strikes and retained its independence despite attacks by the planters' guardias blancas and Callista paramilitary bands.[10] The lesson was not lost on state builders; independent labor worried the "revolutionary family" as much as it frightened the private sector that the regime ultimately sought to nurture.

Article 123 teachers, then, were ordered to devote their energies to the mobilizing, incorporating, and "liberating" dimensions of socialist education; little attention was paid to teaching the three Rs or implementing the SEP's anticlerical and anti-alcohol campaigns. In Daniel Vassallo's zone, teachers in 1935 "more than made up for their academic deficiency with their intense social labor." Vassallo and others ignored "that small sector of people who want their children to attend school only to learn how to read, write, and count."[11] After the March 1934 federal Agrarian Code provided peones acasillados with the right to solicit land reform, teachers in Soconusco busied themselves preparing the paperwork for their communities. When state and federal officials proved too sluggish, radicalized teachers often led land invasions and presented them with a fait accompli. According to Inspector P. Arturo Mota, teachers also "interven[ed] directly with the Agrarian Delegation to remedy some irregularities, because in the past, ejidatarios were granted only rocky, uncultivable lands."[12]

Article 123 teachers were also expected to organize workers into local branches of the federal CTM. This campaign also placed teachers in direct conflict with powerful local interests in Chiapas. Some teachers, like the combative Amadeo Tercero, were up to the task. In 1937, he attempted to form a Rural Workers Syndicate (Sindicato de Trabajadores del Campo) at finca El Retiro, where he taught. According to Tercero, the German plantation administrator—"a member of a Hitlerian organization"—threatened the unionizing workers and later attempted to derail the official registration process by offering bribes to the municipal agent and Tercero himself. The administrator later sent a fellow German employee to Tapachula to bribe and convince authorities to sabotage the union, then went to Tapachula personally for the same purpose. Upon returning to El Retiro, he declared himself disposed to spend thousands of pesos if necessary to break up the union. This battle Tercero won, at least temporarily; shortly after official recognition of the Sindicato, workers at El Retiro negotiated a collective bargaining agreement with management. But planters outmaneuvered the unions because the state's Conciliation and Arbitration Board only granted the right of unionization to those who had worked six consecutive months at the same plantation. As Tercero wrote to President Cárdenas, planters routinely fired workers before they had completed six continuous months, then rehired them on new contracts. In some cases, proprietors had unionizers thrown in jail. This happened in 1935 at El Porvenir, where the municipal president of Pijijiapan locked up teacher Gustavo J. Vázquez, alleging "scandalous activity" and armed assault.[13]

As social activists and enforcers of federal labor laws, Article 123 teachers—against all odds—left an impressive record in Chiapas. Statewide, in 1935 they shut down illegal tiendas de raya on thirty-four plantations, replacing them with consumer cooperatives. Ten teachers organized land invasions, and others called strikes to protest violations of the Federal Labor Law. In Mota's zone, during May and June 1935, twenty-eight communities solicited land reform under the leadership of their federal schoolteachers; nine schools conducted vaccination campaigns; nine created Socialist Mothers' Unions; eight conducted health campaigns against malaria; and teachers at numerous schools led reforestation campaigns, introduced new seeds, oversaw the repair of roads, organized sporting events, and encouraged men to wear pants and women Western-style skirts. Mota's Article 123 teachers also participated in a campaign to standardize and promote the use of national currency in Chiapas, where foreign coins and bills dating from the revolution were still in circulation. Lastly, Article 123 teachers in southern Chiapas helped non-Mexicans (usually Guatemalans) apply for citizenship or naturalization papers, a requirement if they were to be eligible for agrarian reform.[14]

While teachers actively developed the unionization and agrarian campaigns in Chiapas's Article 123 schools, other social campaigns were consciously overlooked. Even though the SEP's misunderstood sex education program was never fully implemented, teachers' surveys asked if the program had been applied anyway. For teacher Carlota Aguilar at finca El Carmen, sexual education was taught "by encouraging children to tell the truth and by creating habits of proper hygiene, thereby destroying all vestiges of an inferiority complex."[15] Humberto Castellanos López at finca El Pataste provided an identical answer on his annual work report. So did Mercedes Serrano de Palacios at finca Despoblado. The uniformity of this bizarre response suggests that SEP authorities in Tuxtla instructed teachers how to finesse the SEP's questionnaire. The importance of the state-building project in Soconusco may have been too great to risk on such a socially explosive campaign.

The SEP's nation-building campaign was also given little attention in Chiapas's Article 123 schools, surprising given Soconusco's remarkably diverse population and its proximity to neighboring Guatemala. Mestizos; various national and foreign Maya ethnicities; Chinese coolies and merchants; Guatemalan, Jamaican, and Polynesian debt peons; German bankers; and British, German, Japanese, Turkish, North American, and Spanish traders and planters called Soconusco home, at least temporarily. Tapachula, the commercial nerve center of the region, became known as "the tropical Babel."[16] Nevertheless, in Chiapas's Article 123 schools most teachers did little more than file citizenship papers, encourage residents to consume national (as opposed to Guatemalan) products, and apply federal immigration and labor laws against Guatemalan laborers. Inspectors made only occasional mention of "castellanization" campaigns among seasonal indigenous workers. Even civic holidays were celebrated without the fanfare seen in federal rural schools.[17]

Even if the SEP was relatively disinterested in fully developing its nation-building campaign in the Article 123 schools, several teachers turned their own individual sense of Mexican nationalism against foreign planters. Tercero, for example, wrote the Mexican Congress in 1937 proposing the complete nationalization and socialization of Soconusco's coffee plantations, since "the wealth of the region is in the hands of French, English, Spanish, Italian, and predominately German capital." Tercero's plan would exclude "assassins, thieves, evildoers, and foreigners" from becoming industrial partners. Tercero also enforced Mexican immigration and labor laws. "As revolutionary socialist teachers, we have the obligation of ensuring that the production centers in the coffee producing region, which are in predominately German hands, do not hire Guatemalan laborers in place of Mexicans," he wrote. Planters favored Guatemalans because they "do not know our labor laws, which means that they agree to work for low wages, they accept excessive work loads, they work more than eight hours daily, and they tolerate bad treatment from the plantation owner."[18]

That a handful of Germans openly sympathized with the Nazis in the mid- to late 1930s only added credibility to accusations of racist, brutal treatment of indigenous workers. Once planters of German descent were blamed for enganche, the tienda de raya, and indigenous alcoholism, the ladino elite that participated in and profited from these institutions were effectively let off the hook. The "black legend" of German coffee planters has stuck, even if some observers like Ernesto Parres in the 1920s noted that "the Indians who work on haciendas owned by Germans live in better conditions than those that work with our compatriots." He continued:

> This is shameful, but it must be said: the Mexican hacendados in this region are retrograde in everything related to improving the life of the Indian. They do not provide schools, and the Indians live in worse conditions than the animals.[19]

Chiapas's Article 123 teachers downplayed the SEP's cultural campaigns because state building was so important and so urgent on the plantations. Agrarian reform and unionization served multiple ends; both tended to pacify a restless rural population while simultaneously creating loyal clients indebted to the federal government. Agraristas were incorporated into the CCM and the CNC, while rural proletarians became members of the CTM and the CROM. The constitutional congress of the PRM cemented the labor and peasant blocs into the corporate structure of the new Mexican state in March 1938. So important was the teachers' state-building mission that they soft-pedaled inflammatory, vague, and counter-productive sexual education and defanaticization campaigns. In the cost-benefit analysis of state building, agrarianism and unionization offered the greatest potential returns.

The Planters Strike Back

As Article 123 teachers in lowland Chiapas monitored labor conditions, unionized workers, prepared land-reform requests, and taught basic skills in their classrooms, they engaged in the daily, contested process of state formation, and opposition was fiercest from those who felt their traditional power threatened. Most planters initially resisted the SEP on legal grounds. The entire federal project derived from one ambiguous sentence found in the revised Federal Labor Law requiring proprietors to "establish and sustain elementary schools on behalf of their workers' children when their land is situated more than three kilometers from population centers, and only when the number of school-aged children exceeds twenty."[20] Recalcitrant planters and their lawyers scrutinized this sentence and subjected every word to rigorous analysis. SEP attempts to force compliance through fines and threats of confiscation of property were frequently met with well-prepared legal appeals. Planters who filed appeals had their fines frozen; others simply used their influence or bought off local authorities to evade payment.

Most of the planters' appeals concerned terms that appeared in the legislation like *hijos de los trabajadores* (workers' children), *centro rural* (rural center), and *comunidad* (community). Immediately after federalization in January 1934, for example, several planters subjected the word *trabajador* (worker) to a particular, self-serving definition, claiming that their workers were not trabajadores but in fact *aparcereros* (sharecroppers) or *arrendatarios* (renters). Esther Castellanos C., owner of finca Chactajal in Ocosingo, insisted that "the sharecropper is a *business partner* (*socio*), not a *worker* (trabajador); consequently, Section XIII of Article 111 of the Federal Labor Law can in no way apply when sharecroppers are involved."[21] Director of Rural Education Rafael Ramírez disagreed, ruling that since sharecroppers and renters were still dependent proletarians, landowners were required to educate them under the terms of the Federal Labor Law.[22]

Typically, the SEP found itself paralyzed by legal appeals of this type and by the often contradictory decisions that resulted. When federalization of the schools took place in 1934, the SEP was still struggling to coalesce as an institution. Planters seized the opportunity to exploit internal divisions and sow confusion. As Alberto Terán, Director of Article 123 Schools, observed, "On many occasions the representatives of the Ministry of Education hand down resolutions favorable to proprietors only because they do not subject the matter to official legislation, either because they wish to favor the proprietors, or they are working outside of their jurisdiction, or simply because they do not consult with their superiors." The SEP's own Fiscal Court (Tribunal Fiscal) decided many legal appeals in favor of proprietors "based on faulty information supplied by Federal Treasury Offices or on information presented by the proprietors themselves."[23]

Landowners exploited other weaknesses in the federal legislation. By law, school rosters were valid only when signed by the proprietor or his/her designated representative. Planters and their lawyers quickly learned that refusal to sign a roster could freeze the SEP in its tracks. The SEP's Director of Federal Education in Chiapas, Raúl Isidro Burgos, repeatedly attempted to circumvent this obstructionist tactic by waiving the signature requirement. However, SEP lawyers in Mexico City rebuffed his proposals. Evidently, the SEP was interested in preserving the requirement as a check against overzealous teachers and inspectors who, motivated by ideology, pedagogical zeal, or financial incentives, might fudge attendance figures to establish more schools.

Preemptive or simulated land reform was another tactic employed by savvy landowners to forestall Article 123 schools. In the north-central municipality of Simojovel, several ranchers moved their resident debt peons to one extreme of their properties, which they subsequently donated to the peons in acts of apparent charity. By relieving themselves of their resident workers, ranchers also spared themselves a meddlesome Article 123 teacher and school while maintaining control of their dependent labor pool.[24] Simulated land reform, whereby proprietors "sold" tracts of land to family members, was another tactic used to preempt the SEP and agraristas, although the practice was not widespread in coastal Chiapas, where most properties tended to be relatively modest in size.

Planters also manipulated the three-kilometer distance requirement. Federal law required municipal authorities to make a declaration concerning the distance between schools, and wealthy planters like coffee magnate Enrique Braun easily convinced them to produce declarations sympathetic to their cause. In 1938, SEP officials in Mexico City resolved a distance dispute at Braun's finca El Achotal in Braun's favor. Their resolution overlooked the testimonies of SEP teachers, inspectors, and officials who had insisted that the distance to the nearest school exceeded three kilometers. The SEP's Mexico City authorities closed the school and attempted to bill the teacher's salary to Raúl Isidro Burgos, the state's Director of Federal Education![25] Burgos was incensed. Accusatory letters were fired back and forth, evidence of a growing rift between activist education officials in Tuxtla and an increasingly conservative SEP. By the time the dust settled, the school at El Achotal had been closed and Burgos had been replaced by conservative Jacinto Téllez.

International market conditions also conspired against the stability and viability of the Article 123 schools. Unfortunately for the SEP, its major Article 123 campaign coincided with some of the worst years for export agriculture in Soconusco. Coffee prices dipped in late 1936 and did not recover until World War II. Enrique Braun cited "the miserable condition of the global coffee market" in one of his requests to have a teacher's assistant dropped from his payroll.[26] Several planters did not survive the 1930s and were absorbed either by their larger neighbors or their banks (usually German or British firms). Even the wealthy and powerful Braun and Luttman families had to borrow large sums of money on onerous terms; all were subject to the oscillations of the international coffee market.[27] Conditions in Chiapas's coffee zone were so grim that in late 1936 the Tapachula branch of the Banco Nacional de México temporarily suspended operations.[28]

Although times were tough, taxes on the coffee industry still constituted between 60 and 80 percent of all state revenue from agriculture and roughly one-third of all state income in Chiapas. Naturally, the state government accommodated planters in hopes of reviving the sector. After the coffee harvests of 1936 and 1937, the state's Conciliation and Arbitration Board obligingly revised the terms of the planters' collective labor contracts so that they could dismiss workers. Herbert Luttman in 1937 was allowed to reduce the workday on his finca La Alianza to five hours a day, three days a week. But the board prohibited him from laying off more than 20 percent of his workforce of 182 peones acasillados.[29] Alejandro Córdoba in 1938 was allowed to reduce his workforce from 96 to 50, with preference going to Mexicans and unionized workers. Otto Pohlenz was allowed to give his acasillados part-time work, provided he gave them land to grow their own food. And the list goes on; in early 1938, the biggest names in Chiapanecan coffee were allowed to "readjust" their labor arrangements, including the Giesemann, Gephardt, Widmaier, and Spohn interests.[30]

As thousands of workers lost their jobs, the school-aged population on the plantations dropped precipitously. In spring 1938 a report from an education inspector in Soconusco underscored the effects of the crisis in coffee. "Overall conditions really must be taken into account," he wrote. "Most plantations can give their workers only three days of work per week, and many have abandoned production entirely, leaving thousands of workers in misery." This explains why "attendance figures at the majority of the Article 123 schools in this zone have dropped at an alarming rate."[31]

As a last resort, if appeals to the SEP, the judicial system, and the Conciliation and Arbitration Board had failed, planters could often corrupt local government institutions. P. Arturo Mota, inspector from Comitán, complained that the SEP's fines had little effect on the finqueros and never resulted in the prompt payment of teachers' salaries because "the Directors of the Public Credit Offices do not initiate legal action so as to avoid difficulties with the planters, many of whom are the Directors' friends or relatives." The Treasury office in Comitán in particular "never [took] measures to ensure that property owners pay their fines." In June 1935, this branch had failed to collect sixty-nine fines from just six finqueros.[32] The SEP was equally frustrated in Soconusco. In 1936, Chiapas's director of federal education, Rafael Bolio Yenro, wrote that the toothless fines of the SEP had the same effect on the finqueros "as the League of Nations' sanctions have against the dictator Mussolini."[33] When local forces were unified in their opposition to the SEP, the federal government appeared anything but a Leviathan.

Planter and Rancher Resistance: Some Case Studies

The weakness of the SEP was most brazenly exposed by the powerful; in 1941, Terán admitted as much, claiming that "many powerful firms are not complying with the law, while a great number of smaller plantations are."[34] The SEP's dealings with brothers Enrique and Fernando Braun highlight the tenacity of elite resistance. The sons of U.S. citizens of German descent, Enrique and Fernando Braun were born in Sonora during the early Porfirian years. When they arrived in Tapachula some twenty years later, they served as middlemen, trafficking in bread, then skins, and finally coffee. Enrique married into a landed family (Salas), while Fernando became jefe político of Soconusco. It was largely the efforts of Fernando that kept the Porfiriato alive in Soconusco as late as 1914. As a Porfirian and later as a Huertista, his savage extermination of Madero sympathizers in Soconusco earned him much notoriety. Using a deft combination of capital and political clout, both brothers accumulated many properties during the late Porfirian and revolutionary years.[35]

By the mid–1930s, Enrique Braun was Chiapas's most powerful planter. He owned the better part of the municipalities of Unión Juárez and Cacahoatán in Soconusco, and was supporting seven teachers and five schools on five of his properties. He employed over one thousand workers. His opposition to the schools stemmed not so much from the cost that they represented, which surely was minimal, as from the intrusion of radicalized teachers and SEP functionaries in his domains. According to the residents on his fincas El Achotal and San Rafael, his aim was to demonstrate "that for him there are no laws, nor is there anyone to enforce them."[36] The zone inspector for this region was the energetic Daniel Vassallo, who never failed to hold Braun's wealth and his German heritage against him. The two fought impassioned battles over several schools as Braun used every conceivable means to sink the SEP's project. His obstructionism followed predictable patterns. His first move was usually to deny that the property existed or claim that it was part of a larger plantation where a school had already been established. At a later date, Braun would argue that another school existed within three kilometers of the proposed site. Still later he would contest the SEP's school rosters in attempts to dismiss teachers and their assistants. Finally he would resort to a legal appeal through the court system.

One such battle was fought at his finca Santo Domingo. On August 17, 1934, Braun's bookkeeper reported that only twenty-six students attended school there, where one teacher and an assistant had been appointed. In order to maintain both instructors at the school, SEP guidelines specified that at least fifty students be in regular attendance. According to Vassallo, however, Braun's foreman had told all women living on the property that morning to report to the coffee mill, knowing that the women would instead send their children to work for them. Braun then sent his bookkeeper to the school to take attendance, where a relatively empty classroom illustrated that the assistant was unnecessary. Once this ruse failed, Braun asked the SEP to authorize a new school roster to determine the exact number of students on his plantations. When the SEP refused to grant his request, he claimed that the original school rosters were illegal, since he had not been present to authorize them.[37] When SEP authorities in Chiapas reminded him that one of his foremen had signed the roster, thereby legalizing it, Braun provided his own roster, which the SEP ignored.

Sensing that Vassallo and the state's Director of Federal Education Pérez would not budge, Braun took his grievance to a higher level. He later bragged to Vassallo that "he had been drinking with the Director of the SEP" in Mexico City, where all had been resolved in his favor. The assistant was suspended without pay. Braun's victory was short-lived, however. Vassallo and the SEP's state authorities soon confirmed that attendance figures at Santo Domingo merited two teachers. The assistant was quickly reinstated.[38]

The showdown at Santo Domingo was but one of many feuds that Braun had with Vassallo. On repeated occasions Braun wrote to the SEP requesting a new zone inspector, since "Vassallo constantly attacks my interests with false declarations" and "is incompetent, and his horrible spelling is proof of his extremely deficient mental capacities."[39] Vassallo responded that for Braun the only good inspector was a weak inspector. Despite being offered bribes from planters seeking exemption from supporting schools, Vassallo founded seventy-three Article 123 schools during the first eighteen months of federalization, more than any other inspector in Mexico. Both he and Director of Federal Education Pérez received national recognition and one thousand pesos for their efforts. Vassallo's colleague P. Arturo Mota took second place and was awarded five hundred pesos.[40] Vassallo founded so many schools that three new zones were created out of his original zone during the 1935 school year.

Abelardo Cristiani, a former Mapache general from Comitán, also manipulated the law, school rosters, and—eventually—government institutions. Cristiani claimed that the workers who lived on his coffee finca Santa Rita were not peones acasillados but in fact small-scale proprietors. Zone inspector P. Arturo Mota investigated the matter and found that the residents of Santa

Rita were in fact peones acasillados, obliging Cristiani to maintain a school. Cristiani retaliated by sending his workers with school-age children to two other plantations that he owned in order to bring Santa Rita's school-age population under twenty. He also prohibited his workers from selling food to the teacher and refused to build a school and pay the teacher's salary. When the SEP imposed fines, he resorted to legal appeal. Cristiani lost his case with the state's district judge, but "the Treasury Office in Comitán did not even take the first steps to collect" the imposed fines.[41]

Nor did the matter end here. Unsatisfied with the results of his hearing in Tuxtla, Cristiani appealed directly to the highest levels of the SEP, where a backroom deal was cut: dozens of SEP fines against him were dropped, and he was not required to cover the back salaries of Santa Rita's first teacher (who had abandoned the post after going months without pay). Later, in 1942, a partial expropriation of his hacienda brought the school-age population on Santa Rita to under twenty, and the school was closed.[42] Cristiani continued to manipulate the various dependencies of the SEP, the judiciary, and local bureaucracy in hopes of closing the Article 123 schools on his other properties. In 1944 a friend of his at the Civil Treasury Office in San Cristóbal was caught falsifying payment receipts showing that Cristiani had paid his teachers, when in fact he had not.[43]

Another case involving Cristiani again proved the SEP weak and perhaps corruptible at the highest levels. Cristiani resorted to a loose interpretation of the federal labor law, preemptive land reform, manipulated school rosters, and finally influence to avoid paying Ramiro Trujillo Fernández, the Article 123 teacher at his hacienda Juncaná. After the SEP levied eighteen fines against Cristiani and the Supreme Court rejected his legal appeal, it appeared that he would finally be forced to pay the fines and seventeen months' salary owed to Trujillo. However, Cristiani appealed to the SEP's very own Judicial Department, which canceled the fines and ruled that he had never been required to support the schools on his property. The incredulous director of federal education in Chiapas, Raúl Isidro Burgos, wrote Trujillo that "we have no idea why the Judicial Department came to such a determination." In November 1938, the Federal Treasury Office agreed to pay Trujillo for work he performed in 1935 and 1936 but later reneged. In 1940, Cristiani still owed 1,260 pesos each to Trujillo and to Guillermo Meza, another Article 123 teacher who shared Trujillo's fate on a different Cristiani plantation.[44]

Banana plantation owners in Chiapas also used hard economic times, threats, and legal appeals to undermine Article 123 schools on their properties.

Most plantations were in the northern district of Pichucalco, where navigable rivers linked production sites to the exporters of Villahermosa, Tabasco, and the markets of the southern United States. In 1937 a blight called *chamusco* (or "*mal de hoja*") ravaged the banana plantations of the region to such an extent that the Southern Banana Corporation of Villahermosa suspended operations. Subsequently, even growers unaffected by the disease had trouble getting their product to North American markets. Manuel Saury, owner of finca Santa Rosalía in Pichucalco, used this situation and an apparent decrease in student population to appeal to the SEP for closure of the school on his plantation. "Unfortunately, Saury is resorting to every means possible to dislodge workers with families from Santa Rosalía . . . and send them to other plantations where schools were closed last year," wrote the Article 123 teacher there.[45] His request for school closure denied, Saury challenged the SEP's ruling in a district court and lost. He later stopped paying teacher Nestor Gutiérrez, claiming that he had not shown up for work. He finally took his legal appeal to the nation's Supreme Court but lost when SEP authorities produced telegrams proving, among other things, that Saury had threatened Gutiérrez's life. At the cost of considerable time and effort, the SEP scored a rare unqualified victory in the Saury case, and the Article 123 school at Santa Rosalía limped along well into the 1940s. One of Saury's fellow planters, Manuel Armendariz, fared better when he demonstrated to the SEP that the state's Conciliation and Arbitration Board had canceled his collective contract with his workers due to the chamusco in 1940.[46] The Article 123 school on his aptly named banana plantation Despoblado was closed after a school census turned up fewer than twenty school-age children.

The strength and determination of the Chiapanecan plantocracy was such in the middle 1930s that SEP officials in Chiapas had trouble finding lawyers to represent them in their legal cases. During 1934 and 1935 nearly a dozen legal appeals were heard in the district court in Tuxtla and the Supreme Court in Mexico City. According to Septimio Pérez Palacios, who directed the SEP in Chiapas when the Article 123 schools were federalized, "No lawyer in Tuxtla would agree to represent me even though many were friends of mine because they [represented] the coffee magnates and ranchers."[47] Many planters' appeals were locked up in the courts for years; in late 1941, fines imposed in 1934 and 1935 were still pending at various stages in the Mexican judicial system.[48] This lengthy process suited planters, since they were usually exempted from supporting schools while their cases were being heard.

In the final analysis, did planter opposition to the Article 123 schools pay off? After all, the expenses associated with sustaining a school and teacher were minimal. Article 123 teachers were the worst paid among federal teachers. Proprietors rarely constructed new schools or new houses for the teachers; usually an old barn or storage shed was converted for the purpose. Furthermore, those who most resisted the SEP were the wealthiest planters, for whom the schools represented a negligible expense. In all likelihood, the costs of fighting the SEP exceeded those of simply cooperating with and sustaining the schools.

Nevertheless, resistance to the Article 123 program was both widespread and adamant. In a report to SEP authorities in Mexico City, Septimio Pérez Palacios painted a grim picture of these schools at their strongest moment—that is, in 1935. "During January a good number of Article 123 schools did not operate," he wrote. Most teachers had to subsist from four to six months without pay while the SEP imposed fines on the planters and took appropriate legal action. "The fines and legal activity do not guarantee one single cent for the teacher, because our legislators overlooked the matter," Pérez wrote. "It is thus no small matter to find heroic people willing to confront hunger and possible assassination in terribly isolated and inhospitable locales."[49] Three years later, in April 1938, 24 of a total of 113 Article 123 schools were vacant because teachers refused the posts, suggesting the limits to SEP state building in Soconusco.[50]

Ironically, the Article 123 program was being shelved just as the Cárdenas administration was beginning to flex its muscles in Soconusco. The perhaps inevitable retreat of popular education in Chiapas in the late 1930s corresponded almost simultaneously with the federal government's most dramatic moves against Soconusco's plantocracy. Article 123 teachers played a critical role in preparing the groundwork for this shift. Viewed in this light, their struggles were not in vain.

The Eclipse of German Influence in Soconusco

Until spring 1939, planters and ranchers in Chiapas had been remarkably adept at rejecting the intrusions and innovations of central government in Mexico City. Through various violent and nonviolent means, they had thwarted or undermined Porfirian taxation, Carrancista labor legislation, the Federal labor Law in 1931, and the Article 123 schools. They had also been able to control the pace of land reform. Such was the strength of the state's ranchers and planters that Cárdenas did not dare attempt a major land distribution until late in his sexenio, when the land reform movement was slowing down in other parts of the country. To have pushed major reform earlier would have invited open confrontation at a time when the federal government was still in a position of relative weakness.

Cardenista land reform in Chiapas coincided with shifting foreign and domestic winds that made ethnic German planters suddenly vulnerable. Early in the sexenio, broad sectors of the Mexican population sympathized with European fascism, including many planters and merchants in Chiapas with German, Italian, and Spanish ties. Tapachula's Club Alemán (German Club), which featured a Nazi flag and an enormous portrait of Hitler, threw rowdy parties every April 20 to commemorate the Führer's birthday. These parties, which included eulogies to Hitler and Nazism, were celebrated openly and received local press coverage.[51] Elsewhere in Mexico, right-wing groups like the nationalist, anti-Semitic, anti-communist Camisas Doradas (Gold Shirts), the Sinarquistas, and the Spanish Falange became so active that Cárdenas felt compelled to relocate the ideological struggle to the battlefields of the Spanish Civil War. In March 1937 Mexico became the only Western country to sell arms to the Spanish Republic.[52]

As the Cárdenas administration and its allies in labor, education, and the political left attempted to mobilize support for the Spanish Republic and a more general "popular front" against fascism, local conditions also conspired against ethnic Germans. In Chiapas, the deplorable state of the coffee industry forced many Mexican planters to sink into debt with German creditors. In May 1938, Mexico City's colony of Chiapanecos warned that Soconusco was "controlled by German and Spanish latifundistas and capitalists, by Nazis and the Spanish Falange, who either own the land directly or loan money at usurious rates."[53] The "black legend" of ethnic German labor practices took hold at this time, singling out Germans for the worst abuses of indigenous debt peonage. Nationalism, envy, and charges of unfair and exclusionary business practices had many Chiapaneco politicians calling for the internment of Germans even before Mexico entered World War II.[54]

Land reform finally came to Soconusco in March 1939. It would be the most dramatic moment in agrarismo's otherwise dark history in Chiapas. Cárdenas's friend Governor Efraín Gutiérrez chose a reactionary and suddenly very vulnerable Mexican of German descent as his principal target: Enrique Braun. Cardenistas correctly identified Braun with the state's Callista faction and with the murders of several strikers and union leaders on his plantations. According to García de León, Braun also afforded the governor with the opportunity to extract a lucrative bribe; for Gutiérrez, complete immunity from expropriation had a 300,000-peso price tag. Braun could not pay the hefty sum, since world coffee prices had hit their lowest point in decades. An embittered Braun reportedly replied, "Screw yourself 300,000 times and give the land to the Indians."[55]

Nearly half of the 7,988 hectares expropriated in March came from Braun's property; lands from Eureka, Santo Domingo, Alpujarras, La Central, Tonintaná, Buenavista, Highlands, Sta. Teresa Guarumo, San Rafael, Cerro del Carmen, La Trinidad, and El Desengaño were used to create six ejidos.[56] By law, Braun was left with at least 300 hectares of land on each of his properties. Knowing that he had been singled out, he complained bitterly to Cárdenas that "all of my properties, reflecting forty years of hard work, were affected, while most plantations in Soconusco went untouched."[57] What made this expropriation exceptional was not the quantity of land, which was quite modest, but the fact that Braun's plantations were among the most productive in Mexico. The expropriation was also controversial because most of the beneficiaries of the reform were recently naturalized Guatemalans.[58] Finally, the expropriation was rich in symbolic meaning: it suggested the dawn of a new age, when powerful ranchers and planters in Chiapas would be forced to occasionally submit to federal control.

In time, Braun turned his "white" unions on the ejidatarios. He and other planters also attempted to bankrupt the fledgling ejidos by refusing to process or purchase ejido coffee for export during the 1939–1940 harvest. After ejidatarios retaliated by seizing a few processing plants, Governor Gutiérrez forced planters to process the crop and found a North American buyer.[59] Later in 1940, Gutiérrez and President Cárdenas would seize the moment and expropriate land from most remaining large coffee plantations in Soconusco and Mariscal.

Ironically, agrarian reform—which Article 123 teachers actively facilitated—often forced the closure of Article 123 schools because it reduced the resident population on rural properties. In Braun's case the SEP closed down the Article 123 schools at La Florida, Alpujarras, Buenavista, La Trinidad, and Eureka and opened federal rural schools on each of the new ejidos.[60] On a national level, agrarian reform was the culprit in nearly four out of every five Article 123 school closures between 1934 and 1941 (1,063 of 1,368). In Chiapas, where Article 123 schools had been under serious attack before the 1939 and 1940 expropriations, only 20 percent of the state's remaining schools were closed as a result of the reform. However, the mere possibility of expropriation had the effect of discouraging even well-intentioned planters from building or repairing schools on their properties.[61]

Shortly after the expropriations of 1939–1940 had confirmed the new strength of central government in Chiapas, international events dealt the ethnic German planter class another serious blow. World War II had the effect of turning the German plantocracy into pariahs practically overnight. A formerly improbable alliance between the Mexican government and the United States put the German plantations at the mercy of the U.S. war effort and placed many of their ethnic German owners in an internment camp in Perote, Veracruz.

Despite the noisy saber-rattling of U.S. oil executives, U.S.-Mexican relations were on the mend very shortly after the March 1938 oil expropriation. In June 1940, following the stunning victories of the German blitzkrieg in Europe, representatives from the United States and Mexico set aside their differences and discussed a possible military alliance. Cárdenas's successor, Manuel Ávila Camacho (1940–1946), also welcomed the opportunity to enter into an industrial partnership with the United States and used the new relationship as a pretext for abandoning Cardenista populism. Seventeen days before the Japanese attack on Pearl Harbor, representatives from the two countries renegotiated Mexico's outstanding debts (some dating from the Porfiriato), settled personal-property claims, signed a reciprocal trade agreement, and hammered out a settlement to the troublesome petroleum conflict, all under terms highly favorable to Mexico. Before either country entered the war, then, Mexico had committed itself to supporting the U.S. war effort, even if this was not popular among many sectors of the Mexican population.[62]

Mexico officially entered the war on May 25, 1942, after German submarines torpedoed two Mexican oil tankers in the Gulf of Mexico. In June a presidential decree established the Junta Intersecretarial Relativa a Propiedades y Negocios del Enemigo (Board of Enemy Properties and Businesses) to determine which German and Japanese businesses would be temporarily sequestered by the government. A Junta de Administración y Vigilancia de la Propiedad Extranjera (Board of Administration and Supervision of Foreign Property) managed these businesses and was staffed by known enemies of agrarismo, such as Luis Cabrera.[63] The sequestration lasted until 1946, and 80 percent of the businesses placed under government custody were German.

The true beneficiaries of the temporary interventions were the North Americans. The embassy in Mexico City recommended which ethnic German businesses should be placed in government custody. The Junta

Intersecretarial acted on virtually every U.S. recommendation, even when the suspected fifth columnists were naturalized Mexicans or Mexicans by birth. Businesses in strategic sectors like the chemical and pharmaceutical industries were confiscated regardless of the proprietor's sympathies with the Nazi regime. Others were targeted if they directly competed with North American interests. In 1942, sixty-seven of the seventy-five coffee plantations in ethnic German hands in Chiapas were sequestered, including La Alianza, La Esperanza, Hamburgo, Liquidámbar, Prusia, El Retiro, and Santa Rita. Two banana plantations owned by ethnic Germans and a handful of merchant and trading houses in Tapachula and Tuxtla were also seized.[64]

When the order came for the Germans to leave their plantations behind, few Chiapanecos protested. Many seized the opportunity to buy German and Dutch radios, electronic devices, dishes, oil lamps, and furniture at rock-bottom prices. Most of the biggest names in Chiapanecan coffee were unceremoniously sent packing to Mexico City or the internment camp at Perote, Veracruz, including the Kahles, the Giesemanns, the Pohlenzes, and the Hammers.[65]

During the four years that the federal government ran the plantations through the Fideicomisos Cafetaleros de Tapachula (Coffee Fiduciary of Tapachula), the SEP had the opportunity to breathe new life into the beleaguered Article 123 circuit in Chiapas. Instead, it let existing Article 123 schools wither on the vine as the fiduciary ran the plantations into the ground. As told by Benjamin, "Officials of the fiduciary were neither good businessmen nor social reformers." Corruption was rampant and "despite the increase in coffee prices during the war, production in impounded plantations dropped by more than half during the sequestration."[66] The fiduciary's administrators also violated federal labor laws by suppressing all strikes and hiring Guatemalans because they worked for less than the minimum wage; the difference between the Guatemalans' salaries and the fictitious Mexicans' salaries was likely pocketed by administrators.[67] Naturally, the educational provisions of Article 123 went ignored. The SEP routinely failed to fill vacancies and established only a handful of schools during the years when the fiduciary ran the plantations. Clearly the SEP and the federal government were more interested in enforcing federal labor law when a largely foreign planter class was picking up the tab. Meanwhile, as the following chapter will detail, workers continued to insist on their right to schooling even though they realized that the days of educational populism were but distant memories.

Article 123 Schools: The Steady Downward Slide

[The eventual return of coffee plantations to their ethnic German owners] represented the end of major land reform in Soconusco; it also presaged the end of the Article 123 experiment in Chiapas. By the mid-1940s the schools had arguably outlived their usefulness. After the Mexican state institutionalized its corporate structure in 1938, the central government's state-building needs became less urgent. Demographic change and shifting labor regimes also boded ill for the schools: a growing population, increased Guatemalan migration, and the conversion of some coffee plantations into ranch land translated into a growing day-wage labor pool and a diminished need for resident workers. The owner of El Vergel in Motozintla spoke for most planters when he said that he preferred "the single day-laborer, who arrives at the plantation only when needed" as opposed to the resident worker, "who lived on the plantation with his family, which created a large population of school-aged children and implied an elevated expense for [me]."[68]

It is well known that following the dramatic expropriation of foreign-held oil fields in March 1938, the Cárdenas administration pursued a more moderate course. Historians have debated for decades whether economic crisis and intense domestic and international opposition forced this reorientation or whether it simply reflected the president's conspiratorial state-building aims.[69] In 1938 Cárdenas suspended the much-celebrated Cultural Missions; according to the SEP's 1938–1939 *Memoria*, they had become "revolutionary shock brigades," inconvenient anachronisms at a time when the Cardenista state had moved from mobilization to consolidation.[70] Official speeches and articles in *El Maestro Rural* contained fewer references to class conflict and anticlericalism. Beginning in 1938, the SEP began withdrawing some of its most radical textbooks. One year later Jacinto Téllez, the new Director of Federal Education in Chiapas, initiated a demobilization campaign that targeted Amadeo Tercero and other activist Article 123 teachers. Téllez immediately began transferring radical teachers to other communities in Chiapas or exiled them to other, more settled states. After the Adolfo Giesemann company lobbied an accommodating SEP, Tercero received his orders to transfer as punishment for having attended meetings of peasants and coffee-pickers. Even the Tapachula branch of the state's official, tame teachers' union, the STERM (Sindicato de Trabajadores de la Enseñanza de la República), declared a strike to protest his and other transfers. In its strike manifesto, the teachers demanded that the SEP conduct full investigations into cases like Tercero's before taking planter complaints at face value. Tercero was allowed to finish the year at El Retiro, but by the next year he had been transferred to another school.[71]

The defensive, angry tone of the strike manifesto suggests that teachers in Tapachula knew by early 1939 that the SEP's real commitment to socialist education was over. Other teachers seemed bewildered by the shifting ideological positions of the SEP and the unions. Rubén Aguilar Pola, Article 123 teacher at finca Realidad, wrote President Cárdenas in May 1939 with a simple question. "Illustrious leader," he began, "with all due respect, what is the role of the rural teacher at this time? Should we follow the direction of the STERM and the Director of Federal Education in Chiapas, or do we continue agitating on behalf of the masses?"[72]

In time, the conservative reorientation of the SEP and the federal government became demoralizing for activist teachers and inspectors. Existing Article 123 schools slipped into disuse and new schools were not established, especially when the fiduciary began running most of Soconusco's coffee plantations. In 1943, inspector Francisco Ovilla complained to his superiors in Mexico City that "teachers have not been named to fill vacant positions in my zone. This is especially unpardonable in the case of the Article 123 schools." Ovilla charged that SEP bureaucrats could not find the time to fill a few vacancies "because they spend all their time talking, knitting, and even reading novels during working hours."[73]

By 1945, two-thirds of the schools operating in 1938 were closed; planter opposition, the growing conservatism of the SEP and the Mexican state in general, and the effect of the fiduciary in particular took their toll. Another 15 percent of the schools operating in 1938 were closed in the 1950s; another 8 percent closed in the 1960s, and the remaining 10 percent closed in the 1970s.[74]

Conclusion

In the 1930s, the SEP's state-building project in zones of export agriculture was undermined not by the marginalized and the dispossessed, but by a resourceful planter and rancher class. While rural proletarians supported the schools and their teachers, Chiapas's rural elite hammered away at the program with a combination of legal appeals, influence, bribery, and intimidation; such were the "weapons of the strong." In the words of Alan Knight, these were "arguably, the most effective deterrents to the full implementation of the Cardenista project, and the surest guarantee that it would fail." While on the one hand Sinarquistas, certain caciques, and a handful of business leaders attempted to confront Cardenista radicalism head-on, a much larger and ultimately more successful coalition "recognized that the revolutionary state was here to stay, that it made more sense to connive intelligently at its deradicalisation than to strive quixotically for its destruction."[75] By using the "weapons of the strong," elite Chiapanecos immediately put the Article 123 program on the defensive until the SEP adopted an orientation more to their liking.

Ironically, while finqueros enjoyed considerable success in undermining the Article 123 program, the Mexican state grew stronger on other fronts in Chiapas during the Cardenista years. In other words, the planter and rancher class won the battle with the SEP but seemed to lose the war. Although the majority of Article 123 schools had been closed down by the early 1940s, teachers at these schools had still managed to initiate land-reform requests, incorporate workers and peasants into official unions, and perform various functions as labor inspectors, immigration officials, and agents of an emerging nation-state. Thanks in part to the work of Article 123 teachers, by 1939 conditions in Chiapas were finally ripe for land reform, and Governor Gutiérrez took the symbolic step of targeting the formerly untouchable Enrique Braun. After most German coffee plantations were sequestered in 1942, the federal government and the SEP passed on the opportunity to carry out more land reform and revive the Article 123 program. Although the Ávila Camacho government certainly lacked the will to pursue such a course, the federal government had outgrown its need for a popular, mobilizing educational program. Resistance on the part of Chiapas's ranchers and planters certainly precipitated the downfall of the Article 123 program, but its ultimate demise came at the behest of the SEP itself. ◆

Part Four

The COLLAPSE of EDUCATIONAL POPULISM after 1940

Chapter Ten

The 1940s

"Thermidor" in Chiapas

> If we continue without a school, our children and all of today's youth will remain in a lamentable state as in the times when the Governments did not concern themselves with education and these young people will be at the mercy of vicious exploiters. It seems that we are condemned to continue suffering this state of backwardness and ignorance; it seems as if we never had the right to elevate ourselves through the school which represents progress.
>
> —*From Municipal Agent Abelardo Morales and forty-eight signers to Director of Federal Education Jacinto E. Téllez in Tuxtla Gutiérrez, November 6, 1943*

The history of state and nation building through education in Chiapas is a study in contrasts after 1940. Without question, the trend toward demobilization—so clearly seen late in the Cárdenas period—was accelerated. Shortly after President Manuel Ávila Camacho took office, it was reported that the SEP had lost forty teaching positions in Chiapas, and two inspector's posts (in Pichucalco and Simojovel) were vacant.[1] In 1941, schools were closed in dozens more communities due to budget cuts. When the SEP closed schools due to epidemics like onchocerciasis, there was often no money to rehire the teacher and reopen the school once the epidemic had passed. Ideologically, Marxist notions that had been in vogue in the mid-1930s were now dismissed as "*exóticas*." Inspectors who continued to politicize, unionize, and agitate for agrarian reform were told to desist. Municipal governments also passed laws meant to tame activist teachers.[2] The slogan "For a classless society," so frequently used in the correspondence of official peasant, worker, and teacher unions in the 1930s, took on a new meaning. No longer was the goal a classless society of proletarians; now the objective was national unity, where class and ethnic distinctions and divisions were to be glossed over in the interests of national security and economic modernization. This implied a dramatic reshaping of SEP indigenismo, which had evolved toward a more plural vision late in the Cárdenas period.

There was, however, a silver lining. The early 1940s offer evidence that the SEP's efforts in the 1930s had not been in vain. Socialist education had won the loyalties of most mestizos. Grassroots support for SEP teachers and schools was greatest in Soconusco, where rural proletarians came to regard federal teachers as their natural allies against capitalists in the export sector. Ironically, several communities that had been indifferent, even hostile to federal schooling around 1930 were among those most adamantly defending or requesting schools one decade later.[3]

Penury and Purges: An Overview

In the early 1940s, education's share of the federal budget shrank as rural priorities took a back seat to urban, industrializing Mexico. While education represented 13.6 percent of the federal budget in 1937 and 13 percent in 1938, its slice of the federal pie shrank to 11.2 percent in 1941 and only 8.8 percent in 1943.[4] Inspectors and teachers were quick to feel the impact. Inspector José Inés Estrada, based in Comitán, complained in 1941 that the SEP was unable to provide his schools with basic materials. At the start of the school year his teachers had requested books, notebooks, pencils, erasers, ink, and other supplies for the more than 4,800 enrolled students. The SEP in Tuxtla sent a mere handful of books and enough notebooks and pencils for just 50 students. Notably frustrated, Estrada took matters into his own hands. He took control of his schools' ejidal plots out of the hands of the ejidal bosses and turned them over to the schools' education committees. Estrada hoped that the fruits and vegetables grown on the plots would help pay for school materials "since I cannot hope for economic assistance from the Federation, the state government, the local governments or even the parents."[5]

In 1941 the SEP in Mexico City sent one of its general inspectors to Chiapas. The inspector, Salvador Caballero Méndez, called particular attention to the appalling conditions under which federal teachers and students labored in the state. At the model school ("Escuela Tipo") in Tuxtla, ideally a paragon of SEP pedagogy, Caballero Méndez found demoralized, almost abusive teachers and an unsatisfactory infrastructure. The school's primitive outhouses gave off noxious, unhealthy odors that afflicted two classrooms and the small-industries workshop. The rural schools he visited utterly lacked notebooks, and two and sometimes three students were expected to share books. To make matters worse, these books often did not correspond to the students' scholastic level. Despite the SEP's strategy to promote sports as an antidote to alcoholism, Caballero Méndez wrote that all schools lacked sporting equipment.

The inspector then unexpectedly praised the new state governor, ex-Cardenista Rafael Pascacio Gamboa, for his commitment to state education. In fact, Caballero Méndez found that the state's schools were much more attractive, better provisioned, and better attended than those of the SEP.[6] The rollback in federal education had already taken its toll. Even though Chiapas's state government willfully abandoned rural primary education in the 1920s and early 1930s, it had now seized the initiative from the SEP in much of the state. Governor Grajales had been the first to fully appreciate the advantages of using docile state teachers as a hedge against radical federal teachers. His successors continued to invest in state education; by 1944, the state controlled 446 schools, up from just 90 in 1927. Although the SEP still administered more schools (584) and held a numerical advantage of almost two to one in the countryside (489 to 250), the presence of the state's schools and its teachers could not be ignored.[7]

When he was not lobbying the SEP for healthy budgets, Jacinto Téllez, the SEP's director of federal education in Chiapas since 1939, continued to suffocate radical pedagogy. Many inspectors now omitted mention of "social action" in their bimonthly reports. Others moderated their activities and their prose in official correspondence. Reforms to the agrarian code made it more difficult to expropriate land, and teachers lost their pivotal role in filing agrarian reform requests as the process increasingly became the domain of peasant unions and officials from the agrarian department. As a safe alternative to provocative agrarian and labor advocacy, most teachers concentrated on hygiene campaigns. In P. Arturo Mota's zone around Ocozocuautla (west of Tuxtla Gutiérrez), every school had a Brigade of Home Visitors that conducted hygienic inspections of peasant homes. In 1940, Mota wrote that peasants were no longer sleeping, cooking, and eating on the floor; rather, they slept in beds that they themselves built, they ate at tables, and women cooked at waist-high hearths. In 1941, students in Mota's zone celebrated National Hygiene Week by drying up swampy areas, and teachers tried to convince villagers to plant trees and avoid slash-and-burn agricultural techniques. Mota and Epigmenio de León, both veterans of the SEP's more radical years, also noted that teachers in their lower Grijalva valley schools campaigned to "liberate women from the dictatorship of the *metate*," the flat stone used by women for grinding corn. Women were reportedly happy to start using the hand-powered *molino de nixtamal*.[8]

Mota's transformation from a fearless revolutionary firebrand into a tamed hygienist and social worker was quite remarkable. During the socialist education period he led land invasions, worked actively to arm his teachers, and made frequent allusion to the proletarian class struggle against capitalist oppressors. He was violently attacked for his efforts. But by 1941, Mota had completely changed his tune. "Having calmed the communist demagoguery that in previous years was at its apogee among the teachers," he wrote Téllez, "those in this zone, excepted the hardened communist agitator Martín Ferrera Martínez, managed to complete their duties." Mota also reported with evident satisfaction that he had not held a single pedagogy meeting in his zone, since they had served the ends of "agitators."[9]

Another inspector who changed with the shifting ideological winds was Manuel Castellanos. Although Castellanos seems to have lost his will to fight as early as 1936, the decline of federal support for rural education and indigenismo after 1940 accelerated the disarticulation of the SEP's project in the highlands. In 1941, Castellanos's social campaigns consisted of combating alcoholism, witchcraft, poor hygiene, locust plagues, typhoid fever, fanatical behavior, the apparent lack of respect for human life, and a poor diet. This amounted to attacking the symptoms of a brutally impoverished lifestyle, not the causes. Teachers held chats and conferences and gave theatrical presentations explaining that meteorological phenomena, illness, and bad harvests had natural, scientific (and not spiritual) causes. Castellanos noted in his annual report the "interesting" observation that all school expenses in his zone were being met by the Tzotzils themselves and that attendance had improved, even among girls.[10] Urbina's muchachos were using the threat of fines and jail time to manufacture this apparent "support" for SEP schools.

The newly apolitical Castellanos was a far cry from the determined activist who had fought enganche, alcohol merchants, and corrupt ladino municipal presidents and their fundamentally unfair taxation practices in 1935 and 1936. No longer challenging the victimizers, he blamed the victims. In the following excerpt from his October 1942 report, Castellanos strikes a detached, paternalistic, dismissive tone that harkens to an earlier age.

> Knowing that the Indians commit a great number of assassinations, especially due to witchcraft; that they are liars and attached to alcohol . . . that they are spiteful and obstinate in their passions; that they feel

> an innate hatred toward the mestizo . . . in other words, that the ethical principles that guide their lives are distinct from those that constitute the base of our civilization, I have recommended that all of the teachers in the zone use every means at their disposal to attend to the extremely important moral aspect of education, forming in said Indians feelings and habits that will make them more human.[11]

In part, Castellanos had ceded political and economic space to Urbina and his scribes, but he was also adjusting his actions and his reports to the more conservative winds blowing from Tuxtla Gutiérrez and Mexico City.

Téllez's "purge and transfer" policy continued to draw fire from the CTM-affiliated STERM in Tapachula. In 1941 this official teachers' union complained that Téllez had arbitrarily transferred seventeen teachers for political and/or ideological reasons and had ignored STERM requests to transfer teachers whose lives were at risk. Weeks later the STERM in Mexico City wrote to the SEP requesting Téllez's removal. The National Syndicate of Education Workers (Sindicato Único Nacional de Trabajadores de la Enseñanza) also sounded off, accusing Téllez of hiring, transferring, and firing teachers at will.[12] Undaunted, Téllez defended inspectors who deducted from teachers' salaries for days missed due to "communist agitation."[13] In early 1942, he wrote his superiors in Mexico City that "it is urgently necessary to transfer out of this state federal teachers who are hardened communist agitators who neglect their true work as teachers . . . and simply dedicate themselves to agitating and unjustly disorienting the workers and peasants of this state."[14] He expelled at least fifteen teachers that year, drawing protest from dozens of peasant communities in the coastal lowlands where all the transfers were taking place. He also fired his nemesis, zone inspector Francisco Ovilla, whom he described as "red to the bone" (*de hueso colorado*). Luis Flores, head of the education committee at Acapetahua, compared Téllez's actions to those of fifth columnists, who "subjugate the democratic peoples of Europe, persecuting and attacking the best civil servants."[15]

Later in 1942, after Mexico entered the war on the side of the Allies (which now included the Soviet Union), the anti-communist rhetoric and policy cooled off somewhat. Following negotiations in Mexico City between the teachers' unions, the state government, and the SEP, "communists" expelled earlier in the year were allowed to return to their posts in Chiapas. Naturally they were expected to give up their "constant agitation" and dedicate themselves instead to the "decent" work for which they were paid.[16]

Téllez not only reflected the new administration's interest in shifting attention away from agrarian reform, but he was openly disdainful of the peasantry. During the 1930s, SEP centralism had forced all education zones in Chiapas to adhere to a school calendar that saw classes start in early February and end in late November. This calendar overlapped with the springtime sowing season, the summer rainy season, and the fall harvest. Many students had spotty attendance during the spring sowing season, skipped school when summer rains made roads and rivers impassable, and abandoned the classroom in the fall when their labor was needed in local fields or on lowland plantations. In other words, the demands of rural life often made the indirect costs of sending a child to school prohibitive and accounts for much of the resistance to public schooling in Chiapas in the 1920s and 1930s. In 1939, the state's education zone inspectors and the federal inspector general attempted to modify the calendar in Chiapas's seventh zone, which hugged the border with Guatemala and sent thousands of mestizo and Mam peasants to Soconusco for the coffee harvest every fall. According to the zone inspector, the seasonal migration to the coffee zone more than halved school attendance figures. To accommodate this seasonal migration, the inspectors agreed to move final exams to the first ten days of October and initiate the following school year on January 2. Even though the authorities in Mexico City approved of the measure, Téllez did not.[17]

The matter was revisited two years later, and again Téllez dismissed the possibility of adjusting regional school calendars to agricultural cycles. Similar proposals by municipal presidents were also rejected.[18] Rather than accommodate the rhythms of rural life, Téllez fought them. He argued, against all evidence, that children's labor was not needed in the fields in Chiapas. "Modifying the school calendar," he wrote, "would reward the terrible custom of using defective methods in agricultural work, such as using boys to lead oxen in the fields, which is unnecessary and is not seen in any other region of the Republic."[19] Téllez stuck to his guns, and parents continued to pull their children out of school as needed.

Although complaints against Téllez poured in from private citizens, ejidos, and teachers' unions, he outlasted all of his predecessors because he fulfilled a key function for the Ávila Camacho administration. He demobilized the countryside and promised the president that his teachers would help "intensify the production of peasants and workers and would avoid strikes by means of persuasion and preventative measures."[20] He was especially notorious for freezing the establishment of Article 123 schools. So blatant were his stalling tactics that he was reprimanded by a conservative SEP in 1944 for not ordering school rosters. But Téllez did not have to worry. Unlike his activist predecessors, who had locked horns with Chiapas's governors and were promptly dismissed, Téllez enjoyed the support of governor Rafael Pascacio Gamboa, who in 1944 still insisted on calling Téllez's detractors "communists."[21]

The Conservative Rollback . . . and Beyond

Of course, the conservative backlash was felt outside of the classroom as well. Among the first to suffer its ill effects were the ejidatarios of Soconusco, whose victories in 1939 and 1940 proved short-lived. Many Cardenista institutions like the ejidal banks, marketing agencies, and cooperative societies were transformed from tools of emancipation into mechanisms of control. By 1942 Soconusco's ejidatarios were literally at war with officials of the Ejidal Bank in Tapachula. That year in April, the Central League of Agrarian Communities wrote to President Ávila Camacho complaining that coffee ejidatarios were still alienated from the fruits of their labors; those who formerly controlled production had been replaced by a new owner, "which calls itself the Bank."[22] Two months later, representatives from several coffee fincas met at the offices of the Ejidal Bank to finalize the purchase of Enrique Braun's coffee milling machinery at his fincas Santo Domingo, La Trinidad, and La Central. Also purchased were three hundred hectares of land from Santo Domingo. The 800,000-peso price tag negotiated by the bank was exceedingly high, especially since Braun's properties were about to be sequestered for at least the duration of World War II. Furthermore, the expense promised to decimate the million-peso reserve that coffee ejidatarios had built following the 1941–1942 harvest. It appears that the bank and the Ávila Camacho administration agreed to such generous indemnifications as a means of winning the support of conservative business interests. Workers further hypothesized that the bank set such high prices because it wanted to see collective agriculture fail. When members of the Central League of Agrarian Communities sought an audience with the bank's assistant manager in late July 1942, he chased them from his office, "calling them Guatemalans and other words."[23]

Once news of the Braun deal became public, the office of the presidency was swamped with letters from ejidatarios in Soconusco alleging that the bank had unleashed a "white terror." Anyone who questioned the bank's appropriation of ejidatario funds was "accused of being a reactionary and an agitator, etc; his loan was suspended, they took away his work and chased him from the ejido."[24] Workers in Cacahoatán complained that they were still "Slaves of Capital" and not "Free Citizens," because the true beneficiaries of the Ejidal Bank were people "favored by the bank, who benefit from the sweat and sacrifice of others."[25] These ejidatarios, as well as those from the municipality of Unión Juárez, claimed that the bank's exploitation was "worse than that endured before the Revolution."[26] Members of Chiapas's main coffee workers' union (Sindicato Único de la Industria del Café del Soconusco) repeated the accusation that bank employees manipulated votes and local politics and incarcerated resistant workers.[27]

CTM-affiliated workers throughout Mexico expressed solidarity with Soconusco's coffee workers throughout the summer of 1942. From Tamaulipas came a telegram asking why the Ejidal Bank was paying finqueros like "millionaire Enrique Braun" exorbitant prices for outdated machinery and additional lands.[28] Ejidatarios at La Laguna in Coahuila, the site of President Cárdenas's most dramatic land expropriation, wrote that "we have also had to taste the bitter fruits of the behavior of some employees of the Ejidal Bank." They demanded that Ávila Camacho order a full investigation into the purchase of Enrique Braun's assets and the Bank's sale arrangements with coffee merchants in Tapachula.[29] However, the Ávila Camacho administration had little interest in addressing these rural matters at a time when Mexico was industrializing in partnership with its wartime ally, the United States.

The Death and Resurrection of Indigenous "Incorporation"

Alexander Dawson has recently argued that federal indigenismo in the 1930s gave indigenous people the opportunity to contest and shape indigenista policy. Indigenous resistance to the SEP's program at the Casa del Estudiante Indígena led to more pluralism and participation at many boarding schools, and eventually indigenous people were encouraged to literally speak out and make demands on the state at the Regional Indigenous Congresses (*Congresos Regionales Indígenas*) convoked periodically by the Cárdenas administration. Dawson concludes that the generation of young men nurtured and educated in the 1930s became *indígenas capacitados*, important interlocutors between their communities and the state, in subsequent decades. Although some abused their positions of authority and responsibility, others pressed for material improvement and some measure of cultural autonomy in their communities.[30]

In some ways, Chiapas represents the exception to Dawson's findings. SEP boarding schools in the state were by no means plural. Teachers were mestizo; indigenous languages were not spoken; relations between the school and the community were typically antagonistic; and schools were often established in former convents, often near aguardiente distilleries or cemeteries, and generally lacked land for agricultural practices. Coercive means were commonly used to recruit students. However, as Dawson argues, indigenous interlocutors did emerge from SEP rural schools, boarding schools, and state indigenista institutions. These men, Urbina's scribes and municipal secretaries, would eventually control the political and economic life of the highlands.

The year 1940 represented the apogee of federal indigenismo in Mexico, but it also revealed the naked reality of state indigenismo in Chiapas. Early that year, the stubborn thesis of "incorporation" was truly under siege. Ironically, the charge was led by Moisés Sáenz, who had so adamantly championed the incorporationist cause one decade earlier. Reflecting his new belief that "the Indian problem is different from that of campesinos," Sáenz proposed a federal Department of Indian Affairs (Departamento de Asuntos Indígenas, or DAI) in 1935.[31] By 1938 the DAI was controlling both the Cultural Missions and the indigenous boarding schools. One year later, Luis Chávez Orozco was named to direct the DAI. Chávez Orozco believed that Mexico's indigenous peoples should be respected as autonomous nations within the greater Mexican nation. He defended the right of Indian groups to maintain their own language and customs. Although these views were at odds with those of Cárdenas, the president respected them out of deference to his friendship with both Chávez Orozco and Sáenz and their many years of indigenista activities.[32]

The pluralists seemingly had the last word at the Interamerican Indigenist Conference held in Pátzcuaro, Michoacán, in March 1940. According to Dawson, the conference represented "a key moment in the convergence of anthropological knowledge and political decision making in Mexico." After several participants endorsed bilingual education, Cárdenas gave a speech in favor of "Mexicanizing the Indian." Cárdenas was committed to a partnership with the social sciences to forge a more modern and democratic society, but talk of cultural heterogeneity threatened to divide and unravel the rural coalition that he needed to survive politically.[33] His words went unheeded, as representatives from all participating countries at the conference signed a declaration stating that "[t]he old theory of the incorporation of the Indian to civilization—a pretext used to better exploit and oppress the aboriginal peoples—has been discarded."[34] In its place, the Congress endorsed bilingual bicultural education and integral development, of which education would be but one aspect.

The focus of national indigenismo then shifted to Chiapas. President Cárdenas called for a Regional Indigenous Congress to be held in Las Casas in May of that year. Luis Chávez Orozco chose Chiapanecan Ángel M. Corzo to organize the event. Typically, in the weeks ahead of the conferences, teachers and DAI employees (many, if not most of them mestizos) helped indigenous communities select representatives and draft petitions. To a large extent, these interventions permitted federal institutions like the SEP and the DAI to set the congresses' agendas. Representatives usually called for roads, land, credit, tools, and special, separate-but-equal "Indian schools" taught by bilingual, bicultural teachers who resided in their communities.[35] Ironically, indigenous peoples "incorporated" themselves into the political system in order to advance proposals calling for economic assistance (part of the Cardenista plan) and cultural autonomy (which threatened Cardenista nation building).

The actual proceedings of the congress in Chiapas were overshadowed by a bitter struggle between the federal DAI and the state's Department of Indigenous Protection. Corzo did everything possible to marginalize Erasto Urbina, his department, and his municipal secretaries and scribes. Governor Gutiérrez was also left out of the loop; neither Corzo nor Chávez Orozco informed him of their plans, nor did he receive an invitation to attend the inauguration ceremonies until the day of the event. At stake was nothing less than the control of the state's indigenous population. Corzo's objective, and quite possibly that of Chávez Orozco, was to condemn the Gutiérrez government for the meager returns on its indigenista policy, especially with respect to agrarian reform, and subsequently take federal control of Indian affairs in Chiapas.[36]

Corzo had his work cut out for him. As Governor Gutiérrez bluntly observed in a letter to President Cárdenas, the state's indigenous population was "controlled by Erasto Urbina."[37] That spring, Urbina managed the highland vote ahead of the 1940 presidential elections, later boasting to Governor Gutiérrez that he had "almost destroyed" (*derrotado*) the supporters of General Juan Andreu Almazán.[38] Almazán was in fact defeated in the elections, amid violence and widespread allegations of fraud, and Urbina became a representative to the state legislature. Following the elections, certain federal teachers of the STERM criticized his dictatorial tactics and accused him of exploiting Indians. Urbina's allies in the STI and other CTM affiliates then lined up behind him and penned a viciously degrading attack on the "pseudoeducators." After first accusing teachers of harboring "antipatriotic" and "exotic" communist ideas, the letter condemned them as "myopic, microcephalic reactionaries" with "decadent bourgeois" tendencies.[39] The accusations may have been contradictory, but it was clear that Urbina would vehemently defend his cacicazgo.

Naturally, in the weeks and days ahead of the regional congress, the state's Department of Indian Protection launched a furious counterattack against Corzo and the federal DAI. Urbina tried to impose his scribes as delegates at the congress and accused Corzo of mobilizing "all of the enemies of the state government" and inviting mestizo agitators. He also suggested to Gutiérrez that his office supervise the telephone office in Las Casas during May and June "so that our opponents will not have free use of the phone lines for their machinations."[40] In this tense climate, the division between state and federal institutions grew sharper. Manuel Castellanos, for one, did not know whether to accept Corzo's invitation to attend the congress or decline, knowing that once the DAI officials returned to Mexico City, there would be nothing preventing the state government from taking reprisals.[41]

Given the tremendous tension leading up to the congress, the event itself was rather uneventful. Some weeks later the DAI tried to send a team of agrarian engineers to Chiapas to resolve some of the problems generated by Urbina's hastily executed expropriations in the highlands. Gutiérrez responded defensively and it appears the matter was dropped.[42] In any case, both he and Cárdenas were due to leave office at the end of the year, and the panorama for indigenista activity would soon change more drastically than either man could have imagined.

Cárdenas's successor, Ávila Camacho, was unsympathetic to indigenismo and gave indigenistas neither the financial resources nor the political capital needed to influence federal policy. After taking office in December 1940, he immediately replaced Chávez Orozco as director of the DAI and named him ambassador to Honduras in 1941. Moisés Sáenz, Mexico's ambassador to Peru, died in Lima. Ángel Corzo, now Oficial Mayor of the DAI, began accusing certain DAI employees of communist tendencies in 1941. The indigenista climate in Mexico suddenly became extremely hostile to all suggestions of pluralism, bilingualism, and self-determination.[43] By 1942, the DAI's range of influence had sharply narrowed. After Mexico entered World War II, new SEP director Octavio Véjar Vázquez resurrected the thesis of "incorporation" on the grounds of national unity. "Since the cohesion of the fatherland can only rise from an identical spiritual formation, it is indispensable that the school be the same for all

Mexicans regardless of their political or religious affiliation, their race or class," wrote Véjar Vázquez.[44] The SEP standardized its curriculum for urban and rural schools so that students in Mexico City and Toluca used the same materials as students in Mitontic and Tenejapa. Social, ethnic, and geographic difference now meant nothing to the SEP, even at a rhetorical level. After twenty years of slowly evolving toward a curriculum that appreciated difference, the SEP reverted back to the failed incorporationist project championed by its founder, Vasconcelos.

Manuel Castellanos may have moderated his approach to federal education, but he was still independent enough to recognize that the SEP's renewed admonitions against bilingual education spelled doom to highland schools. In 1941 he still encouraged teachers in his zone to use the *dialecto* in order to later teach reading and writing in Spanish. Bilingual education, he believed, was "the best way to achieve a rapid psychological transformation in the Indians, so that by their own free will they adopt better forms of life." He flatly stated in a 1942 report that "it is not possible to develop in these schools the same programs developed in urban schools," and he continued to encourage his teachers to use Tzotzil. Where teachers did not know the indigenous language, Castellanos recommended that they learn it and apply it in their classrooms.[45] While this is hardly surprising given Castellanos's experience, it is revealing that he would report it to his superiors in spite of their insistence on "national unity" and monolingual, monocultural pedagogy. Castellanos and other inspectors in indigenous regions had built a convincing case for the utility of bilingual education as a strategy of "incorporation" and integration. The INI would vindicate Castellanos's position in 1952 when it opened bilingual bicultural schools of its own in the highlands.

Folk Support for the Socialist School

The picture of federal education in the 1940s has so far been bleak, characterized by inadequate budgets, a myopic director of federal education, an ideological purge, and a reversal in indigenista policy. However, at another level, the legacy of SEP populism was paying lasting dividends. Beginning in the mid-1930s, mestizo attitudes toward federal schooling changed remarkably. The new, more popular textbooks, the radicalized and better-prepared teachers, the social campaigns, the sporting festivals, and teacher support for land reform helped win mestizo support. Letters and petitions suggest that the culture of schooling began to take hold, especially among communities that participated in the export sector and benefited most directly from the

SEP's program of socialist education. Literacy was becoming an increasingly important skill as the Mexican state began intervening in the lives of rural Chiapanecans as never before. After the SEP muted its anticlerical campaign, mestizo peasants found fewer reasons to oppose its schools. Not surprisingly, the results of the SEP's 1938 survey of federal teachers showed that nearly four in five mestizo communities supported the federal rural schools (78 percent). Four years later, 87 percent of these schools were still in operation, despite increasing demands on the SEP's more modest budgets. Parents not only sent their children to school, but they frequently provided money for school construction and repair and paid for teachers' aides.

Without question, the initial popularity of federal schools in mestizo Chiapas after 1935 can be attributed to the teachers' roles as promoters of agrarian reform. Throughout Mexico, the timing of the agrarian reform and the role played by teachers largely determined a community's response to teachers and schooling. In Puebla, for example, where many ejidatarios received their lands before 1930, SEP teachers were denied a role in the process. With little to offer rural *poblanos*, they struggled belatedly to insert themselves in local agrarian and community politics. In Sonora during the early 1930s, on the other hand, SEP teachers participated in a redistributive state-building project and promoted agrarian reform.[46] Teachers in Chiapas played similar roles. The SEP's director in Chiapas in 1935, Elpidio López, wrote that the SEP's schools were better received in areas where agrarista communities had been established, like the central lowland zones of Ocozocuautla and Chiapa de Corzo.[47] In 1936, Inspector Héctor Eduardo Paniagua explained that all teachers in his zone were leaders of their communities in matters of agrarian reform. "Wherever there is a teacher, we have filed a request for ejidos," he wrote. "In this way, we have managed to win campesino affections for the school."[48] Naturally, the SEP expected better attendance and greater cooperation from communities that had benefited from SEP-facilitated land reform.

As rural Chiapanecos responded favorably to the SEP's "socialist" orientation, the demand for rural schools suddenly outstripped supply. The SEP received literally hundreds of petitions and letters penned by parents, students, unions, and members of education, ejido, and agrarian committees requesting schools and complaining of local obstructers. Letters commonly expressed the belief that free, lay education was one of the great conquests of the revolution and a necessary component for the enjoyment of full citizenship. At La Providencia, for example, the agrarian committee wrote President Cárdenas and the SEP demanding a federal rural school, seeing "no reason why we would be denied this benefit of the Revolution, for which we have fought and shed blood."[49] Villagers also demanded well-trained and energetic teachers. At Tuixcum, in the municipality of Motozintla, education committee members and local ejido officials lobbied successfully in 1938 against two female teachers who failed to give final exams and showed no interest in teaching. One year later, they again wrote to complain that the local SEP inspector had failed to name two new teachers to fill the vacancies.[50] In January 1941, Director of Federal Education Téllez implored the SEP to at least maintain funding at the levels sustained in past years "in order to satisfy the just demands for schools that we constantly receive."[51] Now that demand had outstripped supply, the SEP became more selective and only attempted to provide teachers where villagers had already built a school, a home for the teacher, and extracurricular "annexes."

When shrinking SEP budgets failed to meet the growing demand for schools and literacy, communities wrote impassioned letters of protest to Téllez and Presidents Cárdenas and Ávila Camacho. At the town of Miramar in Soconusco, education committee members and residents in 1939 asked Téllez to send a teacher to their school. They had made the request before and their frustration with the SEP was clearly evident. "Today we can truly say that the conquests of the Revolution have not brought us any benefit," they wrote, appropriating SEP discourse and claiming their right to the "bread of knowledge." Miramar's residents also referred to Cárdenas's highly vaunted literacy campaign, asking how they were to become literate "if they deny us a school and the number of illiterates actually increases." The letter ends with a veiled threat to take their request to the SEP and President Cárdenas, "and we will say that, here, perhaps because we are poor and ignorant, they do not tend to us."[52] As if to underscore the urgency of the matter, most of the letter's fifty-seven signatories "signed" with their thumbs.

One month later Téllez responded, pledging to send a teacher as soon as he had studied the 1940 budget. It was an empty promise. Four years later, forty-nine residents from Miramar signed another highly charged letter to Téllez, who was still at the helm. No response from the SEP. Miramar's residents sent yet another letter in 1945, complaining again that its more than one hundred school-age children would never shed their ignorance. Later that year, after a six-year delay, the SEP finally sent a teacher.[53]

The statistical and anecdotal evidence for the popularity of SEP socialism among mestizos is even more convincing in Soconusco's embattled Article

123 schools. The 1938 federal teachers' survey showed that a startling 90 percent of the Article 123 schools and teachers enjoyed the support of parents and workers. As in the federal rural schools, the initial popularity of the Article 123 schools was due to the broad social mandate of federal teachers who labored as advocates of land reform, enforcers of federal labor legislation, and unionizers. Coffee workers at finca Argentina wrote to President Cárdenas in 1940 requesting a school with the hope that the appointed Article 123 teacher would enforce the terms of the 1931 Federal Labor Law. As the workers told it, the federal education zone inspector in the area was "the only authority who supports us . . . because neither the federal nor state labor inspectors have done us justice, due to management obstructions." The owners at Argentina consistently failed to pay the minimum wage, refused to provide land for cultivation, and denied access to medical care. Management also fired eleven workers with children in order to keep the school roster low. Despite these layoffs, SEP inspectors found over fifty school-age children at Argentina, and a school was established. Some months later, however, the owner ordered local police and authorities from Tapachula and Tuxtla Chico to dislodge the families of unionized workers. "They threw our families' possessions into the street, issued threats, and broke into the schoolhouse destroying all of the supplies that the federal education inspector had given us. Teacher Bruno Balboa was threatened and chased from the plantation by the pistol-brandishing owner," yet workers continued to support the school.[54] Representatives of the school's agrarian committee penned these letters of protest; under the guidance of their teacher, workers had applied for ejidal plots and elected officials to present their claims. They understood that once the school disappeared, so too did their main advocate for federal unionization and land reform.

Workers at other plantations in Soconusco also appreciated the expanded social roles played by their teachers. Amadeo Tercero's most adamant supporters were his students and their parents, thanks to the role he played as local adviser on agrarian issues. In a letter addressed to President Cárdenas in 1938, El Retiro's Rural Workers Syndicate defended Tercero, writing

> We respectfully but energetically protest against the anti-revolutionary maneuvers of the foreign capitalist reactionaries represented mainly by the Syndicate of Coffee Growers of Soconusco. . . . We refute all of their dirty, shameless lies. The federal teachers are providing us with a price-

> less orientation, because it is true classist ideology based on scientific socialism and supported by historic materialism.[55]

Workers on Enrique Braun's finca El Achotal weighed in when Braun went to Mexico City to argue his case with SEP director Rafael Ramírez. In a letter to President Cárdenas, education committee members wrote that "we know perfectly well that the owner, a principal member of the bourgeoisie that dominates this region, is defending himself in Mexico City against our efforts . . . and we ask that you recognize our school and our teacher, Professor Rómulo Delgado Quevedo."[56] At finca Numancia, in the border town of Cacahoatán, members of the Rural Workers Syndicate wrote to defend their teachers against "the slanderous newspaper articles printed in Chiapas and Mexico City which condemn the wholly proletarian and revolutionary labors of the federal teachers in Chiapas and especially in Soconusco . . . where we still suffer under the whip of national and international capitalism. . . . Thanks to the work of the teachers, all of us are now organized and conscious of our true role as citizens."[57]

In a rural society of high illiteracy rates, sophisticated letters that speak of historic materialism and the rights of citizenship should raise our suspicions. At the most basic level, we cannot even be sure who was penning these letters, or for what purpose. Even though much of Soconusco's resident rural proletariat had become politically literate as a result of years of intense social and political struggle, the myriad thumbprint signatures on the letters and petitions—roughly half of all total signatures in Soconusco in the 1930s—suggest a good many signers were functionally illiterate and may not have known what they were signing. Yet these letters corroborate information found in teachers' and inspectors' reports, and the planters' pitched opposition to the Article 123 teachers' activities suggests that the teachers were in fact effective grassroots advocates.

If we accept that grassroots support for the Article 123 schools in the 1930s can be explained largely by the role that teachers played as labor inspectors and catalysts to land reform, how do we explain their continuing popularity after 1940, when the federal government brought land reform to a crawl and suppressed the populist dimensions of rural education? In the late 1930s and early 1940s, when most of the Article 123 schools were closed due to finquero intransigence, agrarian reform, and government intervention during World War II, the SEP received dozens of letters from concerned parents and ejidatarios who petitioned to have federal rural schools established immediately in their place. Some sent along their own rough school rosters and appointed education committees in anticipation of a school opening. Most of them were disappointed by the SEP's apathetic response. Still, workers demanded schools as a right of modern citizenship, even after it had become painfully apparent that the SEP was no longer committed to a populist agenda.

The following case illustrates the persistence of grassroots support as much as the reluctance of the federal government to hold itself to the same laws as the private sector. In 1944, members of the Banana Syndicate (Sindicato Único de Trabajadores de la Industria Platanera, Agrícola y Similares) wrote to SEP director Jaime Torres Bodet twice to solicit a school for the banana plantation El Alcázar. Distance and student population requirements had been met, but the SEP clearly had an interest in delaying the establishment of the school. In June and November 1946, Chiapas' Workers Federation (Federación de Trabajadores del Estado de Chiapas) wrote to inquire about the delays. After Huixtla's Regional Federation of Workers (Federación Regional de Trabajadores de Huixtla) wrote in December 1946, the SEP ordered a second school census, but no further action was taken. Another census was taken in 1949, and the school was finally opened in 1950, six years after workers made the initial request.[58] Not coincidentally, the SEP opened the school just as the fiduciary was about to sell the plantation to Christian Bernstorff in 1950.[59] Bernstorff was no more interested in sustaining the school than the fiduciary had been, and it was shut down two years later.

Even though rosters at El Alcázar never showed fewer than forty-five school-age children, the SEP was reluctant to ask the fiduciary to pay for the school, though Article 123 teachers were the worst paid among federal teachers and in most cases the infrastructure was already in place. The workers who requested the school knew that the federal government would not enact land reform, and they were already members of official unions. Evidently, they were convinced that their children needed a couple of years of formal education, and they were determined to compel the fiduciary to pay for it.

Amadeo Tercero's former school at finca El Retiro suffered a similar fate at the hands of the fiduciary. Between July 1943, when the plantation passed to official hands, and August 1944, the local branch of the CTM-affiliated Coffee Syndicate of Soconusco (Sindicato Único de Trabajadores de la Industria del Café del Soconusco), the plantation's education committee, and a teachers' group wrote eight letters requesting that the SEP fill the vacancy at the school. Again, the workers already enjoyed nominal union representation, and they understood that the fiduciary was not about to permit land reform. In the words of the education committee, "We need education to meet the needs of our country, because if we remain ignorant, we will continue to be victimized by the Nazi-fascist capital that exists in Soconusco. We also need to know our rights as citizens."[60] Two months later, the union wrote President Ávila Camacho with increasing consternation. "Since last year we have been without an Article 123 teacher. We do not understand why the federal authorities in Tuxtla have not attended to this matter in light of our repeated requests."[61] Workers and parents at El Retiro had to wait until 1946 before the SEP would name a teacher to their school, the same year in which the fiduciary returned most sequestered properties to their owners.

Conclusion

Socialist education was swept into the dustbin of history long before President Miguel Alemán officially put an end to the matter in December 1946, when he called it "one of the country's most unfortunate" experiences. After 1940, SEP activists like Amadeo Tercero and Francisco Ovilla were purged, the gains of ejidatarios of Soconusco were compromised, SEP indigenismo went backward in time, and the ranks of Article 123 schools were thinned. Many SEP teachers and inspectors had to change their stripes in order to survive. P. Arturo Mota was one of these survivors. In the 1940s, he tamed the activist zeal and Marxist rhetoric that had inspired him to create dozens of Article 123 schools in the middle 1930s. In the late 1940s he got his reward when he embarked upon a modest career as a representative to the state legislature. Another survivor was Jacinto Téllez, who stayed at the helm of the SEP in Chiapas for six years, much longer than any of his predecessors. Enjoying the support of Chiapas's state governors (and little else), Téllez orchestrated the rollback of Cardenista populism. In 1945 yet another survivor—Manuel Castellanos—replaced him. Castellanos changed with the times too and ceded the highlands to Erasto Urbina's scribes and to what Jan Rus has called the "*comunidad revolucionaria institucional*."

If we look elsewhere, though, it becomes clear that SEP socialism paid enormous dividends in ladino Chiapas, especially along the coast. Despite the high indirect costs of schooling, parents demanded education as a right of Mexican citizenship. Peasant support for official education in Mexico was not without precedent. Rockwell's study of schooling in Tlaxcala shows municipalities seeking federal schools during the 1920s and 1930s in order to join federal agrarian movements. Vaughan found considerable support for socialist education among the settlers on the left bank of the Yaqui River in the 1930s. They too perceived that populist education and literacy could open doors for them in the new Mexican state.[62] What makes grassroots support for education in much of rural Chiapas so noteworthy is that the state utterly lacked a tradition of patriotic liberalism and Porfirian education. It remained on the margins of the Mexican state and was still plagued by a terribly inadequate infrastructure and by tenacious local forces that sought to undermine the school. Yet after roughly twenty years spent trying to interest rural Mexicans in schooling, the SEP suddenly found itself unable to meet grassroots demand. ◆

Conclusion

The Zapatista Rebellion in Historical Context

> My arrival to the mountains of southeastern Mexico [in 1983], to the jungle, was accidental. . . . They needed someone to teach literacy and the history of Mexico.
>
> The *compañeros* of the first group . . . had a lot of political experience already. . . . They had also been in prison, suffered torture, all of that. But they also demanded what they called the "political word" [*la palabra política*]: history. The history of this country and of the struggle. So that was the task I arrived with.
>
> —*Subcomandante Marcos, October 24, 1994*

How did the SEP's schools and teachers transform rural Chiapas in the 1920s and 1930s? And how does the history of rural education in Chiapas before 1945 help us to understand the tremendous upheaval that has gripped parts of the state in recent years?

In September 1914, Carrancista general Jesús Agustín Castro entered Tuxtla Gutiérrez vowing to make Chiapanecan cowards "feel the effects of the Revolution."[1] The Mapache resistance prevented him from carrying out his threat, leaving it to the SEP to bring the revolution to Chiapas after 1920. In the end, of course, the "revolution" was not all that "revolutionary," and the reforms of the 1930s were largely corrupted or swept aside in the 1940s. Still, Chiapas was forever changed, thanks in part to SEP projects and protagonists.

During this critical period of Mexican state formation, SEP teachers introduced Chiapanecos to the reforms and institutions of the central government. In the middle 1930s, as the SEP and its teachers adopted an increasingly radical agenda and channeled workers and peasants into federal institutions, rural Chiapanecos became central actors in epic showdowns between state and federal government. The twin triumphs of the Cardenista state in Chiapas—the imposition of Efraín Gutiérrez in 1936 and the land expropriations of 1939–1940—were savored by workers, peasants, and teachers with federal affiliations. The role played by SEP schools and teachers in these struggles created a popular legacy in education that the SEP later struggled to live down.

Even though rural schooling lost some ground in Chiapas in the early 1940s, the experiment in radical pedagogy had been a success in most mestizo communities. Teachers had facilitated agrarian reform, fought violators of federal labor legislation, imparted basic literacy skills, organized public health campaigns, and challenged local caciques, enganchadores, and alcoholeros before other branches of the federal government could or would. Not all teachers were competent, committed social activists, and many failed as community organizers and pedagogues. Yet rural Chiapas in 1940 was vastly different from how it had been ten years earlier, and federal rural teachers played significant roles in this transformation. Communities that had shunned schooling came to embrace it; their pleas for schools by 1940 appropriated a discourse of popular nationalism and citizenship first introduced by teachers. Communities celebrated patriotic and sporting festivals with more regularity and enthusiasm, thereby engaging in "everyday" types of state and nation formation. Lastly, many rural Chiapanecos became politicized and gained literacy skills that they would use in future dealings with state and federal institutions.

The SEP's "Cultural Revolution" in Chiapas

Assessing the SEP's campaign to change the *mentalité* of rural Chiapanecos is more difficult. This cultural project was not new. Even Porfirian schools attempted to promote secular thought, sobriety, responsible citizenship, and patriotism. What made the SEP's project novel was its utopian faith, its intensity, and its ambitious scope. The socialist education program of the middle and late 1930s was the most concerted campaign to transform Mexican mentalité since the mass religious conversions of the sixteenth century. Of course, campaigning for change is one matter; effectively forging more rational, modern, sober Mexican citizens is quite another.

Let us first turn to the matter of secularization. In 1937, just as the federal anticlerical policy was running out of steam, Francisco Ovilla declared that in the Tzotzil municipality of Bochil "religious fiestas are gradually losing their religious character due to the constant efforts of the school. They are being transformed into commercial, sporting, and cultural fiestas."[2] In 1941, Daniel Tamayo reported that in his predominately mestizo zone of Villa

Flores, "fanaticism . . . has been extinguishing itself, despite the fact that religious freedom and priests have been once again allowed."[3] Ovilla, however, was a notorious radical and a member of the Communist Party who may simply have found in Bochil what he was looking for; in Villa Flores, "fanaticism" may have extinguished itself in the absence of equally fanatical PNR party cadres who literally stoked the anticlerical fires in fall 1934. Even if we take these and other observations at face value and conclude that most rural Chiapanecos underwent a gradual process of secularization during our period of study, which is likely, it is difficult to determine the extent of the SEP's role in the process. Rural health clinics, market forces, the mass media, and other trappings of modernity also exerted considerable secularizing impulses.[4]

It is also important to recall that the Catholic Church in Chiapas had been in retreat ever since the Liberal reforms of the 1850s. PNR anticlericals in the late 1920s and early 1930s ascribed to the Church more wealth and influence than it actually had. The Jacobin attack against the Church was likely used to distract Chiapanecos from the lack of real reforms in agrarian and labor policy. In 1950, the bishop of Chiapas had only thirty priests and forty-six nuns to serve more than nine hundred thousand believers in the state. Only in the 1960s did the Church initiate its second spiritual conquest in Chiapas. Bishop Samuel Ruiz along with Jesuits (who translated the Bible into Tzeltal), Marists, Dominicans, and others introduced "Indian theology" (*teología india*), a subset of liberation theology, to the pioneer settlements in eastern Chiapas.[5] Tzotzil, Tzeltal, Tojolabal, Ch'ol, and ladino catechists used the story of Exodus as a means of relating to and discussing the settlers' own flight to a new "promised land."[6] If the postrevolutionary government largely imagined the Catholic threat of the late 1920s and 1930s, this progressive, grassroots Catholic movement prepared the terrain in eastern Chiapas for a very real challenge to the PRI in the 1990s.

The SEP's noisy, persistent anti-alcohol campaign was a more categorical failure. No evidence suggests that the SEP's work inside or outside of the classroom had any impact on the alcohol-consumption patterns of rural Chiapanecos. Naturally, the SEP received little help from state and municipal authorities, for whom alcohol taxes constituted a major source of revenue.

Lastly, let us consider the SEP's nation-building campaign in Chiapas. Although the SEP's attempt to replace religious services with nationalist celebrations in 1935 was short-lived and unpopular, most patriotic, cultural, and especially sporting events were very well received and contributed to the surge in support for SEP schooling in the late 1930s and 1940s. Patriotic festivals were given particular importance in the southern border towns that had passed to Mexican control in 1882. Whereas Mexicans of Guatemalan descent were considered suspect citizens in the 1920s and 1930s, the Cardenista land expropriations and the SEP's cultural campaigns tended to mitigate anti-Guatemalan hysteria after 1940.

Still, assessing the impact of SEP-sponsored nationalism is risky business, even where the SEP had established schools and sunk deep roots. The transformation of the Zapata legacy is particularly illustrative. In the 1930s, Zapata appeared in SEP textbooks stripped of his drinking, his gambling, his womanizing, and his fatal opposition to Carranza. He was transformed into "the intransigent of the revolution, an immaculate symbol of the emancipation of the rural masses . . . humbl[y] clothed in sandals and the white cotton uniform of the Morelian peasantry."[7] In the words of Vaughan, "Concepts of rebellion, struggle, and the right to social justice were etched into the core of the Mexican cultural nation and legitimated as intrinsic to national identity."[8]

Naturally, the Mexican government could not control how angry students, peasants, and insurgents would apply these lessons in later years. In 1968, after university students in Mexico City invoked Zapata in their tragic challenge to the PRI, the regime lost the monopoly it had enjoyed over its revolutionary heroes. Zapata once again became an oppositional figure. His image was used throughout the 1970s and 1980s as Mexico's economic and political system suffered under the weight of collapsing oil prices, spiraling debt payments, peso devaluations, hyperinflation, and official corruption.

If the SEP could not control the appropriation of its heroes in places like Mexico City, where a relatively effective school infrastructure was in place, what could it expect in indigenous Chiapas, where infrastructure was almost always inadequate? The Tzotzil, Tzeltal, Ch'ol and Tojolabal migrants who colonized the *Selva* after 1940 not only came from communities where the SEP and its nation-building message had generally not taken root, but they made their new homes on the frontier, where SEP infrastructure lagged behind the rate of settlement. (In 1994, nearly half of the population there had had no schooling, and more than half over the age of fifteen could not read or write.[9]) Even when the SEP managed to build schools in eastern Chiapas, its teachers were no longer inspired by the revolutionary nationalist ideology that had driven many SEP teachers and inspectors in the 1930s.

Lynn Stephen's recent comparative study of mainly indigenous ejidatarios in Oaxaca and eastern Chiapas illustrates how communities' experiences with land reform, government officials, and federal education can have critically divergent political implications. Where predominately Zapotec villagers in central Oaxaca received land and supported SEP schools in the 1930s, Zapata became part of a narrative of struggle, perseverance, kept promises, and gratitude. By contrast, in eastern Chiapas, Tojolabal settlers had mostly negative experiences with far-off state and federal agrarian-reform officials in the 1960s, 1970s, and 1980s. SEP schools played a minimal or nonexistent role in their lives. Like the other political and economic refugees who settled in the Lacandón rain forest after 1940, the Tojolabals were largely free to come up with their own ideas about Zapata and were open to unofficial interpretations of his legacy. As we now know, the image of Zapata that emerged was an oppositional one.[10]

To conclude, the SEP can only point to mixed success in its overtly cultural campaigns between 1921 and 1940. Its impact on the state's overall process of secularization is difficult to determine, and powerful alcohol interests and the state government boldly undermined its sobriety campaign. Its patriotic celebrations helped win the support of mestizos for SEP schools, but its message could not sink roots in indigenous communities, where SEP schools themselves enjoyed a precarious existence. In broader terms, however, the school itself had important cultural implications for rural Chiapas. During and after the introduction of socialist education, most mestizo and a few indigenous communities embraced the rural school, the messages it imparted, and the skills that it taught. Soon, demand for rural schooling began to outstrip supply; the culture of schooling had caught on. Today, rural Chiapanecos (including the Zapatistas) continue to demand effective schools, teachers, and curricula.

The Cardenista Legacy in the Highlands

Although the Tzotzil and Tzeltal highlands underwent profound changes during this period, it was not as SEP idealists had planned. By the late 1930s, Castellanos and the SEP had ceded the highlands to Erasto Urbina and the state government. Urbina continued to indirectly manage the Department of Indian Protection in the early 1940s, even as he served as deputy to the state legislature and municipal president of Las Casas. During this time, some department delegates did struggle to improve the conditions of the highland Maya, but their aims were very modest. For example, instead of striving to eliminate the illegal tienda de raya altogether they merely checked that workers were not paid in scrip and that prices at the stores were not too high. The department wrote letters on behalf of indigenous communities that supposedly wanted federal teachers, but its agents also worked with the SEP in Tuxtla to root out known activists. State director Téllez generally agreed with the department's recommendations and transferred or fired teachers without even investigating the charges, prompting still more protests from Section 7 of the STERM.[11]

In 1942 the department launched its own modest education project. Itinerant male teachers, usually scribes, were assigned to teach Spanish literacy at highland schools. Mexican anthropologist Ricardo Pozas noted that these men did a brisk business selling excused absences to parents. He observed one of these teachers give a class at the Colonia Agraria Belisario Domínguez (part of Chamula) "with a huge pistol in his belt."[12] Another renowned anthropologist, Alfonso Villa Rojas, noted that the federal teacher in the Tzeltal municipality of Oxchuc ensured attendance through a practice known as *sacar prenda*. The teacher sent older students to the homes of truants and collected some article of clothing or a tool. The truant would have to go to school the next day to retrieve the article. The teacher, who was monolingual in Spanish, sometimes took the items himself, with a pistol in his holster. As Villa Rojas observed, "On various occasions the house of the teacher looked like a clothing warehouse: there you would find *sarapes*, machetes, large hoes, [and] hats."[13] When the federal inspector visited the school, he was surprised to note that the teacher still had not learned Tzeltal, even though he had been teaching there for four years; none of the students understood Spanish, even though the school had been in operation for seven.

Meanwhile, Urbina's scribes grew more powerful. As Pozas noted in the middle 1940s, "They exploit every opportunity to cement their prestige and their political power. Everyone knows that they are the ones who relate with the government in Las Casas and the state." Moreover, "it is also well-known that the scribes have permanent power, because they never change." In the 1940s they were coached to assume religious cargoes and become *principales*. As principales, they penetrated their communities' traditional religious hierarchies and further legitimated themselves. Pozas also observed how the scribes/principales eliminated potential competitors. After identifying the most promising students, they worked together to prevent them from completing the sixth grade and becoming scribes themselves. This ensured that power and influence remained concentrated in the original scribes' hands.[14]

The contradictory impact of Cardenista indigenismo in highland Chiapas is personified in its chief architect, Erasto Urbina. During a ten-year period he rose from a humble immigration official to become a Cardenista election official; director of the Department of Social Action, Culture, and Indigenous Protection; founder and director of the STI; director of the municipal PNR; a federal deputy; and municipal president of Las Casas. Anthropologists researching the highlands in the early 1940s invariably met with Urbina before beginning their work. He left strong impressions. In 1943, Fernando Cámara Barbachano met the indigenista while he was municipal president of Las Casas. Cámara noted that Urbina played the part of an all-knowing cacique when dealing with indigenous people. In one-on-one conversation with Cámara, the indigenista "reclined in his chair, raised his head, crossed his leg, lit a cigarette and began talking." Cámara found his attitude "pedantic and presumptuous."[15]

Two years later, Ricardo Pozas was more circumspect. "Don Erasto Urbina has a very debatable personality," he wrote. Pozas noted that Urbina gave many speeches in the late 1930s condemning ladinos until he met Vicente Lombardo Toledano, the Marxist who headed the CTM during the Cárdenas years. Lombardo explained to Urbina that the class struggle superseded all others, including the ethnic struggle between Indians and non-Indians. "This rectification may be what led him to hand himself over to the ladinos," wrote Pozas acidly. Urbina also "rectified" his previous anticlerical beliefs. "The man who once launched the most vehement attacks against the clergy began associating with Eduardo Flores, one of the most important priests in Ciudad Las Casas, and attended the funeral of the priest Lino Morales, who was regarded by the fanatics of Ciudad Las Casas as a saint." One of the side effects of Urbina's ideological metamorphosis was the accumulation of private property; as Pozas noted, "The agrarian leader was transformed into the owner of one of the best fincas in the Cacaté region." Ever enigmatic, Urbina insisted on his socialist and anticlerical beliefs when speaking with Pozas, a Marxist anthropologist. In closing, Pozas noted that Urbina "seemed a little bitter and felt that his political power was diminishing." (Urbina was right. In 1946, one year after the interview, the state government abolished his STI and fired all department officials who had been associated with him and the reforms of the Cardenista period. Urbina himself was transferred out of the state.) Pozas concluded his lengthy observation with the thought that "maybe the time is not yet ripe to judge Erasto Urbina's work with the Indians, which was largely positive."[16]

Perhaps Urbina's short-term impact *was* positive, but over the long term, his legacy placed the highlands on the road to disaster. By the late 1930s his scribes had already become "labor union officers, heads of their municipal agrarian committees, leaders of the local branches of the official party . . . and representatives to the regional committee of the [CNC]."[17] By the early 1940s these men had also penetrated their communities' parallel, "traditional" hierarchies. Once Mexico's one-party state learned that it could control entire indigenous communities by co-opting a relatively small number of "traditional" leaders, the PRI ensured their loyalty by letting them control access to federal patronage benefits like agrarian reform and teaching jobs. In exchange, the former scribes were expected to keep the peace and provide votes for the PRI at election time. The "closed corporate communities" that anthropologists believed they had found in the 1950s were in fact tied economically to lowland plantations and bound politically to Tuxtla Gutiérrez and far-off Mexico City.[18]

From Indigenismo to Insurrection

After the SEP retreated in the highlands, a new federal institution emerged to take its place. In 1948, anthropologist Alfonso Caso convinced the administration of President Miguel Alemán to create the INI. The strategy offered by Caso and his fellow culturalists (both Mexican and foreign) was a tame one, consisting of "integral regional development" through bilingual indigenous "promoters." The INI opened its first experimental Coordinating Center (Centro Coordinador) in San Cristóbal in 1951. As its name suggests, the Coordinating Center was to coordinate the work of government agencies and provide the anthropological insight needed to facilitate "development." This approach left untouched the overriding structural factors that kept indigenous Mexicans in a marginal and terribly impoverished condition.

Shortly after the Coordinating Center opened its doors, it ran headlong into the alcohol monopoly of Hernán and Moctezuma Pedrero. The ensuing clash pitting federal indigenistas against the monopoly and its patrons in the state government had the effect of compromising the INI's already modest program. While the Pedreros lost their monopoly status to produce and sell aguardiente, the INI privatized its cooperatives and some of its other operations in the highlands.[19] This shift in the INI's development policy greatly favored Urbina's scribes/principales, who became the business partners of the Pedreros and other wealthy ladinos. Coincidentally, aguardiente consumption did fall in the highlands shortly after this compromise, but not as the result of a top-down public health campaign led by the SEP or the INI. Beginning in the late 1950s, many of Urbina's scribes/principales operated Coca-Cola and Pepsi monopolies. Soon the soft drinks had not only become

the refreshment of choice in the highlands, but their use became ubiquitous in Tzotzil and Tzeltal religious rituals.[20] The power of the market proved more effective than the best-laid plans of federal social engineers.

The INI's experience in highland Chiapas was not without isolated achievements. One of these was its program of bilingual bicultural education. During the early 1950s the INI recruited and trained bilingual community leaders, most of them Urbina's scribes/principales, to teach reading and writing in their native tongues and in Spanish. These bilingual bicultural *promotores* also led sanitation and vaccination campaigns, introduced new farming techniques, established cooperatives, introduced piped water, and facilitated road construction.[21]

However, as in the 1940s, the scribes/principales prevented potential rivals from finishing school and reserved places in the schools for their own families. In 1975, 80 percent of the promotores in Chamula were related to Urbina's scribes. In Mitontic, 100 percent of the promotores were related to the original scribes, and nearly all of the seventy-odd students who had completed the sixth grade in that municipality were named Rodríguez and were members of the ruling family. In some communities, like Chalchihuitán, Chenalhó, and Mitontic, the career path from scribe to teacher to municipal authority became practically institutionalized.[22]

The contradiction between the tremendous political and economic control of the scribes/principales and the democratizing effects of the federal government's education and development policies produced important political convulsions in the 1960s. In Chamula, growing numbers of frustrated young people protested the caciques' transportation monopolies and their corruption. In an unprecedented move, in 1970 these dissidents ran an opposition candidate in Chamula's municipal elections and would do so again in 1973 and 1976. The caciques responded by attacking (and sometimes killing) the dissidents, burning their homes, and expelling them from Chamula on the grounds that they had violated the community's "traditional unity and respect for hierarchy."[23] The INI and especially the state's indigenista institution, the DAI, turned a blind eye to the violence and murders, aided and abetted cacique corruption, and managed elections in favor of the caciques. Before the start of the 1969–1970 school year the INI fired all of the teachers involved in protesting the graft of Chamula's municipal president, one of Urbina's original scribes. In another egregious case of state complicity with highland caciquismo, in 1976 the state's indigenista agency provided trucks to transport beaten and humiliated dissidents out of

Chamula following elections in which their candidate, naturally, lost. The state agency, now called the Chiapas Development Program, or PRODESCH (Programa de Desarrollo de Chiapas), justified its role by explaining that the mass expulsions were, in its words, an "expression of the popular, traditional will of the community." Convinced that their own control of the highlands was at stake, and its vast reserve of PRI votes at risk, the INI and PRODESCH "capitulated to its own creatures, the scribes/principales."[24]

After 1971 the INI and the PRODESCH granted the same blanket immunity to scribes/principales in all of the Tzotzil and Tzeltal communities in the highlands. Five years later, communities such as Chalchihuitán, Tenejapa, Mitontic, Zinacantán, Chenalhó, and Oxchuc began expelling dissidents.[25] Many of the *expulsados* became Protestants and settled in the outskirts of San Cristóbal; many others made the longer journey to the Selva in eastern Chiapas.

The year 1974 represents a crucial turning point for indigenous dissidents in Chiapas. To commemorate the 500th anniversary of the birthday of Bartolomé de Las Casas, the state government sponsored an Indigenous Congress in San Cristóbal de Las Casas. Indigenous people had little to celebrate. A particularly brutal form of resident peonage was still alive and well in Simojovel, north of San Cristóbal. Indigenous people were still thrown in San Cristóbal's jails if caught in town after dark. And North American anthropologists tell of returning from fieldwork in Chamula and having trash thrown at them simply for wearing Chamulan ponchos.[26]

Governor Manuel Velasco Suárez asked Bishop Samuel Ruiz to assist in organizing the conference. Ruiz was determined to turn the state government's populist ploy into a meaningful event where indigenous communities could air their long-standing grievances. In 1973, one year before the congress was to take place, Ruiz's hand-picked organizers traveled to indigenous communities and asked them to select representatives to the congress. The communities were also told to prepare their denunciations and demands along four broad themes—land, commerce, education, and health. At the congress, the Tzotzil, Tzeltal, Tojolabal, and Ch'ol representatives realized that they shared similar grievances in spite of their historic and ethnic differences. Below is an excerpt from their summary of denunciations related to education.

> It is a very bad system of education. Even the teaching is bad.
>
> . . . What they teach is of no use for the improvement of the community.
>
> . . . It is an education that prepares the children for exploitation.

> . . . Those who finish the sixth year know nothing, they become exploiters following the example of their teachers.
>
> . . . There is a lack of schools.
>
> . . . Schooling is incomplete. For example, there is a school that has been going for 38 years, and no one has finished the primary grades.
>
> Most of the teachers and INI agents give a bad example.
>
> . . . They do not respect the older girls in school. There are many cases of rape.
>
> . . . They do not keep the schedule.
>
> . . . They are merchants and exploit the students.
>
> . . . They run cantinas.
>
> . . . They get drunk.
>
> . . . They are ashamed of being Indians. They do not respect the custom of their communities.
>
> Ladino teachers . . . think they are superior.
>
> . . . They do not teach well because they do not know the Indian language, and the children do not know Spanish.[27]

Congress organizers hoped to use this common ground as a springboard for future collective action. Their plans were foiled by a concerted PRI counterattack and by political and ideological divisions. An opportunity was lost, at least for the moment. Meanwhile, in 1978 coletos unveiled a statue to Diego de Mazariegos. It was the only monument to a conquistador to be found in all of Mexico. The battle lines were hardening.[28]

Countdown to Rebellion

A combination of long-standing problems and short-term triggers carried parts of the state to the point of rebellion in 1994 and have provided the Zapatistas with remarkable levels of support since then in spite of the government's determined counter-insurgency campaign. Let us briefly recount the major explanatory arguments.

We begin with land. Three generations of rural Chiapanecos have had mostly frustrating experiences with the federal land-reform program. Furthermore, the astonishing demographic growth of indigenous communities meant that land that once adequately sustained communities in the 1940s and 1950s became insufficient within a generation. In the 1980s, men in land-starved municipalities like Chamula who typically worked part of the year in lowland plantations suddenly had to compete with Guatemalan war refugees willing to work for even less. Furthermore, the increased use of herbicides and commercial fertilizer in agriculture reduced the demand for field hands.[29]

In the Selva, where the land is nutrient-poor and where indigenous refugees settled in the tens of thousands, the situation was not much better. Stephen reported that the population of the Tojolabal ejido of Guadalupe Tepeyac more than doubled from 1955 to 1965. Ejidos like Guadalupe Tepeyac applied for more land but had to wait years before it was granted; meanwhile, their populations continued to grow. In the 1970s, the population of the Selva grew by 40 percent. Exacerbating matters in the middle 1980s was Chiapas's governor, General Absalón Castellanos Domínguez. One of the state's richest cattlemen, his Comitán-based family was notoriously known for being the "bosses of the Selva." (The Castellanos and Domínguez clans played important roles in leading the Mapache resistance of 1914–1920.) During his tenure, Castellanos further handcuffed agrarian reform in the Selva by handing out 4,714 "certificates of inaffectability" to fellow cattle ranchers, placing at least 70 percent of their land beyond the reach of agrarian reform programs. In fact, the number of certificates doled out by Castellanos was more than all of Chiapas's previous state governors combined.[30]

Economic crises in the 1980s induced the Mexican government to agree to the neoliberal economic reforms of the international banking community. One of the principal casualties was revolutionary nationalism, including agricultural protectionism. The Mexican government reduced the assistance it gave to corn and coffee producers, the latter of which saw world coffee prices collapse in 1989. To ease the pain (and bolster the PRI's allies at a time when government largess was otherwise shrinking), President Carlos Salinas (1988–1994) channeled federal development money (most notably, PRONASOL [Programa Nacional de Solidaridad] funds) to the highlands and parts of the Selva like Guadalupe Tepeyac, where a large, modern hospital was built. While Salinas offered the carrot, his governor in Chiapas, General Patrocinio González Garrido, employed the stick. His 1990 penal code criminalized public protest, and many activists served lengthy jail terms simply for organizing demonstrations. As the prisons filled, the state government continued to rig elections in favor of the PRI.[31]

Meanwhile, in the frontier communities of the Selva, there were no political parties and the PRI had not hooked the leadership into its co-optive/repressive mechanisms. The settlers belonged to an alphabet-soup of diverse regional peasant organizations that were independent of the PRI's

CNC. They shared an impoverished lifestyle and had common enemies. Building on the relationships that had been established at the 1974 Indigenous Congress, a pan-indigenous class consciousness emerged that superceded their identities as Tzeltals, Tzotzils, Tojolabals, and Ch'ols. The settler ejidos governed themselves democratically, by consensus. Officeholders were instructed by colonists and catechists to govern by obeying (*mandar obedeciendo*).[32]

In late 1983, three mestizos established themselves in this politically receptive corner of Chiapas with the intention of fomenting revolution. They were members of the pro-Cuban, anti-imperialist FLN, the Fuerzas de Liberación Nacional (Forces of National Liberation). The EZLN, the Ejército Zapatista de Liberación Nacional, was one of the FLN's combat units. One of the mestizos was Rafael Sebastián Guillén Vicente, alias Subcomandante Marcos, whose 1980 undergraduate thesis was titled "*Filosofía y educación*."[33] Marcos tells that he and his comrades were accepted into the communities only after they translated their political message into indigenous languages and came to appreciate local cultures and local histories of struggle. The FLN's urban, Marxist agenda was consequently "contaminated" and transformed. As Marcos tells it, the EZLN is "the product of a hybrid, of a confrontation, of a collision in which, fortunately I believe, we lost."[34]

In 1990, as the EZLN meticulously built its base in eastern Chiapas and the state's political and economic crises worsened, the SEP published its plan to modernize education in indigenous Chiapas. It called for pedagogy "congruent with the socioeconomic, cultural, and political development of the Indians" that would "link these cultures with the national culture to reconcile interests, rights and obligations that will tend to strengthen national identity."[35] Such a pedagogy was unlikely, however, when out of its 6,529 teachers in indigenous Chiapas, only 31 percent had normal-school training; an even greater percentage had not even graduated from high school. As in the 1930s, textbooks arrived late and in insufficient numbers. Indigenous communities were often sent bilingual teachers that spoke a native tongue not their own. In any case, most bilingual teachers preferred using Spanish in the classroom and thereby transmitted the dominant culture to students who felt disconnected from the learning process. When bilingual teaching materials were available, most teachers either refused to use them or lacked the training to do so. Moreover, the SEP still struggled to maintain adequate indigenous boarding schools in Chiapas. Now called Albergues Escolares, the SEP openly described them as "Centers of Misery," much as Corzo might have labeled them in the middle 1930s.[36]

The final, short-term triggers to the rebellion are well known. Chief among these was the suspension of agrarian reform. To prepare the groundwork for Mexico's entry into the North American Free Trade Agreement, in 1992 President Carlos Salinas abandoned those provisions in Article 27 that authorized agrarian reform and protected communal landholding. Twenty-eight percent of the pending land claims at Mexico's Ministry of Agrarian Reform were from Chiapas, a state that has just 5 percent of the national population. At this point, Stephen reports, many ejidos voted for war.[37]

State and Nation Building and the Zapatistas

On January 1, 1994, the day that NAFTA took effect, the Zapatistas declared themselves in rebellion against the Mexican government and seized several towns. They skillfully appropriated the revolutionary nationalist language, ideas, and symbols first and most emphatically introduced by the SEP in the 1930s. They named themselves after the "intransigent of the revolution," they called their base "Aguascalientes" after the city of the same name where eighty years earlier Zapatista, Villista, and Carrancista armies had met as the "Sovereign Revolutionary Convention," and they adroitly used the imagery of the Mexican flag. Never a separatist movement, the new Zapatismo claimed the rights of national citizenship for Mexico's most marginalized indigenous communities. For decades, the federal government labored to construct an "imagined community" of Mexicans; in 1994, neoliberal technocrats in the PRI paid a price for turning their backs on that nation.

After twelve days of fighting, the Zapatistas accepted President Salinas's offer of a cease-fire. A few weeks later, negotiations between the two sides commenced in San Cristóbal. The Zapatistas presented thirty-four demands, many of which echoed those made twenty years earlier in the same city at the Indigenous Congress. Some of these were rooted in the immediate postrevolutionary period. Surely SEP teachers in the 1930s would have identified with the Zapatistas' call for the application of the federal labor law, an improved health care system, and more and better schools and teachers. (Most pro-Zapatista indigenous communities in Chiapas expelled SEP teachers from their midst as soon as the rebellion commenced.) Some of the Zapatistas' political demands included calls for effective democracy, the revocation of González's 1990 penal code, and an end to the expulsions from highland communities. Another set of demands lambasted federal indigenismo and pointed the way to a more plural view of the Mexican nation, calling for political, economic, and cultural (including judicial) autonomy for indigenous communities.[38] Such demands would likely have resonated with Cardenista progressives in the late 1930s like former DAI director Luis Chávez Orozco.

Since March 1994, the history of contemporary Zapatismo has oscillated between utopian euphoria and the grueling reality of military occupation and paramilitary aggression. In August 1994, just ahead of national presidential elections, the Zapatistas presented their alternative national vision at the National Democratic Convention held at their base in Aguascalientes. In December of that year, they established more than thirty autonomous municipalities in their strongholds. The fledgling government of Ernesto Zedillo countered in February 1995 with a military invasion of Zapatista territory, the "unmasking" of Marcos, and the detention of top Zapatistas. Later that year, however, negotiations began between Zapatista and federal representatives in San Andrés Larráinzar. In 1996, they signed the San Andrés Peace Accords on Indigenous Rights and Culture. The Zedillo administration in Mexico City later refused to sign these accords into law, and the Zapatistas broke off talks. Political stalemate ensued; meanwhile, the state-level PRI and its revolving-door governors armed anti-Zapatista paramilitaries and precipitated a number of atrocities, most notably the December 1997 massacre of forty-five pacifists at Acteal. More stalemate followed.

By the year 2000, the Zapatistas had few concrete gains to show for their efforts. Although supporters in their municipal strongholds enjoyed unprecedented autonomy over cultural policy, education, and legal practice, the PRI/government continued to use its resources to divide and weaken them. Yet the argument can be made that the Zapatistas played a pivotal role in Mexico's ongoing transition to democracy. In July 2000, for the first time in seventy-one years, the PRI was defeated in a presidential election, and outgoing president Zedillo immediately recognized the outcome and congratulated the winner, the candidate from the National Action Party (Partido de Acción Nacional, or PAN), Vicente Fox. During the campaign, the PRI could not overcome its grave crisis of legitimacy, and no phenomenon had done more to tarnish that legitimacy than Zapatismo. The opposition's victory was even sweeter in Chiapas, where seven weeks later a coalition of opposition parties carried the governor's race, also a historic first. The victors of the summer of 2000 promised to open dialogue with the Zapatistas, and hope was rekindled.

Shortly after taking office, President Fox invited the Zapatistas to Mexico

City to present to the national congress a proposal for constitutional reforms based on the San Andrés Accords. It was pure political theater pitting the marketing genius of the former Coca-Cola executive against the wily, enigmatic Marcos. Guarded by a federal escort, busloads of Zapatistas, their supporters, and the press wove their way to Mexico City. In March 2001 Zapatistas occupied Mexico City's Zócalo for the first time since late 1914. They presented their draft to congress and returned home. In April, the Mexican Congress altered key components of the law, then passed it. The furious Zapatista leadership lashed out in the national press, then dropped off the national radar. Some observers speculated that they had become an anachronism in a Mexico that now seemed to be moving toward true political pluralism.

Why did the Zapatista rebellion occur in Chiapas and not in some other state like Oaxaca, Guerrero, or Veracruz, likewise characterized by political violence, grinding poverty, and marginalized indigenous populations? Certainly the idiosyncratic course of the Mexican revolution between 1914 and 1920 greatly handicapped efforts to connect Chiapas to the modern state and nation that emerged in Mexico after 1920. Until the middle 1930s, the federal government's chief state- and nation-building institution, the SEP, struggled to build and maintain schools and was unable to promote development or initiate agrarian and labor reforms. Socialist education and revolutionary nationalism won over most mestizo communities after 1935, but SEP indigenismo had unintended and ultimately rather sinister consequences in the highlands. By 1940 the rollback of Cardenista populism was in full swing, even as communities came to embrace the culture of schooling; by the middle 1940s it was "business as usual" in Chiapas.

Fifty years passed. The delayed, incomplete, and corrupted nature of state and nation building in Chiapas prevented government from resolving the state's most pressing political, economic, and social problems. The grievances that produced the insurrection were not unique to Chiapas, but the institutions charged with resolving such matters seemed singularly unable to do so. As the hunger for land grew, so too did frustration with the agrarian reform process. Caciquismo in the highlands flourished, nurtured and protected by the state and federal government. As the political system became increasingly corrupt, the state's repressive apparatus became more active. Schooling in the highlands remained ineffective and culturally insensitive; in the Selva, it was generally not available at all, leaving settlers with few options.

In this setting, when neoliberal economic policies induced the federal government to abandon the revolutionary nationalism that it had promoted for decades, indigenous Chiapanecos (whose parents and grandparents likely rejected the SEP's schools, if they were exposed to them at all) reappropriated that potent discourse. Their rebellion not only upset the political order in Chiapas and Mexico and grabbed international headlines, but it has forced Mexican society to conceptualize a multiethnic nation. Still, it is hard not to see the Zapatistas as one act in Chiapas's long, tragic play. They, like Jesús Agustín Castro and Carlos Vidal in the nineteen teens and twenties; and Governor Efraín Gutiérrez and Inspectors Castellanos, Mota, and Vassallo in the 1930s; and the INI in the 1950s; and the Congreso Indígena in the 1970s were ultimately unable to reverse centuries of marginalization, exploitation, institutionalized racism, and scarcity in Chiapas. ◆

Notes

Introduction

The epigraph is from Thomas Benjamin, "A Time of Reconquest: History, the Maya Revival, and the Zapatista Rebellion in Chiapas," *American Historical Review* 105, no. 2 (April 2000): 450.

1. Most of these books and articles were published by Harvard's prolific Chiapas project (1957–1980). Project director Evon Vogt recently defended the community study methodology in his memoirs; see Vogt, *Fieldwork among the Maya: Reflections on the Harvard Chiapas Project* (Albuquerque: University of Mexico Press, 1994), 350. For a critique of the Harvard Project's approach, see Cynthia Hewitt de Alcántara, *Anthropological Perspectives on Rural Mexico* (Boston: Routledge & Kegan Paul, 1984), 60; and Jan Rus, "Rereading Tzotzil Ethnography: Recent Scholarship from Chiapas, Mexico" in *Pluralizing Ethnography: Comparison and Representation in Maya Cultures, Histories, and Identities,* eds. John M. Watanabe and Edward F. Fischer (Santa Fe: School of American Research Press, 2004).

2. See, for example, George Collier with Elizabeth Lowery Quaratiello, *Basta! Land and the Zapatista Rebellion in Chiapas* (Oakland: Institute for Food and Development Policy, 1999 [1994]); Antonio García de León, *Fronteras interiores: Chiapas: una modernidad particular* (México: Oceano, 2002); Diana Guillén, *Chiapas 1973–1993: Mediaciones, política e institucionalidad* (México, D.F.: Instituto Mora, 1998); Neil Harvey, *The Chiapas Rebellion: The Struggle for Land and Democracy* (Durham, N.C.: Duke University Press, 1998); Lynn Stephen, *¡Zapata Lives!* (Berkeley: University of California Press, 2002); and Sonia Toledo Tello, *Historia del movimiento indígena en Simojovel, 1970–1989* (Tuxtla: Universidad Autónoma de Chiapas, 1996).

3. Thomas Benjamin, *A Rich Land, a Poor People: Politics and Society in Modern Chiapas* (Albuquerque: University of New Mexico Press, 1989); Antonio García de León, *Resistencia y utopía: Memorial de agravios y crónica de revueltas y profecías acaecidas en la provincia de Chiapas durante los últimos quinientos años de su historia*, 2 vols. (México: Ediciones Era, 1985); and Jan Rus, various, especially "The 'Comunidad Revolucionaria Institucional': The Subversion of Native Government in Highland Chiapas, 1936–1968," in *Everyday Forms of State Formation: Revolution and the Negotiation of Rule in Modern Mexico*, ed. Gilbert M. Joseph and Daniel Nugent (Durham, N.C.: Duke University Press, 1994), 265–300.

4. Adrian Bantjes, *As If Jesus Walked on Earth: Cardenismo, Sonora, and the Mexican Revolution* (Wilmington, Del.: Scholarly Resources Inc., 1998); Marjorie Becker, *Setting the Virgin on Fire* (Berkeley: University of California Press, 1995); and Ben Fallaw, *Cárdenas Compromised: The Failure of Reform in Postrevolutionary Yucatán* (Durham, N.C.: Duke University Press, 2001).

5. Alan Knight, "Cardenismo: Juggernaut or Jalopy?" *Journal of Latin American*

Studies 26 (1994): 73–107.

6. Mary Kay Vaughan, *Cultural Politics in Revolution: Teachers, Peasants, and Schools in Mexico (1930–1940)* (Tucson: University of Arizona Press, 1997).

7. Thomas Benjamin, *La Revolución: Mexico's Great Revolution as Memory, Myth and History* (Austin: University of Texas Press, 2000), 14. See also Benedict Anderson, *Imagined Communities: Reflections on the Origins and Spread of Nationalism* (New York: Verso, 1991 [1983]).

8. David Brading, *The First America: The Spanish Monarchy, Creole Patriots, and the Liberal State, 1492–1867* (Cambridge: Cambridge University Press, 1991); see also Nicola Miller, *In the Shadow of the State: Intellectuals and the Quest for National Identity in Twentieth-century Spanish America* (New York: Verso, 1999); and Ricardo Pérez Montfort, *Estampas de nacionalismo popular mexicano: Ensayos sobre cultura popular y nacionalismo* (México: CIESAS, 1994).

9. Gustavo Esteva, "The Meaning and Scope of the Struggle for Autonomy," *Latin American Perspectives* 28, no. 2 (March 2001): 120; and Guillermo de la Peña, "Poder local, poder regional: Perspectivas socioantropológicas," *Poder local, poder regional*, ed. Jorge Padua and Alain Vanneph (México: El Colegio de México/CEMCA, 1986), 43.

10. Guy Thomson, "Liberalism and Nation-Building in Mexico and Spain during the Nineteenth Century," in *Studies in the Formation of the Nation State in Latin America*, ed. James Dunkerley (London: Institute of Latin American Studies, 2002), 190; see also Florencia Mallon, *Peasant and Nation: The Making of Postcolonial Mexico and Peru* (Berkeley: University of California Press, 1995); and Thomson, with David G. LaFrance, *Patriotism, Politics, and Popular Liberalism in Nineteenth-Century Mexico: Juan Francisco Lucas and the Puebla Sierra* (Wilmington, Del.: Scholarly Resources Inc., 2002 [1999]).

11. John M. Hart, *Revolutionary Mexico: The Coming and Process of the Mexican Revolution* (Berkeley: University of California Press, 1987).

12. Alan Knight, *The Mexican Revolution*, 2 vols. (Lincoln: University of Nebraska Press 1990 [1986]), I:2.

13. Natividad Gutiérrez, *Nationalist Myths and Ethnic Identities: Indigenous Intellectuals and the Mexican State* (Lincoln: University of Nebraska Press, 1999), 2–24.

14. Emphasis in original. Eric J. Hobsbawm, *Nations and Nationalism since 1780: Programme, Myth, Reality* (Cambridge: Cambridge University Press, 1992 [1990]), 12.

15. John Dewey, "Mexico, 1926," in *John Dewey's Impressions of Soviet Russia and the Revolutionary World: Mexico-China-Turkey*, ed. William W. Brickman (New York: Teachers College, Columbia University, 1964 [1929]), 123.

16. Robert H. Holden, *Mexico and the Survey of Public Lands: The Management of Modernization, 1876–1911* (DeKalb: Northern Illinois University Press, 1994), 66–67.

17. Juan Pedro Viqueira, "Chiapas y sus regiones," in *Chiapas: Los rumbos de otra historia*, ed. Juan Pedro Viqueira and Mario Humberto Ruz (México: UNAM, 1995), 19–40.

Chapter 1

The epigraph is reproduced in Marie-Odile Marion Singer, *El agrarismo en Chiapas (1524–1940)* (México, D.F.: Instituto Nacional de Antropología e Historia, 1988), 78.

1. Instituto Nacional de Antropología e Historia, Archivo Histórico de la Institución (hereafter INAHAHI), Serie: Depto. Monumentos Artísticos, Arqueológicos e Históricos, Caja 35, Exp. 2471, Circular II-114-235, from Jefe del Depto. de Enseñanza Primaria y Normal Joaquín Jara Díaz to Inspectores y Directores de la Ed. Fed., dated Sept. 7, 1935.

2. Christine Eber, *Women and Alcohol in a Highland Maya Town* (Austin: University of Texas Press, 1995), 19–20; Kevin Gosner, *Soldiers of the Virgin: The Moral Economy of a Colonial Maya Rebellion* (Tucson: University of Arizona Press, 1992), 30–42, 47–68; Murdo MacLeod, *Spanish Central America: A Socioeconomic History, 1520–1720* (Berkeley: University of California Press, 1973), 68–79, 91–95, 235–40; and Robert Wasserstrom, *Class and Society in Central Chiapas* (Berkeley: University of California Press, 1983), 32–106.

3. Prudencio Moscoso Pastrana, *México y Chiapas: Independencia y federación de la provincia chiapaneca* (México, 1974), 162–64, Documento número 13, signed by Fernando Jph. del Valle, dated from the Sala Capitular de Chiapa, Oct. 29, 1821.

4. Benjamin, *A Rich Land*, 7–8; and Roderic Ai Camp, *La cuestión chiapaneca: Revisión de una polémica territorial* (Tuxtla Gutiérrez, Chis.: H. Congreso del estado de Chiapas, LV Legislatura, 1984), 10–14.

5. Benjamin, *A Rich Land*, 8; Jan de Vos, *Las fronteras de la frontera sur* (Villahermosa, Tabasco: Universidad Juárez Autónoma de Tabasco y CIESAS, 1993), 90.

6. Benjamin, *A Rich Land*, 8–11; Camp, *La cuestión chiapaneca*, 23–28; de Vos, *Las fronteras de la frontera sur*, 91–94; "Acta por la cual los representantes de los ayuntamientos del Partido de Soconusco deciden ser parte de la provincias unidas del Centro de América, separándose de Chiapa," in Matías Romero, *Bosquejo histórico de la agregación a México de Chiapas y Soconusco* (México: Imprenta del Gobierno, 1877), 500–501.

7. Benjamin, *A Rich Land*, 11.

8. De Vos, *Las fronteras de la frontera sur*, 102–5.

9. Benjamin, *A Rich Land*, 56; de Vos, *Las fronteras de la frontera sur*, 102–11; and Jan de Vos, *Oro verde: La conquista de la Selva Lacandona por los madereros tabasqueños, 1822–1949* (México: Fondo de Cultura Económica, 1988), 103–9.

10. De Vos, *Las fronteras de la frontera sur*, Documento No. 19, 152; Daniela Spenser, "Soconusco: The Formation of a Coffee Economy in Chiapas," in *Other Mexicos: Essays on Regional Mexican History, 1876–1911*, ed. Thomas Benjamin and William McNellie (Albuquerque: University of New Mexico Press, 1984), 124–27.

11. Benjamin, *A Rich Land*, 38–39; García de León, *Resistencia*, 1: 173; and Holden, *Mexico and the Survey of Public Lands*, 66–69.

12. Friedericke Baumann, "Terratenientes, campesinos, y la expansión de la agricultura capitalista en Chiapas, 1896–1916," *Mesoamérica* 4 (1983): 15ff.; Daniela Spenser, "Los inicios del cultivo del café en Soconusco," 77–78; and Brígida von Mentz, "Las empresas alemanas en México (1920–1942)," in *Los empresarios alemanes*, I: 184–86. In 1910, only the Federal District had more foreign residents than the state of Chiapas.

13. Benjamin, *A Rich Land*, 42, 48.

14. Ibid., 48–50; Rus, "Coffee and the Recolonization of Highland Chiapas, Mexico: Indian Communities and Plantation Labor, 1892–1912," in *The Global Coffee Economy in Africa, Asia, and Latin America, 1500–1989*, ed. Steven Topik and W. Clarence-Smith (Cambridge: Cambridge University Press, 2003), 262–64, 267–72, 277; and Spenser, "Los inicios del cultivo del café en Soconusco," 80.

15. Rus, "Contained Revolutions," 4–5.

16. Rus, "Coffee and the Recolonization of Highland Chiapas," 278.

17. Baumann, "Terratenientes", 14–16, 53; and Rus, "Coffee and the Recolonization of Highland Chiapas," 280.

18. Baumann, "Terratenientes", 60–62; and Salvador Guzmán López, Jan Rus, and Socios de la Unión "Tierra Tzotzil," *Kipaltik* (San Cristóbal de Las Casas, Chis.: El Taller Tzotzil, 1999).

19. Rus, "Coffee and the Recolonization of Highland Chiapas," 258, 283–85.

20. Ibid., 278.

21. Rus, "Contained Revolutions," 9.

22. Moisés González Navarro, *La vida social, Historia Moderna de México*, ed. Daniel Cosío Villegas, vol. 2, *El Porfiriato* (Tomo 4) (México: Editorial Hermes, 1957), 230–31.

23. *Discurso del Coronel Francisco León, Gobernador de Chiapas, ante la XIX Legislatura del Estado, al abrir ésta sus sesiones ordinarias el 16 de septiembre* (Tuxtla: Imprenta del Gobierno, dirigida por Félix Santaella, 1896), 9.

24. *Informe oficial del Gobernador de Chiapas, C. Coronel Francisco León, rendido ante la XX Legislatura del Estado, al abrir ésta su primer período de sesiones ordinarias en el segundo año de su ejercicio, el 16 de septiembre de 1898* (Tuxtla: Imprenta del Gobierno dirigida por Félix Santaella, 1898), 12.

25. Colección Porfirio Díaz, Rollo 132/XXI, #13944, León to Díaz, 15 Aug. 1896. My thanks to Friedl Baumann for sharing with me Thomas Benjamin's notes from this archive.

26. *Reglamento Interior de la Escuela Normal para Profesoras* (Tuxtla: Imprenta del Gobierno del Estado, dirigida por Félix Santaella, 1903), 3–4.

27. *Anuario estadístico del Estado de Chiapas, formado por la Sección de Estadística de la Secretaría General de Gobierno, a cargo del ciudadano J. Abel Cruz*, Año de 1908, I: 47–48.

28. Mary Kay Vaughan, *The State, Education, and Social Class in Mexico, 1880–1928* (DeKalb: Northern Illinois University Press, 1982), 42.

29. "Programas detallados para las escuelas de 1a, 2a, y 3a clase," Dir. Gen. de Instrucción Pública del Estado de Tabasco (San Juan Bautista, Tabasco: Imprenta de M. Gaburcio M., 1896), 14; Vaughan, *The State, Education, and Social Class*, 22–28.

30. Stephen E. Lewis, "Citizenship, Education, and Revolution in San Juan Bautista, Tabasco, 1894–1917," *MACLAS Latin American Essays* vol. VIII (1994): 8–9.

31. Bancroft Library, Colección Tabasco, "Programa detallado para las escuelas dirigidas por maestros ambulantes" (San Juan Bautista, Tabasco: Gobierno del estado libre y soberano de Tabasco, 1898), 4.

32. Alfonso Caparrozo, "Algunas consideraciones metodológicas acerca de la

enseñanza de la Instrucción Cívica" (San Juan Bautista, Tabasco: Tipografía "La Ilustración," 1902), 9.

33. Francisco Bulnes, *The Whole Truth About Mexico; President Wilson's Responsibility* (New York: M. Bulnes book company, 1916), 324. See also Luz Elena Galván de Terrazas, *Los maestros y la educación en México* (México: CIESAS, 1985).

34. García de León, *Resistencia*, 2: 101–33.

35. Rus, "Contained Revolutions," 14–15.

36. Benjamin, *A Rich Land*, 42, 106–10; García de León, *Resistencia*, 2: 22–33; Jan Rus, "Whose Caste War? Indians, Ladinos, and the Chiapas 'Caste War' of 1869," in *Spaniards and Indians in Southeastern Mesoamerica: Essays on the History of Ethnic Relations*, ed. Murdo J. MacLeod and Robert Wasserstrom (Lincoln: University of Nebraska Press, 1983), 127–68.

37. Benjamin, *A Rich Land*, 120–22; Alicia Hernández Chávez, "La defensa de los finqueros en Chiapas, 1914–1920," in *Historia Mexicana* XXVIII (3) (enero–marzo 1979): 355–56; Knight, *The Mexican Revolution*, 2: 237–42; Prudencio Moscoso Pastrana, *El pinedismo en Chiapas, 1916–1920* (México, 1960), 18–34; Archivo Histórico del Estado de Chiapas (hereafter AHECh), Fondo Documental Fernando Castañon Gamboa, 1039.1, Circular Núm. 17, Gobierno Preconstitucional del Estado de Chiapas, signed by Oficial Mayor Santiago A. Vázquez, dated from Tuxtla, Dec. 29, 1915.

38. Archivo Histórico del Municipo de San Cristóbal de Las Casas (hereafter AHMSCLC), 1917, Tomo 2, Borrador de Circulares, 1917, "Dado en el Palacio del Gobierno Constitucionalista del Estado, en Tuxtla Gutiérrez, a los treinta días del mes de octubre de mil novecientos catorce. J. A. Castro, General de Brigada, Gobernador y Comandante Militar del Estado de Chiapas. Jose C. Rangel, Secretario Gen."

39. *Memoria del Primer Congreso Pedagógico del Estado de Chiapas: Convocado por el Ciudadano Gobernador y comandante Militar del Estado y reunido en la Ciudad de Tuxtla Gutiérrez, del 10 de diciembre del año de 1914 al 17 de enero de 1915* (Tuxtla: Imprenta del Gobierno del Estado, 1916), 9–10, 39–41, 105–11.

40. Ibid., 23–24.

41. *Informe general que rinde a la Secretaría de Estado y del Despacho de Gobernación, el C. Gobernador y comandante Militar del Estado de Chiapas, C. Gral. Blas Corral* (Tuxtla: Oficina de Información y Propaganda del Gob. del Estado, 1916), 77.

42. Daniela Grollová, "Los trabajadores cafetaleros y el Partido Socialista Chiapaneco, 1920–1927," in *Chiapas: Los rumbos de otra historia* (México: UNAM, 1995), 202.

43. Gary H. Gossen, "Who is the Comandante of Subcomandante Marcos?" in *Indigenous Revolts in Chiapas and the Andean Highlands*, ed. Kevin Gosner and Arij Ouweneel (Amsterdam: CEDLA, 1996), 115.

44. "Apuntes y Memoria de Mons. Belisario Trejo, 1855–1920," *Boletín del Archivo Histórico Diocesano* IV (4) (noviembre 1991): 51.

45. Benjamin, *A Rich Land*, 124–25.

46. Marion Singer, *El agrarismo en Chiapas*, 78.

47. Benjamin, *A Rich Land*, 127–28, 137; García de León, *Resistencia*, 2: 68, Marion Singer, *El agrarismo en Chiapas*, 75, 78.

48. Rus, "Contained Revolutions," 15.

49. Calixta Guiteras Holmes, *Cancuc: Entografía de un pueblo tzeltal de los altos de Chiapas, 1944* (Tuxtla: Gobierno del Estado de Chiapas e Instituto Chiapaneco de Cultura, 1992), 139; see also Archivo General de la Nación (hereafter AGN), Ramo Obregón-Calles (hereafter O-C), 104-CH-19, "Problemas sociales y económicos del estado de Chiapas," from Agustín Farrera to Calles, dated Jan. 1925.

50. Rus, "Contained Revolutions," 2.

51. Fideicomiso Archivos Plutarco Elías Calles y Fernando Torreblanca (hereafter FAPECFT), Fondo Álvaro Obregón, "División Libre de Chiapas," 11030500, Exp. 423, Inv. 3298, Fo. 16, signed by Gral. Carlos A. Vidal and Gral. Tiburcio Fernández Ruiz, Feb. 8, 1920.

52. Benjamin, *A Rich Land*, 142; Marion Singer, *El agrarismo en Chiapas*, 96–97; Moscoso, *El pinedismo en Chiapas*, 287–96.

53. Benjamin, *A Rich Land*, 150–51.

54. Ibid., 151; María Eugenia Reyes Ramos, *El reparto de tierras y la política agraria en Chiapas, 1914–1988* (México: UNAM, 1992), 48–49.

55. AHMSCLC, 1915/2, "Circulares de la Dirección General del Ramo, 1915," Número 65, Fo. 1, "Instrucciones para los Delegados de Instrucción Pública," from Dir. Gen. de Instrucción Pública, J. O. Guzmán, dated April 1915.

56. Ibid., Número 78, Fo. 1, from Secretario de la Dirección Alejandro Navas to the Inspector de la 5a. Zona Escolar in San Cristóbal de Las Casas, dated from Tuxtla, July 15, 1915.

57. Ibid., "Circulares de la Dirección General del Ramo, 1915," Circular Núm. 8, Número 65, Fo. 9, signed by Dir. Gen. J. O. Guzmán and Secretario Alejandro Navas G., dated May 19, 1915.

58. Ibid., Número de órden 66, Fo. 14, "Notas de la Delegación," from Sub-Delegado de Instrucción Pública del Municipio de San Andrés to Inspector de la 5a. Zona Escolar Julio M. Corzo, dated July 1, 1915.

59. Ibid., Número de órden 94, Fos. 1–14, "Informativo sobre la conducta de los Directores de las Escuelas Urbanas Oficiales del municipio de Santiago del Departamento de Las Casas," from Directora del Municipio de Santiago, Maurilia Villafuerte, to Dir. de Instrucción Pública del Estado, Tuxtla, dated from San Cristóbal, Dec. 5, 1915.

60. *Periódico Oficial del Gobierno Constitucionalista del Estado de Chiapas*, Tuxtla Gutiérrez, July 31, 1919, Tomo XXXVI, Núm. 43, pp. 2–6.

61. Archivo Histórico de la Secretaría de Educación Pública (hereafter AHSEP), DE, Caja 3158 (682), Exp. 3, Fo. 87, from Prof. Conferencista en Chiapa y Las Casas Federico A. Corzo, to Jefe del DECI de la SEP, dated from México, D.F., April 28, 1922.

62. Ernesto Meneses Morales, coord., *Tendencias educativas oficiales en México 1911–1934* (México: Centro de Estudios Educativos, A.C., 1986), 184–89; Vaughan, *The State, Education, and Social Class*, 97.

63. AHSEP, DE, Caja 3126 (38), Exp. 68, Fo. 23, from Mauro Calderón, Delegación de

la SEP, Chiapas, to Jefe del DE de la SEP, México, D.F., dated from Tuxtla, Feb. 22, 1922.

64. Ibid., Exp. 68, Fos. 32–33, from Mauro Calderón, Jefe de la Delegación de la SEP, Chiapas, "Informe que rinde el Delegado en el Estado de Chiapas, al Jefe del Depto. Escolar de la Secretaría de Educación Pública Federal," dated from Tuxtla, Aug. 8, 1922.

65. The debate over Vasconcelos's proposal is covered by Claude Fell, *José Vasconcelos: Los años del águila (1920–1925)* (México: Universidad Nacional Autónoma de México, 1989), 62–69; and Meneses, coord., *Tendencias educativas oficiales en México 1911–1934*, 294–301.

66. *Informe que rinde el C. Gobernador Constitucional del Estado, General de División Tiburcio Fernández Ruiz, ante la H. Legislatura del mismo, al abrir ésta su primer período de sesiones ordinarias en el 20. año de su ejercicio* (Tuxtla Gutiérrez, Chiapas: Imprenta del Gobierno, 1921), 26.

67. Ibid., 20.

Chapter 2

The epigraph is reprinted in *México íntegro* (México: SepSetentas, 1982 [1939]) 153, 154.

1. Adolfo Gilly, *La revolución interrumpida* (México: El Caballito, 1971); Knight, *The Mexican Revolution*; and Knight, "Revolutionary Project, Recalcitrant People: Mexico, 1910–40," in *The Revolutionary Process in Mexico: Essays on Political and Social Change, 1880–1940*, ed. Jaime E. Rodríguez O. (Los Angeles: UCLA Latin American Center Publications, 1990), 228–29.

2. For more information on Vasconcelos, see Fell, *José Vasconcelos: Los años del águila (1920–1925)*, and Luis A. Marentes, *José Vasconcelos and the Writing of the Mexican Revolution* (New York: Twayne Publishers, 2000). Vasconcelos discussed his work as head of the SEP in *El desastre* in *Memorias*, vol. 2 (México: Fondo de Cultura Económica, 1982 [1939]), 9–598. On his frustrated bid for the presidency, see John Skirius, *José Vasconcelos y la cruzada de 1929* (México: Siglo XXI Editores, 1978), 140–43, 165.

3. AHSEP, DE, Caja 3148 (61), Exp. 2, Fos. 1–2, "Extracto del informe general que rinde el C. Delegado Mauro Calderón, relativo a la educación en el Estado de Chiapas," from Calderón to SEP, México, D.F., dated from Tuxtla, 1922.

4. Elsie Rockwell, "Schools of the Revolution: Enacting and Contesting State Forms in Tlaxcala, 1910–1930," in *Everyday Forms of State Formation*, 170–208.

5. AGN, O-C, Chiapas, Gobernador, 428-CH-8, Circular #6, from Srio. Gen. Interino Dr. F. Rincón, dated from Tuxtla, June 13, 1923; AHSEP, DECI, Caja 766 (691), Exp. 81, Fos. 3–4, from Gobernador Interino Manuel Encarnación to SEP, México, D.F., dated from Tuxtla, May 1923.

6. AGN, O-C, Chiapas, Gobernador, 428-CH-8, "Memorándum sobre la situación actual del Estado de Chiapas, que presenta su Gobernador Interino a los C.C. Presidente de la República y Secretario de Gobernación," by Gobernador Interino Manuel Encarnación, dated from Tuxtla, June 14, 1923.

7. Ibid., Circular #5, signed by Secretario Gen. Dr. F. Rincón, dated from Tuxtla, May 26, 1923; AHSEP, DECI, Caja 766 (691), Exp. 81, Fos. 3–4, from Gobernador Interino Manuel Encarnación to SEP, México, D.F., dated from Tuxtla, May 1923.

8. See, for example, "Las escuelas de Tapachula pasarán al control Escolar," *El Eco del Sureste*, Año I, Núm. I, Huixtla, June 23, 1933, p. 1; see also AHECh, Fondo Documental Fernando Castañón Gamboa, 1060, Años 1925 y 1926, "Circulares, decretos, y otras comunicaciones," Sección de Instrucción Pública, signed by Secretario Gen. de Gobierno Lic. José Castañón to Pres. Municipal Coapilla-Mezcalapa, dated from Tuxtla, Feb. 15, 1926.

9. AHSEP, DECI, Caja 689 (764), Exp. 6, Fo. 54, "Informe de la laboriosidad, idoneidad y conducta de cada uno de los profesores que atienden las distintas 'Casas del Pueblo' establecidas hasta hoy en la zona de esta misión," from Ernesto Parres, Misionero de Cultura Indígena y Educación Pública, dated from Motozintla, Dec. 1, 1923.

10. AHSEP, DEF Caja 1667 (1339), Exp. 8, from Parres to Jefe del'DECI, México, D.F., dated from Huixtla, Dec. 16, 1922.

11. AHSEP, DEI, Año de 1924, Caja 823 (754), Exp. 23, Fo. 103, from Parres to Oficina Principal del Timbre, Tuxtla, dated from Tapachula, May 8, 1924; see also Fo. 151, from Oficial Mayor Moisés Sáenz to Secretario de Hacienda y Crédito Público in México, D.F., dated from México, D.F., Oct. 9, 1924.

12. AHSEP, DECI, Caja 825 (756), Exp. 30, Fo. 14, "Informe que el Maestro Rural de la 'Casa del Pueblo' de la Villa de Tuxtla Chico, rinde al Profesor Misionero de Cultura Indígena," from Prof. Octavio Ángel Soto, dated June 20, 1924; and Caja 823 (754), Exp. 23, Fo. 317, from Parres to Dir. de Ed. y Cultura Indígena, SEP, México, D.F., dated from Tapachula, April 8, 1924.

13. AHSEP, DE, Caja 3158 (682), Exp. 3, Fo. 77, from Federico A. Corzo, Profesor Conferencista y Misionero en Chiapa y Las Casas, to Jefe del DECI de la SEP, México, D.F., dated from San Cristóbal, April 18, 1922.

14. Fell, *José Vasconcelos: Los años del águila (1920–1925)*, 236.

15. AHSEP, DECI, Caja 765 (690), Exp. 1, Fos. 25–26, from Maestro Misionero Núm. 112 Gilberto Tello to Dir. de Educación y Cultura Indígena Enrique Corona, México, D.F., dated from Cancuc, April 7, 1923.

16. R. Aída Hernández Castillo, *Histories and Stories from Chiapas: Border Identities in Southern Mexico* (Austin: University of Texas Press, 2001), 34; Daniela Spenser, *El Partido Socialista Chiapaneco: Rescate y reconstrucción de su historia* (México: CIESAS, Ediciones de la Casa Chata, 1988), 11–18.

17. Benjamin, *A Rich Land*, 142–43.

18. Archivo del Estado de Chiapas (hereafter AECh), Tomo XIV, 1923, from residents of San Pedro Remate to Pres. de la República, dated from San Pedro Remate, Dec. 5, 1922. I am grateful to Friedl Baumann for sharing this document with me and providing her insights on this section.

19. AHSEP, DEF, Caja 1667 (1339), Exp. 82, from Diputado Federal 1st District in Chiapas José Castañón to SEP, dated Jan. 9, 1922.

20. Ibid., Fo. 69, "Informe que el Director de la Escuela Rural de San Pedro Remate, Municipio de La Grandeza, Chiapas, rinde a la SEP," dated from San Pedro Remate, May 2, 1922.

21. Ibid., Fo. 112, from Gob. Int. Const. Amadeo Ruiz to Srio. Ed. Pública Federal, dated from Tuxtla, May 16, 1922.

22. Ibid., Fos. 115–16, from Maestro Rural Juan Eduardo Paniagua to Jefe del DECI de la SEP, dated from San Pedro Remate, May 31, 1922; on parents keeping their children in school in 1924, see Parres's report in AHSEP, DECI, Caja 823 (754), Exp. 23, Fo. 74, "Informe de fin de año," dated from Tapachula, Dec. 13, 1924.

23. Spenser, *El Partido Socialista Chiapaneco*, 124–26; "Más de cinco mil jornaleros de las fincas cafeterias proyectan una huelga, la que de efectuarse, será de fatales consecuencias," *La Frontera del Sur*, Tapachula, Año 1, Núm. 11, Sept. 24, 1922.

24. AHSEP, DEF, Caja 1667 (1339), Exp. 8, Fo. 19, from Pres. Muni. de Motozintla Eliseo Melgar to Jefe del DECI, México, D.F., dated from Motozintla, Dec. 5, 1922.

25. Ironically, in 1926 Parres himself was accused of misusing federal funds and was forced to resign his post as Director General of Federal Education in Chiapas.

26. AHSEP, DEF, Caja 1667 (1339), Exp. 82, Fos. 130, from Maestro Rural Juan Eduardo Paniagua to Jefe del DECI, México, D.F., dated from San Pedro Remate, Dec. 15, 1922.

27. Benjamin, *A Rich Land*, 152–56.

28. FAPECFT, Luis Espinosa (Dip.), Gav. 29, Exp. 68, Inv. 1899, Fo. 6, to Gen. Plutarco Elías Calles, Ministerio de Gobernación, from Raúl Marina Flores, dated Aug. 10, 1921; Rus, "The 'Comunidad Revolucionaria Institucional,'" 269–72.

29. AHSEP, DE, Caja 751 (673), Exp. 42, Fo. 82, 99, Misionero Elpidio López, al Jefe del DE de la SEP, México, D.F., dated from Motozintla, March 14 and May 20, 1922.

30. FAPECFT, Raymundo E. Enríquez (Ing.), Gav. 28, Exp. 51, Leg. 1/9, Inv. 1780, Fo. 4, from Ing. Raymundo Enríquez to Gen. Plutarco Elías Calles, Nov. 23, 1923.

31. FAPECFT, Luis Espinosa (Dip.), Gav. 29, Exp. 68, Inv. 1899, Fo. 8–11, 14, from Diputados Luis Espinosa and Jaime A. Solís to Srio. de Gobernación Calles, dated from México, D.F., Feb. 15, 1923.

32. FAPECFT, Álvaro Obregón, Gav. 56, Exp. 5, Leg. 2/13, Inv. 4038, Fo. 95, to Pres. Obregón, from Ejército Reorganizador del Estado Libre y Soberano de Chiapas, dated from Campamento Pacayal, March 4, 1923; see also Manuel Mendoza (Gral.), Gav. 52, Exp. 92, Inv. 3666, to Gral. Calles from Gral. Manuel Mendoza, dated from Tonalá, Feb. 28, 1923.

33. FAPECFT, Álvaro Obregón, Gav. 56, Exp. 5, Leg. 2/13, Inv. 4038, to Pres. Obregón, México, D.F., from Srio. de Gobernación Gral. P. Elías Calles, dated from Tapachula, Feb. 21, 1923.

34. FAPECFT, Fondo Plutarco Elías Calles, Fausto Ruiz C. (Gral.), Gav. 67, Exp. 101, Leg. 2/2, Inv. 5161, Fo. 93, to Gral. Plutarco Elías Calles, Hda. Soledad de la Mota, from Gen. Brigadier Fausto Ruiz, dated from Tuxtla, Oct. 6, 1923.

35. AGN, O-C, Rendiciones rebeldes, 101-R2-D, from Victórico Grajales to Saúl Ochoa in Villaflores, dated from Chiapa de Corzo, Jan. 10, 1924.

36. Benjamin, *A Rich Land*, 158–60; García de León, *Resistencia*, 2: 178–79; Linda B. Hall, *Oil, Banks, and Politics: The United States and Postrevolutionary Mexico, 1917–1924* (Austin: University of Texas Press, 1995), 155–73; Carlos Macías, ed., *Plutarco Elías Calles: Correspondencia personal (1919–1945)* (México: Fideicomiso Archivos Plutarco Elías Calles y Fernando Torreblanca, 1993), 254–63, 503; AGN, O-C, Rendiciones rebeldes, 101-R2-D, from J. D. Martínez Rojas to Presidente, dated

from San Cristóbal, Sept. 21, 1924; and 101-R2-CH, from Srio. Relaciones Exteriores Aaron Sáenz to Pres. Álvaro Obregón, dated from México, D.F., Oct. 25, 1924; FAPECFT, Fondo Raymundo E. Enríquez (Ing.), Gav. 28, Exp. 51, Leg. 1/9, Inv. 1780, Fo. 10, from Dirección Gen., Partido Socialista de Soconusco, to Sr. Gen. Plutarco Elías Calles, dated from Tapachula, April 4, 1924.

37. AGN, O-C, 805-CH-20, from Lic. N. C. Ríos, Agente del Ministerio Público Federal, to Fernando Torreblanca, México, D.F., dated from Tapachula, Oct. 4, 1927.

38. AGN, Ortiz Rubio, (1931) 4531A.-, from Comunidades Agrarias de Soconusco (PNR); Confederación Sindical de Trabajadores de Chiapas (PNR); Partido Socialista Revolucionario Chiapaneco (P.N.R., integrado por obreros y campesinos, con 28 partidos organizados en todo el estado), dated from México, D.F., Aug. 1931; Benjamin, *A Rich Land*, 175–80; Grollová, "Los trabajadores cafetaleros y el Partido Socialista Chiapaneco," 212.

39. AHSEP, DECI, Caja 823 (754), Exp. 19, Fo. 1, from Misionero Núm. 110 Arnulfo E. Niño to Jefe del Depto., SEP, México, D.F., dated from Arriaga, Chiapas, March 31, 1924; under same classification see Fos. 27–29 from Parres to DECI, SEP, México, D.F., dated from Tapachula, Aug. 23, 1924.

40. AHSEP, DEI, Año 1924, Caja 823 (754), Exp. 23, Fo. 345, from Prof. Misionero Ernesto Parres to DECI, SEP, México, D.F., dated from Tapachula, April 11, 1924.

41. Ibid., Exp. 16, Fos. 27–28, from Prof. Antonio Prado to Misionero de Cultura Indígena Ernesto Parres, Tapachula, dated from Acapetagua, May 5, 1924.

42. AHSEP, DE, Caja 3148 (61), Exp. 61, Fos. 23, 24, from Delegado Mauro Calderón to Oficial Mayor de la SEP, México, D.F., dated from Tuxtla, April 19 and May 1, 1924.

43. Ibid., Fo. 32, "Cuadro estadístico mensual de las escuelas primarias que funcionaron en el mes de agosto de 1924," from Delegado Mauro Calderón to SEP, México, D.F., dated from Tuxtla, Sept. 12, 1924.

44. AHSEP, DEF, Chiapas, Caja 4659 (79), Exp. 17, Fos. 1–2, from Dir. de Ed. Fed. Lisandro Calderón to Jefe Técnico de las Escuelas Federales, Depto. de Enseñanza Pública y Normal, SEP, México, D.F., dated from Tuxtla, Feb. 26, 1925; and *El sistema de escuelas rurales en México* (México: TGN, 1927), 110.

45. Among Dewey's most influential works are *The School and Society* (Chicago: University of Chicago Press, 1963 [1899]); *The Child and the Curriculum* (Chicago: University of Chicago Press, 1902); and *Democracy and Education* (New York: Free Press, 1966 [1916]). Several years after his retirement he traveled to Mexico to serve as chair of the Commission on Inquiry into the Charges Made against Leon Trotsky (1937–1938). Dewey subsequently issued two reports: *The Case of Leon Trotsky* (New York: Merit Publishers, 1968 [1937]); and *Not Guilty* (New York: Harper, 1937).

46. AHSEP, DECI, Caja 823 (754), Exp. 23, Fo. 79, "Informe de fin de año" from Prof. Misionero Ernesto Parres, dated from Tapachula, 13 Dec. 1924; under same classification see Fo. 4, Zona Escolar de Tapachula, from Dir. del DECI Enrique Corona to Parres, dated from México, D.F., March 17, 1924.

47. Vaughan, *The State, Education, and Social Class*, 179–80.

48. Enrique Krauze, "La escuela callista," *Historia de la Revolución Mexicana,*

período 1924–1928: La reconstrucción económica (México: El Colegio de México, 1977), 298.

49. Dewey, "Mexico, 1926," 121–22, 124; John Collier, "Mexico: A Challenge," *Progressive Education* 9 (Feb. 1932): 95–98.

50. AHSEP, DGEPET, Chiapas, Caja 6060 (10), Exp. 1309, Fos. 7–8, "Informe sintético de visitas de inspección," from Florentino Guzmán, dated from Ocuilapa, May 20, 1927.

51. AHSEP, DEF, Informes Chiapas, Caja 1195, from Inspector J. Jesús Ixta to Dir. de Ed. Fed. in Tuxtla, dated from San Cristóbal, April 14, 1928.

52. AHSEP, DECI, Caja 823 (754), Exp. 23, Fos. 316–17, from Misionero Ernesto Parres to DECI, SEP, México, D.F., dated from Tapachula, April 8, 1924.

53. AHSEP, DEF, Informes Chiapas, Caja 895, Exp. 1520/2, from Inspector Epigmenio de León to DEF, Tuxtla, dated from Chiapa de Corzo, Aug. 18, 1932.

54. AHSEP, DEF, Caja 1730 (1241), Exp. 1886, Fo. 17, "Informe de las actividades desarrolladas en la tercera zona escolar, estado de Chiapas, correspondiente al mes de noviembre de 1929. Rendido por el Insp. Epigmenio de León," dated from Chiapa de Corzo, Dec. 3, 1929.

55. Ibid., Fos. 2–3.

56. Ángel Cabellos Quiroz and Carlos Carrizales Barreto, "Las Escuelas Artículo 123 en Coahuila, 1926–1940" (Tesina inédita. Universidad Autónoma Metropolitana Iztapalapa, 1992), 259; Engracia Loyo, "Escuelas Rurales 'Artículo 123' (1917–1940)" *Historia Mexicana* 40, no. 2 (1991): 305–6.

57. AHMSCLC, 1915/2, Número de órden 38, Fo. 1, "1915—Municipio San Felipe Ecatepec, Padrón Escolar, Dept. Las Casas," from Delegado de Instrucción Pública Luis M. Flores, dated from San Felipe Ecatepec, Oct. 15, 1915; *Noticia estadística sobre la educación pública en México correspondiente al año de 1928*, (México, D.F.: TGN, 1930), 382–83.

58. *Periódico Oficial*, Tuxtla, Chiapas, June 16, 1926. Tomo XLIII, Num. 24, Decreto 69, Artículo 1, p. 2; see also AHSEP, Dir. de Ed. Fed., Informes, Chiapas, Caja 979, Exp. 1446/2, Fos. 204–5, from Gobernador Carlos A. Vidal to Secretario de Educación Pública Dr. J. M. Puig Casauranc, México, D.F., Jan. 30, 1926.

59. *Periódico Oficial del Gobierno Constitucionalista del Estado de Chiapas*, Tuxtla, Chiapas, Tomo XXXV, Núm. 24, May 11, 1918; Núm. 25, May 18, 1918; and Núm. 26, May 25, 1918.

60. AHSEP, DEF, Chiapas, Caja 827, Fo. 6, from Benjamín Martínez to Jefe del DER, SEP, México, dated from Huixtla, Dec. 1926.

61. *Informe rendido por el Gobernador Interino Constitucional de Chiapas C. Dip. José María Brindis, en virtud de licencia temporal concedida al Gobernador Constitucional C. Ing. Raymundo E. Enríquez ante la XXXIII Legislatura del Estado, en el segundo año de su ejercicio, el 1 de Nov. de 1931*, 52; *Noticia estadística*, 382–85.

62. AHSEP, SP, Caja 4468 (4595), Exp. 1, Fo. 101–2, from DGEET Alberto Terán, Oficina de Escuelas Art. 123, to Secretario del Ramo, México, D.F., dated from México, D.F., Nov. 7, 1941; AHSEP, DEF, Chiapas, Caja 1560 (935), Exp. 28, Fos. 3–69.

63. INAH, Instituto Nacional de Antropología e Historia (hereafter INAH),

Biblioteca "Manuel Orozco y Berra," Archivo de la Palabra, Papeles de Familia, Erasto Urbina García, "El despertar de un pueblo—Memorias relativas a la evolución indígena en el estado de Chiapas" (unpublished manuscript, dated 1944), 9, 16–17.

64. AHSEP, DEF, Chiapas, Caja 5298 (280), Exp. 43, Fo. 4, from Secretario de la DEF Salvador Lorenzano R., dated from Tuxtla, July 26, 1936; *Memoria relativa al estado que guarda el ramo de educación pública el 31 de agosto de 1934*, II: 53, 58.

65. Moisés Sáenz, *Carapan: Bosquejo de una experiencia* (Morelia, Mich.: Talleres linotipográficos del gobierno del Estado, 1969 [1936]), 37.

66. Vaughan, *The State, Education, and Social Class*, 148–50; James W. Wilkie, *La Revolución Mexicana: Gasto federal y cambio social* (México: Fondo de Cultura Económica, 1978 [1967]), 192–95.

67. *Informe rendido por el Gobernador Constitucional de Chiapas C. Ing. Raymundo E. Enríquez ante la XXXIII Legislatura del Estado, en el segundo año de su ejercicio, el 1 de noviembre de 1930*, 34, 36–37; and *Noticia estadística*, 144, 148–49, 272–73, 308–9.

68. *Noticia estadística*, 146–47.

Chapter 3

The epigraph is from AHSEP, DE, Caja 3126 (38), Exp. 68, Fos. 23–27, from Delegación de la SEP, Edo. de Chiapas, to Jefe del DE de la SEP, México, D.F., dated from Tuxtla, Feb. 22, 1922.

1. Rockwell, "Schools of the Revolution," 186–204; Dorothy Tanck de Estrada, *Pueblos de indios y educación en el México Colonial, 1750–1821* (México, D.F.: El Colegio de México, Centro de Estudios Históricos, 1999), 153–206, 281–83; and Vaughan, *Cultural Politics*, 108–12.

2. Alan Knight, "Racism, Revolution, and *Indigenismo*: Mexico, 1910–1940," in *The Idea of Race in Latin America, 1870–1940*, ed. Richard Graham (Austin: University of Texas Press, 1990), 82.

3. Alexander S. Dawson, *Indian and Nation in Revolutionary Mexico* (Tucson: University of Arizona Press, 2004), xiv–xx, 6.

4. Rick Anthony López, "*Lo más mexicano de Mexico*: Popular Arts, Indians, and Urban Intellectuals in the Ethnicization of Mexican Postrevolutionary National Identity, 1921–1972" (Ph.D. diss., Yale University, 2001), chapter 3, pp. 4, 6; see also Manuel Gamio, *El gobierno, la población, el territorio* (México: Departamento de Talleres Gráficos de la Secretaría de Fomento, 1917), 5.

5. Knight, "Racism, Revolution, and *Indigenismo*," 83.

6. Rick Anthony López, "The Noche Mexicana and the Exhibition of Popular Arts of 1921: Two Ways of Indianizing Mexican National Identity," in *The Eagle and the Virgin: National Identity, Memory and Utopia in Mexico, 1920–1940*, ed. Mary Kay Vaughan and Stephen E. Lewis (Durham, N.C.: Duke University Press, 2005).

7. Rick Anthony López, "The India Bonita Contest of 1921 and the Ethnicization of Mexican National Culture," *Hispanic American Historical Review* 82, no. 2 (May 2002): 291–328; Ricardo Pérez Montfort, "Indigenismo, Hispanismo y Panamericanismo en la cultura popular mexicana de 1920 a 1940," in *Cultura e identidad nacional*, ed. Roberto Blancarte (México: Consejo Nacional para la Cultura y

las Artes and Fondo de Cultura Económica, 1994), 354.

8. López, "*Lo más mexicano de Mexico*," chapter 3; see also Andrés Molina Enríquez, *Los grandes problemas nacionales* (México: Ediciones del Instituto Nacional de la Juventud, 1964 [1908]).

9. Racial determinism is the belief that "racial" or biological factors, rather than material and cultural ones, "determine" aptitude and character traits.

10. Dawson, *Indian and Nation*, 11; Nancy Leys Stepan, "*The Hour of Eugenics*": *Race, Gender, and Nation in Latin America* (Ithaca, N.Y.: Cornell University Press, 1991), 67–68; Alexandra Minna Stern, "From Mestizophilia to Biotypology: Racialization and Science in Mexico, 1920–1960," in *Race and Nation in Modern Latin America*, ed. Nancy P. Applebaum, Anne S. Macpherson, and Karin Alejandra Rosemblatt (Chapel Hill: The University of North Carolina Press, 2003), 190–91; José Vasconcelos, *The Cosmic Race/La raza cósmica*, trans. and intro. by Didier T. Jaén (Baltimore: Johns Hopkins University Press, 1997), 16.

11. José Vasconcelos, *A Mexican Ulysses: The Autobiography of José Vasconcelos*, trans. and ed. W. Rex Crawford (Bloomington: Indiana University Press, 1963), 169.

12. *La Casa del Estudiante Indígena: 16 meses de labor en un experimento psicológico colectivo de indios. Febrero de 1926–junio de 1927*, Publicaciones de la SEP (México: TGN, 1927), 24.

13. AHSEP, DE, Caja 3126 (38), Exp. 68, Fos. 23–27, from Delegación de la SEP, Chiapas, to Jefe del DE de la SEP, México, D.F., dated from Tuxtla, Feb. 22, 1922.

14. Rafael Ramírez, "La incorporación indígena por medio del idioma castellano," *El Maestro Rural* 3, no. 2 (June 15, 1933): 5–6.

15. Knight, "Racism, Revolution, and *Indigenismo*," 73–75.

16. AHSEP, DECI, Caja 689 (764), Exp. 1, Fo. 4, "El problema educativo indígena en Chiapas," by Missionary Federico A. Corzo, dated from México, D.F., July 4, 1922.

17. *La Vanguardia*, Tuxtla, March 4, 1934; cited in Hernández Castillo, *Histories and Stories from Chiapas*, 28.

18. "Chamulan" is often used to refer to the Tzotzil Maya who inhabit the Chiapas highlands. Technically speaking, however, Chamulans are only those Tzotzils who reside in the municipality of Chamula.

19. Ironically, by the late 1950s the INI's corps of teachers in highland Chiapas totaled roughly one hundred. AHSEP, DECI, Caja 689 (764), Exp. 1, Fos. 7–8, "El problema educativo indígena en Chiapas," by Misionero Federico A. Corzo, dated from México, D.F., July 4, 1922.

20. Ibid., Fo. 4.

21. AHSEP, DECI, Caja 823 (754), Exp. 22, Fos. 35–39, "Informe que rinde el Prof. Ricardo Sánchez de la comisión que se le confirió en el estado de Chiapas," from Misionero Ricardo Sánchez, dated from México, D.F., Dec. 3, 1924; AHSEP, DE, Caja 3126 (38), Exp. 68, Fos. 23–27, from Delegación de la SEP, Edo. de Chiapas, to Jefe del DE de la SEP, México, D.F., dated from Tuxtla, Feb. 22, 1922.

22. AHMSCLC, 1925, Tomo 2, "Al Ciudadano Pres. del Consejo Municipal. San Cristóbal Las Casas," from Manuel Pérez, Pascual Patistán y otros, copied by Secretario Gen. de Gobierno M. V. Aguirre, Tuxtla, Feb. 3, 1925.

23. AHMSCLC, 1929, Tomo 2, "Correspondencia de fuera del distrito, Febrero de 1929," from Ayuntamiento de San Cristóbal de Las Casas to Gobernador del Estado; and Rus, "Contained Revolutions," 22–26.

24. AHSEP, DEF, Informes Chiapas, Caja 1195, from Inspector J. Jesús Ixta to Dir. de Ed. Fed., Tuxtla, dated from San Cristóbal, April 14, 1928; AHSEP, DGEPET, Chiapas, Caja 6117 (st.), Exp. 45, Fos. 3–7, from Dir. de Ed. Fed. Erasto Valle to Gobernador, Tuxtla, dated from Tuxtla, 24 June 1930; see also Frans Blom with Oliver La Farge and the Tulane University Expedition to Middle America, *Tribes and Temples: A Record of the Expedition to Middle America Conducted by the Tulane University of Louisiana in 1925* (New Orleans: Tulane University Press, 1926–1927), 356.

25. AHMSCLC, 1925, Tomo 2, Número 2358, from Srio. Gral. de Gob. José Castañón to Pres. Muni. San Cristóbal Las Casas, dated from Tuxtla, May 28, 1925.

26. AHSEP, 689 (764), Exp. 6, Fo. 54, "Informe de la laboriosidad, idoneidad y conducta de cada uno de los profesores que atienden las distintas 'Casas del Pueblo' establecidas hasta hoy en la zona de esta misión," from Misionero Ernesto Parres dated from Motozintla, Dec. 1, 1923.

27. Prof. Marcos E. Becerra, "El Internado Indígena Regional 'Plutarco Elías Calles' establecido recientemente en San Cristóbal L.C.," in *Chiapas: Revista Mensual*, Tuxtla, vol. 1, no. 1 (Oct. 1928): 12–13.

28. AHSEP, DEF, Informes, 1652 (4763), Exp. 1778/1, Fos. 115–18, from Dir. de Ed. Fed. Eduardo Zarza to Jefe del DER, México, D.F., dated from Tuxtla, Sept. 1, 1928. See also AHSEP, DEF, Informes Chiapas, 1195, no folio, from Dir. de Ed. Fed. Eduardo Zarza to Jefe del DERPFICI, SEP, México, D.F., dated from Tuxtla, Dec. 31, 1928.

29. AHSEP, DEF, Informes, 1652 (4763), Exp. 1778/1, Fos. 116.

30. AHSEP, DGEPET, Chiapas, Caja 6095 (45), Exp. 14, Fos. 1–2, "Anexo al Informe Sintético de la Escuela Rural en Chamula, Las Casas, Chis.," from Inspector José Macías Padilla, dated July 1926.

31. AHSEP, DGEPET, Caja 6119 (69), Exp. 36, Fo. 8, "Magdalenas, Municipio de San Andrés, Distrito de Las Casas. Escuela Rural para Niños," from Inspector José Macías Padilla, dated 1926.

32. AHSEP, DEF, Caja 1827, Fos. 29–32, from Inspector Ángel M. Corzo to Jefe del Dept. de Escuelas Rurales e Incorporación Cultural Indígena, dated from Comitán, Feb. 23, 1927.

33. Fell, *José Vasconcelos: Los años del águila (1920–1925)*, 255; José Gálvez, "Proyecto para la organización de las misiones federales de educación," in *Las Misiones Culturales (1923–1973)*, by Augusto Santiago Sierra (México: SepSetentas, 1973), 78.

34. Pérez Montfort, *Estampas*, 117–30; Vaughan, *Cultural Politics*, 99, 184.

35. *Las Misiones Culturales en 1927: las Escuelas Normales Rurales* (México: Publicaciones de la SEP, 1928), 172–78.

36. AHSEP, DMC, Caja 1805 (st.); 1932 (1180), Exp. 26, Fo. 2, from Trabajadora Social Sara Valero de Marines to Jefe de la Misión Cultural Ing. Marcelino Murieta, dated from Chiapa de Corzo, Dec. 19, 1928; under same classification, Exp. 11, Fo. 1, from Jefe de la Misión Antonio Amaya to Jefe de las Misiones Culturales José

Guadalupe Nájera, México, D.F., dated from La Grandeza, Dec. 15, 1928.

37. AHSEP, DMC, Caja 1804 (st.); 1931 (1179), Exp. 1, Fo. 1, "Instituto social celebrado en Chiapa de Corzo," from Trabajadora Social de la Misión Cultural Sara Valero de Marines to Dir. de las Misiones Culturales J. Guadalupe Nájera, dated from México, D.F., Jan. 10, 1929.

38. AHSEP, DMC, Caja 1805 (st.); 1932, (1180), Exp. 2, Fo. 5, "Informe de los trabajos realizados en el Cuarto Instituto Social verificado en La Grandeza, Chiapas," from Jefe de la Misión Antonio Amaya to Jefe de Misiones Culturales José Guadalupe Nájera, SEP, México, D.F., dated Jan. 1929.

39. AHSEP, DEF, Chiapas, Caja 1560 (935), Exp. 11, Fo. 121, "Informe de julio," from Dir. de Ed. Fed. Septimio Pérez Palacios to Secretario de Educación Pública, DERP-FII, México, D.F., dated from Tuxtla, Aug. 1, 1933.

40. *Memoria relativa al estado que guarda el ramo de Educación Pública el 31 de agosto de 1933*, Tomo II, Documentos (México: TGN, 1933), 45.

41. Ibid., Fo. 65, "De todo aprendimos," by "Grillo," newspaper unknown, 1933.

42. Gonzalo Aguirre Beltrán, *Teoría y práctica de la educación indígena* (México, D.F.: Fondo de Cultura Económica, 1992 [1973]), 100.

43. AHSEP, SP, Caja 4302 (471), Exp. 16, Fo. 71, from Visitador Especial Manuel Mesa A. to SEP, dated from México, D.F., June 24, 1932.

44. *La Casa del Estudiante Indígena*, 45–46.

45. AHSEP, DER, Casa del Estudiante Indígena, Caja 1628 (2339), Exp. 1, Fo. 71, from Federico Ruiz, Pres. Muni. de San Cristóbal Las Casas, Chiapas, Aug. 14, 1926; also Fos. 72–82. Macías was later reprimanded because three of the boys were underage (*sumamente pequeños*).

46. *La Casa del Estudiante Indígena*, 46.

47. Ibid., 59–60, 97.

48. AHSEP, DER, Caja 6214 (16), Exp. 36, Fos. 1–2, "Memorandum" from Jefe del Depto. Rafael Ramírez to Secretario del Ramo, Encargado del Despacho, dated from México, D.F., Oct. 27, 1930.

49. AGN, Cárdenas, Leyes, Proyectos diversos, 545.3/147, "Al margen de las afirmaciones presidenciales sobre el problema social de la incorporación indígena a la vida nacional," by Prof. Rafael Molina Betancourt, sent to Secretario Particular, Presidencia de la República, dated June 30, 1936.

50. Sáenz, *México íntegro*, 154.

51. Guillermo Palacios, "Postrevolutionary Intellectuals, Rural Readings and the Shaping of the 'Peasant Problem' in Mexico; *El Maestro Rural*, 1932–1934," *Journal of Latin American Studies* 30 (1998): 318; and Sáenz, *Carapan*, 178.

52. AHSEP, DEF, Informes, 1652 (4763), Exp. 1778/1, Fo. 100, from Dir. de Ed. Fed. Eduardo Zarza to Jefe del DER, SEP, México, D.F., dated from Tuxtla, July 26, 1928; under same classification, see Fo. 119, Sept. 1, 1928.

53. AHSEP, DER, Caja 1560 (935), Exp. 11, Fo. 102, from Dir. de Ed. Fed. Septimio Pérez Palacios to Secretario de Educación Pública, DERPF in México, D.F., dated from Tuxtla, July 1, 1933.

Chapter 4

1. See various chapters in *The Eagle and the Virgin*; and Desmond Rochfort, *Mexican Muralists: Orozco, Rivera, Siqueiros* (New York: Universe, 1994).

2. AGN, Cárdenas, Exp. 542.1/299, from Delegado Gral. de la CCM de Chiapas Fidel Alberto López Trujillo to Cárdenas, México, D.F., from Tapachula, May 11, 1935; also AGN, Cárdenas, Campañas Nacionalistas, Exp. 404.1/2238, from Oficial Mayor Dr. Guillermo T. Padilla, Secretario de la Economía Nacional, to Gobernador del Estado, Tuxtla, dated from México, D.F.; and *El Sur de México*, Tapachula, Año XVII, Núm. 937, Aug. 27, 1942, p. 3. For more information on the campaigns against the Chinese and Mexicans of Chinese descent, see Moisés González Navarro, *Los extranjeros en México y los mexicanos en el extranjero 1821–1970*, Tomo II (México: El Colegio de México, 1994), 163–78; and Gerardo Rénique, "Sonora's Anti-Chinese Racism and Mexico's Postrevolutionary Nationalism, 1920s–1930s," in *Race and Nation in Modern Latin America*, 211–36.

3. Brading, *The First America*, 674.

4. Adrian A. Bantjes, "Idolatry and Iconoclasm in Revolutionary Mexico: The De-Christianization Campaigns, 1929–1940," *Mexican Studies/Estudios Mexicanos* 13, no. 1 (winter 1997): 88–89.

5. Knight, *The Mexican Revolution*, I: 402–4; Jean Meyer, *La Cristiada*, vol. II (México: Siglo Veintiuno Editores, 1991 [1973]), 212–31; and Patience Schell, *Church and State Education in Revolutionary Mexico City* (Tucson: University of Arizona Press, 2003), 3, 9–12.

6. Schell, *Church and State Education in Revolutionary Mexico City*, 14.

7. Meneses, coord., *Tendencias educativas oficiales en México 1911–1934*, 503–5; J. M. Puig Casauranc, *La cuestión religiosa en relación con la educación pública en México* (México: TGN, 1928), 11–12; and Schell, *Church and State Education in Revolutionary Mexico City*, 180.

8. Knight, "Revolutionary Project," 246.

9. Meyer, *La Cristiada*, III: 260–71; Jennie Purnell, *Popular Movements and State Formation in Revolutionary Mexico* (Durham, N.C.: Duke University Press, 1999), 72–110.

10. John A. Britton, *Educación y radicalismo en México: Los años de Bassols (1931–34)* (México: SepSetentas, 1976), 35–36; Ma. Eugenia Espinosa Carbajal y Jorge Ernesto Mesta Martínez, *Narciso Bassols: Un intelectual olvidado* (México: Subsecretaría de Servicios Educativos para el D.F., 1994), 14, 21; *Memoria de la SEP 1932*, II: 228–32; and Meneses, coord., *Tendencias educativas oficiales en México 1911–1934*, 598, 606.

11. Mary Kay Vaughan, "Cambio ideológico en la política educativa de la SEP: Programas y libros de texto, 1921–1940," in *Escuela y sociedad en el periodo cardenista*, ed. Susana Quintanilla and Mary Kay Vaughan (México: Fondo de Cultura Económica, 1997), 86.

12. Juan Pedro Viqueira, "Éxitos y fracasos de la evangelización en Chiapas (1545–1859)," in *La iglesia Católica en México*, ed. Nelly Sigaut (Zamora: El Colegio de Michoacán, 1997), 91–92.

13. AHSEP, DEF, Chiapas, Caja 827, Exp. 1452/21, Fo. 21, from Inspector José Macías

Padilla to Dir. de Ed. Fed. in Tuxtla, dated from San Cristóbal de Las Casas, March 25, 1926; see also from Macías to Calles, Sept. 12, 1926.

14. *Periódico Oficial*, Tuxtla, Chiapas, Tomo XLV, Núm. 6, Feb. 8, 1928, p. 2; AGN, O-C, 101-R2-G2.

15. AHSEP, DEF, Informes, 1652 (4763), Exp. 1779/2, Fos. 12–13, "Acta que demuestra las infracciones a las leyes constitucionales y del ramo de Instrucción Pública," signed by state inspector Gilberto Tello N., federal inspector Benjamín P. Martínez, and others, Tapachula, March 27, 1928.

16. "Unofficial" priests and pastors could still say mass in private homes, do baptisms, and tend to the sick.

17. Meyer, *La Cristiada*, II: 148–56; Archivo General del Estado (hereafter AGE), Asuntos de Culto Público Religioso (hereafter ACPR), Soconusco, Zona 2, 1932, from Pres. Muni. San Cristóbal de Las Casas Plinio García to Comandante de Policía, dated from San Cristóbal, April 18, 1932.

18. AGE, ACPR, Las Casas, Zona 6, from Obispo Anaya to Señor Cura, dated from San Cristóbal, March 10, 1932.

19. Ibid., various, see also in Soconusco, Zona 2, from Cura Párroco José Ramírez to Pres. Municipal of Cacahoatán Odilón Cisneros, dated from Tapachula, May 13, 1932.

20. AGE, ACPR, Las Casas, Zona 6, from Enríquez to Gral. Leonardo M. Hernández, Comandante del 39 Regimento de Caballería in San Cristóbal de Las Casas, dated from Tuxtla, Oct. 5, 1932.

21. Ibid., Zona 6, from Bishop Anaya to Enríquez, dated from San Cristóbal, Nov. 15, 1932.

22. Adrian A. Bantjes, "Saints, Sinners, and State Formation: Local Religion and Cultural Revolution in Mexico," in *The Eagle and the Virgin.*

23. AHSEP, DEF, Informes Chiapas, Caja 956, Exp. 1581/6, from Inspector José Vázquez Luna to DER, SEP, México, D.F., dated from Comitán, Nov. 30, 1933.

24. AGN, 542.1/20, "Informe detallado que el suscrito eleva a la muy ilustre consideración del C. Presidente Constitucional de la República con motivo de la comisión que se sirvió conferirle en esta entidad federativa," from Pres. Municipal of Tuxtla Gutiérrez Gustavo López Gutiérrez, dated from Tuxtla, Jan. 1, 1935; AGN, Cárdenas, Atropellos autoridades civiles, 542.1/20, from Liga Central de Comunidades Agrarias del Estado de Chiapas adherida a la CCM to Cárdenas, dated from Mexico City, 11 Dec. 1934; FAPECFT, Fondo Plutarco Elías Calles, Victórico Grajales, Gav. 37, Exp. 45, Leg. 2/11, Inv. 2497, Fos. 110–15, México, D.F., June 30, 1933; "El Diputado Ángel M. Corzo fue Desaforado," *La Vanguardia*, Tuxtla, March 31, 1929.

25. AGN, Cárdenas, Elecciones Chiapas, 544.2/6, from M. E. Guzmán to Secretario Particular Luis I. Rodríguez, dated from México, D.F., Aug. 28, 1935, 8.

26. FAPECFT, Fondo Plutarco Elías Calles, Victórico Grajales, Gav. 37, Exp. 45, Leg. 2/11, Inv. 2497, to Secretaría de Gobernación y Guerra, Circular Núm. 7, from Grajales to Presidente Municipal ____, dated from Tuxtla, Feb. 23, 1933; "Los fanáticos alteraron el orden en Villa Las Rosas y Simojovel," in *La Vanguardia*, March 19, 1933.

27. José Villalobos, "¡Guerra al Fanaticismo!" in *La Vanguardia*, April 9, 1933, Año V, Núm. 209, p. 3.

28. AHMSCLC, 1933/3, Núm. 281, Fo. 4, expediente relativo a la campaña de desfanatización, "Circular a los señores empleados Municipales," from Pres. Municipal Ciro Domínguez C. and Secretario Humberto Marín Orantes, dated from San Cristóbal, Feb. 23, 1933.

29. Ibid., Núm. 2380, Fo. 7, from Secretario Gen. de Gobierno Dr. Samuel León, Sección de Gobernación y Guerra, to Pres. Muni. Ciro Domínguez C., dated from Tuxtla, Nov. 17, 1933.

30. Ibid., Núm. 1454, Fo. 13, from Pres. Muni. Ciro Domínguez C. and Secretario Humberto Marín Orantes, to Comandante de Policía, dated from San Cristóbal, Nov. 22, 1933; "El Presidente Municipal de San Cristóbal L.C., tolera las funciones religiosas," *Renovación*, Tuxtla, Nov. 18, 1933; personal communication, Jan Rus, July 1995.

31. *Informe que el C. Gobernador Constitucional del Estado de Chiapas Victórico R. Grajales rinde a la H. XXXV Legislatura*, 1934, pp. 4–5.

32. *Periódico Oficial del Gobierno del Estado de Chiapas*, decree number 132, Tuxtla, Feb. 28, 1934, vol. LI, Núm. 9, pp. 2–3.

33. AHMSCLC, 1934/4, Fo. 1, "Expediente relativo al cierra temporal de los Templos de esta Ciudad. Mes de abril 1934," Circular Núm. 22, from Secretario Gen. Interino Lic. José L. Burguete, Sección de Gobernación, Justicia y Guerra, dated from Tuxtla, April 19, 1934.

34. AGN, Cárdenas, Ley de Cultos, 547.2/2, various; AHMSCLC, 1934/4, Fo. 5, "Muy digno Señor Presidente . . . ," dated April 25, 1934, unsigned.

35. "El Obispo y todos los curas salieron de Chiapas," *Liberación*, Tuxtla Gutiérrez, Oct. 21, 1934.

36. "El sacerdote José Ramírez incineró varios fetiches," *Liberación*, Tuxtla Gutiérrez, Dec. 9, 1934.

37. "Notable evolución en nuestros pueblos indígenas," *Liberación*, Tuxtla Gutiérrez, Dec. 2, 1934; see also AHSEP, DER, Caja 1332 (191), Exp. 8, Fo. 14, "Informe de enero i febrero," from Inspector Manuel Castellanos to Dir. de Ed. Fed. Elpidio López in Tuxtla, dated from Ciudad Las Casas, April 6, 1935; Rus, "The 'Comunidad Revolucionaria Institucional,'" 271.

38. AHSEP, DER, Caja 1582 (957), Exp. 1, Fo. 4, "Informe General de 1933," from Inspector Epigmenio de León G. to Secretario de Educación Pública, México, D.F., dated from Tuxtla, Dec. 5, 1933; Andrés Aubry, *Los obispos de Chiapas* (San Cristóbal de Las Casas, Chiapas: INAREMAC, 1990), 74.

39. AHSEP, DER, Caja 1332 (191), Exp. 15, Fo. 65, "Informe anual de labores," from Inspector Héctor Eduardo Paniagua to Dir. de Ed. Fed. in Tuxtla, dated from Frontera Comalapa, Nov. 14, 1935.

40. "Programa especial de la campaña socialista y desfanatizante," in *La escuela socialista de Chiapas*, coord. Elpidio López (Tuxtla: Talleres Linotipográficos del Gobierno del Estado, 1935), 120, 132–35, 191–95.

41. AHSEP, DER, Caja 1375 (236), Exp. 18, Fo. 17, "Relación de las escuelas federales que han cambiado de denominación en el presente año," from Dir. de Ed. Fed. Elpidio López, dated from Tuxtla, Feb. 1, 1935.

42. AHSEP, DER, Caja 1332 (191), Exp. 3, Fo. 35, "Informe General de Labores," from

Inspector P. Arturo Mota to Secretario de Educación Pública, DERPF, México, D.F., dated Dec. 19, 1934; Fo. 11, 12, from Inspector P. Arturo Mota to SEP, DER, dated Nov. 5, 1935.

43. Ibid., Exp. 3, Fo. 39, from P. Arturo Mota to López in Tuxtla, dated from Comitán, March 29, 1935.

44. Ibid., Exp. 8, Fo. 14, from Inspector Manuel Castellanos to López in Tuxtla, dated from Ciudad Las Casas, April 6, 1935.

45. Ibid., Exp. 7, Fo. 31, from Inspector Manuel Fernando Molina to Dir. de Ed. Fed. in Tuxtla, dated from Tuxtla, Nov. 30, 1935.

46. Ibid., Exp. 15, Fos. 37–38, "Informe sintético de labores," from Inspector Héctor Eduardo Paniagua to Dir. de Ed. Fed. in Tuxtla, dated from Frontera Comalapa, Aug. 10, 1935.

47. AHSEP, DGEPET, Chiapas, Caja 6095 (45), Exp. 6, Fo. 63, from Maestro Rural Gaspar Díaz to Agente Fiscal Subalterno de la Oficina Federal de Hacienda in Motozintla, dated from Bella Vista, Aug. 22, 1935.

48. AHSEP, DGEPET, Caja 5324/5356 (304), Exp. 22, Fos. 27–28, from Dir. Gen. Rafael Méndez Aguirre to Inspector Rubén M. Rincón in Tuxtla, dated from México, D.F., Oct. 22, 1936.

49. Adrian Bantjes, "Burning Saints, Molding Minds: Iconoclasm, Civic Ritual, and the Failed Cultural Revolution," in *Rituals of Rule, Rituals of Resistance: Public Celebrations and Popular Culture in Mexico*, ed. William H. Beezley, Cheryl English Martin, and William E. French (Wilmington, Del.: Scholarly Resources Inc., 1994), 277.

50. Knight, "Revolutionary Project," 253.

Chapter 5

1. Meneses, coord., *Tendencias educativas oficiales en México 1934–1964*, 44.

2. See the following overviews: Britton, *Educación y radicalismo en México*, 2 vols.; Meneses, coord., *Tendencias educativas oficiales en México 1934–1964*, 1–231; David L. Raby, *Educación y revolución social en México* (México: SepSetentas, 1974); and Victoria Lerner, *Historia de la Revolución Mexicana: La educación socialista* (México: El Colegio de México, 1987).

3. Héctor Aguilar Camín and Lorenzo Meyer, *In the Shadow of the Mexican Revolution: Contemporary Mexican History, 1910–1989*, trans. Luis Alberto Fierro (Austin: University of Texas Press, 1996 [1993]), 109; Britton, *Educación y radicalismo en México*, I: 117–26; Susana Quintanilla, "El debate intelectual acerca de la educación socialista," in *Escuela y sociedad*, 53.

4. Britton, *Educación y radicalismo en México*, I: 118–42; Lerner, *Historia de la Revolución Mexicana*, 11–31; Vaughan, *Cultural Politics*, 29–31.

5. Samuel Ramos, *Veinte años de educación en México* (México: Imprenta Universitaria, 1941), 66.

6. Vaughan, *Cultural Politics*, 34.

7. Lerner, *Historia de la Revolución Mexicana*, 83–94; Meneses, coord., *Tendencias educativas oficiales en México 1934–1964*, 49–51; Raby, *Educación y revolución social en México*, 39–42.

8. Quintanilla, "El debate intelectual acerca de la educación socialista," 56–57;

Humberto Tejera, "La educación socialista," *El Maestro Rural* 7: 5–7.

9. Becker, *Setting the Virgin on Fire*, 41; Britton, *Educación y radicalismo en México. II. Los años de Cárdenas*, 24–26; "La educación socialista y la escuela rural," *El Maestro Rural* 11 (1 Dec. 1934): 3; Lerner, *Historia de la Revolución Mexicana*, 58–61; Meneses, coord., *Tendencias educativas oficiales en México 1934–1964*, 40; and Vaughan, "Cambio ideológico," 91.

10. Lerner, *Historia de la Revolución Mexicana*, 94–98; Engracia Loyo, "Lectura para el pueblo," in *La educación en la historia de México*, ed. Josefina Zoraida Vázquez (México: El Colegio de México, 1992), 272–85; Vaughan, *Cultural Politics*, 38–42.

11. AHSEP, DER, Caja 1375 (236), Exp. 10, Fo. 6, "Plan General de Trabajo," from López and Dir. Gral. de Educ. Pública Ángel M. Corzo to SEP, México, D.F., dated from Tuxtla, Feb. 1, 1935.

12. Ibid., Fo. 68, from López to SEP, DER, México, D.F., dated from Tuxtla, 1935.

13. Ibid., Fos. 7, 9–10, from López and Dir. Gen. de Ed. Pública del Estado Ángel M. Corzo, to SEP, México, D.F., dated from Tuxtla, Feb. 1, 1935.

14. "Acción de la escuela socialista," in *La escuela socialista en Chiapas*, 54–61; AHSEP, DGEPET, Caja 5324/5356 (304), Fo. 14, from Inspector Armando Guerra to Dir. de Ed. Fed. Rafael Bolio Yenro, Tuxtla, dated from Comitán, May 26, 1936.

15. AHSEP, DER, Caja 1375 (236), Exp. 10, Fo. 30, from López to Secretario de Educación Pública, DER, México, D.F., dated from Tuxtla, March 27, 1935.

16. AHSEP, DEF, Chiapas, Caja 5300 (282), Exp. 33, Fo. 16, from López to DER, México, D.F., dated from Tuxtla, May 29, 1935.

17. Ibid., Fos. 15–17.

18. AHSEP, Dir. de Ed. Fed., Informes, Chiapas, Caja 979, Exp. 1602/3, Fos. 83–87, from Dir. de Ed. Fed. Septimio Pérez Palacios to Jefe del DER Rafael Ramírez, SEP, México, D.F., dated from Tuxtla, May 7, 1933.

19. Septimio Pérez Palacios, "Mi labor en el sector educativo," in *Los maestros y la cultura nacional, 1920–1952*, vol. 5, *Sureste* (México: Museo Nacional de Culturas Populares, y Dirección Gen. de Culturas Populares, 1987), 83; see also AHSEP, Caja 979, Exp. 1602/3, Fos. 172–73, from Dir. de Ed. Fed. Septimio Pérez Palacios to Secretario de Ed. Pública, México, D.F., dated from Tuxtla, Dec. 12, 1933.

20. AHSEP, DER, Caja 1375 (236), Exp. 10, Fos. 30, 37, from López to SEP, DER, México, D.F., from Tuxtla, March 27, 1935. Under the same classification, see folio 47, from López to SEP, DER, México, D.F., dated from Tuxtla, May 20, 1935.

21. AHSEP, DER, Caja 1582 (957), Exp. 3, Fo. 5, from Inspector Ricardo Ruelas Pelayo to Secretario de Educación Pública, DER, México, D.F., dated from Yajalón, June 4, 1933.

22. AHSEP, DGEPET, Delegación Chiapas, Caja 5324 (304) Exp. 18, 27–30, from Inspector Andrés Cancúa Neri to Dir. Gral. de Escuelas Primarias Rurales Foráneas Celso Flores Zamora, México, D.F., dated from México, May 7, 1936.

23. AHSEP, DER, Caja 1375 (236), Exp. 10, Fos. 6, 10–11, from López and Dir. Gen. de Ed. Pública del Estado Ángel M. Corzo, to SEP, México, D.F., dated from Tuxtla, Feb. 1, 1935.

24. Ibid., Exp. 29, Fo. 15, "Programa de la clase de historia del movimiento obrero, que el subscrito desarrollará durante el presente instituto . . . ," from Prof. de la

Materia Manuel Castellanos and Jefe de la Misión Cultural Miguel Espinosa, dated from Tenejapa, April 17, 1935; see also Fo. 30 from Espinosa to the SEP in México, D.F., dated from Ocosingo, May 25, 1935.

25. AHSEP, DGEPET, Caja 5324 (304), Exp. 22, Fo. 8, from Inspector Jesús Durán Cárdenas to DEF in Tuxtla, dated from Pichucalco, early March, 1936.

26. AHSEP, DER, Caja 1332 (191), Exp. 3, Fo. 51, from Inspector P. Arturo Mota to Elpidio López, DEF in Tuxtla, dated from Comitán, March 29, 1935.

27. AHSEP, DER, Caja 1375 (236), Exp. 10, Fo. 69, from Comité de Ed. y padres de familia de Villa de Yajalón to Dir. de Ed. Fed., Tuxtla, dated from Villa de Yajalón, Nov. 10, 1935.

28. Ibid., Fo. 21, "Informe bimestral correspondiente a enero y febrero de 1935," from Inspector Benjamín Rojas to López in Tuxtla, dated from Bochil, March 11, 1935.

29. AHSEP, DGEPET, Caja 5324 (304), Exp. 22, Fo. 145, "Relación del Personal que presta servicios en la IX zona del estado de Chiapas con cabecera en Pichucalco y a cargo del Inspector J. Durán Cárdenas," dated from Pichucalco, Dec. 11, 1936.

30. AHSEP, DEF, Chiapas, Caja 5300 (282), Exp. 33, Fo. 15, from López to Secretario de Educación Pública, DER, México, D.F., dated from Tuxtla, May 29, 1935.

31. Ibid., Fo. 17, from López to Secretario de Educación Pública, DER, México, D.F., dated from Tuxtla, May 29, 1935.

32. AHSEP, DER, Caja 1375 (236), Exp. 10, Fo. 52, from López to C. Secretario de la SEP, México, D.F., dated from Tuxtla, May 20, 1935.

33. AHSEP, DER, Caja 1332 (191), Exp. 4, various from Inspector Daniel Vassallo L., to Dir. de Ed. Fed., dated from Tapachula, 1935.

34. AHSEP, DGEPET, Caja 5346 (328), Exp. 10, Fo. 47, from Jefe del DERPF Celso Flores Zamora to Inspector P. Arturo Mota in Tuxtla, dated from México, D.F., Jan. 18, 1935.

35. AHSEP, DER, Caja 1332 (191), Exp. 3, Fo. 60, "Protesta," from Sociedad Magisterial de Comitán, dated from Comitán, April 10, 1935.

36. Ibid., Exp. 3, Fo. 56, from Inspector P. Arturo Mota to López in Tuxtla, dated from Comitán, March 29, 1935. See also AHSEP, DER, Caja 1375 (236), Exp. 10, Fos. 40–41, from López to Secretario de la SEP, DER, dated from Tuxtla, April 20, 1935.

37. "Los problemas educativos estudiados por el C. Presidente," *El Maestro Rural* 8, no. 1 (Jan. 1, 1936): 5.

38. AHSEP, DER, Caja 1375 (236), Exp. 29, Fo. 90, from Jefe de la Misión Miguel Espinosa R. and others to Secretario de la SEP, Depto. de Enseñanza Agrícola y Normal Rural, México, D.F., dated from Villa Ortiz Rubio, Oct. 28, 1935; James Scott, *Weapons of the Weak: Everyday Forms of Peasant Resistance* (New Haven, Conn.: Yale University Press, 1985).

39. AHSEP, DER, Caja 1375 (236), Exp. 7, Fo 3, from "Sociedad" to Dir. de Ed. Fed. in Tuxtla, dated from Ocosingo, March 11, 1935.

40. AHSEP, DGEPET, Caja 6088 (38), Exp. 11, Fo. 37, from Pres. del Comité de Ed. David Fuentes to Dir. de Ed. Fed. Rafael Bolio Yenro in Tuxtla, dated from Escuela Rural Federal Benito Juárez, Metapa, May 27, 1937.

41. Eric Wolf, "Closed Corporate Peasant Communities in Mesoamerica and Central Java," *Southwestern Journal of Anthropology* 13 (1957): 1–18.

42. Juan B. Alfonseca, "La Escuela Rural Federal en los distritos de Texcoco y Chalco (1923–1936)," 9–11, paper presented at the III Congreso Nacional de Investigación Educativa in Mexico City, Oct. 26, 1995.

43. AHSEP, DEPET, Chiapas, Caja 6095 (st.), 6095, (45), Exp. 9, Fo. 48, from Jefe del DER Rafael Ramírez to Dir. de Ed. Fed. in Tuxtla, dated from México, D.F., Nov. 26, 1931.

44. Ibid., Exp. 9, Fo. 50, from Dir. de Ed. Fed. Erasto Valle, to SEP, DER, México, D.F., dated from Tuxtla, Dec. 11, 1931.

45. AHSEP, DER, Caja 1375 (236), Exp. 10, Fo. 63, "Circular número treinta," from López to Inspectores de Educación Federal en Chiapas, dated from Tuxtla, June 28, 1935.

46. Benjamin, *A Rich Land*, 181–82, 188–90.

47. AHSEP, DER, Caja 1375 (236), Exp. 10, Fos. 63–65, "Circular número treinta," from López to Inspectores de Educación Federal en Chiapas, dated from Tuxtla, June 28, 1935.

48. AGN, Cárdenas, Elpidio López, 534.6/226, various telegrams including from Gobernador del Estado de Nuevo León G. Morales Sánchez to Pres. de la República, dated Nov. 10, 1935.

49. *Informe que el C. Gobernador Constitucional del Estado de Chiapas Victórico R. Grajales rinde a la H. XXXV Legislatura* (Tuxtla: Talleres Tipográficos del Gobierno del Estado, 1934), 41–42; *La Vanguardia*, Año V, Núm. 265, May 27, 1934, p. 1.

50. Alicia Civera, "Crisis política y reforma educativa: El estado de México, 1934–1940," in *Escuela y sociedad*, 152–53; Elsie Rockwell, "Reforma constitucional y controversias locales: la educación socialista en Tlaxcala," in *Escuela y sociedad*, 202.

Chapter 6

The epigraph by d'Azeglio is taken from Hobsbawm, *Nations and Nationalism*, 44. The epigraph by Cancúa is from AHSEP, DGEPET, Caja 5324 (304), Exp. 18, Fo. 28, from Cancúa Neri to Jefe del DERPF Celso Flores Zamora in México, D.F.

1. AGN, O-C, Primer centenario independencia, 805-CH-20, from Contador de la Administración del Timbre Francisco Fernández to Obregón, México, D.F., dated from Tuxtla, Sept. 16, 1924.

2. AHSEP, DER, Caja 1375 (236), Exp. 19, Fo. 41, from Jefe del DERPF Celso Flores Zamora to Dir. de Ed. Fed., Tuxtla, dated from México, D.F., May 16, 1935; and Fos. 7, 9, "Plan General de Trabajo," from Elpidio López and Dir. Gral. de Educ. Pública Ángel M. Corzo to SEP, México, D.F., dated from Tuxtla, Feb. 1, 1935; and Pérez, "Mi labor en el sector educativo," 82.

3. Katherine Elaine Bliss, "Gender and the Cultural Politics of Social Hygiene in Revolutionary Mexico," in *The Eagle and the Virgin*.

4. Juan Blasco López, "La fabricación de aguardiente en San Cristóbal en el siglo XIX" (paper delivered at Foro Internacional "El estado de Chiapas: De la Independencia a la Revolución," San Cristóbal de Las Casas, Chiapas, Mexico, March 2002), 11–12.

5. AGN, Portes Gil, Chiapas, Gob. del Estado, 3/669, Leg. 4, from F. Canales,

Subsecretario encargado del despacho, Secretaría de Gobernación to Gobernador, dated from México, D.F., April 22, 1929.

6. Ibid.; Antonio Gutiérrez y Oliveros, *El supulturero de la raza latinoamericana o el cantinero y la conquista pacífica* (México: Casa Unida de Publicaciones, S.A., 1929). On the prominent role of women in federal sobriety campaigns in the 1930s, see Fallaw, *Cárdenas Compromised*, 92–93.

7. AHSEP, DEF, Caja 1730 (1241), Exp. 1886/77–89, Fo. 47, 69 from Insp. José Inés Estrada to Jefe del DERPFII, SEP, México, D.F., dated from Motozintla, July 4, 1930; see also Caja 1652 (4763), Exp. 1838/1, from Insp. Benjamín P. Martínez to Jefe del Depto. Rafael Ramírez, SEP, México, dated from Huixtla, Nov. 24, 1929.

8. Ibid., Exp. 1886/26, from Insp. Juan Vidal to Jefe del DERPFII, dated from San Cristóbal de Las Casas, May 7, 1930; see also Caja 1195, from Dir. de Ed. Fernando Ximello H. to SEP, México, D.F. dated from Tuxtla, Nov. 18, 1929.

9. AGN, Portes Gil, Chiapas, Gob. del Estado, 3/699, Leg. 3, from Manuel Maldonado to Pres. Emilio Portes Gil, Palacio Nacional, México, D.F., dated from San Cristóbal de Las Casas, May 18, 1929.

10. Ibid.

11. AHSEP, DEF, Caja 1730 (1241), Exp. 1886, from Insp. Juan Vidal to Dir. de Ed. Federal, Tuxtla, dated from San Cristóbal de Las Casas, July 22, 1930.

12. Gonzalo Hernández M., "Campaña de temperancia en vez de campaña antialcólica," *El Maestro Rural* 3, no. 9 (Oct. 1, 1933): 14.

13. AHSEP, DER, Caja 1375 (236), Exp. 29, Fo. 26, from Jefe de la Misión Miguel Espinosa and others, to Secretario de Educación Pública, Depto. de Enseñanza Agrícola y Normal Rural in México, D.F, dated from Ocosingo, May 29, 1935.

14. Bliss, "Gender and the Cultural Politics of Social Hygiene in Revolutionary Mexico."

15. AHSEP, DER, Caja 1332 (191), Exp. 4, Fos. 88–91, flyer printed by Huixtla's Comité Local de Cultura, Huixtla, 1935.

16. AHSEP, DEF, Chiapas, Caja 5300 (282), Exp. 2, Fo. 10, oficio núm. 31-1-984, from Subsecretario Gabriel Lucio, DGEPET, Oficina de Acción Social, to Gobernador del Estado, Tuxtla, dated from México, D.F., March 27, 1936.

17. AHSEP, DGEPET, Caja 5324 (304), Exp. 21, Fo. 53, "Informe anual de Labores," from Inspector Héctor Eduardo Paniagua, to Dir. de Ed. Fed. in Tuxtla, dated from Comalapa, Nov. 15, 1936.

18. AHSEP, DER, Caja 1332 (191), Exp. 8, Fo. 11, 45 from Inspector Manuel Castellanos to López in Tuxtla, dated from Ciudad Las Casas, April 6 and Dec. 10, 1935; Ruth Bunzel, "The Role of Alcoholism in Two Central American Cultures," *Psychiatry* 3 (1940): 361—87.

19. Ibid., Fo. 46, "Informe anual," from Castellanos to López in Tuxtla, dated from Ciudad Las Casas, Dec. 10, 1935.

20. AHSEP, DGEPET, Chiapas, Caja 5298 (280), Exp. 38, Fos. 31–32, from Dir. de Ed. Fed. Rafael Bolio Yenro to Gabriel Lucio, Subsecretario de Educación Pública, México, D.F., dated from Tuxtla, April 14, 1936.

21. AHSEP, DGEPET, Caja 5324 (304), Exp. 6, Fo. 10, 123, "Informe bimestral," from

Inspector Daniel Vassallo to Dir. de Ed. Fed. in Tuxtla, dated from Huixtla, March 3 and early July 1936.

22. AHSEP, DEF, Informes Chiapas, Caja 1056; Exp. 1681/10, from Prof. Rodulfo I. Rincón (for Daniel Vassallo) to Educación Federal, Tuxtla, dated from Huixtla, April 10, 1934.

23. Rosario Castellanos, *Balún-Canán* (México: Fondo de Cultura Económica, 1987 [1957]).

24. AHSEP, DGEPET, Caja 5324 (304), Exp. 6, Fo. 11, "Informe bimestral," from Inspector Daniel Vassallo, to Dir. de Ed. Fed. in Tuxtla, dated from Huixtla, March 3, 1936.

25. AHSEP, DEF, Informes, 1652 (4763), Exp. 1778/1, Fo. 314, from Dir. de Ed. Fed. Eduardo Zarza, dated from Tuxtla, Aug. 20, 1928.

26. Bantjes, "Burning Saints, Molding Minds," 261–84; Knight, "Revolutionary Project," 247–59; and Mary Kay Vaughan, "The Construction of Patriotic Festival in Tecamachalco, Puebla, 1900–1946," in *Rituals of Rule*, 213–45.

27. "Editorial: La educación en Chiapas," *La Vanguardia*, Tuxtla, Sept. 13, 1931; also *La Vanguardia*, Tuxtla, p. 3.

28. AHSEP, DER, Caja 1375 (236), Exp. 10, Fos. 3–5. Under the same classification, see also folio 54, from López to Secretario de la SEP, DER, México, D.F., dated from Tuxtla, May 20, 1935.

29. Ibid., Fo. 32, from López to Secretario de la SEP, DER, México, D.F., dated from Tuxtla, March 27, 1935; and Fo. 61.

30. Ibid., Exp. 28, Fo. 1, "Calendario escolar para todas las escuelas primarias dependientes del Gobierno del Estado y de la Federación, para el año escolar de 1935," from Dir. de Educación Pública Ángel M. Corzo and Dir. Fed. de Ed. Septimio Pérez Palacios, dated from Tuxtla, Jan. 3, 1935; *La educación pública en México, desde el 1 de diciembre de 1934 hasta el 30 de noviembre de 1940* (México, D.F.: SEP, 1941), 54–59.

31. AHSEP, DGEPET, Chiapas, Caja 6060 (10), Exp. 1321, Fos. 30–32, from Prof. Manuel García C. y otros, to SEP, dated from El Carrizal, May 26, 1940.

32. AGN, Cárdenas, Rebeliones, Chiapas, 559.1/60, from Lic. Jorge García Granados to Cárdenas, dated from México, D.F., March 8, 1937.

33. Ibid., "Memorándum confidencial," from Secretaría de Relaciones Exteriores, República de Guatemala, April 19, 1939.

34. AGN, Cárdenas, Rebeliones, Chiapas, 559.1/60, from Gen. de Brigada Comandante Ernesto Aguirre Colorado to Gen. de Brigada Subsecretario Encargado del Despacho de la Defensa Nacional, dated from México, D.F., Nov. 5, 1937.

35. AHSEP, DER, Caja 1375 (236), Exp. 19, Fo. 41, from Jefe del Depto. de Enseñanza Rural y Primaria Celso Flores Zamora to Dir. de Ed. Fed., Tuxtla, Chiapas, dated from México, D.F., May 16, 1935.

36. Emphasis in original. AHSEP, DEF, Chiapas, Caja 5298 (280), Exp. 38, Fo. 77, "Estudio de la comunidad 'La Libertad,' municipio de Suchiate, Chis.," from Inspector Daniel Vassallo L., to Dir. de Ed. Fed., Tuxtla, dated from Tuxtla, Jan. 19, 1936.

37. Ibid., Fos. 53–54, "Estudio de las comunidades 'Tuxtla Chico,' 'Metapa,'

'Frontera Hidalgo,' 'Congregación Hidalgo' y 'Manuel Lazos,'" from Inspector Rubén Antonio Rivas to Dir. de Ed. Fed., Tuxtla, dated from Tuxtla, Jan. 19, 1936.

38. Emphasis in original. AHSEP, DEPET, Caja 5324 (304), Exp. 18, Fo. 9, from Inspector Andrés Cancúa Neri to Prof. Celso Flores Zamora, Jefe del DER, México, D.F., dated from Motozintla, Jan. 1936.

39. Ibid., Fos. 1–2, from Inspector Gen. José Dolores Medina to Inspector Andrés Caneda Neri, Motozintla, dated from Jalapa, Veracruz, March 4, 1936.

40. AHSEP, DEF, Chiapas, Caja 5298 (280), Exp. 38, Fos. 54–58, from Jefe de la Oficina de Acción Social Lucas Ortiz B. to DGEPET, México, D.F., dated from México, D.F., June 16, 1936; "Chiapas, baluarte de México ante los paises de Centro y Sud América," *El Informador*, Tuxtla, May 31, 1936.

41. AHSEP, Dirección de Educación, Chiapas, Caja 1332 (191), Exp. 15, Fos. 65–70, "Informe anual de labores," from Inspector Héctor Eduardo Paniagua to Dir. de Ed. Fed., Tuxtla, dated from Frontera Comalapa, Nov. 15, 1935.

42. *Colonia Chiapaneca*, Revista anual de sus actividades, México, D.F., mayo de 1938, p. 22; González Navarro, *Los extranjeros en México*, III: 129.

43. "Ningún movimiento se fragua en Guatemala contra nuestro país," *El Sur de México*, Tapachula, April 7, 1938, pp. 1, 4.

44. "Categóricas declaraciones del Sr. Lic. Carlos Salazar," in *El Liberal Progresista*, Guatemala City, July 22, 1940; *El Sur de México*, Tapachula, Aug. 8, 1940, p. 1.

45. AGN, Cárdenas, Campañas nacionalistas, 533.31/9, from Nefalti Cobón, Sindicato Único de Trabajadores Plataneros de Tonalá y Soconusco, Sección 17, to Cárdenas, dated from Islamapa, June 22, 1938; "Campaña de integración nacional," *Alborada*, Tuxtla, March 26, 1938, p. 3; "Campaña pro-integración nacional," *Alborada*, Tuxtla, April 16, 1938, pp. 1–2. See also *Memoria de la Secretaría de Educación Pública* (septiembre de 1937–agosto de 1938), I: 482–83.

46. AGN, Cárdenas, Conflictos obreros, 533.31, various, including from Sindicato de Trabajadores Plataneros de la Finca Islamapita, member of the Confederación Obrera del Estado Eduardo Tovilla to Cárdenas, México, D.F., dated from Finca Islamapita, June 21, 1938.

47. García de León, *Resistencia*, 2: 212.

48. AHSEP, DEF, Chiapas, Caja 5298 (280), Exp. 2, Fo. 13, from Dir. de Ed. Fed. Rafael Bolio Yenro to Dir. Gral. de Ed. Primaria Urbana y Rural en los Estados Celso Flores Zamora, dated from Tuxtla, Jan. 16, 1936.

Chapter 7

1. Speech given in Pátzcuaro, 1940. *Palabras y documentos públicos de Lázaro Cárdenas 1928–1940* (México: Siglo Veintiuno Editores, 1979), 403.

2. Dawson, *Indian and Nation*, 45; *Memorias de la SEP*, Sept. 1936–Aug. 1937, Tomo 1, p. 401.

3. AHSEP, DER, Caja 1332 (191), Exp. 8, Fo. 44, from Castellanos to Bolio Yenro in Tuxtla, dated from Ciudad Las Casas, Dec. 10, 1935.

4. AHSEP, DGEPET, Caja 5324 (304), Exp. 20, Fo. 19, from Castellanos to Dir. de Ed. Fed. in Tuxtla, dated from Ciudad de Las Casas, May 11, 1936.

5. Isabel M. Zambrano, "Mass Schooling and Everyday Forms of State Formation: Mitontik, Chiapas, Mexico" (unpublished manuscript), 12.

6. AHMSCLC, 1929, Tomo 2, "Correspondencia de fuera del distrito, Mayo de 1929," signed by Inspector de Obreros y Jefe de la Oficina de Control (illegible), Rep. de los Patrones Francisco J. Velasco y N. G. Aguilar, Pres. de la Comisión Síndico Muni. Miguel Utrilla, Reps. de los Trabajadores Librado Guillén y Gustavo E. Paniagua, Secretario Municipal Juan J. Ramírez, dated from San Cristóbal de Las Casas, March 24, 1930.

7. AHMSCLC, 1933, Tomo 5, "Correspondencia con el Gobierno del Estado y varios, Mes de agosto, 1933," No. 172, from Sección de Fomento y Hacienda, Secretario Gen. de Gobierno, Dr. Samuel León to Pres. Municipal, San Cristóbal Las Casas, dated from Tuxtla, Aug. 25, 1933.

8. *Periódico Oficial*, Tuxtla, April 18, 1934, Tomo LI, Núm. 16, pp. 3–4.

9. AHSEP, DER, Caja 1375 (236), Exp. 5, Fo. 3, "Reglamento del Departamento de Acción Social, Cultura y Protección Indígena," signed by Dir. Gen. de Ed. Pública del Estado Ángel M. Corzo, dated from Tuxtla, May 31, 1934.

10. AHSEP, DGEPET, Caja 5324 (304), Exp. 18, Fo. 11, from Inspector Andrés Cancúa Neri to Jefe del DER Celso Flores Zamora in México, D.F., dated from Motozintla, Jan. 1936; also *Informe que el C. Gobernador Constitucional del Estado de Chiapas Victórico R. Grajales, rinde a la H. XXXV Legislatura, de conformidad con el art. 22 de la Constitución Política del Estado, en el 3er. año de su Ejercicio* (Tuxtla Gutiérrez, Chis.: Imprenta del Gobierno, 1935), 29–30.

11. "El niño indígena de Chiapas mejorará en su manera de vestir," *Liberación*, Oct. 7, 1934, pp. 1, 7. See also *Informe que el C. Gobernador Constitucional del Estado de Chiapas Victórico R. Grajales rinde a la H. XXXV Legislatura*, 46.

12. AHSEP, DGEPET, Caja 5324/5356, Exp. 22. Fo. 19, from Inspector Rubén M. Rincón to Dir. de Ed. Fed., Tuxtla, dated from Ocosingo, Nov. 29, 1935.

13. FAPECFT, Fondo Plutarco Elías Calles, Victórico Grajales, Gav. 37, Exp. 45, Leg. 10/11, Inv. 2497, Fo. 498, from Pres. del Comité Pro-vestido Alumno Indígena Victórico R. Grajales, to Gral. de Div. P. E. Calles, El Tambor, Sin., dated from Ciudad Las Casas, April 24, 1935.

14. Hernández Castillo, *Histories and Stories from Chiapas*, 24–27.

15. Dawson, *Indian and Nation*, 35–44; Engracia Loyo, "Los Centros de Educación Indígena y su papel en el medio rural," in *Educación rural e indígena en iberoamérica*, ed. Pilar Gonzalbo Aizpuru (México: El Colegio de México, 1996), 144–45.

16. Loyo, "Centros de Educación Indígena," 153.

17. Alexander S. Dawson, "Savage and Citizen: Indigenismo and the Vagaries of Race in Post-Revolutionary Mexico" (unpublished manuscript), 125.

18. AHSEP, DER, Caja 1560 (935), Exp. 11, Fos. 81–87, from Dir. de Ed. Fed. Septimio Pérez Palacios to Secretario de Educación Pública, DERPF in México, D.F., dated from Tuxtla, June 8, 1933.

19. Ibid., Fos. 103–4, anonymous comments written on a report from Pérez in early July 1933.

20. AHSEP, DGEPET, Caja 5324 (304), Exp. 16, Fos. 4–6, from Inspector Manuel

Fernando Molina to Dir. de Ed. Fed. in Tuxtla, dated from Copainalá, Mezcalapa, Feb. 29, 1936.

21. AHSEP DEF, Chiapas, Caja 5298 (280), Exp. 39, Fos. 50–53, from Jefe de la Sección de Educación Indígena Angel M. Corzo to DEGEPURE, México, D.F., dated from México, D.F., April 9, 1936.

22. Ibid., Fo. 48.

23. Ibid., various; see also Caja 5356/5324 (304), Exp. 20, various, from Castellanos to Bolio Yenro, Tuxtla, dated from Ciudad Las Casas, July–Nov. 1936.

24. AHSEP, DGEPET, Caja 3399 (st.), 5480, Exp. 108, Fo. 29, from Dir. de Ed. Fed. Jacinto E. Téllez to Dir. Gral. de Enseñanza Primaria Urbana y Rural en los Estados, SEP, México, D.F., dated from Tuxtla, April 18, 1941.

25. AHSEP, DER, Caja 1332 (191), Exp. 8, Fos. 10–11, from Castellanos to López in Tuxtla, dated from Ciudad Las Casas, April 6, 1935.

26. Ibid., Fos. 18–20, "Informe de julio i agosto," from Castellanos to Dir. de Ed. Fed. in Tuxtla, Sept. 10, 1935.

27. AHSEP, DGEPET, Caja 5324 (304), Exp. 20, Fo. 8, from Castellanos to Dir. de Ed. Fed. in Tuxtla, dated from Ciudad Las Casas, March 12, 1936.

28. Ibid., Fo. 19, from Castellanos to Dir. de Ed. Fed. in Tuxtla, May 11, 1936.

29. AHSEP, DER, Caja 1332 (191), Exp. 8, various, Castellanos to Dir. de Ed. Fed. in Tuxtla, dated from Ciudad Las Casas, April–Dec. 1935; AHSEP, DGEPET, Caja 5324/5356 (304), Exp. 20, Fos. 40–42, from Castellanos to Bolio Yenro, Tuxtla, Nov. 18, 1936.

30. AHSEP, DGEPET, Caja 5324 (304), Exp. 20, Fo. 20, from Castellanos to Dir. de Ed. Fed. in Tuxtla, May 11, 1936.

31. AHSEP, DER, Caja 1332 (191), Exp. 8, Fo. 11, from Castellanos to López in Tuxtla, dated from Ciudad Las Casas, April 6, 1935.

32. AHSEP, DGEPET, Caja 5324 (304), Exp. 20, Fo. 10, from Castellanos to Dir. de Ed. Fed. in Tuxtla March 12, 1936.

33. Ibid., Fo. 7.

34. Ibid., Fo. 19, May 11, 1936.

35. AHSEP, DGEPET, Caja 5352 (334), Circular Núm. IV-42-132, signed by Manuel Castellanos in Ciudad Las Casas, May 30, 1936.

36. AHSEP, DGEPET, Caja 5324 (304), Exp. 20, Fos. 38 and 41, from Castellanos to Dir. de Ed. Fed. in Tuxtla, dated from Ciudad Las Casas, Sept. 6 and Nov. 18, 1936.

37. AHSEP, DGEPET, Caja 5489 (2788), Exp. 42, Fos. 18–21, from Castellanos to Dir. de Ed. Fed., Feb. 23, 1937.

38. AHMSCLC, various from 1920s and 1930s, including 1929, Tomo 2, "Correspondencia de fuera del distrito, Mayo de 1929," from Carmen Hernández to Gobernador del Estado, dated from San Cristóbal de Las Casas, April 25, 1929; Urbina, "El despertar de un pueblo," 21.

39. AHMSCLC, 1936–1937, from A. Arvea Jiménez, Procurador de Comunidades Indígenas del Depto. de Asuntos Indígenas to Pres. Municipal, dated from Las Casas, May 19, 1936; also Sec. Gral. de Gobierno José L. Burguete in Tuxtla forwarding letter from Jefe del Depto. de Asuntos Indígenas in México, D.F., to Pres. Muni., Ciudad Las Casas, April 3, 1936; see also reply from Pres. Muni. Evaristo Bonifaz to Sec. Gen.

de Gobierno in Tuxtla, dated from Las Casas, April 29, 1936.

40. Ibid., from Oficial Mayor Aristeo Toledo, acting Srio. Gral, relaying message from Proc. de Comunidades Indígenas A. Arvea Jiménez to Pres. Muni. de Ciudad Las Casas, dated from Las Casas, Oct. 26, 1936.

Chapter 8

1. AGN, Cárdenas, Atropellos autoridades civiles, 542.1/20, from Liga Central de Comunidades Agrarias del Estado de Chiapas adherida a la Confederación Campesina Mexicana, dated from México, D.F., Dec. 11, 1934.

2. AGN, Abelardo Rodríguez, 561.31/9-5, "Salario mínimo," from Gobernador Grajales to Sr. Presidente, dated from Tuxtla, Jan. 31, 1934.

3. AGN, Cárdenas, Atropellos autoridades civiles, 542.1/20, from Liga Central de Comunidades Agrarias del Estado de Chiapas to Cárdenas; under same classification see "Informe detallado que el suscrito eleva a la muy ilustre consideración del C. Presidente Constitucional de la República con motivo de la comisión que se sirvió conferirle en esta entidad federativa," from Pres. Municipal of Tuxtla Gutiérrez Gustavo López Gutiérrez, dated from Tuxtla, Jan. 1, 1935; Benjamin, *A Rich Land*, 181–90; and FAPECFT, Fondo Plutarco Elías Calles, Victórico Grajales, Gav. 37, Exp. 45, Leg. 5/11, Inv. 2497, from Grajales to Calles, México, D.F., dated from Tuxtla, Nov. 5, 1933.

4. Benjamin, *A Rich Land*, 191–94; García de León, *Resistencia*, II: 199–204; FAPECFT, Fondo Plutarco Elías Calles, Gav. 28, Exp. 51, Leg. 9/9, Inv. 1780, Fo. 426, from Horacio Moreno and 57 others, Partido Nacional Revolucionario y el Comité Cardenista to Secretario Gen. del Centro Dir. Cardenista, México, DF, from Tuxtla, Aug. 10, 1933.

5. AGN, Cárdenas, 542.1/20, "Memorandum: Resumen de los cargos que organizaciones campesinas, elementos obreros y políticos hacen al gobernador del estado de Chiapas, Coronel Victórico Grajales," dated from Mexico, D.F., Dec. 13, 1934.

6. Ibid., from Liga Central de Comunidades Agrarias del Estado de Chiapas adherida a la Confederación Campesina Mexicana to Cárdenas, dated from Mexico City, Dec. 11, 1934.

7. Ibid., "Informe detallado que el suscrito eleva a la muy ilustre consideración del C. Presidente Constitucional de la República con motivo de la comisión que se sirvió conferirle en esta entidad federativa," from Pres. Municipal de Tuxtla Gutiérrez Gustavo López Gutiérrez, dated from Tuxtla, Jan. 1, 1935, 6, 10.

8. Ibid., various.

9. AGN, Cárdenas, 533/7, from Secretario Particular Luis I. Rodríguez to Grajales, Tuxtla, dated from Palacio Nacional, México, D.F., March 19, 1935.

10. Luis González, *Historia de la Revolución Mexicana Período 1934–1940: Los días del presidente Cárdenas* (México: El Colegio de México, 1988 [1981]), 38; Nora Hamilton, *The Limits of State Autonomy: Post-Revolutionary Mexico* (Princeton: Princeton University Press, 1982), 125.

11. "Adhesion Bloque Socialista de Educación Pública, al Ciudadano Presidente de la República," *El Maestro Rural* 8, no. 1 (Jan. 1, 1936); Luis Javier Garrido, *El partido de la Revolución institucionalizada* (México: Siglo XXI Editores, 1991 [1982]),

186–200; *Palabras y documentos públicos de Lázaro Cárdenas 1928–1940*, 166–67.

12. AGN, Cárdenas, Elecciones gobernador, Chiapas, 544.2/6, from M. E. Guzmán to Secretario Particular Luis I. Rodríguez, dated from México, D.F., Aug. 28, 1935, 1–8.

13. AGN, Cárdenas, Efraín Gutiérrez, 565.1/60, from J. O. Gutiérrez to Cárdenas, dated from México, D.F., Nov. 2, 1935; Cárdenas, Elecciones gobernador, Chiapas, 544.2/6, leg. 7; Benjamin, *A Rich Land*, 193.

14. AGN, Cárdenas, Elecciones gobernador, Chiapas, 544.2/6, from Pres. del Primer Centro Pro-Cárdenas en el Estado Raul García to Cárdenas, dated from Arriaga, April 15, 1936; and under same classification Leg. 7, 4.

15. "Combatir el fanatismo no es atacar credos religiosos," *El Maestro Rural* 8, Núm. 6, March 15, 1936, 3–4; *Palabras y documentos públicos de Lázaro Cárdenas 1928–1940*, 192–93.

16. AGN, Cárdenas, Templos, 547.2/2, from Comité de Resguardo de los Bienes de la Iglesia to Cárdenas, dated from Pijijiapan, Chiapas, April 1936; González, *Historia de la Revolución Mexicana Período 1934–1940: Los días del presidente Cárdenas*, 40, 62–63; Meyer, *La Cristiada*, I: 363–64.

17. AGN, Cárdenas, Ley de Cultos, 547.4/196, from Agente de Correos Felipe F. Villafuerte to Presidente, dated from Teopisca, April 5, 1936.

18. AHSEP, DGEPET, Caja 5324 (304), Exp. 1, Fo. 43, from Inspector Francisco Ovilla's "Informe sintético de las visitas efectuadas durante el bimestre de marzo y abril," dated from Bochil, May 28, 1936.

19. AGN, Cárdenas, Elecciones gobernador, Chiapas, 544.2/6, "Memorandum del Centro Director Pro-Chiapas al Sr. Pres. de la República Lázaro Cárdenas," by Lic. Aquiles Cruz, Presidente del Centro, dated from México, D.F., Oct. 4, 1935, 13.

20. Rus, "The 'Comunidad Revolucionaria Institucional,'" 273–74.

21. AHSEP, DEF, Informes, Caja 866, exp. 1333/5, from Inspector Jesús Ramírez Caloca to Dir. de Ed. Fed., dated from Tuxtla, March 1, 1935; AGN, Cárdenas, Atropellos autoridades civiles, Chiapas, 542.1/20, various.

22. AHSEP, DGEPET, 5489 (2788), Exp. 42, Fos. 69–70, from Inspector Francisco Ovilla to Bolio Yenro, dated from Bochil, Feb. 1937.

23. AHSEP, DEF, Chiapas, Caja 5298 (280), Exp. 38, Fo. 36, from the Comité de Huelga, Federación Magisterial Chiapaneca to Gobernador Constitucional Interino del Estado, dated from Tuxtla, April 16, 1936; AGN, Cárdenas, Escuelas, Chiapas, 542.1/1753, Fo. 2, from Srio. Gral. de la Sociedad de Maestros Victoriano Trinidad to Cárdenas, dated from Tuxtla, March 3, 1936; and John Britton, "Teacher Unionization and the Corporate State in Mexico, 1931–1945," *Hispanic American Historical Review* 59, no. 4 (1979): 674–90.

24. AGN, Cárdenas, Elecciones gobernador, Chiapas, 544.2/6, from Srio. Gen. of the Liga Central de Comunidades Agrarias de Chiapas Luis Liévano to Cárdenas; AHMSCLC, 1936–37, from Manuel Castellanos to Capitán and Jefe de la Guarnición Aurelio Flores, dated from Las Casas, April 8, 1936.

25. AHSEP, DGEPET, Caja 5324 (304), Exp. 6, Fo. 32, from Inspector Daniel Vassallo to Dir. de Ed. Fed. in Tuxtla, dated from Huixtla, May 21, 1936; AGN, Cárdenas, Escuelas, Chiapas, 534.6/271, Fos. 30–36, from José Romero, Srio. Gral. de la Cámara Regional del

Trabajo del Sureste to Cárdenas, dated from Tapachula, April 28, 1936.

26. AHSEP, DEF, Chiapas, Caja 5298 (280), Exp. 38, Fo. 41, Circular Número 12, from Gobernador Constitucional Int. Lic. José L. Burguete and Bolio Yenro, to CC. Presidentes Municipales y CC. Agentes Municipales en el Estado, dated from Tuxtla, April 19, 1936; AHSEP, DGEPET, Caja 5324 (304), Exp. 1, Fos. 1–2, from Inspector Gen. Erasto Valle to Subsecretario del Ramo, SEP, México, D.F., dated from México, D.F., June 8, 1936.

27. "Se constituyó un frente de Maestros Chiapanecos," *El Informador*, Tuxtla, Chis. June 7, 1936, p. 1; see also Joe Foweraker, *Popular Mobilization in Mexico: The Teachers' Movement, 1977–1987* (Cambridge: Cambridge University Press, 1993).

28. AGN, Cárdenas, Elecciones gobernador, Chiapas, 544.2/6, from Dip. Mario E. Balboa to Pres. de la República, dated from México City, June 2, 1936; Benjamin, *A Rich Land*, 193–94.

29. AHSEP, DGEPET Caja 5489 (2788), Exp. 42, Fos. 69–70, from Inspector Francisco Ovilla to Bolio Yenro in Tuxtla, dated from Bochil, Feb. 1937.

30. As Thomas Benjamin notes, the city's 1848 appropriation of Las Casas's name "lent honor to the city that was largely undeserved." Benjamin, "A Time of Reconquest: History, the Maya Revival, and the Zapatista Rebellion in Chiapas," *American Historical Review* 105, no. 2 (April 2000): 425.

31. AHSCLC, 1936, "Resultado de la votación sobre cambio de nombre de la ciudad," from Pres. Muni. Lic. Evaristo Bonifaz y Secretario Alberto R. Pérez, dated from Ciudad Las Casas, Feb. 12, 1936. Emphasis in the original.

32. Benjamin, "A Time of Reconquest," 429–33.

33. AGN, Cárdenas, Elecciones Chiapas, Municipales, 544.5/496, from María M. de Molina to Cárdenas, dated from Las Casas, 30 Sept. 1936; AHSCLC, 1936–37, from Wistano Molina to Juez de Distrito, Tuxtla, dated from Ciudad de Las Casas, Oct. 1. 1936.

34. AHMSCLC, 1936–37, from Pres. Muni. Lic. Evaristo Bonifaz to Juez de Distrito in Tuxtla, dated from Ciudad Las Casas, Oct. 1, 1936.

35. AGN, Cárdenas, Ley de Cultos, 547.4/496, telegram from Josefa Aguilar V. de Cortés to Cárdenas, dated from Las Casas, Jan. 29, 1937; see also Cárdenas, Templos, 547.2/2, telegram from Estela Jiménez, Comisario de Ac. Social, Frente Único Revolucionario de Chiapas to Cárdenas, dated from Las Casas, Jan. 29, 1937.

36. AGN, Cárdenas, Elecciones Chiapas, Municipales, 544.5/496, from Dips. Venancio Corzo and Mario J. Culebro to H. Congreso del Estado, dated from Tuxtla, Feb. 6, 1937.

37. AHMSCLC, 1937/3, from Inspector Manuel Castellanos to Pres. Muni. Gral. Alberto Pineda O., Ciudad Las Casas, June 30, 1937; also 1937/6, from Pres. Muni. Sub. Dip. Isidro Rabasa and Secretario Fidel Molina B. to Oficial de Acuerdos de la Sria. Gral de Gobierno in Tuxtla José Palacios Ochoa, dated from Ciudad Las Casas, Sept. 3, 1937.

38. AGN, Cárdenas, Elecciones Chiapas, Municipales, 544.5/496, from Gutiérrez to Cárdenas, dated from Tuxtla, July 19, 1937.

39. Ibid., telegram from Gen. Comandante 31/a. Zona Militar to Presidente, dated from Tuxtla, July 9, 1937.

40. *Periódico Oficial*, July 20, 1937.

41. AGN, Cárdenas, Elecciones Chiapas, Municipales, 544.5/496, various telegrams from Erasto Urbina, Srio. Gen. del Comité Municipal del P.N.R. in Las Casas, and others.

42. AHMSCLC, 1937/5, from el Pres. Mpal. Salbador [*sic*] Gómez to Señor Presidente Municipal de Ciudad Las Casas, dated Jan. 1, 1937; and telegram from Pres. Municipal Ciudad de Las Casas Alberto Pineda O. to Sec. Gen. de Gobierno, Tuxtla, dated from Ciudad Las Casas, Jan. 2, 1937; see also AGN, Cárdenas, Elecciones Chiapas, Municipales, 544.5/1038, from Cárdenas to Secretario de Gobernación, dated from Palacio Nacional, México, D.F., Dec. 13, 1937; and Rus, "The 'Comunidad Revolucionaria Institucional,'" 275.

43. AHMSCLC, 1937/2, from Secretario Gen. Salvador Gómez Oso and Secretario de Conflictos Nicolás Espinosa to Pres. de la H. Junta Central de Conciliación y Arbitraje del Estado in Tuxtla, dated from Ciudad Las Casas, July 15, 1937; AGN, Cárdenas, Conflictos obreros, 533.31, from Srio. Gen. del Sindicato de Trabajadores Indígenas Salvador López to Cárdenas, México, D.F., dated from Las Casas, Sept. 16, 1939; and Rus, "The 'Comunidad Revolucionaria Institucional,'" 277.

44. AHMSCLC, 1937/6, various, including from Pres. Muni. Subs. Dip. Isidro Rabasa to Pres. Municipal Oxchuc, dated from Ciudad Las Casas, Dec. 13, 1937.

45. Ibid., from Pres. Muni. Subs. Dip. Isidro Rabasa to Jefe de la Oficina Federal de Hacienda, dated from Ciudad Las Casas, Dec. 8, 1937.

46. AGN, Cárdenas, Conflictos obreros, 432.2/253-2-4, from Pres. del Comité Municipal del P.N.R. Erasto Urbina to Cárdenas, dated from Ciudad Las Casas, April 7, 1938.

47. AHMSCLC, 1938/2, minutes of extraordinary session of H. Ayuntamiento Constitucional de Ciudad de Las Casas, dated from Ciudad de Las Casas, May 8, 1938, pp. 1–2; AGN, Cárdenas, Elecciones Chiapas, Municipales, 544.5/496, various, including telegram from Pineda to Cárdenas, dated from Las Casas, July 23, 1937; and telegram from Ciro Coello G., Regidor Primero, Ayuntamiento Constitucional de Cd. Las Casas to Cárdenas, dated from Las Casas, April 13, 1938.

48. AGN, Cárdenas, Elecciones Chiapas, Municipales, 544.5/496, various telegrams from Gutiérrez to Cárdenas, dated from Tuxtla, April 22–25, 1938; "Atento Memorándum que el Gobernador Constitucional del Estado de Chiapas, presenta al Señor Presidente de la República," from Gutiérrez, dated from Tuxtla, April 24, 1939.

49. AHMSCLC, 1938/2, minutes of extraordinary session of H. Ayuntamiento Constitucional de Ciudad de Las Casas, dated from Ciudad de Las Casas, May 8, 1938, 3.

50. AHMSCLC, 1938/1, from Subteniente and Comandante de la Partida y de la Policía José A. Borges to Pres. Muni. Subs. Dip. Isidro Rabasa, dated from Ciudad Las Casas, April 22, 1938; 1938/2, minutes of extraordinary session of H. Ayuntamiento Constitucional de Ciudad de Las Casas, dated from Ciudad de Las Casas, May 8, 1938, p. 3; and AGN, Cárdenas, Elecciones Chiapas, Municipales, 544.5/496, various, including telegram from Comandante de la Zona Antonio Ríos Zertuche to Presidente, dated from Las Casas, April 24, 1938.

51. AGN, Cárdenas, Conflictos obreros, 432.2/253-2-4, from Lic. Roberto Villa, Venancio Corzo and Joaquín Salgado, dated from Ciudad Las Casas, May 1, 1938; see also AGN, Cárdenas, Elecciones Chiapas, Municipales, 544.5/496, telegram from Srio. Generales of Confed. Obrera Chiapas and others to Cárdenas, dated from Tuxtla, May 5, 1938.

52. AHMSCLC, 1938/1, from Alberto Pineda Ogarrio to Juez de Distrito en el Estado, Tuxtla, dated from Ciudad Las Casas, dated May 2, 1938.

53. AHMSCLC, 1938/2, minutes of extraordinary session of H. Ayuntamiento Constitucional de Ciudad de Las Casas, dated from Ciudad Las Casas, May 8, 1938, p. 4.

54. AHMSCLC, 1938/1, from Sub. Tte. Policía del Estado, Comandante de la Partida José A. Borger to Pres. Muni. Alberto Pineda, dated from Ciudad de Las Casas, May 9, 1938; and AGN, Cárdenas, Elecciones Chiapas, Municipales, 544.5/496, various, including telegram from Srio. de Organización de la Liga de Comunidades Agrarias del Estado Felipe Roblero, dated from Tuxtla, May 11, 1938.

55. AGN, Cárdenas, Elecciones Chiapas, Municipales, 544.5/496, telegram from Jefe del Depto. de Acción Social, Cultura y Protección Indígena Erasto Urbina, dated from Ciudad Las Casas, May 10, 1938.

56. Ibid., telegram from Pres. Municipal Alberto Pineda Ogarrio to Cárdenas, dated from Las Casas, Chiapas, May 11, 1938.

57. Ibid., from Cárdenas to Gutiérrez, dated from Palacio Nacional, Mexico City, May 17, 1938.

58. AHMSCLC, 1938/2, various, including from Nicolás Espinosa to Pres. Municipal, Ciudad Las Casas, dated from Ejido Pedernal, May 12, 1938.

59. "Alberto Pineda Ogarrio, Enemigo del Movimiento Sindical," in *Alborada*, Tuxtla, May 14, 1938, p. 1. See also in the same issue "Protesta contra los atropellos de Alberto Pineda Ogarrio," p. 2.

60. AHMSCLC, 1938/2, from Pres. Muni. Alberto Pineda Ogarrio and Secretario Argentino Paniagua to Comandante de Armas, Ciudad Las Casas, dated from Ciudad Las Casas, May 14, 1938; and AGN, Cárdenas, Elecciones Chiapas, Municipales, 544.5/496, from Pres. Muni. Alberto Pineda to Cárdenas in San Luis Potosí, dated from Las Casas, May 25, 1938.

61. AGN, Cárdenas, Elecciones Chiapas, Municipales, 544.5/496, from Erasto Urbina to Cárdenas, dated from Las Casas, June 12, 1938; García de León, *Resistencia*, II: 209–10.

62. AHMSCLC, 1938/2, from Comandante de la Policía Municipal Fernando Cortés P. to Pres. Muni. Alberto Pineda, dated from Ciudad Las Casas, June 14, 1938; and Urbina, "El despertar de un pueblo," 44–45.

63. AGN, Cárdenas, Elecciones Chiapas, Municipales, 544.5/496, various from Sen. Dr. Gustavo Marín to Cárdenas.

64. AHMSCLC, 1939/2, from Manuel Castellanos to CC. Presidentes Municipales Zinacantán, Chamula, Larráinzar, Chenalhó, Tenejapa, and Huixtán, dated from Ciudad de Las Casas, Feb. 22, 1939; Rus, "The 'Comunidad Revolucionaria Institucional,'" 275, 277–78.

65. AGN, Cárdenas, Atropellos autoridades civiles, Chiapas, 542.1/20, from Gutiérrez to Cárdenas, dated from Tuxtla, Oct. 12, 1938.

66. See Bantjes, *As If Jesus Walked on Earth*; Fallaw, *Cárdenas Compromised*; and Knight, "Cardenismo: Juggernaut or Jalopy?"

67. Benjamin, *A Rich Land*, 229; George Collier, "Peasant Politics and the Mexican State: Indigenous Compliance in Highland Chiapas," *Mexican Studies/Estudios*

Mexicanos 3, no. 1 (winter 1987): 82; Hernández Castillo, *Histories and Stories from Chiapas*, 39; Reyes Ramos, *El reparto de tierras y la política agraria en Chiapas, 1914–1988*, 62; Rus, "The 'Comunidad Revolucionaria Institucional,'" 259–60; and Jan Rus, "Managing Mexico's Indians: The Historical Context and Consequences of *Indigenismo*" (Unpublished manuscript, 1976), 24.

68. Benjamin, *A Rich Land*, 236–37; Reyes Ramos, *El reparto de tierras y la política agraria en Chiapas, 1914–1988*, 59–63; and Rus, "The 'Comunidad Revolucionaria Institucional,'" 281–83. See also AHSEP, DGEPET, Caja 5489 (2788), from Castellanos to Dir. de Ed. Fed., Tuxtla, Sept. 4, 1944.

Chapter 9

The epigraph is from correspondence dated from Ismalapa, Chis., July 26, 1938, AHSEP, DGEPET, Chiapas, Caja 6134 (84), Exp. 12, Fo. 29.

1. In May 1936, the geographic breakdown of schools *in operation* in Chiapas shows sixty-five schools in Soconusco. Neighboring Motozintla, which also boasted coffee fincas, had nine schools, while Comitán had eight. The banana plantations in Pichucalco supported six schools. AHSEP, DEF, Chiapas, Caja 5298 (280), Exp. 39, Fos. 44–53, Circular Num. IV-42-132, from Dir. Gen. Celso Flores Zamora, DGEPET, dated May 30, 1936.

2. *Memoria relativa al estado que guarda el ramo de educación pública el 31 de agosto de 1934*, 52.

3. AHSEP, DEnR, Sección Escuelas Artículo 123, Caja 1331 (189), Exp. 11, Fo. 125, from Jefe de la Sección Adolfo Contreras to the Jefe del DEnR, México, D.F., Nov. 7, 1935.

4. AHSEP, SP, Caja 4468 (4595), Exp. 1, Fo. 101, from DGEET Alberto Terán, Oficina de Escuelas Art. 123, to Secretario del Ramo, México, D.F., Nov. 7, 1941.

5. Ibid., Fo. 105, from DGEET Alberto Terán, Oficina de Escuelas Art. 123, to Secretario del Ramo, México, D.F., Nov. 7, 1941; and AHSEP, Delegación Chiapas, Caja 5346 (328), Exp. 7, Fos. 18–19, from Pérez Palacios to SEP, DEnR, México, D.F., dated from Tuxtla, Jan. 8, 1935.

6. AHSEP, DER, Caja 1331 (189), Exp. 11, Fo. 78, "Cuadro que indica las 'escuelas del artículo 123' que funcionaron en el país durante el mes de diciembre de 1934 controladas por la Secretaría."

7. AHSEP, DER, Caja 1375 (236), Exp. 18–19, various; and Caja 1332 (191), Exp. 15, Fos. 37–38, "Informe sintético de labores," Inspector Héctor Eduardo Paniagua, Inspección 13th Zone, to Dir. de Ed. Fed., Tuxtla, dated from Frontera Comalapa, Aug. 10, 1935.

8. AHSEP, DGEPET, Chiapas, Caja 6134 (84), Exp. 12, Fo. 29, from Dir. de la Escuela Rafael Ancheita Aparicio to SEP, Dir. Gen. de Enseñanza Primaria y Normal Rural, SEP, México, D.F., dated from Islamapa, July 26, 1938.

9. AHSEP, DGEPET, Chiapas, Caja 6131 (81), Exp. 22, Fo. 17, from Agente Municipal Celestino Espinosa, dated from finca Julia, Motozintla, Sept. 16, 1937.

10. García de León, *Resistencia*, 2: 190–95.

11. AHSEP, DER, Caja 1332 (191), Exp. 4, Fos. 13, 16–17, "Informe bimestral" and "Informe," from Daniel Vassallo L.; Celso Flores Zamora, "Escuelas del Artículo 123,"

El Maestro Rural 6, no. 6 (March 2, 1935): 22.

12. AHSEP, DGEPET, Caja 5324 (304), Exp. 1, Fo. 40, "Informe de labores por el bimestre julio–agosto," from Inspector P. Arturo Mota to Bolio Yenro in Tuxtla, dated from Ocozocuautla, Sept. 10, 1936.

13. AHSEP, DGEPET, Chiapas, Caja 6130 (80), Exp. 3, Fo. 9, from Amadeo Tercero to Cárdenas, dated from Finca "El Retiro," Jan. 3, 1938; and DER, Caja 1332 (191), Exp. 4, Fo. 29, "Informe bimestral," from Inspector Daniel Vassallo L. to Jefe del DER, Sección de Escuelas Rurales, SEP, México, D.F., dated from Huixtla, Aug. 9, 1935.

14. AHSEP, DER, Caja 1375 (236), Exp. 26, Fos. 16–18, from López to SEP, DER, México, D.F., dated from Tuxtla, Aug. 14, 1935; also Caja 1332 (191), Exp. 3, Fo. 16, Fo. 2, "Informe de labores del 3er. Bimestre, en la parte relativa a las Escuelas rurales y Artículo 123," from Inspector P. Arturo Mota to López in Tuxtla, dated Aug. 5, 1935; and Catherine Nolan-Ferrel, "Campesinos of Questionable Nationality: Government Reform Programs and the Creation of a Mexican Peasantry in Chiapas," paper delivered at Foro Internacional "El estado de Chiapas: De la Independencia a la Revolución," San Cristóbal de Las Casas, Chiapas, Mexico, March 2002, 5, 10.

15. AHSEP, DGEPET, Chiapas, Caja 6135 (85), Exp. 18, Fos. 9–10, "Plan de Trabajo," from School Director Carlota Aguilar, dated from finca El Carmen, June 8, 1938.

16. The cosmopolitan flavor of the Chiapanecan coffee industry is colorfully described in García de León, *Resistencia*, 1: 172–203.

17. AHSEP, DER, Caja 1332 (191), Exp. 3, Fo. 32, "Informe General de Labores," from Inspector P. Arturo Mota to Secretario de Educación Pública, Depto. de Ens. Rural y Primaria Foránea, México, D.F., dated Dec. 19, 1934; and AGN, Cárdenas, Conflictos obreros, 432.2/253-2-4, from Octavio García for the Comité Central of the Sindicato de Trabajadores del Campo to Cárdenas, dated from Finca "El Retiro," June 22, 1938.

18. AHSEP, DGEPET, Chiapas, Caja 6130 (80), Exp. 3, Fo. 10, "Proyecto de ley que se somete a la consideración del H. Congreso de la Unión para su estudio, tendiente a la forma que debe socializarse la riqueza en la región del Soconusco del Estado de Chiapas," from Dir. Escuela Federal Art. 123 Amadeo Tercero, dated from Finca "El Retiro," Dec. 15, 1937.

19. AHSEP, DEF, Caja 1667 (1339), Exp. 8, Fo. 21, from Misionero de Cultura Indígena Ernesto Parres to Jefe del Dept. de Cultura Indígena, dated from Huixtla, Dec. 16, 1922.

20. *Memoria relativa al estado que guarda el ramo de educación pública el 31 de agosto de 1934*, II: 52.

21. AHSEP, DGEPET, Chiapas, Caja 6131 (81), Exp. 489, Fo. 1, from Esther Castellanos C. to Dir. de Ed. Fed. Tuxtla, dated from Chactajal, Ocosingo, Sept. 30, 1934. (Original emphasis.)

22. AHSEP, DERPF, Caja 2384 (148), Exp. 1, Fos. 28–35, Circular No. IV-21-102, from Jefe del DER Rafael Ramírez to CC. Inspectores Generales, Directores de Educación y Profesores Inspectores, dated from México, D.F., June 20, 1934.

23. AHSEP, SP, Caja 4468 (4595), Exp. 1, Fos. 106–19, from DGEET Alberto Terán, Oficina de Escuelas Art. 123, to Secretario del Ramo, México, D.F., dated from México, D.F., Nov. 7, 1941.

24. AHSEP, DGEPET, Chiapas, Caja 6135 (85), Exp. 21, Fos. 12–13, from Dir. de Ed. Fed. Raúl Isidro Burgos to Secretario de Educación Pública, México, D.F., dated from Tuxtla, Dec. 31, 1938.

25. AHSEP, DGEPET, Chiapas, Caja 6131 (79), Exp. 13, Fos. 26–27, from Dir. Gen. Rafael Méndez Aguirre, to DEF in Tuxtla, dated from México, D.F., Aug. 2, 1938.

26. Ibid., Exp. 14, Fo. 26, from Enrique Braun to Secretario de Educación Pública, DGEPURE, México, D.F., dated from Tapachula, Nov. 30, 1937.

27. When he bought "Santo Domingo," Enrique Braun not only had to guarantee the loan with his land, but commit to maintaining one thousand head of cattle and taking out fire insurance. María de los Angeles Ortiz and Bertha Toraya, *Concentración de poder y tenencia de la tierra: El caso de Soconusco*, Cuadernos de la Casa Chata 125 (México: CIESAS, 1985), 107, 123.

28. Archivo de Concentración del Estado de Chiapas (hereafter ACECh), Junta de Conciliación y Arbitraje, 1932–1939, from Luis Santiago de la Torre to Junta Central de Conciliación y Arbitraje, Tuxtla, dated from Tapachula, Jan. 3, 1937.

29. Ibid., from Pres. de la Junta de Conciliación y Arbitraje Lic. Carlos Albores C. to Herbert Luttman, dated from Tuxtla, May 29, 1937; AHSEP, DGEPET, Chiapas, Caja 6135 (83), Exp. 11, Fo. 13, from Secretario de Educación Federal Salvador Lorenzana to Secretario de Educación Pública, DGEPURE, México, D.F., dated from Tuxtla, July 26, 1938; Benjamin, *A Rich Land*, 180.

30. ACECh, Junta de Conciliación y Arbitraje, 1932–1939, various, including from Pres. de la Junta de Conciliación y Arbitraje José Orantes E., Tuxtla, Jan. 31, 1938.

31. AHSEP, DGEPET, Chiapas, Caja 4168 (st.), 3548, (5598), Exp. 45, Fos. 1–2, from Inspector Rafael Hernández Madrigal, to Rafael Méndez Aguirre, SEP, México, D.F., dated April 28, 1938.

32. AHSEP, Delegación Chiapas, DER, Caja 1375 (236), Exp. 13, Fo. 9, 22, from Subsecretario Enseñanza Rural Escuelas Artículo 123 Gabriel Lucio to Secretario de Hacienda y Crédito Público, México, D.F., dated from México, D.F., Sept. 20, 1935. Head of Comitán's Hacienda office Baldomero Dávila responded that Mota "should abstain from making completely false allegations."

33. AHSEP, DGEPET, Caja 5352 (334), Exp. 3, Fo. 67, from Rafael Bolio Yenro to Secretario de Educación Pública, DGEPURE, México, D.F., dated from Tuxtla, March 4, 1936.

34. AHSEP, SP, Caja 4468 (4595), Exp. 1, Fo. 115, from DGEET Alberto Terán, Oficina de Escuelas Art. 123, to Secretario del Ramo, México, D.F., dated from México, D.F., Nov. 7, 1941.

35. García de León, *Resistencia*, 2: 38, 68, 169; Ortiz and Toraya, *Concentración de poder y tenencia de la tierra*, 109.

36. AHSEP, DGEPET, Chiapas, Caja 6131 (79), Exp. 13, Fo. 30, from Secretario General de Educación Daniel Ruiz to Dir. de Ed. Fed., Tuxtla, dated from Jitotol, Aug. 5, 1938.

37. Ibid., Exp. 14, Fo. 7, from Pérez Palacios to Sr. Enrique Braun, Tapachula, dated from Tuxtla, Aug. 24, 1934.

38. Ibid., Exp. 14, Fo. 6, 19, 21, 26.

39. Ibid., Exp. 13, Fo. 11, from Enrique Braun to Dir. de Ed. Fed., Tuxtla, dated from Tapachula, June 17, 1938.

40. Pérez's successor, Elpidio López, claimed that these Article 123 school crusaders sacrificed accuracy and legality in their push to win recognition; see AHSEP, DER, Caja 1375 (236), Exp. 10, Fo. 31, from López to Srio. de Educación Pública, DEnR, México, D.F., dated from Tuxtla, March 27, 1935.

41. AHSEP, DGEPET, Chiapas, Caja 6130 (80), Exp. 514, Fo. 109, from Dir. Gen. de la DGEPET Celso Flores Zamora, to Prof. Guillermo Meza in Comitán, dated from México, D.F., March 19, 1936.

42. Ibid., Fos. 6–143.

43. Ibid., Fo. 170, from Encargado del Depto. de Contaduría Personal Miguel J. Urruchúa to Pag. Civ. Serv. Feds. Cd. Las Casas, dated from México, D.F., Dec. 11, 1944.

44. AHSEP, DEF, Caja 5566 (3371), "Memorándum al Presidente de la República," from Inspector José Inés Estrada, dated from Comitán, March 26, 1940.

45. AHSEP, DGEPET, Chiapas, Caja 6131 (81), Exp. 21, Fo. 15, from Burgos to SEP, DGEPURE, Sección de Escuelas Artículo 123, México, D.F., dated from Tuxtla, Jan. 27, 1938.

46. Ibid., Exp. 31, Fos. 40–41, from Jefe del Depto. Jurídico y de Revisión de Estudios Lic. Germán Fernández del Castillo to DGEPET, dated from México, D.F., Dec. 15, 1944. Armendariz had also been granted a "readjustment" of his labor contract in February 1938; see ACECh, Junta de Conciliación y Arbitraje, 1932–1939.

47. Pérez Palacios, "Mi labor en el sector educativo," 79–80.

48. AHSEP, SP, Caja 4468 (4595), Exp. 1, Fos. 104, 107, from DGEET Alberto Terán, Oficina de Escuelas Art. 123, to Secretario del Ramo, México, D.F., dated from México, D.F., Nov. 7, 1941.

49. AHSEP, Delegación Chiapas, DER, Caja 1375 (236), Exp. 10, Fo. 15, from Pérez Palacios, to SEP, DER, dated from Tuxtla, Feb. 5, 1935.

50. AHSEP, DGEPET, Caja 3593 (st.), 5522, (2973), Exp. 3, Fo. 7, "Escuelas Artículo 123 que funcionaron en el Estado de Chiapas durante el mes de abril de 1938."

51. Gustavo Montiel, *Recordando el Soconusco y su perla* (México: B. Costa-Amic, 1979), 110; "Aniversario del Natalicio del Fuehrer Hitler," in *El Sur de México*, Tapachula, Chiapas, April 21, 1938, p. 1.

52. Pérez Montfort, "Indigenismo, Hispanismo y Panamericanismo en la cultura popular mexicana de 1920 a 1940," 374; Friedrich E. Schuler, *Mexico between Hitler and Roosevelt: Mexican Foreign Relations in the Age of Lázaro Cárdenas* (Albuquerque: University of New Mexico Press, 1998), 55–59.

53. *Colonia Chiapaneca*, Revista Anual de sus Actividades, México, May 1938, 21.

54. "Alemanes y Japoneses en Chiapas serán concentrados a Perote, Ver.," *El Sur de México*, Tapachula, May 11, 1942, p. 1.

55. García de León, *Resistencia*, 2: 213, "Le doy trescientas mil chingadas y que las tierras sean para los indios."

56. Braun's brother Fernando also lost land. "Cómo fue hecha la repartición de tierras en el Soconusco," in *Chiapas Nuevo*, Tuxtla, March 23, 1939, p. 4.

57. AGN, Presidentes, Cárdenas, 404.1/3390, from Enrique Braun to Cárdenas, dated from Tapachula, Sept. 22, 1939.

58. "El pleno reparto de tierras," in *El Sur de México*, Tapachula, March 3, 1939, p. 1; García de León, *Resistencia*, 2: 276.

59. AGN, Cárdenas, 404.1/3390; also AGN, Cárdenas, Conflictos obreros, from Sec. Gen. Liga Comunidades Agrarias del Distrito de Soconusco Enrique Castañeda to Cárdenas, dated from Tapachula, 13 Feb. 1940; also Benjamin, *A Rich Land*, 207.

60. AHSEP, DGEPET, Escuelas Artículo 123, Caja 6131 (79), Exp. 14, Fo. 39, from Téllez to Inspector Bernardo Piedrasanta, dated from Tuxtla, April 21, 1939.

61. AHSEP, SP, Caja 4468 (4595), Exp. 1, Fo. 115, from DGEET Alberto Terán, Oficina de Escuelas Art. 123, to Secretario del Ramo, México, D.F., dated from México, D.F., Nov. 7, 1941; DGEPET, Chiapas, Caja 6130 (80), Exp. 3, Fo. 28, from Prof. Amadeo Tercero to Delegado de la Sección XII del STERM, Colonia El Chaparrón, dated from Finca "El Retiro," Aug. 6, 1938.

62. Stephen R. Niblo, *War, Diplomacy, and Development: The United States and Mexico, 1938–1954* (Wilmington, Del.: Scholarly Resources Inc., 1995), 63–189; and Schuler, *Mexico between Hitler and Roosevelt*, 104–6, 127–34, 166.

63. Von Mentz, "Las empresas alemanas en México (1920–1942)," 214–16.

64. Ibid., 182–86, 216–17. See also in the same volume Daniela Spenser, "Economía y movimiento laboral en las fincas cafetaleras de Soconusco," 276–78, and "La reforma agraria en Soconusco y la contraofensiva del finquero cafetalero," 308–11.

65. Montiel, *Recordando el Soconusco y su perla*, 225; von Mentz, "Las empresas alemanas en México (1920–1942)," 199–202; and "Confisca el gobierno federal las negociaciones alemanas y japonesas afectadas de acuerdo con la nueva ley," *El Sur de México*, Tapachula, June 18, 1942, p. 1.

66. Benjamin, *A Rich Land*, 209.

67. AGN, Ávila Camacho, Exp. 546.2/10, from Jesus Jiménez y Romeo Noriega, Federación Trabajadores Chiapas to Ávila Camacho dated from Tuxtla, Sept. 7, 1944.

68. AHSEP, DGEPET, Chiapas, Caja 6130 (80), Exp. 5, Fo. 47, from Inspector José Gabriel Cifuentes C. to DGEPET, México, D.F., dated from Huixtla, Jan. 17, 1959.

69. These arguments are discussed in Alan Knight, "Cardenismo: Juggernaut or Jalopy?"

70. AHSEP, DER, Caja 1375 (236), Exp. 10, Fos. 50–51, from López to Secretario de la SEP, DER, México, D.F., dated from Tuxtla, May 20, 1935. See also Meneses, coord., *Tendencias educativas oficiales en México 1934–1964*, 86–88.

71. AGN, Cárdenas, 534.5/172, from Cándido López Orozco, A. Mayorga V. y demás firmantes, Directores de las Escuelas Art. 123 de Finca "Segovia," "Hamburgo" y otras, to Cárdenas, México, D.F., dated from Huixtla, Nov. 3, 1938; AHSEP, DGEPET, Chiapas, Caja 6130 (80), Exp. 3, Fo. 41–46, from Sindicato de Trabajadores de la Enseñanza de la República Mexicana, Delegación XII de la Sección VII, to Téllez, Tuxtla, dated from Tapachula, May 15, 1939.

72. AGN, Cárdenas, 534.5/172, from Rubén Aguilar Pola, Maestro Rural Art. 123, Finca "Realidad," to Cárdenas, dated from Tapachula, May 27, 1939.

73. AHSEP, DGEPET, Caja 4162 (st.), 5593 (3542), Exp. 129, Fo. 1., from Inspector Francisco Ovilla to DGEPURE, SEP, México, D.F., dated from Huixtla, June 9, 1943. Folio 2 shows that DGEET Ramón García Ruiz responded strongly to Ovilla's

charges. "Se toma debida nota de la forma indebida e irrespetuosa con que se dirige a esta Secretaría y de la cual se informará a la superioridad, ya que los cargos que usted señala no los podrá comprobar. . . ."

74. This data is based on a forty-school sampling, since closure dates could not be located for nine schools.

75. Knight, "Cardenismo: Juggernaut or Jalopy?" 100; see also John W. Sherman, "Reassessing Cardenismo: The Mexican Right and the Failure of a Revolutionary Regime, 1934–1940," *The Americas*, 54, no. 3 (Jan. 1998): 357–78.

Chapter 10

The epigraph is from correspondence dated from Miramar, Escuintla, November 6, 1943, AHSEP, DGEPET, Chiapas, Caja 6088 (38), Exp. 5, Fos. 22–23.

1. AHSEP, DEF, Informes Chiapas, 1941, 5463 (Caja 2758); Exp. 3382/5, Fos. 94–96, "Memorandum que presenta la Sección Séptimo del Sterm, correspondiente al Estado de Chiapas, por conducto de su Secretario Gen., al Lic. Luis Sánchez Pontón, Secretario de Educación Pública," from Sec. Gen. F. Donato Mota, dated from Tuxtla, Dec. 16, 1940.

2. Ibid., Exp. 3393/23; Fos. 5–11, from Téllez to Dir. Escuela Art. 123 Antonio Salazar Argüello, Finca Prusia, Mpio. Ángel A. Corzo, dated from Tuxtla, July 5, 1941.

3. See, for example, AHSEP, DGEPET, Chiapas, Caja 6060 (10), Exp. 23148, Fos. 7–9. Under the same classification, see Exp. 23927, Fo. 17; Exp. 1314, Fos. 13–14; and Caja 4168 (st); 5598 (3548), Exp. 45, Fos. 1–2.

4. Wilkie, *La Revolución Mexicana*, 193.

5. AHSEP, DEF, Caja 5581 (3530), Exp. 4483/40, Fos. 6–7, from Inspector José María Estrada to Téllez in Tuxtla, dated from Comitán, Nov. 30, 1941.

6. AHSEP, DEF, Informes Chiapas, Caja 5463 (2758), Exp. 3393/23, Fos. 5–11, from Controlador de Primera de la Dir. Gen. de Administración Ing. Salvador Caballero Méndez, dated April 30, 1941.

7. *Noticia estadística sobre la educación pública en México correspondiente al año de 1927* (México: TGN, 1928), 414–19; Roldán Velasco Farrera, *La educación en Chiapas en los últimos cuatro años: 1941–1944* (Tuxtla: Gobierno Constitucional de Chiapas, 1944), 23–24.

8. AHSEP, DEF, Caja 5566 (3371), Exp. 3944/9 Fo. 27, from Inspector Epigmenio de León to Téllez in Tuxtla, dated from Chiapa de Corzo, Dec. 18, 1940; also Caja 5581 (3530), Exp. 4482/29, Fo. 34, "Informe general de labores de la zona, por el año de 1941," from Mota to Téllez in Tuxtla, dated from Ocozocuautla, Dec. 31, 1941.

9. AHSEP, DEF, Chiapas, Caja 5581 (3530), Exp. 4482/29, Fos. 31–32, "Informe general de labores de la zona, por el año de 1941," from P. Arturo Mota to Téllez, dated from Tuxtla, Dec. 31, 1941.

10. Ibid., Fos. 2–4, from Castellanos to Téllez in Tuxtla, dated from Ciudad Las Casas, Dec. 25, 1941.

11. Ibid., Fo. 69, from Castellanos to Téllez in Tuxtla, dated from Ciudad Las Casas, Oct. 1, 1942. See also AHSEP, Escuelas Rurales Federales, Chiapas, 6050, Exp. 7222/19, "Supervisión Escolar," by Castellanos, dated from Sibactel, Tenejapa, April 7, 1943.

12. AHSEP, DGEPET, Caja 3377 (st.); 5462 (2757), Exp. 7, Fo. 1, from Delegación Doce de la Sección VII del STERM/CTM to Téllez in Tuxtla, dated from Tapachula, Jan. 28, 1941; and Fo. 6, from Secretario Gen. Raymundo Flores Fuentes, STERM, to DGEPET Aureliano Esquivel, SEP, México, D.F., dated from México, D.F., Feb. 7, 1941; and AGN, Ávila Camacho, Profesorado Chiapas, 534.6/268, various.

13. AHSEP, DEF, Informes Chiapas, 1941, 5463 (2758); Exp. 3382/5; Fos. 171–73, from Téllez to DGEPURET, SEP, México, D.F., dated from Tuxtla, Dec. 22, 1941.

14. AHSEP, DEF, Chiapas, Caja 5581 (3530), Exp. 9489/2, Fos. 2–3, from Téllez to Lic. Roberto T. Bonilla, Sub-Secretario de Educación Pública, México, D.F., dated from Tuxtla, Jan. 16, 1942.

15. AHSEP, DEF, Chiapas, 5690 (1888); Exp. 4495/82, from Pres. del Comité de Ed. Fed. in Acapetahua Luis Flores to Pres. Ávila Camacho, dated from Acapetahua, May 17, 1942.

16. AHSEP, DEF, Chiapas, Caja 5581 (3530), Exp. 9489/2, Fo. 99, from Rpte. del Gob. del Estado, Dir. de Educación Pública del Estado Joaquín Cruz C., and Rpte. de los HH. Ayuntamientos del Edo. Fidel Martínez, dated from Tuxtla, Aug. 13, 1942.

17. AHSEP, DGEPET, Caja 4203 (st.), 5600 (3585), Exp. 4, Fo. 3, from Inspector Antonio Rodríguez Cano to Téllez in Tuxtla, dated from Motozintla, March 21, 1939; and Fo. 5, from Dir. Gen., DGEPET, Oficina de Directores e Inspectores de Educación, to Téllez, Tuxtla, dated from México, D.F., Dec. 11, 1939.

18. AHSEP, DGEPET, Caja 3404 (st.); 5485 (2784), Exp. 53, Fo. 11, from Pres. Muni. de Cintalapa Ing. Octavio H. Serrano to Secretario de Educación Pública, México, D.F., dated from Cintalapa, July 10, 1941.

19. Ibid., Fo. 7, from Téllez to Dir. Gral. de Enseñanza Primaria Urbana y Rural en los Estados, Oficina de Coord. Técnica, SEP, México, D.F., dated from Tuxtla, Sept. 4, 1941.

20. AGN, Ávila Camacho, Profesorado Chiapas, 534.6/224, from Téllez to Presidente, México, D.F., dated from Tuxtla, Jan. 17, 1942.

21. AHSEP, DGEPET, Caja 6131 (81), Exp. 31, Fos. 40–41, from Jefe del Depto. Jurídico y de Revisión de Estudios Germán Fernández del Castillo to DGEPET, SEP, México, D.F., dated from México, D.F., Dec. 15, 1944; AGN, Ávila Camacho, Profesorado Chiapas, 534.6/268, from Gobernador Rafael P. Gamboa to Sec. Part. del Pres. J. Jesus González Gallo, Palacio Nacional, México, D.F., dated from Tuxtla, July 15, 1944.

22. AGN, Ávila Camacho, Ejidos, Exp. 703.4/238, from Liga Central de Comunidades Agrarias de la República, México, DF, to Presidente, México, D.F., dated April 8, 1942.

23. Ibid., from Pres. del Comité Ejecutivo de la Liga Central de Comunidades Agrarias de la República Lic. Luis Ramírez de Arellano to Presidente, July 28, 1942.

24. Ibid., from Comité de Defensa de los Intereses de los Trabajadores Cafeteros del Soconusco and Comité Central Ejecutivo del Sindicato de Trabajadores de la Industria del Café del Soconusco to Presidente, dated from Tapachula, July 5, 1942.

25. Ibid., from Rosendo Morales and others to Presidente, dated from Cacahoatán, July 15, 1942.

26. Ibid., from Pres. del Comité Ejecutivo de la Liga Central de Comunidades Agrarias de la República Lic. Luis Ramírez de Arellano, to Presidente, dated from México, D.F., July 28, 1942.

27. Ibid., various.

28. Ibid., from Sec. Gen. de la Federación Regional de Trabajadores de C. Victoria (CTM), José Castillo V., to Presidente, dated from Ciudad Victoria, Tamaulipas, July 20, 1942.

29. Ibid., from Unión Central de Sociedades Locales Colectivas de Crédito Ejidal de la Comarca Lagunera, to Presidente, dated from Torreón, Coahuila, July 21, 1942.

30. Dawson, *Indian and Nation*, 153–58.

31. AGN, Cárdenas, Folklore, 533.4/1, Exp. 2, Fos. 217–24, "Sobre la creación de un Departamento de población indígena," by Moisés Sáenz, Sept. 1935.

32. Dawson, *Indian and Nation*, 82–83.

33. Ibid., 83–85.

34. Gonzalo Aguirre Beltrán, ed., *Obra antropológica XII: Lenguas vernáculas* (México: Fondo de Cultura Económica, 1993 [1983]), 344; see also Héctor Díaz Polanco, *La cuestión étnico-nacional* (México, D.F.: Editorial Línea, 1985), 40; and Cecilia Greaves, "Entre la teoría educativa y la práctica indigenista: La experiencia en Chiapas y la Tarahumara (1940–1970)," in *Educación rural e indígena en iberoamerica*, 163.

35. *Departamento de Asuntos Indígenas: Memoria del Primer Congreso Regional Indígena celebrado en Ixmiquilpan, Hgo. 25 a 26 de septiembre de 1936* (México: D.A.A.P., 1938), 13; for more on the regional indigenous congresses, see Dawson, *Indian and Nation*, 96–126.

36. AGN, Cárdenas, Congresos Indígenas, 433/482, to Delegado Agrario Ing. Salvador García Bros in Tuxtla from Jefe de la Zona Ejidal Ing. Carlos Amado Ávila, dated from Ciudad de Las Casas, May 18, 1940.

37. Ibid., from Gobernador Gutiérrez to Presidente, México, D.F., dated from Tuxtla, July 19, 1940, 2.

38. Ibid., from Urbina to Gutiérrez, Tuxtla, dated from Ciudad Las Casas, May 16, 1940.

39. AGN, Cárdenas, Sindicato de Trabajadores Indígenas, 703.4/205, "Carta abierta a la Sección Séptima del S.T.E.R.M. Tuxtla," from Sindicato de Trabajadores Indígenas del Estado de Chiapas and other C.T.M. affiliates in Chiapas, dated from Ciudad Las Casas, Aug. 1940.

40. AGN, Cárdenas, Congresos Indígenas, 433/482, from Urbina to Gutiérrez, dated from Ciudad Las Casas.

41. Ibid., from Gilberto Tello N. to Prof. Alberto Gutiérrez, Tuxtla, dated from Ciudad Las Casas, May 16, 1940.

42. Ibid., telegram from Dir. of DAI Luis Chávez Orozco to Cárdenas, dated from Las Casas, May 27, 1940; also letter from Gutiérrez to Cárdenas, dated from Tuxtla, July 19, 1940, 2.

43. Dawson, *Indian and Nation*, 134–36.

44. Octavio Véjar Vázquez, *Hacia una escuela de unidad nacional* (México: SEP, 1944), 60.

45. AHSEP, DEF, Chiapas, Caja 5581 (3530), Exp. 4483/40, Fos. 59–60, from Castellanos to Téllez in Tuxtla, dated from Ciudad Las Casas, 31 March 1942; AHSEP, DEF, Caja 5484 (2783), Exp. 11, from Castellanos to Téllez in Tuxtla, from Las Casas, various dates.

46. Vaughan, *Cultural Politics*, 65.

47. AHSEP, DEF, Chiapas, Caja 5300 (282), Exp. 33, Fo. 16, from López to Secretario de Educación Pública, DER, México, D.F., dated from Tuxtla, May 29, 1935.

48. AHSEP, DGEPET, Caja 5324 (304), Exp. 21, Fo. 43, from Inspector Paniagua to Dir. de Ed. Fed. in Tuxtla, dated from Comalapa, Aug. 31, 1936.

49. AHSEP, DER, Caja 1375 (236), Exp. 19, Fo. 18, from Pres. del Comité Particular Ejecutivo Agrario "Tenochtitlán" Leonides Ramírez to Cárdenas, México, D.F., dated from "Tenochtitlán," May 20, 1935.

50. AHSEP, DGEPET, Chiapas, Caja 6095 (45), Exp. 9, Fo. 87, from Pres. del Comité de Educación Eleuterio Escobar L. and Pres. del Comisariado Ejidal Fermín Escobar to Srio. de Educación Pública in México, D.F., and Dir. de Ed. Fed. in Tuxtla, dated from Tuixcum, Motozintla, May 7, 1939.

51. AHSEP, DGEPET, Caja 3399 (st); 5480, (2779), Exp. 108, Fo. 11, from Téllez to Dir. Gral. de Enseñanza Primaria Urbana y Rural, México, D.F., dated from Tuxtla, Jan. 31, 1941.

52. AHSEP, DGEPET, Chiapas, Caja 6088 (38), Exp. 5, Fo. 19, from Pres. del Comité de Educación Teófilo Salas y 57 firmas más, to Téllez in Tuxtla, dated from Miramar, Escuintla, Nov. 29, 1939.

53. Ibid., Fos. 25–33.

54. AHSEP, DGEPET, Chiapas, Caja 6132 (82), Exp. 20, Fo. 18, from Trabajadores de la Finca "Argentina," Mpio. de Tuxtla Chico, Sección Num. 40, Sindicato Único de la Industria del Café del Soconusco, to Cárdenas, México, D.F., dated from Poblado "Argentina," Tuxtla Chico, Aug. 16, 1940.

55. AHSEP, DGEPET, Chiapas, Caja 6130 (80), Exp. 3, Fo. 26, from Srio. Gen. del Sindicato de Trabajadores del Campo de la Finca "El Retiro" Octavio García to Cárdenas, México, D.F., dated from Finca "El Retiro," July 12, 1938.

56. AHSEP, DGEPET, Chiapas, Caja 6131 (79), Exp. 13, Fos. 21–23, from Comité de Educación to Cárdenas, México, D.F., dated from Finca "El Achotal," Municipio de Unión Juárez, Soconusco, July 26, 1938.

57. Ibid., Exp. 80, Fo. 23, from Secretario Gen. del Sindicato de Trabajadores del Campo Núm. 25 Ramón Cárdenas to Cárdenas, México, D. F., dated from Cacahoatán, July 12, 1938.

58. Ibid., Exp. 29, Fos. 4, 12, 14, 19–20, Escuela Artículo 123 Finca "El Alcázar," Municipio Acapetahua, various dates.

59. The Fideicomisos held on to certain properties beyond 1946.

60. AHSEP, DGEPET, Chiapas, Caja 6130 (80), Exp. 3, Fo. 80, from Comité de Educación de la Finca "El Retiro," Municipio de Tapachula, Chiapas, to Téllez in Tuxtla, dated from "El Retiro," April 16, 1944.

61. Ibid., Fo. 82, from Comité Ejecutivo, Sección #21 del Sindicato Único de Trabajadores del la Industria del Café del Soconusco to Ávila Camacho, México, D.F., dated from Finca "El Retiro," June 16, 1944.

62. Rockwell "Reforma constitucional y controversias locales," and Vaughan, *Cultural Politics*, 163–88.

Conclusion

The quote by Marcos is from Adolfo Gilly, Subcomandante Marcos, and Carlo Ginzburg, *Discusión sobre la historia* (México, D.F.: Taurus, 1995), 131–32.

1. Benjamin, *A Rich Land*, 119.

2. AHSEP, DGEPET, 5489 (2788); Exp. 42, Fo. 69, from Inspector Francisco Ovilla to Bolio Yenro in Tuxtla, dated from Bochil, Feb. 1937.

3. Ibid., Exp. 18, Fo. 3, from Inspector Daniel Tamayo Luna to Téllez in Tuxtla, dated from Villa Flores, Jan. 27, 1941.

4. Knight, "Revolutionary Project," 230.

5. Shannan Mattiace, *To See with Two Eyes: Peasant Activism and Indian Autonomy in Chiapas, Mexico* (Albuquerque: University of New Mexico Press, 2003), viii.

6. Harvey, *The Chiapas Rebellion*, 62–65, 69–76; John Womack Jr., ed., *Rebellion in Chiapas: An Historical Reader* (New York: New Press, 1999), 30–31, 128–32; and two documents written by Bishop Samuel Ruiz García and reprinted in Womack's anthology: "Evangelisation in Latin America," 119–27; and "In This Hour of Grace," 237–44.

7. Samuel Brunk, *¡Emiliano Zapata! Revolution and Betrayal in Mexico* (Albuquerque: University of New Mexico Press, 1998 [1995]), xii–xiii.

8. Vaughan, *Cultural Politics*, 40.

9. Womack, ed., *Rebellion in Chiapas*, 11.

10. Stephen, *¡Zapata Lives!*, 126–38, 254–62, and 275–80; also Harvey, *The Chiapas Rebellion*.

11. AHSEP, DEF, Chiapas, 5690 (1888); Exp. 4495/82, from Jefe del Depto. de Asuntos Indígenas Isidro Candia to SEP, dated from México, D.F., Jan. 9, 1942; AHMSCLC, 1942, vol. 1, from Jefe de la Delegación de Protección Indígena Ricardo Gómez Lamadrid to Jefe del Depto. de Protección Indígena in Ciudad de Las Casas, dated Jan. 23, 1942.

12. AHMSCLC, 1942, vol. 1, from Jefe del Depto. Artemio Rojas M. to Delegado de Protección Indígena in Yajalón, dated from Ciudad Las Casas, June 16, 1942; also Instituto Nacional Indigenista, Centro de Documentación "Juan Rulfo" (hereafter INICDJR) Ricardo Pozas Arciniega, "Chamula, field notes, 1945," 317, 333.

13. Alfonso Villa Rojas, *Notas sobre la etnografía de los indios tzeltales de Oxchuc, Chiapas, México* (Microfilm Collection of Manuscripts on Middle American Cultural Anthropology, 7) (University of Chicago Library, Chicago, 1946), entry dated Aug. 21, 1942, p. 580.

14. INICDJR, Ricardo Pozas, "Chamula" manuscript, 317.

15. INICDJR, Fernando Cámara Barbachano, "Diario etnográfico. Expedición para trabajo de campo etnológico en el Municipio de Tenejapa, Chis.," 5.

16. INICDJR, Ricardo Pozas Arciniega, "Chamula, field notes, 1945," 93–94. Some of the entries are dated 1946.

17. Rus, "The 'Comunidad Revolucionaria Institucional,'" 278.

18. Ibid., 267.

19. Ibid., 289; INICDJR, Julio de la Fuente, Coordinador, *Comisión del estudio del*

problema del alcoholismo en Chiapas, INI, 1954 (estudio no publicado), vols. 1–4, Tomo IV; and Stephen E. Lewis, "Dead-end caudillismo and entrepreneurial caciquismo in Chiapas, 1910–1955," in *Caudillos and Caciques*, ed. Alan Knight and Wil Pansters (forthcoming, Institute of Latin American Studies).

20. Jan Rus, personal communication, Oct. 5, 2002.

21. Studies of the INI are few in number and usually official in origin. The classic statement of indigenous education in Chiapas and throughout Mexico remains Aguirre Beltrán, *Teoría y práctica*. Also useful is Ulrich Köhler, *Cambio cultural dirigido en los Altos de Chiapas: Un estudio sobre la antropología social aplicada* (México: INI y SEP, 1975 [1969]); and *Realidades y proyectos; 16 años de trabajo. Memorias, vol. X* (México, D.F.: INI, 1964).

22. Luz Olivia Pineda, *Caciques culturales (El caso de los maestros bilingües en los Altos de Chiapas)* (Puebla: Altres Costa-Amic, 1993), 174–75; Jan Rus, personal communication, Oct. 4, 2002; Rus, "The 'Comunidad Revolucionaria Institucional'," 288; Zambrano, "Mass Schooling and Everyday Forms of State Formation," 25–36.

23. Jan Rus, "The Struggle against Indigenous Caciques in Highland Chiapas: Religion, Exile and the Rise of Pluralism, 1965–1993," paper presented at Caudillos and Caciques conference at Oxford, September 2002, 8.

24. Ibid., 9–14.

25. Ibid., 15.

26. Benjamin N. Colby and Pierre L. Van Den Berghe, "Ethnic Relations in Southeastern Mexico," *American Anthropologist* 63, no. 4 (1961): 779–81; Margaret Ann Ryan, "Chiapas Observed: the Impact of Researchers on Rural Mexico" (unpublished master's thesis, UC Berkeley, 1996), 20; and Toledo, *Historia del movimiento indígena en Simojovel, 1970–1989*, 79–99.

27. Womack, ed., *Rebellion in Chiapas*, 157–58. See also García de León, *Fronteras interiores*, 168–69; and Harvey, *The Chiapas Rebellion*, 77–78.

28. Benjamin, "A Time of Reconquest," 425–28, 434; García de León, *Fronteras interiores*, 173; Stephen, *¡Zapata Lives!*, 115–19; Womack, ed., *Rebellion in Chiapas*, 148–58.

29. Collier, *Basta!*, 93–106.

30. Harvey, *The Chiapas Rebellion*, 62, 148–55; Reyes Ramos, *El reparto de tierras y la política agraria en Chiapas, 1914–1988*, 119, 141; Stephen, *¡Zapata Lives!*, 113; Womack, ed., *Rebellion in Chiapas*, 199.

31. Collier, *Basta!*, 141–44; Harvey, *The Chiapas Rebellion*, 183–86; Andres Oppenheimer, *Bordering on Chaos* (New York: Little, Brown, 1998 [1996]), 55–56, 75; Womack, ed., *Rebellion in Chiapas*, 228–29.

32. García de León, *Fronteras interiories*, 105; Harvey, *The Chiapas Rebellion*, 65–66; Xóchitl Leyva Solano, "Regional, Communal, and Organizational Transformations in Las Cañadas," *Latin American Perspectives* 28, no. 2 (March 2001): 22–23, 32; and June Nash, "The Reassertion of Indigenous Identity: Mayan Responses to State Intervention in Chiapas," *Latin American Research Review* 30, no. 3: 24–27.

33. Rafael Sebastián Guillén Vicente, "Filosofía y educación (prácticas discursivas y prácticas ideológicas)" (unpublished undergraduate thesis, Universidad Nacional Autónoma de México, 1980).

34. Gilly, Marcos, and Ginsberg, *Discusión sobre la historia*, 139.

35. SEP, Subsecretaría de Educación Elemental, Dirección Gen. de Educación Indígena, *Programa para la modernización de la educación indígena: Chiapas (1990–1994)*, 1990, 7.

36. Ibid., 12–13, 45; Pineda, *Caciques culturales.*

37. García de León, *Fronteras interiores*, 61; Harvey, *The Chiapas Rebellion*, 186–94; Stephen, *¡Zapata Lives!*, 141.

38. Harvey, *The Chiapas Rebellion*, 204.

References

Archival Sources

In Mexico City

Archivo General de la Nación (AGN)
All references can be found in Ramo Presidentes.
Archivo Histórico de la Secretaría de Educación Pública (AHSEP)
Colección Porfirio Díaz
Fideicomiso Archivos Plutarco Elías Calles y Fernando Torreblanca (FAPECFT)
Instituto Nacional de Antropología e Historia, Archivo Histórico de la Institución (INAHAHI)
Instituto Nacional de Antropología e Historia (INAH), Biblioteca "Manuel Orozco y Berra"
Instituto Nacional Indigenista, Centro de Documentación "Juan Rulfo" (INICDJR)

In Chiapas

Archivo de Concentración del Estado de Chiapas (ACECh)
Archivo del Estado de Chiapas (AECh)
Archivo General del Estado (AGE)
Archivo Histórico del Estado de Chiapas (AHECh)
Archivo Histórico del Municipio de San Cristóbal de Las Casas (AHMSCLC)
Servicios Educativos para Chiapas (SECh)

In the United States

Bancroft Library, Berkeley, Calif.

Key to AHSEP Abbreviations

DE Departamento Escolar
DECI Departamento de Educación y Cultura Indígena
DEF Dirección de Educación Federal
DEFET Dirección de Educación Federal en los Estados y Territorios
DEI Departamento de Educación Indígena
DEnR Departamento de Enseñanza Rural
DEPET Dirección de Educación Primaria en los Estados y Territorios
DER Departamento de Escuelas Rurales
DERPFII Departamento de Escuelas Rurales, Primarias Foráneas e Incorporación Indígena
DERPR Departamento de Enseñanza Rural y Primaria Foránea
DGEPET Dirección General de Educación Primaria en los Estados y Territorios

DGEPURE Dirección General de Enseñanza Primaria, Urbana y Rural en los Estados
DMC Dirección de Misiones Culturales
DGEET Director General de Enseñanza en los Estados y Territorios
SP Secretaría Particular

Published References

Aguilar Camín, Héctor, and Lorenzo Meyer. *In the Shadow of the Mexican Revolution: Contemporary Mexican History, 1910–1989*. Trans. Luis Alberto Fierro. Austin: University of Texas Press, 1996 (1993).

Aguirre Beltrán, Gonzalo, ed. *Obra antropológica XII: Lenguas vernáculas*. México: Fondo de Cultura Económica, 1993 (1983).

———. *Teoría y práctica de la educación indígena*. México, D.F.: Fondo de Cultura Económica, 1992 (1973).

Alfonseca, Juan B. "La Escuela Rural Federal en los distritos de Texcoco y Chalco (1923–1936)." Paper presented at the III Congreso Nacional de Investigación Educativa in Mexico City, Oct. 26, 1995.

Anderson, Benedict. *Imagined Communities: Reflections on the Origins and Spread of Nationalism*. New York: Verso, 1991 1983).

Aubry, Andrés. *Los obispos de Chiapas*. San Cristóbal de Las Casas, Chiapas: INAREMAC, 1990.

Bantjes, Adrian A. *As If Jesus Walked on Earth: Cardenismo, Sonora, and the Mexican Revolution*. Wilmington, Del.: Scholarly Resources Inc., 1998.

———. "Burning Saints, Molding Minds: Iconoclasm, Civic Ritual, and the Failed Cultural Revolution." In *Rituals of Rule, Rituals of Resistance: Public Celebrations and Popular Culture in Mexico*. Edited by William H. Beezley, Cheryl English Martin, and William E. French. Wilmington, Del.: Scholarly Resources Inc., 1994, 261–84.

———. "Idolatry and Iconoclasm in Revolutionary Mexico: The Dechristianization Campaigns, 1929–1940." *Mexican Studies/Estudios Mexicanos* 13:1 (winter 1997): 87–120.

Baumann, Friedericke. "Terratenientes, campesinos y la expansión de la agricultura capitalista en Chiapas, 1896–1916." *Mesoamérica* (1982): 8–63.

Becker, Marjorie. *Setting the Virgin on Fire: Lázaro Cárdenas, Michoacán Peasants, and the Redemption of the Mexican Revolution*. Berkeley: University of California Press, 1995.

Benjamin, Thomas. *La Revolución: Mexico's Great Revolution as Memory, Myth, and History*. Austin: University of Texas Press, 2000.

———. *A Rich Land, a Poor People: Politics and Society in Modern Chiapas*. Albuquerque: University of New Mexico Press, 1989.

———. "A Time of Reconquest: History, the Maya Revival, and the Zapatista Rebellion in Chiapas." *American Historical Review* 105, no. 2 (April 2000): 417–50.

Blasco López, Juan. "La fabricación de aguardiente en San Cristóbal en el siglo XIX." Paper delivered at Foro Internacional "El estado de Chiapas: De la Independencia a la Revolución," San Cristóbal de Las Casas, Chiapas, Mexico, March 2002.

Bliss, Katherine Elaine. *Compromised Positions: Prostitution, Public Health, and Gender Politics in Revolutionary Mexico City*. University Park, Pa.: Pennsylvania State University Press, 2001.

———. "Gender and the Cultural Politics of Social Hygiene in Revolutionary Mexico." In *The Eagle and the Virgin: National Identity, Memory and Utopia in Mexico, 1920–1940*. Edited by Mary Kay Vaughan and Stephen E. Lewis. Durham, N.C.: Duke University Press, 2005.

Blom, Frans, with Oliver La Farge and the Tulane University Expedition to Middle America. *Tribes and Temples: A Record of the Expedition to Middle America Conducted by the Tulane University of Louisiana in 1925*. New Orleans: Tulane University Press, 1926–27.

Boyer, Christopher. *Becoming Campesinos: Politics, Identity, and Agrarian Struggle in Postrevolutionary Michoacán, 1920–1935*. Stanford: Stanford University Press, 2003.

Brading, David. *The First America: The Spanish Monarchy, Creole Patriots, and the Liberal State, 1492–1867*. Cambridge: Cambridge University Press, 1991.

Brickman, William W., ed. *John Dewey's Impressions of Soviet Russia and the Revolutionary World: Mexico—China—Turkey*. New York: Teachers College, Columbia University, 1964 (1929).

Britton, John A. *Educación y radicalismo en México*. 2 vols. México: SepSetentas, 1976.

———. "Teacher Unionization and the Corporate State in Mexico, 1931–1945." *Hispanic American Historical Review* 59:4 (1979): 674–90.

Brunk, Samuel. *¡Emiliano Zapata! Revolution and Betrayal in Mexico*. Albuquerque: University of New Mexico Press, 1998 (1995).

Bulnes, Francisco. *The Whole Truth About Mexico—President Wilson's Responsibility*. New York: M. Bulnes Book Company, 1916.

Bunzel, Ruth. "The Role of Alcoholism in Two Central American Cultures." *Psychiatry* 3 (1940): 361–87.

Cabellos Quiroz, Ángel, and Carlos Carrizales Barreto. "Las Escuelas Artículo 123 en Coahuila, 1926–1940." Tesina inédita. Universidad Autónoma Metropolitana Iztapalapa, 1992.

Camp, Roderic Ai. *La cuestión chiapaneca: Revisión de una polémica territorial*. Tuxtla Gutiérrez, Chis.: H. Congreso del estado de Chiapas. LV Legislatura, 1984.

Cancian, Frank. *The Decline of Community in Zinacantán*. Stanford: Stanford University Press, 1992.

Castellanos, Rosario. *Balún-Canán*. México: Fondo de Cultura Económica, 1987 (1957).

Civera Cerecedo, Alicia. "Crisis política y reforma educativa: El estado de México, 1934–1940." In *Escuela y sociedad en el periodo cardenista*. Edited by Susana Quintanilla and Mary Kay Vaughan. México: Fondo de Cultura Económica, 1997, 141–65.

Cockroft, James D. "El maestro de primaria en la Revolución mexicana." *Historia mexicana* XVI:4 [64] (abril–junio): 565–87.

Colby, Benjamin N., and Pierre L. Van Den Berghe, "Ethnic Relations in Southeastern Mexico." *American Anthropologist* 63, no. 4 (1961).

Collier, George. "Peasant Politics and the Mexican State: Indigenous Compliance in Highland Chiapas." *Mexican Studies/Estudios Mexicanos* 3, no. 1 (winter 1987): 71–98.

———, with Elizabeth Lowery Quaratiello. *Basta! Land and the Zapatista Rebellion in Chiapas*. Oakland, Calif.: Institute for Food and Development Policy, 1999 (1994).

Collier, John. "Mexico: A Challenge." *Progressive Education* 9 (Feb. 1932): 95–98.

Dawson, Alexander S. *Indian and Nation in Revolutionary Mexico*. Tucson: University of Arizona Press, 2004.

———. *Savage and Citizen: Indigenismo and the Vagaries of Race in Post-Revolutionary Mexico*. Unpublished manuscript.

De Vos, Jan. *Las fronteras de la frontera sur*. Villahermosa, Tabasco: Universidad Juárez Autónoma de Tabasco y CIESAS, 1993.

———. *Oro verde: La conquista de la Selva Lacandona por los madereros tabasqueños, 1822–1949*. México: Fondo de Cultura Económica, 1988.

Dewey, John, ed. *The Case of Leon Trotsky*. New York: Merit Publishers, 1968 (1937).

———. *The Child and the Curriculum*. Chicago: University of Chicago Press, 1902.

———. *Democracy and Education*. New York: Free Press, 1966 (1916).

———. *Not Guilty*. New York: Harper, 1937.

———. *The School and Society*. Chicago: University of Chicago Press, 1963 (1899).

Díaz Polanco, Héctor. *La cuestión étnico-nacional*. México, D.F.: Editorial Línea, 1985.

Eber, Christine. *Women and Alcohol in a Highland Maya Town: Water of Hope, Water of Sorrow*. Austin: University of Texas Press, 1995.

Espinosa Carbajal, Ma. Eugenia, and Jorge Ernesto Mesta Martínez. *Narciso Bassols: Un intelectual olvidado*. México: Subsecretaría de Servicios Educativos para el D.F., 1994.

Esteva, Gustavo. "The Meaning and Scope of the Struggle for Autonomy." *Latin American Perspectives* 28, no. 2 (March 2001): 120–48.

Fallaw, Ben. *Cárdenas Compromised: The Failure of Reform in Postrevolutionary Yucatán*. Durham, N.C.: Duke University Press, 2001.

Fell, Claude. *José Vasconcelos: Los años del águila (1920–1925)*. México: Universidad Nacional Autónoma de México, 1989.

Foweraker, Joe. *Popular Mobilization in Mexico: The Teachers' Movement, 1977–1987*. Cambridge: Cambridge University Press, 1993.

Galván, Luz Elena. *Los maestros y la educación pública en México*. México: CIESAS, Ediciones de la Casa Chata, 1985.

Gamio, Manuel. *Forjando patria*. México: Editorial Porrúa, 1960 (1916).

———. *El gobierno, la población, el territorio*. México: Departamento de Talleres Gráficos de la Secretaría de Fomento, 1917.

García de León, Antonio. *Fronteras interiores: Chiapas: Una modernidad particular*. México: Editorial Oceano de México, 2002.

———. *Resistencia y utopía: Memorial de agravios y crónica de revueltas y profecías acaecidas en la provincia de Chiapas durante los últimos quinientos años de su historia*. 2 vols. México: Ediciones Era, 1985.

Garrido, Luis Javier. *El partido de la Revolución institucionalizada*. México: Siglo XXI Editores, 1991 (1982).

Gilly, Adolfo. *La revolución interrumpida*. México: El Caballito, 1971.

———, with Subcomandante Marcos and Carlo Ginzburg. *Discusión sobre la historia*. México, D.F.: Taurus, 1995.

González, Luis. *Historia de la Revolución Mexicana Período 1934–1940: Los días del presidente Cárdenas*. México: El Colegio de México, 1988 (1981).

González Navarro, Moisés. *Los extranjeros en México y los mexicanos en el extranjero, 1821–1970*. México: El Colegio de México, 1994.

———. *La vida social*. In *Historia Moderna de México*. Edited by Daniel Cosío Villegas. Vol. 2, *El Porfiriato* (Tomo 4). México: Editorial Hermes, 1957.

Gosner, Kevin. *Soldiers of the Virgin: The Moral Economy of a Colonial Maya Rebellion*. Tucson: University of Arizona Press, 1992.

Gossen, Gary H. "Who Is the Comandante of Subcomandante Marcos?" In *Indigenous Revolts in Chiapas and the Andean Highlands*. Edited by Kevin Gosner and Arij Ouweneel. Amsterdam: CEDLA, 1996.

Greaves, Cecilia. "Entre le teoría educativa y la práctica indigenista: La experiencia en Chiapas y la Tarahumara (1940–1970)." In *Educación rural e indígena en iberoamérica*. Edited by Pilar Gonzalbo Aizpuru. México: El Colegio de México y Madrid: Universidad Nacional de Educación a Distancia, 1996, 161–78.

Grollová, Daniela. "Los trabajadores cafetaleros y el Partido Socialista Chiapaneco, 1920–1927." In *Chiapas: Los rumbos de otra historia*. Edited by Juan Pedro Viqueira and Mario Humberto Ruz. México: UNAM, 1995, 195–214.

Guillén, Diana. *Chiapas, 1973–1993: Mediaciones, política e institucionalidad*. México, D.F.: Instituto Mora, 1998.

Guillén Vicente, Rafael Sebastián. "Filosofía y educación (prácticas discursivas y prácticas ideológicas)." Undergraduate thesis, Universidad Nacional Autónoma de México, 1980.

Guiteras Holmes, Calixta. *Cancuc: Etnografía de un pueblo tzeltal de los altos de Chiapas, 1944*. Tuxtla Gutiérrez: Gobierno del Estado de Chiapas e Instituto Chiapaneco de Cultura, 1992.

Gutiérrez y Oliveros, Antonio. *El sepulturero de la raza latinoamericana o el cantinero y la conquista pacífica*. México: Casa Unida de Publicaciones, S.A., 1929.

Guzmán López, Salvador, Jan Rus, and Socios de la Unión "Tierra Tzotzil." *Kipaltik*. San Cristóbal de Las Casas, Chis.: El Taller Tzotzil, 1999.

Hall, Linda B. *Oil, Banks, and Politics: The United States and Postrevolutionary Mexico, 1917–1924*. Austin: University of Texas Press, 1995.

Hamilton, Nora. *The Limits of State Autonomy: Post-Revolutionary Mexico*. Princeton: Princeton University Press, 1982.

Hart, John M. *Revolutionary Mexico: The Coming and Process of the Mexican Revolution*. Berkeley: University of California Press, 1987.

Harvey, Neil. *The Chiapas Rebellion: The Struggle for Land and Democracy*. Durham, N.C.: Duke University Press, 1998.

Hernández Castillo, R. Aída. *Histories and Stories from Chiapas: Border Identities in Southern Mexico*. Austin: University of Texas Press, 2001.

Hernández Chávez, Alicia. "La defensa de los finqueros en Chiapas, 1914–1920." *Historia Mexicana* XXVIII:3 (enero–marzo 1979).

Hewitt de Alcántara, Cynthia. *Anthropological Perspectives on Rural Mexico*. Boston: Routledge & Kegan Paul, 1984.

Hobsbawm, Eric J. *Nations and Nationalism since 1780: Programme, Myth, Reality*. Cambridge: Cambridge University Press, 1992 (1990).

Holden, Robert H. *Mexico and the Survey of Public Lands: The Management of Modernization, 1876–1911*. DeKalb: Northern Illinois University Press, 1994.

Knight, Alan. "Cardenismo: Juggernaut or Jalopy?" *Journal of Latin American Studies* 26 (1994): 73–107.

———. *The Mexican Revolution*. 2 vols. Lincoln: University of Nebraska Press 1990 (1986).

———. "Racism, Revolution, and *Indigenismo*: Mexico, 1910–1940." In *The Idea of Race in Latin America, 1870–1940*. Edited by Richard Graham. Austin: University of Texas Press, 1990, 71–113.

———. "Revolutionary Project, Recalcitrant People: Mexico, 1910–40." In *The Revolutionary Process in Mexico: Essays on Political and Social Change, 1880–1940*. Edited by Jaime E. Rodríguez O. Los Angeles: UCLA Latin American Center Publications, 1990, 227–64.

Köhler, Ulrich. *Cambio cultural dirigido en los Altos de Chiapas: Un estudio sobre la antropología social aplicada*. México: INI y SEP, 1975 [1969].

Krauze, Enrique. "La escuela callista." In *Historia de la Revolución Mexicana, período 1924–1928: La reconstrucción económica*. México: El Colegio de México, 1977.

Lerner, Victoria. *Historia de la Revolución Mexicana: La educación socialista*. México: El Colegio de México, 1987.

Lewis, Stephen E. "Citizenship, Education, and Revolution in San Juan Bautista, Tabasco, 1894–1917." *MACLAS Latin American Essays*. Vol. VIII (1994): 3–19.

———. "Dead-End Caudillismo and Entrepreneurial Caciquismo in Chiapas, 1910–1955." In *Caudillos and Caciques*, ed. Alan Knight and Wil Pansters. Forthcoming, Institute of Latin American Studies.

Leys Stepan, Nancy. *"The Hour of Eugenics": Race, Gender, and Nation in Latin America*. Ithaca: Cornell University Press, 1991.

Leyva Solano, Xóchitl. "Regional, Communal, and Organizational Transformations in Las Cañadas." *Latin American Perspectives* 28, no. 2 (March 2001): 20–44.

Lomnitz, Claudio. *Deep Mexico, Silent Mexico: An Anthropology of Nationalism (Public Worlds)*. Minneapolis: University of Minnesota Press, 2001.

López, Rick. "The India Bonita Contest of 1921 and the Ethnicization of Mexican National Culture." *Hispanic American Historical Review* 82, no. 2 (May 2002): 291–328.

———. "*Lo más mexicano de Mexico:* Popular Arts, Indians, and Urban Intellectuals in the Ethnicization Mexican Postrevolutionary National Identity, 1921–1972." Ph.D. diss., Yale University, 2001.

———. "*The Noche Mexicana* and the Exhibition of Popular Arts of 1921: Two Ways of Indianizing Mexican National Identity." In *The Eagle and the Virgin: National Identity, Memory and Utopia in Mexico, 1920–1940*. Edited by Mary Kay Vaughan and Stephen E. Lewis. Durham, N.C.: Duke University Press, 2005.

Loyo Bravo, Engracia, ed. "Los Centros de Educación Indígena y su papel en el medio rural." In *Educación rural e indígena en iberoamérica*. Edited by Pilar Gonzalbo Aizpuru. México: El Colegio de México y Madrid: Universidad Nacional de Educación a Distancia, 1996, 139–59.

———. "Escuelas Rurales 'Artículo 123' (1917–1940)." *Historia Mexicana* 40, no. 2 (1991), 299–336.

———. "Lectura para el pueblo." In *La educación en la historia de México*. Edited by Josefina Zoraida Vázquez. México: El Colegio de México, 1992.

Macías, Carlos, ed. *Plutarco Elías Calles: Correspondencia personal (1919–1945)*. México: Fideicomiso Archivos Plutarco Elías Calles y Fernando Torreblanca, 1993.

MacLeod, Murdo. *Spanish Central America: A Socioeconomic History, 1520–1720*. Berkeley: University of California Press, 1973.

Mallon, Florencia E. *Peasant and Nation: The Making of Postcolonial Mexico and Peru*. Berkeley: University of California Press, 1995.

Marentes, Luis A. *José Vasconcelos and the Writing of the Mexican Revolution*. New York: Twayne Publishers, 2000.

Marion Singer, Marie-Odile. *El agrarismo en Chiapas (1524–1940)*. México, D.F.: Instituto Nacional de Antropología e Historia, 1988.

Mattiace, Shannan L. *To See with Two Eyes: Peasant Activism and Indian Autonomy in Chiapas, Mexico*. Albuquerque: University of New Mexico Press, 2003.

Meneses Morales, Ernesto, coord. *Tendencias educativas oficiales en México 1911–1934*. México: Centro de Estudios Educativos, A.C., 1986.

———. *Tendencias educativas oficiales en México 1934–1964*. México: Centro de Estudios Educativos, Universidad Iberoamericana, 1988.

Meyer, Jean. *La Cristiada*. 3 vols. México: Siglo Veintiuno Editores, 1991 (1973).

Miller, Nicola. *In the Shadow of the State: Intellectuals and the Quest for National Identity in Twentieth-Century Spanish America*. New York: Verso, 1999.

Modiano, Nancy, and Antonio Pérez Hernández. "Educación." In *El indigenismo en acción: XXV aniversario del Centro Coordinador Indigenista Tzeltal-Tzotzil, Chiapas*. Edited by Gonzalo Aguirre Beltrán, Alfonso Villa Rojas, Agustín Romano Delgado and others. México: INI y SEP, 1976.

Molina Enríquez, Andrés. *Los grandes problemas nacionales*. México: Ediciones del Instituto Nacional de la Juventud, 1964 (1908).

Montiel, Gustavo. *Recordando el Soconusco y su perla*. México: B. Costa-Amic, 1979.

Moscoso Pastrana, Prudencio. *México y Chiapas: Independencia y federación de la provincia chiapaneca*. México, 1974.

———. *El pinedismo en Chiapas, 1916–1920*. México, 1960.

Nash, June. "The Reassertion of Indigenous Identity: Mayan Responses to State Intervention in Chiapas." *Latin American Research Review* 30, no. 3 (1995): 7–41.

Niblo, Stephen R. *War, Diplomacy, and Development: The United States and Mexico, 1938–1954*. Wilmington, Del.: Scholarly Resources Inc., 1995.

Nolan-Ferrell, Catherine. "Campesinos of Questionable Nationality: Government Reform Programs and the Creation of a Mexican Peasantry in Chiapas." Paper delivered at Foro Internacional "El estado de Chiapas: De la Independencia a la Revolución," San Cristóbal de Las Casas, Chiapas, Mexico, March 2002.

Oppenheimer, Andres. *Bordering on Chaos*. New York: Little, Brown, 1998 (1996).

Ortiz, María de los Angeles, and Bertha Toraya. *Concentración de poder y tenencia de la tierra: El caso de Soconusco*. Cuadernos de la Casa Chata 125. México: Ciesas, 1985.

Palabras y documentos públicos de Lázaro Cárdenas, 1928–1940. México: Siglo Veintiuno Editores, 1979.

Palacios, Guillermo. "Postrevolutionary Intellectuals, Rural Readings and the Shaping of the 'Peasant Problem' in Mexico; *El Maestro Rural*, 1932–1934." *Journal of Latin American Studies* 30 (1998): 309–39.

de la Peña, Guillermo. "Poder local, poder regional: Perspectivas socioantropológicas." In *Poder local, poder regional*. Edited by Jorge Padua and Alain Vanneph. México: El Colegio de México/CEMCA, 1986.

Pérez Montfort, Ricardo. *Estampas de nacionalismo popular mexicano: Ensayos sobre cultura popular y nacionalismo*. México: CIESAS, 1994.

———. "Indigenismo, Hispanismo y Panamericanismo en la cultura popular mexicana de 1920 a 1940." In *Cultura e identidad nacional*. Compiled by Roberto Blancarte. México: Consejo Nacional para la Cultura y las Artes and Fondo de Cultura Económica, 1994.

Pérez Palacios, Septimio. "Mi labor en el sector educativo." In *Los maestros y la cultura nacional, 1920–1952*, vol. 5, *Sureste*. México: Museo Nacional de Culturas Populares, y Dirección General de Culturas Populares, 1987.

Pineda, Luz Oliva. *Caciques culturales (El caso de los maestros bilingües en los Altos de Chiapas)*. Puebla: Altres Costa-Amic, 1993.

Purnell, Jennie. *Popular Movements and State Formation in Revolutionary Mexico*. Durham, N.C.: Duke University Press, 1999.

Quintanilla, Susana. "El debate intelectual acerca de la educación socialista." In *Escuela y sociedad en el periodo cardenista*. Edited by Susana Quintanilla and Mary Kay Vaughan. México: Fondo de Cultura Económica, 1997, 47–75.

Raby, David L. *Educación y revolución social en México*. México: SepSetentas, 1974.

Ramos, Samuel. *Veinte años de educación en México*. México: Imprenta Universitaria, 1941.

Rénique, Gerardo. "Sonora's Anti-Chinese Racism and Mexico's Postrevolutionary Nationalism, 1920s–1930s." In *Race and Nation in Modern Latin America*. Edited by Nancy P. Applebaum, Anne S. Macpherson, and Karin Alejandra Rosemblatt. Chapel Hill: University of North Carolina Press, 2003, 211–36.

Reyes Ramos, María Eugenia. *El reparto de tierras y la política agraria en Chiapas, 1914–1988*. México: UNAM, 1992.

Rockwell, Elsie. "Reforma constitucional y controversias locales: la educación socialista en Tlaxcala, 1935–1936." In *Escuela y sociedad en el periodo cardenista*. Edited by Susana Quintanilla and Mary Kay Vaughan. México: Fondo de Cultura Económica, 1997, 196–228.

———. "Schools of the Revolution: Enacting and Contesting State Forms in

Tlaxcala, 1910–1930." In *Everyday Forms of State Formation: Revolution and the Negotiation of Rule in Modern Mexico*. Edited by Gilbert Joseph and Daniel Nugent. Durham, N.C.: Duke University Press, 1994, 170–208.

Romero, Matías. *Bosquejo histórico de la agregación a México de Chiapas y Soconusco y de las negociaciones sobre límites entabladas por México con Centro América y Guatemala*. México: Imprenta de Gobierno, 1877.

———. *Cultivo del café en la costa meridional de Chiapas*. Tuxtla Gutiérrez: H. Congreso del Estado, 1991 (1876).

Rus, Jan. "Coffee and the Recolonization of Highland Chiapas, Mexico: Indian Communities and Plantation Labor, 1892–1912." In *The Global Coffee Economy in Africa, Asia, and Latin America, 1500–1989*. Edited by Steven Topic and W. Clarence-Smith. Cambridge: Cambridge University Press, 2003, 257–85.

———."The 'Comunidad Revolucionaria Institucional': The Subversion of Native Government in Highland Chiapas, 1936–1968." In *Everyday Forms of State Formation: Revolution and the Negotiation of Rule in Modern Mexico*. Edited by Gilbert M. Joseph and Daniel Nugent. Durham, N.C.: Duke University Press, 1994, 265–300.

———. "Managing Mexico's Indians: The Historical Context and Consequences of *Indigenismo*." Unpublished manuscript, 1976.

———. "Rereading Tzotzil Ethnography: Recent Scholarship from Chiapas, Mexico." *In Pluralizing Ethnography: Comparison and Representation in Maya Cultures, Histories, and Identities*. Edited by John M. Watanabe and Edward F. Fischer. Santa Fe: School of American Research Press, 2004.

———. "The Struggle against Indigenous Caciques in Highland Chiapas: Religion, Exile and the Rise of Pluralism, 1965–1993." Paper presented at Caudillos and Caciques conference at Oxford, September 2002.

———. "Whose Caste War? Indians, Ladinos, and the Chiapas 'Caste War' of 1869." In *Spaniards and Indians in Southeastern Mesoamerica: Essays on the History of Ethnic Relations*. Edited by Murdo J. MacLeod and Robert Wasserstrom. Lincoln: University of Nebraska Press, 1983, 127–68.

———, and George Collier. "A Generation of Crisis in the Central Highlands of Chiapas: The Cases of Chamula and Zinacantán, 1974–2000." In *Mayan Lives, Mayan Utopias: The Indigenous Peoples of Chiapas and the Zapatista Rebellion*. Edited by Jan Rus, Rosalva Aída Hernández Castillo, and Shannan L. Mattiace. New York: Rowman & Littlefield Publishers, 2003, 33–61.

———, and Robert Wasserstrom. "Civil-Religious Hierarchies in Central Chiapas: A Critical Perspective." *American Ethnologist* 7, no. 3 (August 1980): 466–78.

Ryan, Margaret Ann. "Chiapas Observed: The Impact of Researchers on Rural Mexico." Master's thesis, UC Berkeley, 1996.

Sáenz, Moisés. *Carapan: Bosquejo de una experiencia*. Morelia, Mich.: Talleres linotipográficos del gobierno del Estado, 1969 (1936).

———. *México íntegro*. México, D.F.: SEP/Fondo de Cultura Económica, 1982 (1939).

Schell, Patience A. *Church and State Education in Revolutionary Mexico City*. Tucson: University of Arizona Press, 2003.

Schuler, Friedrich E. *Mexico between Hitler and Roosevelt: Mexican Foreign Relations in the Age of Lázaro Cárdenas*. Albuquerque: University of New Mexico Press, 1998.

Scott, James. *Weapons of the Weak: Everyday Forms of Peasant Resistance*. New Haven, Conn.: Yale University Press, 1985.

Sherman, John W. "Reassessing Cardenismo: The Mexican Right and the Failure of a Revolutionary Regime, 1934–1940." *The Americas* 54, no. 3 (January 1998): 357–78.

Sierra, Augusto Santiago. *Las Misiones Culturales (1923–1973)*. México: SepSetentas, 1973.

Skirius, John. *José Vasconcelos y la cruzada de 1929*. México: Siglo XXI Editores, 1978.

Spenser, Daniela. "Economía y movimiento laboral en las fincas cafetaleras de Soconusco." In *Los empresarios alemanes, el Tercer Reich y la oposición de derecha a Cárdenas*, Tomo I. By Brígida von Mentz, Ricardo Pérez Montfort, Verena Radkau, and Daniela Spenser. México: CIESAS, Ediciones de la Casa Chata, 1988, 231–78.

———. "Los inicios del cultivo del café en Soconusco y la inmigración extranjera." In *Los empresarios alemanes, el Tercer Reich y la oposición de derecha a Cárdenas*, Tomo I. By Brígida von Mentz, Ricardo Pérez Montfort, Verena Radkau, and Daniela Spenser. México: CIESAS, Ediciones de la Casa Chata, 1988, 61–87.

———. *El Partido Socialista Chiapaneco: Rescate y reconstrucción de su historia*. México: CIESAS. Ediciones de la Casa Chata, 1988, 279–311.

———. "La reforma agraria en Soconusco y la contraofensiva del finquero cafetalero." In *Los empresarios alemanes, el Tercer Reich y la oposición de derecha a Cárdenas*, Tomo I. By Brígida von Mentz, Ricardo Pérez Montfort, Verena Radkau, and Daniela Spenser. México: CIESAS, Ediciones de la Casa Chata, 1988.

———. "Soconusco: The Formation of a Coffee Economy in Chiapas." In *Other Mexicos: Essays on Regional Mexican History, 1876–1911*. Edited by Thomas Benjamin and William McNellie. Albuquerque: University of New Mexico Press, 1984, 123–43.

Stephen, Lynn. *¡Zapata Lives! Histories and Cultural Politics in Southern Mexico*. Berkeley: University of California Press, 2001.

Stern, Alexandra Minna. "From Mestizophilia to Biotypology: Racialization and Science in Mexico, 1920–1960." In *Race and Nation in Modern Latin America*. Edited by Nancy P. Applebaum, Anne S. Macpherson, and Karin Alejandra Rosemblatt. Chapel Hill: University of North Carolina Press, 2003, 187–210.

Tanck de Estrada, Dorothy. *Pueblos de indios y educación en el México Colonial, 1750–1821*. México, D.F.: El Colegio de México, Centro de Estudios Históricos, 1999.

Thomson, Guy. "Liberalism and Nation-Building in Mexico and Spain during the Nineteenth Century." In *Studies in the Formation of the Nation State in Latin America*. Edited by James Dunkerley. London: Institute of Latin American Studies, 2002, 189–211.

———, with David G. LaFrance. *Patriotism, Politics, and Popular Liberalism in Nineteenth-Century Mexico: Juan Francisco Lucas and the Puebla Sierra*. Wilmington, Del.: Scholarly Resources Inc., 2002 (1999).

Toledo Tello, Sonia. *Historia del movimiento indígena en Simojovel, 1970–1989*. Tuxtla Gutiérrez: Universidad Autónoma de Chiapas, 1996.

Vasconcelos, José. *The Cosmic Race/La raza cósmica*. Translated with an introduction by Didier T. Jaén. Baltimore: Johns Hopkins University Press, 1997 (1925).

———. *El desastre* in *Memorias*. Vol. 2. México: Fondo de Cultura Económica, 1982 (1939), 9–598.

———. *A Mexican Ulysses. The Autobiography of José Vasconcelos*. Translated and edited by W. Rex Crawford. Bloomington: Indiana University Press, 1963.

Vaughan, Mary Kay. "Cambio ideológico en la política educativa de la SEP: Programas y libros de texto, 1921–1940." In *Escuela y sociedad en el periodo cardenista*. Edited by Susana Quintanilla and Mary Kay Vaughan. México: Fondo de Cultura Económica, 1997, 76–108.

———. "The Construction of Patriotic Festival in Tecamachalco, Puebla, 1900–1946." In *Rituals of Rule, Rituals of Resistance*. Edited by William Beezley, Bill French, and Cheryl Martin. Wilmington, Del.: Scholarly Resources Inc., 1994, 213–45.

———. *Cultural Politics in Revolution: Teachers, Peasants, and Schools in Mexico (1930–1940)*. Tucson: University of Arizona Press, 1997.

———. *The State, Education, and Social Class in Mexico, 1880–1928*. DeKalb: Northern Illinois University Press, 1982.

Véjar Vázquez, Octavio. *Hacia una escuela de unidad nacional*. México: Secretaría de Educación Pública, 1944.

Velasco Farrera, Roldán. *La educación en Chiapas en los últimos cuatro años: 1941–1944*. Tuxtla Gutiérrez: Gobierno Constitucional de Chiapas, 1944.

Villa Rojas, Alfonso. *Notas sobre la etnografía de los indios tzeltales de Oxchuc, Chiapas, México*. Microfilm Collection of Manuscripts on Middle American Cultural Anthropology, 7. University of Chicago Library, Chicago, 1946.

Viqueira, Juan Pedro. "Chiapas y sus regiones." In *Chiapas: Los rumbos de otra historia*. By Juan Pedro Viqueira and Mario Humberto Ruz. México: UNAM, 1995,. 19–40.

———. "Éxitos y fracasos de la evangelización en Chiapas (1545–1859)." In *La iglesia Católica en México*. Edited by Nelly Sigaut. Zamora: El Colegio de Michoacán, 1997, 69–98.

Vogt, Evon Z. *Fieldwork among the Maya: Reflections on the Harvard Chiapas Project*. Albuquerque: University of Mexico Press, 1994.

von Mentz, Brígida. "Las empresas alemanas en México (1920–1942)." In *Los empresarios alemanes, el Tercer Reich y la oposición de derecha a Cárdenas*, Tomo I. By Brígida von Mentz, Ricardo Pérez Montfort, Verena Radkau, and Daniela Spenser. México: CIESAS, Ediciones de la Casa Chata, 1988, 19–59.

Wasserstrom, Robert. *Class and Society in Central Chiapas*. Berkeley: University of California Press, 1983.

Wilkie, James W. *La Revolución Mexicana: Gasto federal y cambio social*. México: Fondo de Cultura Económica, 1978 (1967).

Wolf, Eric. "Closed Corporate Peasant Communities in Mesoamerica and Central Java." *Southwestern Journal of Anthropology* 13 (1957): 1–18.

Womack, John Jr., ed. *Rebellion in Chiapas: An Historical Reader*. New York: New Press, 1999.

Zambrano, Isabel M. "Mass Schooling and Everyday Forms of State Formation: Mitontik, Chiapas, Mexico." Unpublished manuscript.

Periodicals

Alborada. 1938–1939. Tuxtla Gutiérrez, Chis.
Boletín del Archivo Histórico Diocesano. 1991. San Cristóbal de Las Casas, Chis.
Chiapas Nuevo. 1939. Tuxtla Gutiérrez, Chis.
Chiapas: Revista Mensual. 1928. Tuxtla Gutiérrez, Chis.
Colonia Chiapaneca. 1938. México, D.F.
El Eco del Sureste. 1933. Huixtla, Chis.
El Financiero. 1994. 1998. México, D.F.
La Frontera del Sur. 1922. Tapachula, Chis.
El Informador. 1936. Tuxtla Gutiérrez, Chis.
La Jornada. 1994, 1996, 1998. México, D.F.
Liberación. 1934. Tuxtla Gutiérrez, Chis.
El Liberal Progresista. Guatemala City, 1940.
El Maestro Rural. 1933–1937. México, D.F.
El Noticiero del Sureste. 1933. San Cristóbal de Las Casas, Chis.
Renovación. 1933. Tuxtla Gutiérrez, Chis.
El Sur de México. 1938–1940, 1942. Tapachula, Chis.
El Universal. 1994, 2003. México, D.F.
La Vanguardia. 1929, 1931–1934. Tuxtla Gutiérrez, Chis.

State and Federal Government Publications

Anuario estadístico del Estado de Chiapas, formado por la Sección de Estadística de la Secretaría General de Gobierno, a cargo del ciudadano J. Abel Cruz. Año de 1908. Vol. 1.

Caparrozo, Alfonso. "Algunas consideraciones metodológicas acerca de la enseñanza de la Instrucción Cívica." San Juan Bautista, Tabasco: Tipografía "La Ilustración," 1902.

Departamento de Asuntos Indígenas: Memoria del Primer Congreso Regional Indígena celebrado en Ixmiquilpan, Hgo. 25 a 26 de septiembre de 1936. México: D.A.A.P., 1938.

Diario Oficial. Various. México, D.F.

Discurso del Coronel Francisco León, Gobernador de Chiapas, ante la XIX Legislatura del Estado, al abrir ésta sus sesiones ordinarias el 16 de septiembre. Tuxtla Gutiérrez: Imprenta del Gobierno, dirigida por Félix Santaella, 1896.

Informe general que rinde a la Secretaría de Estado y del Despacho de Gobernación, el C. Gobernador y comandante Militar del Estado de Chiapas, C. Gral. Blas Corral. Tuxtla Gutiérrez: Oficina de Información y Propaganda del Gob. del Estado, 1916.

Informe oficial del Gobernador de Chiapas, C. Coronel Francisco León, rendido ante la XX Legislatura del Estado, al abrir ésta su primer período de sesiones ordinarias en el segundo año de su ejercicio, el 16 de septiembre de 1898. Tuxtla Gutiérrez: Imprenta del Gobierno dirigida por Félix Santaella, 1898.

Informe que el C. Gobernador Constitucional del Estado de Chiapas Victórico R. Grajales rinde a la H. XXXV Legislatura. Tuxtla Gutiérrez: Talleres Tipográficos del Gobierno del Estado, 1934.

Informe que el C. Gobernador Constitucional del Estado de Chiapas Victórico R. Grajales, rinde a la H. XXXV Legislatura, de conformidad con el art. 22 de la Constitución Política del Estado, en el 3er. año de su Ejercicio. Tuxtla Gutiérrez, Chis.: Imprenta del Gobierno, 1935.

Informe que rinde el C. Gobernador Constitucional del Estado, General de División Tiburcio Fernández Ruiz, ante la H. Legislatura del mismo, al abrir ésta su primer período de sesiones ordinarias en el 20. año de su ejercicio. Tuxtla Gutiérrez, Chiapas: Imprenta del Gobierno, 1921.

Informe rendido por el Gobernador Constitucional de Chiapas C. Ing. Raymundo E. Enríquez ante la XXXIII Legislatura del Estado, en el segundo año de su ejercicio, el 1 de noviembre de 1930. Tuxtla Gutiérrez, Chis.: Talleres Tipográficos del Gob. del Estado, 1930.

Informe rendido por el Gobernador Interino Constitucionalista de Chiapas C. Dip. José María Brindis, en virtud de licencia temporal concedida al Gobernador Constitucional C. Ing. Raymundo E. Enríquez ante la XXXIII Legislatura del Estado, en el segundo año de su ejercicio, el 1 de noviembre de 1931. Tuxtla Gutiérrez: Talleres Tipográficos del Gob. del Estado, 1931.

Instituto Nacional Indigenista. *Realidades y proyectos; 16 años de trabajo. Memorias*, vol. X. México, D.F.: INI, 1964.

López, Elpidio, coord. *La escuela socialista de Chiapas*. Tuxtla Gutiérrez, Chis.: Talleres Linotipográficos del Gobierno del Estado, 1935.

Memoria del Primer Congreso Pedagógico del Estado de Chiapas. Convocado por el Ciudadano Gobernador y comandante Militar del Estado y reunido en la Ciudad de Tuxtla Gutiérrez, del 10 de diciembre del año de 1914 al 17 de enero de 1915. Tuxtla Gutiérrez: Imprenta del Gobierno del Estado, 1916.

Periódico Oficial del Gobierno Constitucionalista del Estado de Chiapas. Various. Tuxtla Gutiérrez, Chiapas.

"Programa detallado para las escuelas dirigidas por maestros ambulantes." San Juan Bautista, Tabasco: Gobierno del estado libre y soberano de Tabasco, 1898.

"Programas detallados para las escuelas de 1a, 2a, y 3a clase." Dirección General de Instrucción Pública del Estado de Tabasco. San Juan Bautista, Tabasco: Imprenta de M. Gaburcio M., 1896.

Puig Casauranc, J. M. *La cuestión religiosa en relación con la educación pública en México*. México: Talleres Gráficos de la Nación, 1928.

Reglamento Interior de la Escuela Normal para Profesoras. Tuxtla Gutiérrez: Imprenta del Gobierno del Estado, dirigida por Félix Santaella, 1903.

SEP. *Boletín de la SEP*. 1924.

———. *La Casa del Estudiante Indígena: 16 meses de labor en un experimento psicológico colectivo de indios. Febrero de 1926–junio de 1927*. Publicaciones de la Secretaría de Educación Pública. México: Talleres Gráficos de la Nación, 1927.

———. *La educación pública en México, desde el 1 de diciembre de 1934 hasta el 30 de noviembre de 1940*. México, D.F.: Secretaría de Educación Pública, 1941.

———. *Memoria que indica el estado que guarda el ramo de Educación Pública el 31 de agosto de 1931*. México: Talleres Gráficos de la Nación, 1931.

———. *Memoria relativa al estado que guarda el ramo de Educación Pública el 31 de agosto de 1933*. Tomo II. Documentos. México: TGN, 1933.

———. *Memoria relativa al estado que guarda el ramo de Educación Pública el 31 de agosto de 1934*. Tomo II, Documentos. México: TGN, 1934.

———. *Memoria de la Secretaría de Educación Pública (septiembre de 1937–agosto de 1938)*. Tomo I, 2da. parte. México: D.A.P.P, 1938.

———. *Las Misiones Culturales en 1927: Las Escuelas Normales Rurales*. México: Publicaciones de la Secretaría de Educación Pública, 1928.

———. *Noticia estadística sobre la educación pública en México correspondiente al año de 1927*. México: Talleres Gráficos de la Nación, 1928.

———. *Noticia estadística sobre la educación en México correspondiente al año de 1928*. México, D.F.: Talleres Gráficos de la Nación, 1930.

———. *El sistema de escuelas rurales en México*. México: Talleres Gráficos de la Nación, 1927.

———. Subsecretaría de Educación Elemental, Dirección General de Educación Indígena. Programa para la modernización de la educación indígena: Chiapas (1990–1994), 1990.

Index